Lecture Notes in Computer Science   13126

Luca Ardito · Andreas Jedlitschka ·
Maurizio Morisio · Marco Torchiano (Eds.)

Product-Focused
Software Process Improvement

22nd International Conference, PROFES 2021
Turin, Italy, November 26, 2021
Proceedings

 Springer

Editors
Luca Ardito ⓘ
Politecnico di Torino
Torino, Italy

Maurizio Morisio ⓘ
Politecnico di Torino
Torino, Italy

Andreas Jedlitschka ⓘ
Fraunhofer Institute for Experimental
Software Engineering
Kaiserslautern, Rheinland-Pfalz, Germany

Marco Torchiano ⓘ
Politecnico di Torino
Torino, Italy

ISSN 0302-9743   ISSN 1611-3349 (electronic)
Lecture Notes in Computer Science
ISBN 978-3-030-91451-6   ISBN 978-3-030-91452-3 (eBook)
https://doi.org/10.1007/978-3-030-91452-3

LNCS Sublibrary: SL2 – Programming and Software Engineering

This Springer imprint is published by the registered company Springer Nature Switzerland AG
The registered company address is: Gewerbestrasse 11, 6330 Cham, Switzerland

Preface

On behalf of the PROFES Organizing Committee, we are proud to present the proceedings of the 22nd International Conference on Product-Focused Software Process Improvement (PROFES 2021). Due to the COVID-19 outbreak, the conference was held in a hybrid format on November 26, 2021.

Since 1999, PROFES has established itself as one of the top recognized international process improvement conferences. In the spirit of the PROFES conference series, the main theme of PROFES 2021 was professional software process improvement (SPI) motivated by product, process, and service quality needs.

PROFES 2021 is a premier forum for practitioners, researchers, and educators to present and discuss experiences, ideas, innovations, as well as concerns related to professional software development and process improvement driven by product and service quality needs. PROFES especially welcomes contributions emerging from applied research to foster industry-academia collaborations of leading industries and research institutions.

The technical program of PROFES 2021 was selected by a committee of leading experts in software process improvement, software process modelling and empirical software engineering. Two Program Committees were formed from qualified professionals: one for the full and short tracks and one for the industrial track. This year, 36 full research papers were submitted. After a thorough evaluation that involved at least three independent experts per paper, 14 full technical papers were finally selected (39% acceptance rate). In addition, we had 5 industry paper submissions, 3 of which we accepted for the final program. Furthermore, we received 7 short paper submissions, of which 3 were accepted.

Each submission was reviewed by at least three members from the PROFES Program Committees. Based on the reviews and overall assessments, the program chairs took the final decision on acceptance.

The technical program consisted of the following sessions: Agile and Migration, Requirements, Human Factors, and Software Quality.

Continuing the open science policy adopted since PROFES 2017, we encouraged and supported all authors of accepted submissions to make their papers and research publicly available.

We are thankful for the opportunity to have served as chairs for this conference. The Program Committee members and reviewers provided excellent support in the papers. We are also grateful to all authors of submitted manuscripts, presenters, keynote speakers and session chairs, for their time and effort in making PROFES 2021 a success. We would also like to thank the PROFES Steering Committee members for their guidance and support in the organization process.

October 2021

Luca Ardito
Andreas Jedlitschka
Maurizio Morisio
Marco Torchiano

Organization

General Chair

Maurizio Morisio   Politecnico di Torino, Italy

Program Co-chairs

Andreas Jedlitschka   Fraunhofer IESE, Germany
Marco Torchiano   Politecnico di Torino, Italy

Industry Papers Co-chairs

Alessandra Bagnato   Softeam, France
Michael Klaes   Fraunhofer IESE, Germany

Short Paper Co-chairs

Riccardo Coppola   Politecnico di Torino, Italy
Barbara Russo   Free University of Bozen Bolzano, Italy

Journal First Chair

Antonio Vetrò   Politecnico di Torino, Italy

Proceedings Chair

Luca Ardito   Politecnico di Torino, Italy

Local Arrangement Chair

Mariachiara Mecati   Politecnico di Torino, Italy

Web Co-chairs

Simone Leonardi   Politecnico di Torino, Italy
Diego Monti   Politecnico di Torino, Italy

Program Committee Members (Full Research Papers, and Short Papers)

Andreas Jedlitschka   Fraunhofer IESE, Germany
Marco Torchiano   Politecnico di Torino, Italy

Sousuke Amasaki	Okayama Prefectural University, Japan
Maria Teresa Baldassarre	University of Bari, Italy
Andreas Birk	SWPM, Germany
Luigi Buglione	ETS, Canada
Danilo Caivano	University of Bari, Italy
Marcus Ciolkowski	QAware GmbH, Germany
Bruno da Silva	California Polytechnic State University, USA
Maya Daneva	University of Twente, The Netherlands
Michal Dolezel	Prague University of Economics and Business, Czech Republic
Christof Ebert	Vector Consulting Services GmbH, Germany
Davide Falessi	University of Rome Tor Vergata, Italy
Michael Felderer	University of Innsbruck, Austria
Xavier Franch	Universitat Politècnica de Catalunya, Spain
Ilenia Fronza	Free University of Bozen-Bolzano, Italy
Lina Garcés	UNIFEI, Brazil
Carmine Gravino	University of Salerno, Italy
Noriko Hanakawa	Hannan University, Japan
Jens Heidrich	Fraunhofer IESE, Germany
Helena Holmström Olsson	University of Malmö, Sweden
Martin Höst	Lund University, Sweden
Frank Houdek	Daimler AG, Germany
Letizia Jaccheri	Norwegian University of Science and Technology, Norway
Andrea Janes	Free University of Bozen-Bolzano, Italy
Marcos Kalinowski	Pontifical Catholic University of Rio de Janeiro, Brazil
Petri Kettunen	University of Helsinki, Finland
Jil Klünder	Leibniz Universität Hannover, Germany
Marco Kuhrmann	University of Passau, Germany
Filippo Lanubile	University of Bari, Italy
Jingyue Li	Norwegian University of Science and Technology, Norway
Tomi Männistö	University of Helsinki, Finland
Kenichi Matsumoto	Nara Institute of Science and Technology, Japan
Sandro Morasca	Università degli Studi dell'Insubria, Italy
Silverio Martínez-Fernández	Universitat Politècnica de Catalunya, Spain
Juergen Muench	Reutlingen University, Germany
Anh Nguyen Duc	University College of Southeast Norway
Edson Oliveirajr	State University of Maringá, Brazil
Paolo Panaroni	INTECS, Italy
Oscar Pastor Lopez	Universitat Politècnica de València, Spain
Dietmar Pfahl	University of Tartu, Estoi
Rudolf Ramler	Software Competence Center Hagenberg, Austria
Daniel Rodriguez	University of Alcalá, Spain
Bruno Rossi	Masaryk University, Czech Republic

Gleison Santos   Federal University of the State of Rio de Janeiro, Brazil
Giuseppe Scanniello   University of Basilicata, Italy
Kurt Schneider   Leibniz Universität Hannover, Germany
Ezequiel Scott   University of Tartu, Estonia
Outi Sievi-Korte   Tampere University, Finland
Martin Solari   Universidad ORT Uruguay, Uruguay
Viktoria Stray   University of Oslo, Norway
Michael Stupperich   Daimler AG, Germany
Burak Turhan   University of Oulu, Finland
Rini Van Solingen   Delft University of Technology, The Netherlands
Stefan Wagner   University of Stuttgart, Germany
Hironori Washizaki   Waseda University, Japan
Dietmar Winkler   Vienna University of Technology, Austria

Program Committee Members (Industry Papers)

Alessandra Bagnato   Softeam, France
Michael Klaes   Fraunhofer IESE, Germany
Monalessa Barcellos   UFES, Brazil
Rafael de Mello   CEFET-RJ, Brazil
Maurizio Morisio   Politecnico di Torino, Italy
Jari Partanen   Bittium Wireless Ltd, Finland
Federico Tomassetti   Strumenta, Italy
Edoardo Vacchi   Red Hat, Italy
Rini Van Solingen   Delft University of Technology, The Netherlands

Contents

Human Factors

Software Quality

Agile and Migration

Implications on the Migration from Ionic to Android

Maria Caulo[1], Rita Francese[2], Giuseppe Scanniello[3(✉)] ⓘ,
and Genoveffa Tortora[2]

[1] Potenza, Italy
[2] University of Salerno, Fisciano, Italy
{francese,tortora}@unisa.it
[3] University of Basilicata, Potenza, Italy
giuseppe.scanniello@unibas.it

Abstract. In our past research, we presented an approach to migrate apps implemented by a cross-platform technology (*i.e.,* Ionic-Cordova-Angular) toward a native platform (*i.e.,* Android). We also conducted a study to assess if there was a difference in the user experience and in the affective reactions of end-users when they used the original version of an app and its migrated version. Since we were also interested to study the perspective of developers, we successively conducted a controlled experiment to study possible differences, *e.g.,* in terms of source code comprehension and affective reactions, when developers dealt with the original and migrated versions of a given app. In this paper, we present and discuss implications from both these studies and discuss them from both researchers' and practitioners' perspectives. For example, one of the most important takeaway results from the practitioners' perspective is: it is worthy to develop an app by using a cross-platform technology (*e.g.,* for time-to-market reasons) and then to assess if this app is ready for the market; if this happens, its migration to a native technology is a good option so letting the app penetrate more the market.

Keywords: Android · Ionic · Migration · User experience

1 Introduction

Migration means transferring an application to a new target environment holding the same features as the original application [6]. Migrating applications is relevant to consolidate past knowledge and to preserve past investments [12]. We can conjecture that the use of a migrated application should not affect how the end-user perceives it as compared with its original version, in terms of performances and User Interface (UI) interaction. This is to say that one of the success factors in the migration is that the end-user does not perceive any difference when using the original and migrated apps.

M. Caulo—Independent Researcher.

L. Ardito et al. (Eds.): PROFES 2021, LNCS 13126, pp. 3–19, 2021.
https://doi.org/10.1007/978-3-030-91452-3_1

To reduce the development cost and time-to-market many mobile-cross-platform development technologies have been proposed [14]. Their main advantage is that apps are developed once and delivered for a number of hardware/-software platforms. Cross-platform development can be also adopted for rapid prototyping. For example, start-uppers often have to release their mobile app in a very short time on many platforms (*e.g.,* iOS, Android) and they have neither time nor money and so cross-platform development represents the only possible solution. The results from an industrial survey [15] indicated that cross-platform development is largely adopted because it is less risky than native development. Respondents in this survey also thought that a cross-platform app should be preferred when not much money can be invested in native development. Once the value of cross-platform apps has been assessed with real users (*e.g.,* through beta-testing), these apps could be re-implemented or migrated towards native platforms (*e.g.,* Android or iOS). As an example, a Stack Overflow user asks some suggestions on how to substitute an Ionic app with a native Android one in the Google Play store, because he is *"planning to start a startup and currently not in a position to afford individual development for various platforms."*[2]. Further motivations for migrating to a native platform are represented by cross-platform development downsides [26,33], such as: *(i)* cross-platform frameworks often provide a worse user experience, *(ii)* they provide only limited access to native APIs, and *(iii)* developers must rely on the continuous development of the cross-platform frameworks to adapt changes of the changing native APIs.

In [9], we presented an approach to migrate apps implemented by cross-platform technology (*i.e.,* Ionic-Cordova-Angular) toward a native platform (*i.e.,* Android). We conducted a user study to investigate if there was a difference in the user experience[1] (UX) when using the cross-platform app version and the migrated one. We also took into account users' affective reactions[2]. Since we were also interested to study the perspective of developers, we successively conducted a controlled experiment to study possible differences when developers dealt with the source code of the original and migrated apps. The participants were novice developers (*i.e.,* graduate students), who were asked to comprehend, identify, and fix faults in the source code of the original and migrated apps. The results of such an experiment were presented in [8].

To summarize, we present a combined discussion of the results of our research previously presented in [8] and [9]. This allowed us to derive new results—from both the end-user's and developer's perspectives—that improved our body of knowledge on the relevance of approaches to migrate cross-platform apps toward a native platform considering researchers' and practitioners' perspectives.

---

[1] In the ISO 9241-210 [18], the user experience is defined as "a person's perceptions and responses that result from the use or anticipated use of a product, system or service". One of the most important components (*i.e.,* Usability, Adaptability, Desirability, and Value) of the user experience is usability.

[2] Affect is a concept used in psychology to describe the experience of feeling or emotion.

2   Related Work

Our study concerns the comparison between cross-platform and native apps. Comparing our study with those focused on performances (*i.e.*, [4, 11]), we differ from them on: *(i)* specific technologies considered (*i.e.*, design); *(ii)* aim of the study; and *(iii)* method applied. When considering those studies which compare cross-platform and native apps by means of user tests (*i.e.*, [3, 28, 30]), we differ from the studies of Malvolta *et al.* [28] and Noei *et al.* [30] for the design (*e.g.*, metrics and attributes to evaluate apps), the method used (*e.g.*, we do not mine opinions on the Google Play Store), and, also, the aims (*i.e.*, we do not only compare two versions of a given app but also evaluate our migration approach when applied on a real case). The research of Angulo and Ferre [3] might seem the most similar to that conducted in our user study: they also compared native and cross-platform tools used to deploy the same app by means of user tests. But our study differs from theirs in substantial ways. First, the aim: we do not only investigate end-users' opinions on the two versions of the app (*i.e.*, UX), but also measure their affective states (*i.e.*, Pleasure, Arousal, Dominance, and Liking). Second, the design: we have one experimental object in two versions: an Android app developed with Ionic-Cordova-Angular technologies and the same app implemented in native Android, while they have one experimental object in four versions: the native ones (Android and iOS) and the cross-platform ones (Titanium Android, and Titanium iOS). Then, the involved participants used their own smartphone, while we made the participants use the same smartphone; moreover, we did not make the participants execute specific tasks, while they did. The GUI of the native and the Titanium version (in both the cases of iOS and Android) significantly differ from one another, while in our case the GUIs are very similar, in a way that it was hard for the participants to distinguish one version from the other. Finally, the cross-platform technology they adopted was Titanium, while we use Ionic-Cordova-Angular technologies. As a consequence of all these differences, their conclusions involve several comparisons among Android and iOS (both native and Titanium), while in our case we focus on the differences between the native Android version and the Ionic-Cordova-Angular Android version. Concerning the developers' perspective, we do not focus on the selection of the most convenient cross-platform technology to suggest to developers, as made in [13, 14, 16, 17, 33], as well as we do not investigate the challenges concerning the developing phase, but we compare affective reactions that developers feel while executing three tasks on existing source code of the two aforementioned versions of the same app and also measure differences on the correctness of the results of their tasks. The work by Que *et al.* [32] might seem the most similar to that conducted in our controlled experiment but the most important differences concern the method used to conduct their research. Indeed, they did not execute an experiment with practitioners to make comparisons between cross-platform and native technologies in terms of ease of coding, debug/test, and distribution stage, but they make comparisons in theory.

3   Overall Assessment

The main RQ we investigated in our integrated study follows:

How does the migration of mobile applications from the Ionic Framework to Native code impact the end-user's and developer's experience/satisfaction?

The rationale behind this RQ is that: when migrating a cross-platform app towards a native platform, it is advisable that the UX and affective reactions improve when end-users deal with the migrated version of the app, and the maintenance and the evolution are easier for the migrated version of the app (or at least comparable). To this end, we conducted two empirical investigations: *(i)* a user study and *(ii)* a controlled experiment. The former aimed at comparing the affective reactions of end-users and their UX when using a cross-platform app and its migrated version. The latter aimed at studying if there is a difference when comprehending source code and performing fault fixing tasks on a cross-platform app and its migrated version.

To conduct both the investigations, we followed the guidelines by Wohlin *et al.* [40] and Juristo and Moreno [20]. We reported these studies on the basis of the guidelines suggested by Jedlitschka *et al.* [19]. In this paper, we limited ourselves to the presentation of the main aspects of both studies. The interested reader can find more details in our technical report (TR), available at bit.ly/3xIjjSJ.

3.1   User Study

In this section, we present the design and the results of our user study. The goal of this study was to evaluate the difference (if any) between apps developed by using cross-platform and native technologies from the perspective of the end-users. We compared the original version of an app, namely Movies-app [1], with that migrated to Android (see TR for details) in terms of affective reactions (*i.e.,* Pleasure, Arousal, Dominance, and Liking) of end-users, as well as the UX that they reached. If we observe a difference in favor of the Android migrated version of Movies-app with respect to these two aspects, we can speculate that the migration from Ionic-Cordova-Angular to Android impacts the end-user's experience.

Experimental Units. Initially, 19 people accepted to take part in the study, while 18 actually participated. The background of the participants can be summarized as follows: 12 people had a Bachelor Degree (ten in Computer Science and two in Mathematics); four people had a Master's Degree (three in Computer Engineering and one in Mathematics); one had a Ph.D. in Computer Science and one had a Scientific High School Diploma. Except for the latter participant, all the others were graduate students at the University of Basilicata.

Experimental Material and Tasks. The experimental objects (as already mentioned) consisted of the two versions of Movies-app: the original one and the migrated one. The experiment referred to a version of Movies-App which was available on GitHub. It is worth mentioning that the official Ionic website has recently adopted Movies-App as a demo app.[3] We asked the participants to freely use both versions of Movies-app.

We collected affective reactions by requiring participants to filling in the SAM [5] questionnaire. It considered the following dimensions evaluated on a nine-point scale for Pleasure, Arousal, and Dominance. As Koelstra *et al.* [25] did, we included the Liking dimension.

As for UX, we relied on the 26 statements by Laugwitz *et al.* [27]. These authors defined these statements to evaluate the quality of interactive products (*e.g.*, software). Each statement is made of two adjectives that describe some opposite qualities of products (*e.g.*, annoying and enjoyable). According to their objectives, these statements are grouped into the following six categories: Attractiveness, Perspicuity, Efficiency, Dependability, Stimulation, and Novelty.

Experiment Design. We opted for a *factorial crossover* [38] design. The number of periods (*i.e.*, Order) and treatments (*i.e.*, Technology) is the same and the treatment is applied only once [38]. We randomly assigned the participants into two groups, G_1 and G_2, both made of nine members. Each participant used both versions of the app. Participants in G_1 firstly used the Android version and then the Ionic-Cordova-Angular one, while vice-versa for G_2.

Hypotheses and Variables. We considered two independent variables: *Technology* and *Order*. The first indicates the technology used to implement the app. Therefore, Technology is a categorical variable with two values: Android and Ionic (abbreviating Ionic-Cordova-Angular). The Order variable indicates the order in which a participant used the version of the app (also known as *sequence* in the literature).

To measure affective reactions, we used four dependent variables (one for each dimension of SAM plus Liking). To measure UX, we used six dependent variables, one for each of the six categories of UEQ (User Experience Questionnaire), *e.g.*, Attractiveness. To obtain a single value for each category we summed the scores of each statement in that category. This practice to aggregate scores from single statements is widespread [39]. We formulated and tested the following parameterized null hypothesis.

- $H0_X$: *There is no statistically significant difference between the Android and Ionic Apps with respect to X.*

Where X is one of the dependent variables (*e.g.*, Liking).

Procedure. We performed the following sequential steps.

1. We invited Ph.D. and Master's students in Computer Science and Mathematics at the University of Basilicata and students enrolled in the course of

---

[3] https://ionicacademy.com/ionic-4-app-api-calls/.

Advanced Software Engineering of the Master's Degree in Computer Engineering from the same University. We also invited people working in the Software Engineering Laboratory at the University of Basilicata. They had to fill in a pre-questionnaire to gather demographic information. This design choice allowed us to have participants with heterogeneous backgrounds.
2. We randomly split the participants into two groups: G_1 and G_2.
3. The study session took place under controlled conditions in a research laboratory.
4. Depending on the group, each participant freely used a version of the Movies-app and then filled in the SAM+Liking questionnaire (first) and UEQ (later).
5. Each participant freely used the other version of the Movies-app and then filled in the SAM+Liking questionnaire (first) and UEQ (later).

All the participants used the same smartphone[4] when using both the versions of Movies-app.

Analysis Procedure. To test the null hypothesis, we used the ANOVA Type Statistic (ATS) [7]. It is used (*e.g.,* in Medicine) to analyze data from rating scales in factorial designs [22]. We built ATS models as follows:

$$X \sim Technology + Order + Technology : Order. \tag{1}$$

Where the dependent variable is X and Technology and Order are the manipulated ones. Technology:Order indicates the interaction between Technology and Order. This model allows determining if Technology, Order, and Technology:Order had statistically significant effects on a given dependent variable X. In the case of a statistically significant effect of a factor, we planned to use Cliff's δ effect size. It is conceived to be used with ordinal variables [10] and assumes the following values: *negligible* if $|\delta| < 0.147$, *small* if $0.147 \leq |\delta| < 0.33$, *medium* if $0.33 \leq |\delta| < 0.474$, or *large* if $|\delta| \geq 0.474$ [34].

To verify if an effect is statistically significant, we fixed (as customary) α to 0.05. That is, we admit 5% chance of a Type-I-error occurring [40]. If a p-value is less than 0.05, we deemed the effect as statistically significant.

3.2   User Study Results

Android vs. Ionic with Respect to Affective Reactions of End-Users. Median values seem to suggest that the participants in both G_1 and G_2 obtained more positive affective reactions when dealing with the migrated version of Movies-app. The smallest difference between Ionic and Android is for the Pleasure dimension. The median values are seven and 6.5, without considering the participants' distributions between the groups, respectively. As for G_1 the median values are the same, *i.e.,* 7, whatever is the Technology. As for Liking,

---

[4] Umidigi A3, a Dual-Sim smartphone equipped with Android 8.1.0, 5.5" screen with 720 × 1440 resolution points, 3300mAh capacity battery, 2 GB RAM, 16 GB of expandable memory, MediaTek MT6739 processor.

Table 1. Median values for Attractiveness, Perspicuity, Efficiency, Dependability, Stimulation, and Novelty.

| | Android | | | | | | Ionic | | | | | |
	Attract.	Perspicuity	Efficiency	Depend.	Stimulation	Novelty	Attract.	Perspicuity	Efficiency	Depend.	Stimulation	Novelty
G_1	33	27	23	23	19	18	28	24	17	18	18	16
G_2	23	25	23	21	18	14	28	26	18	22	18	12
Total	32.5	26.5	23	22.5	19	17	28	24.5	17.5	19	18	14

the difference between the two versions of Movies-app (without considering the participants' distributions between the groups) is very clear: eight for Android and six for Ionic. The median values for G_1 are eight for Android and seven for Ionic, while the median values for G_2 are six for Android and five for Ionic.

The results of our statistic inference suggest a statistically significant difference with respect to Liking. Therefore, we can reject $H0_{Liking}$ ($p - value = 0.0494$) with a *medium* effect size (0.383), and then we can postulate that the participants liked more the migrated version of Movies-app than its original version. As for Liking, we also observed a significant interaction between the two independent variables. This interaction is significant also for Pleasure. This means that there is a combined positive effect of Technology and Order for these two dependent variables.

> **We observed that there is a slight preference for the app migrated to the Android platform, although this is statistically significant only for the Liking dimension with a medium effect size.**

Android vs. Ionic with Respect to the UX. In Table 1, we report the median values for the dependent variables measuring the UX grouped by G_1 and G_2. The median values by grouping observations only considering Technology are also shown (*i.e.,* Total row). The median values seem to suggest that the participants, in general, expressed more positive UX when dealing with the migrated version of Movies-app. The smallest difference between the two versions of this app can be observed for the category Stimulation. Descriptive statistics also show the following pattern: the participants in G_1 (those administered first with the Android version of Movies-app) were more positive with respect to the migrated version of the app as compared with the participants in G_2 (those administered first with the Ionic-Cordova-Angular version). The only exception is Efficiency since the values are 23 for both groups.

The results our statistic inference indicate a statistical significant difference with respect to Efficiency ($p - value = 0.0004$) with a *large* effect size (0.67). Therefore, we can assert that the participant found the Android version of the app to be more efficient than its original version since we were able to reject the null hypothesis $H0_{Efficiency}$. We also observed a significant interaction between Technology and Order for Novelty. This means that there is a combined positive effect of these two independent variables.

> **The UX is better for the app migrated to the Android platform although the effect of Technology is significant only for Efficiency, where the size of the effect is large.**

3.3   Controlled Experiment

If through the controlled experiment we observe a difference in the source code comprehensibility and fault identification and fixing when dealing with the two versions of Movies-app, we can speculate that the migration from Ionic to that platform impacts the developers' experience. We were also interested in assessing how developers perceive source code comprehension tasks and fault identification and fixing tasks. Therefore, we also focused on both affective reactions. A positive (or negative) effect of a technology (Ionic-Cordova-Angular vs Android) with respect to affective reactions might imply that a developer is more (or less) effective when performing these kinds of tasks.

Experimental Units. The participants were 39 students of the "Enterprise Mobile Applications Development" course at the University of Salerno (Italy). This course focused on the study of Ionic-Cordova-Angular technologies. The average age of participants was 24. At the time of the experiment, participants were 39 months (on average) experienced with programming and ten months (on average) experienced with mobile programming, in particular. They passed the programming exams with a rating of 27.4/30 on average. The participants before the "Enterprise Mobile Applications Development" course passed the "Mobile Development" course, which was focused on Android.

Experimental Material. We used the source code of two versions of Movies-app. Its code is not very complex and it is small enough to allow good control over participants. The problem domain of this app can be considered familiar to the participants. The reader can find further details in our TR. We used the SAM [5] questionnaire to gather affective reactions of participants when accomplishing comprehension and fault identification and fixing tasks. We also included the Liking dimension in addition to those considered in the SAM questionnaire.

Tasks. We asked the participants to perform three tasks in the following order:

1. *Comprehension Task.* We defined a comprehension questionnaire composed of six questions that admitted open answers. The questions of this questionnaire were the same for both the groups of participants; those administered with the source code of the Ionic-Cordova-Angular version of Movies-app and those administered with the source code of its migrated version.
2. *Fault Identification.* Similar to Scanniello *et al.* [35], we seeded (four) faults in the source code of the two versions of the app. We asked the participants to fix these faults providing them with a fault report for each seeded one. The bug report was the same independently from the app version. We seeded faults by applying mutation operators (*i.e.*, predefined program modification rules) by Kim *et al.* [23]. We asked the participants to document where they believed each fault was in the source code. It is worth mentioning that we seeded faults in the source code which the participants did not have to analyze to answer the

questions of the comprehension questionnaire. However, we could not prevent that the participants could have analyzed the faulty source code during the comprehension tasks. This threat to conclusion validity equally affects fault identification (and fixing) results for both the versions of Movies-app.

3. *Fault Fixing.* Participants had to fix the faults they identified. We asked them to work with a fault at a time. Faults do not interfere with one another.

4. *Post questionnaire.* It included a SAM+Liking questionnaire for each task the participants accomplished.

Hypotheses and Variables. As made for the user study, we considered Technology as the independent variable (or manipulated factor). This variable indicates the technology with which the app was implemented. As for the source-code comprehension task, we used *Comprehension* as the dependent variable. It measures the correctness of understanding of a participant given a version of Movies-app by analyzing the answers provided to the comprehension questionnaire. We used an approach based on that by Kamsties *et al.* [21] that computes the number of correct responses to the questions of that questionnaire. The dependent variable *Comprehension* assumes values between zero and six (*i.e.*, the number of questions in the comprehension questionnaire). A value close to six indicates that a participant comprehended the source code very well. A fault is successfully identified if the participant correctly marked the source code where the fault was seeded. We named the variable counting the faults correctly identified as *Correctness of Fault Identification.* This variable assumes values between zero and four (*i.e.*, the number of faults). The higher the value the better it is. As for the fault fixing task, we defined the variable: *Correctness of Fault Fixing.* It counts the number of seeded faults the participants correctly fixed in the source code of the experimental object. Also, *Correctness of Fault Fixing* assumes values between zero and four (*i.e.*, the number of faults). The higher the value the better it is.

As for affective reactions, we considered four dependent variables (one for each dimension of SAM plus the Liking one) for each kind of task the participants performed: comprehension, fault identification, and fault fixing.

We tested the following parametrized null hypothesis.

– $H1_X$: *There is no statistically significant difference between the participants who were administered with the cross-platform and the native versions of Movies-app with respect to X (i.e., one of the considered dependent variables).*

Experiment Design. We used the *one factor with two treatments* design [40]. We randomly divided the participants into two groups: Ionic (*i.e.*, control group) and Android (*i.e.*, treatment group). The participants in the first group were asked to accomplish only the experiment tasks on the version of Movies-app implemented by using Ionic-Cordova-Angular technology. The participants in the second group were asked to accomplish the tasks only on the version of such app migrated to Android. The participants in the Ionic group were 20, while those in the Android one were 19.

Procedure. The experimental procedure included the following sequential steps.

1. We invited all the students and asked them to fill in the pre-questionnaire to gather their demographic information.
2. We randomly split the participants into two groups: Ionic and Android.
3. The experiment session took place under controlled conditions in a laboratory at the University of Salerno. All the used PCs had the same (Hardware/Software) configuration.
4. The participant performed the comprehension task by answering the questions of the comprehension questionnaire.
5. We asked the participants to deal with each fault at a time. The participants could pass to the next fault only when they either fixed the previous fault or were aware that they could not identify/fix it.
6. Participants filled in the post-questionnaire by rating affective reactions.
7. Participants compressed and archived their version of the app with the source code they modified. We then collected all those versions.

Analysis Procedure. We carried out the following steps:

- We undertook the descriptive statistics.
- To test the null hypotheses, we planned to use either an unpaired t-test or the Mann-Whitney U test [29]. Unlike the t-test, the Mann-Whitney U test does not require the assumption of normal distributions. To study the normality of data, we use the Shapiro-Wilk W test [36]. Regarding this test, a p-value lower than a fixed α indicates that data are not normally distributed. In the case of a statistically significant effect of Technology, we planned to compute effect size (Cohen's d or Cliff's δ) to measure the magnitude of such a difference. We applied a non-parametric statistical analysis (Mann-Whitney U test [29]) when considering affective reaction. If any statistically significant difference is found, we measure its extent through Cliff's δ.

As we did for the data analysis of the user study, we fixed α to 0.05 to verify if an effect is statistically significant.

3.4   Controlled Experiment Results

In Table 2, we report the descriptive statistics and the results of the statistical tests performed (*i.e.*, p-values).

Android vs. Ionic with Respect to Source-Code Comprehension. As for *Comprehension*, descriptive statistics (Table 2) do not show a huge difference in the source-code comprehension the participants achieved in the Ionic and Android groups. Descriptive statistics indicate that the participants in the Ionic group answered the questions of the comprehension questionnaire better: the mean and median values are 0.625 and 0.667, respectively; while the mean and

Table 2. Descriptive Statistics of Comprehension and Correctness of Fault Identification and Fixing.

Technology	Comprehension				Correctness of fault identification				Correctness of fault fixing			
	Mean	Std. Dev	Median	p-value	Mean	Std. Dev	Median	p-value	Mean	Std. Dev	Median	p-value
Android	0.5	0.266	0.5	0.109	0.882	0.255	1	0.971	0.829	0.289	1	0.935
Ionic	0.625	0.152	0.667		0.9	0.189	1		0.850	0.235	1	

median values for the Android group are both 0.5. The results of the Shapiro-Wilk W test suggest that data were not normally distributed in the Ionic group (p-value = 0.007). For such a reason, we performed the Mann-Whitney U test. The returned p-value is 0.109, *i.e.,* there is no statistically significant difference between the comprehension that the participants in the two groups achieved.

> **The results of the Mann-Whitney U test do not allow us to reject the null hypothesis, thus we could not observe a statistically significant difference in the comprehensibility of the source code written in either Android or Ionic-Cordova-Angular technologies.**

Android vs. Ionic with Respect to Fault Identification. Descriptive statistics (Table 2) suggest that all the participants achieved high correctness in the identification of the faults. The mean values for the *Correctness of Fault Identification* are 0.882 and 0.9 for Android and Ionic, respectively. The results of the Shapiro-Wilk W test show that data did not follow a normal distribution: the p-values are 1.294e−06 for Android and 1.422e−06 for Ionic. The results of the Mann-Whitney U test do not indicate any statistically significant difference between the data in the two groups since the p-value is 0.971.

> **The results of the statistical inference do not allow us to reject the null hypothesis, thus, also in this case, we could not observe a statistically significant difference in the identification of faults in the source code written in either Android or Ionic-Cordova-Angular technologies.**

Android vs. Ionic with Respect to Fault Fixing. As we could suppose, for *Correctness of Fault Fixing* we observed a pattern similar to *Correctness of Fault Identification*. The participants in the groups achieved high correctness in the fixing of the faults in both the versions of Movies-app (see Table 2). Data were not normally distributed since the Shapiro-Wilk W test returned 2.04e-05 and 2.656e-05 as the p-values for the Android and Ionic groups, respectively. Then, we applied the Mann-Whitney U test and we obtained 0.935 as the p-value.

> **We did not observe a statistically significant difference in the fixing of faults in the source code written in either Android or Ionic-Cordova-Angular technologies.**

Android vs. Ionic with Respect to the Affective Reactions of Developers. As Sullivan and Artino [37] suggest, we used median values and frequencies as descriptive statistics of the dependent variables PLS_K, ARS_K, DOM_K, and LIK_K (where K is the kind of task, *i.e.,* source code comprehension and fault identification and fixing). In Table 3, we report the median values and

Table 3. Median values and statistical test results for the affective reactions of the participants in the study.

Technology	PLS_{Comp}	ARS_{Comp}	DOM_{Comp}	LIK_{Comp}	PLS_{Ident}	ARS_{Ident}	DOM_{Ident}	LIK_{Ident}	PLS_{Fix}	ARS_{Fix}	DOM_{Fix}	LIK_{Fix}
Android	7	7	8	7	8	7	8	8	8	7	8	8
Ionic	7.5	6.5	9	8	8	7.5	9	8	8	7.5	8	8.5
p-value	0.988	0.503	0.106	0.326	0.352	0.626	0.206	0.912	0.538	0.966	0.768	0.59

the p-values of the statistical test performed. As for the Comprehension task, there is not a huge difference between the dependent variables (*i.e.*, PLS_{Comp}, ARS_{Comp}, DOM_{Comp}, and LIK_{Comp}) in the two groups. However, the medians for the Ionic group were always higher than the Android group ones, except for ARS_{Comp}. The Mann-Whitney U test returned p-values higher than 0.05 for all the dependent variables, hence there is no statistically significant difference between the affective reactions of the two groups.

Also for the Fault Identification task, there is not a huge difference between the two groups. Medians of dependent variables of the Ionic group were always greater or equal to the Android group ones. The Mann-Whitney U test returned p-values higher than 0.05 for all the dependent variables signifying that there is no statistically significant difference between the affective reactions of both the groups. The analysis of the data from the Fault Fixing task allowed identifying the same pattern as we identified for the Fault Identification task.

> The affective reactions of developers in the two groups do not show a statistically significant difference when dealing with a cross-platform app and its migrated version to comprehend source code and identify and fix faults in that code.

4   Overall Discussion

In this section, we discuss implications and future extensions related to the results of both our studies. We conclude this section by discussing the threats that could have affected the validity of the obtained results.

4.1   Implications and Future Extensions

We delineate a number of practical implications from the researcher and the practitioner perspectives. We also suggest possible future directions for research. We believe that one of the values of our paper concerns the body of knowledge on the relevance of approaches to migrate cross-platform apps toward a native platform and how to use this body of knowledge for future research.

- End-users' opinions are in favor of the Android (migrated) version of Movies-app in terms of Liking and Efficiency. However, UEQ statements measuring how generally appealing the two apps are (*i.e.*, Attractiveness, Perspicuity, Stimulation, and Novelty) seem not to highlight any preference for either technology. Thus, we conjecture that the Liking dimension might be influenced by the performance of the apps perceived by end-users. This point has implications for the practitioner, who could invest initial efforts in the development of apps through a cross-platform technology (*e.g.*, for time-to-market or prototyping reasons) and then she could decide to migrate such apps towards a native technology to have a better UX and let the app affirm in the market.

- Overall results of the controlled experiment suggest that novice developers did not find a huge difference between the two studied technologies (Ionic-Cordova-Angular and Android) in terms of the source-code comprehension and the correctness of fault identification and fixing (although a slight difference in the size of the two versions of the app). Furthermore, the affective reactions of developers seem not to be affected when performing tasks as well as the difficulty perceived to accomplish them (see TR). This outcome might be relevant to the practitioner. In particular, our study seems to support one of the main results by Francese *et al.* [15]; *i.e.*, cross-platform development is valuable when an app has to be run in different hardware/software platforms. That is, native technology should be preferred in all the other cases.
- Outcomes of the controlled experiment also suggest future research on the design and the implementation of native and cross-platform apps. However, our experiment is based on tasks concerning existing source code, but there could be found a difference in the use of these technologies when conducting implementation tasks. This point is of interest to the researcher.
- The researcher could be interested to study if the shown outcomes hold also for apps developed by cross-platform technologies different from those considered in our research (*i.e.*, Ionic-Cordova-Angular) when migrating them towards a native platform (*e.g.*, Android as we did, but also iOS or others). An experimental approach similar to that used (user study and a controlled experiment) could be adopted.
- The adoption of a migration approach should also consider the cost for its application. This aspect, not considered in this paper, is of particular interest for the practitioner. In fact, it could be crucial knowing whether it is less costly to migrate an apps developed by cross-platform technology to a native platform rather than to re-engineer it. Obviously, this aspect is also relevant for the researcher because she could define predictive models to quantify costs and benefits to migrate or re-engineer cross-platform app. Our research contributes to justify further work on this subject.
- The experiment object is of a specific kind of apps, *i.e.*, the entertainment universe. The researcher and the practitioner could be interested in studying whether our results also hold for different kinds of apps. It could be also of interest for the researcher to study whether our outcomes scale to applications more complex and larger than that studied.
- The diffusion of a new technology/method is made easier when empirical evaluations are performed and their results show that such a technology/method solves actual issues [31]. The results of our investigations suggest that migrating cross-platform apps towards a native platform matters from the practitioner perspective. This outcome could increase the diffusion of such a kind of migration approach and the definition of new ones. These points are clearly relevant for both the practitioner and the researcher.

4.2   Threats to Validity

Internal Validity. A possible threat to Internal Validity is voluntary participation (*selection threat*). We embedded the experiment in a University course and did not consider experiment scores to grade participants in that course.

To deal with *threat of diffusion or treatment imitations*, we monitored participants and asked back material to prevent them from exchanging information in the controlled experiment. We also prevented the diffusion of the experimental material by gathering it at the end of the tasks from all participants.

Another threat might be *resentful demoralization*—participants assigned to a less desirable treatment might not perform as well as they normally would. This kind of task is present only in the controlled experiment.

Construct Validity. A possible threat is concerned to the *threat of hypotheses guessing* could be present. Although the participants were not informed about our goals, they might guess them and change their behavior accordingly. To deal with this kind of threat we did not disclose the goals to the participants.

To mitigate *evaluation apprehension threat*, we reassured participants in the controlled experiments that their data were treated anonymously. We also asked the participants to sign a consent form to use their data.

Conclusion Validity. We involved participants with a different background in the user study and then the *threat of random heterogeneity of participants* could be present. In the controlled experiment, participants followed the same course, underwent the same training, and had a similar background.

Reliability of measures is another threat to conclusion validity. We used well-known and widely used measures in both studies.

Low statistical power refers to the ability of the test to reveal a true pattern in the data. If the power is low, there is a risk that an erroneous conclusion is drawn from data. To partially deal with this kind of threat we used robust and sensitive statistical tests [24].

External Validity. The participants in the controlled experiment were graduate students. This could pose some threats to the generalizability of the results to the population of professionals developers (*threat of interaction of selection and treatment*). The studied technology is relatively novel and then we can speculate that participants are more experienced than many professionals.

The experimental object might affect external validity (*threat of the interaction of setting and treatment*). In particular, Movies-app could be not representative of the universe of real-world apps.

5   Conclusion

Results suggest that migrating cross-platform apps developed by Ionic-Cordova-Angular towards Android matters from both the developers' and end-users' perspectives. This main outcome allows formulating the most important practical takeaway message from our research: it is worthy to develop an app by using a cross-platform technology (*e.g.*, for time-to-market reasons) and then to assess if this app is ready for the market; if this happens its migration to a native technology is a good option to provide better support to the UX so letting the app penetrate more the app market.

References

1. Movies-App. https://github.com/okode/movies-app
2. The Stackoverflow comment. https://stackoverflow.com/questions/34986098/migrating-from-hybrid-app-to-native-app-at-later-point-of-time
3. Angulo, E., Ferre, X.: A case study on cross-platform development frameworks for mobile applications and UX. In: Proceedings of HCI (2014)
4. Biørn-Hansen, A., Rieger, C., Grønli, T.-M., Majchrzak, T.A., Ghinea, G.: An empirical investigation of performance overhead in cross-platform mobile development frameworks. Empir. Softw. Eng. **25**(4), 2997–3040 (2020). https://doi.org/10.1007/s10664-020-09827-6
5. Bradley, M.M., Lang, P.J.: Measuring emotion: the self-assessment manikin and the semantic differential. J. Behav. Ther. Exp. Psychiatry **25**(1), 49–59 (1994)
6. Brodie, M.L., Stonebraker, M.: Legacy Information Systems Migration: Gateways, Interfaces, and the Incremental Approach (1995)
7. Brunner, E., Dette, H., Munk, A.: Box-type approximations in nonparametric factorial designs. J. Am. Stat. Assoc. **92**(440), 1494–1502 (1997)
8. Caulo, M., Francese, R., Scanniello, G., Spera, A.: Dealing with comprehension and bugs in native and cross-platform apps: a controlled experiment. In: Franch, X., Männistö, T., Martínez-Fernández, S. (eds.) PROFES 2019. LNCS, vol. 11915, pp. 677–693. Springer, Cham (2019). https://doi.org/10.1007/978-3-030-35333-9_53
9. Caulo, M., Francese, R., Scanniello, G., Spera, A.: Does the migration of cross-platform apps towards the android platform matter? An approach and a user study. In: Franch, X., Männistö, T., Martínez-Fernández, S. (eds.) PROFES 2019. LNCS, vol. 11915, pp. 120–136. Springer, Cham (2019). https://doi.org/10.1007/978-3-030-35333-9_9
10. Cliff, N.: Ordinal methods for behavioral data analysis (1996). https://books.google.it/books?id=bIJFvgAACAAJ
11. Corral, L., Sillitti, A., Succi, G.: Mobile multiplatform development: an experiment for performance analysis. Proc. Comput. Sci. **10**, 736–743 (2012)
12. De Lucia, A., Francese, R., Scanniello, G., Tortora, G.: Developing legacy system migration methods and tools for technology transfer. Softw. Pract. Exp. **38**, 1333–1364 (2008)
13. El-Kassas, W.S., Abdullah, B.A., Yousef, A.H., Wahba, A.: ICPMD: integrated cross-platform mobile development solution. In: International Conference on Computer Engineering and Systems, pp. 307–317 (2014)
14. El-Kassas, W.S., Abdullah, B.A., Yousef, A.H., Wahba, A.M.: Taxonomy of cross-platform mobile applications development approaches. Ain Shams Eng. J. **8**(2), 163–190 (2017)
15. Francese, R., Gravino, C., Risi, M., Scanniello, G., Tortora, G.: Mobile app development and management: results from a qualitative investigation. In: Proceedings of International Conference on Mobile Software Engineering and Systems, pp. 133–143 (2017)

16. Heitkötter, H., Hanschke, S., Majchrzak, T.A.: Evaluating cross-platform development approaches for mobile applications. In: Cordeiro, J., Krempels, K.-H. (eds.) WEBIST 2012. LNBIP, vol. 140, pp. 120–138. Springer, Heidelberg (2013). https://doi.org/10.1007/978-3-642-36608-6_8

17. Heitkötter, H., Kuchen, H., Majchrzak, T.A.: Extending a model-driven cross-platform development approach for business apps. Sci. Comput. Program. **97**, 31–36 (2015)

18. Ergonomics of human system interaction - Part 210: Human-centered design for interactive systems. Standard, International Organization for Standardization (2009)

19. Jedlitschka, A., Ciolkowski, M., Pfahl, D.: Reporting experiments in software engineering. In: Shull, F., Singer, J., Sjøberg, D.I.K. (eds.) Guide to Advanced Empirical Software Engineering, pp. 201–228. Springer, London (2008). https://doi.org/10.1007/978-1-84800-044-5_8

20. Juristo, N., Moreno, A.: Basics of Software Engineering Experimentation. Springer, Heidelberg (2001). https://doi.org/10.1007/978-1-4757-3304-4

21. Kamsties, E., von Knethen, A., Reussner, R.: A controlled experiment to evaluate how styles affect the understandability of requirements specifications. Inf. Soft. Technol. **45**(14), 955–965 (2003)

22. Kaptein, M., Nass, C., Markopoulos, P.: Powerful and consistent analysis of likert-type ratingscales, vol. 4, pp. 2391–2394 (2010)

23. Kim, S., Clark, J.A., McDermid, J.A.: The rigorous generation of java mutation operators using hazop technical report (1999)

24. Kitchenham, B., et al.: Robust statistical methods for empirical software engineering. Empir. Softw. Eng. **22**(2), 579–630 (2016)

25. Koelstra, S., et al.: DEAP: a database for emotion analysis using physiological signals. IEEE Trans. Affect. Comput. **3**(1), 18–31 (2012)

26. Latif, M., Lakhrissi, Y., Nfaoui, E.H., Es-Sbai, N.: Cross platform approach for mobile application development: A survey. In: Proceedings of International Conference on Information Technology for Organizations Development, pp. 1–5 (2016)

27. Laugwitz, B., Held, T., Schrepp, M.: Construction and evaluation of a user experience questionnaire. In: Holzinger, A. (ed.) USAB 2008. LNCS, vol. 5298, pp. 63–76. Springer, Heidelberg (2008). https://doi.org/10.1007/978-3-540-89350-9_6

28. Malavolta, I., Ruberto, S., Soru, T., Terragni, V.: End users' perception of hybrid mobile apps in the google play store. In: Proceedings of International Conference on Mobile Services, pp. 25–32 (2015)

29. Mann, H.B., Whitney, D.R.: On a test of whether one of two random variables is stochastically larger than the other. Ann. Math. Statist. **18**(1), 50–60 (1947)

30. Noei, E., Syer, M.D., Zou, Y., Hassan, A.E., Keivanloo, I.: A study of the relation of mobile device attributes with the user-perceived quality of android apps. In: Proceedings International Conference on Software Analysis, Evolution and Reengineering, p. 469 (2018)

31. Pfleeger, S.L., Menezes, W.: Marketing technology to software practitioners. IEEE Softw. **17**(1), 27–33 (2000)

32. Que, P., Guo, X., Zhu, M.: A comprehensive comparison between hybrid and native app paradigms. In: Proceedings of International Conference on Computational Intelligence and Communication Networks, pp. 611–614 (2016)

33. Rieger, C., Majchrzak, T.A.: Towards the definitive evaluation framework for cross-platform app development approaches. J. Syst. Softw. **153**, 175–199 (2019)

34. Romano, J., Kromrey, J.: Appropriate statistics for ordinal level data: should we really be using t-test and Cohen's d for evaluating group differences on the NSSE and other surveys? (2006)
35. Scanniello, G., Risi, M., Tramontana, P., Romano, S.: Fixing faults in C and java source code: abbreviated vs. full-word identifier names. ACM Trans. Softw. Eng. Methodol. **26**(2), 6:1–6:43 (2017)
36. Shapiro, S., Wilk, M.: An analysis of variance test for normality. Biometrika **52**(3–4), 591–611 (1965)
37. Sullivan, G., Artino, A.: Analyzing and interpreting data from Likert-type scales. J. Grad. Med. Educ. **5**, 541–2 (2013)
38. Vegas, S., Apa, C., Juristo, N.: Crossover designs in software engineering experiments: benefits and perils. IEEE Trans. Softw. Eng. **42**(2), 120–135 (2016)
39. Watson, D., Clark, L.A., Tellegen, A.: Development and validation of brief measures of positive and negative affect: the PANAS scales. J. Pers. Soc. Psychol. **54**(6), 1063 (1988)
40. Wohlin, C., Runeson, P., Höst, M., Ohlsson, M., Regnell, B., Wesslén, A.: Experimentation in Software Engineering. Springer, Heidelberg (2012). https://doi.org/10.1007/978-3-642-29044-2

The Migration Journey Towards Microservices

Hamdy Michael Ayas[✉], Philipp Leitner, and Regina Hebig

Chalmers | University of Gothenburg, Gothenburg, Sweden
{ayas,philipp.leitner,hebig}@chalmers.se

Abstract. Organizations initiate migration projects in order to change their software architecture towards microservices and ripe the many benefits that microservices have to offer. However, migrations often take place in unstructured, non-systemic, and trial-and-error manners, resulting in unclarity and uncertainty in such projects. In this study, we investigate 16 software development organizations that migrated towards microservices and we chart their detailed migration journey. We do so by conducting an interview survey using some of the tools from Grounded Theory in 19 interviews from 16 organizations. Our results showcase the evolutionary and iterative nature of the migration journey at an architectural-level and system-implementation level. Also, we identify 18 detailed activities that take place in these levels, categorized in the four phases of 1) designing the architecture, 2) altering the system, 3) setting up supporting artifacts, and 4) implementing additional technical artifacts.

Keywords: Microservices · Migrations · Grounded theory · Process

1 Introduction

Microservices is a type of service-oriented architecture, that many organizations developing software adopt, resulting to the appearance of many microservices migration projects. A Microservices Based Architecture (MSA) provides benefits like scalability, maintainability, time to market [9] and sometimes it is a way to help transitioning to the cloud [15]. Unavoidably, there are many practices that direct organizations on how to develop or migrate towards such MSAs and it is important to investigate them in detail. Empirical evidence on migration projects can bring light to such practices as well as prepare practitioners for the expected migration journey and what activities such a journey entails [23]. Hence, studying and understanding how companies make their transitions towards MSAs can also provide a detailed theoretical basis to researchers on the different aspects of migrations [13]. Also, there is a need in empirically investigating the details of migrations comprehensively from different points of view [5].

Migration projects are not simple, since migrating a system towards microservices (from a monolithic architecture) is a long endeavour with many things to

L. Ardito et al. (Eds.): PROFES 2021, LNCS 13126, pp. 20–35, 2021.
https://doi.org/10.1007/978-3-030-91452-3_2

consider and an inherent complexity [19]. This is mainly due to the distributed nature of designing and developing MSAs [18,27]. Also, current approaches often need exhaustive specifications of the migrating system, which limits the practical applicability of different decomposition approaches, making migration processes unstructured and non-systemic [6]. Research and best practices stemming from industry provide some approaches on migrations, covering many aspects [1,19].

However, it is not always clear how aspects of migrations connect to each other and how migration activities take place in relation to one another. On the one hand, microservices migrations are characterized by overarching patterns like decomposing the old system or introducing new technologies [2]. On the other hand, microservices migrations have practical activities that are more specific and narrow in scope, operationalizing these overarching patterns [9,14]. For example, migrations entail technical activities that actually take place in the code (e.g. actually splitting the code-base into small services) [11]. Therefore, there is an observed shortage of approaches that are pragmatic in describing accurately different migration activities, on different levels of abstraction and their relations [9]. Also there are not many studies organizing rigorously and systematically aspects that describe precedent migrations [6].

We address this by aggregating the migration journey that 16 migrating software development organizations went through and separating the activities they do in different levels of abstraction. We do so by conducting an interview survey using some of the techniques from Grounded Theory in 19 interviews with engineers from companies of different size, industries, and geographical regions. All interviewed developers have been part of their companies' migration journeys towards microservices. Our analysis is re-using qualitative interview data gathered as part of a different study, that focuses on the decision-making taking place in microservices migrations [16]. We address the following research question:

RQ1: *What is the migration journey that companies go through when transitioning towards microservices?*

RQ1.1: On what different levels can the migration journey take place on?
RQ1.2: What do those different levels of the migration journey entail?

Our results showcase that changes in microservices migrations take place in two modes of change. These are: *1) the architectural-level and 2) the system-level.* In addition, we describe the iterative nature of the migration journey in different modes of pace in each level. These modes of pace are longer-term changes on the architectural-level and shorter-term changes on the other level. We provided details on the different levels of the journey in 4 reoccurring, thematic phases that are *1) Make design decisions, 2) Alter the system, 3) Setup supporting artifacts, and 4) Implement additional technical artifacts.* This structure and understanding of migrations can be used to identify solutions for accelerating the required change. The resulting journey can help researchers distinguish between the different modes of change happening during migrations. Similarly, practitioners can use these different modes to maintain their scope to the appropriate mode when migrating.

2   Related Work

Microservices are a way of structuring systems into loosely coupled pieces that are developed and operated independently, each with its own individual resources [26]. These individual pieces communicate with each other to compose a complete system [27]. Usually there is a large leap between a monolith and a microservice architecture [18]. A migration/transition is the crucial project that takes the software development organization through the leap [12,23]. Therefore, there are many fundamental differences between a software application based on a monolithic architecture and a system based on microservices [19]. However, we still need to understand more in detail these differences and how the transition between the two architectures can possibly take place.

Migrating to a microservice-based architecture can be very rewarding for organizations because microservices promise to enable many benefits [19,21]. The migration journey is often very helpful to improve the developed system [1]. Hence, organizations are very often extremely motivated to migrate towards microservice-based architectures and there are many potential ways to do so [19]. Microservices promise improvements in many aspects like scalability, maintainability and continuous development [5]. Specifically, resource-demanding parts of a software application can be scaled independently and unburden the rest of the system. Also, the modular organization of the system with minimal dependencies allows improved maintainability [7]. In addition, the flexibility in service design that can be achieved enables a lot of potential in continuous delivery of new business value [8]. All these benefits are promised for the completion of the migration. However, it is not clear how they can be achieved in intermediary stages and have tangible benefits during the migration.

Microservices are increasingly getting widely adopted by different organizations and therefore, research on microservice migration projects gains popularity [12]. Previous research investigated the area surrounding the architectural characteristics of microservices migrations [2,9], as well as how it relates to the overall development process [23]. In addition, existing research provides several solutions on how to technically enact a migration. These solutions include splitting a system, transforming the code of an application or identifying services in a monolith [10]. In addition, such solutions often provide tools on how to identify and decompose services, assuming a technical and deterministic viewpoint on the migration [11]. This is not always ideal, as migrations are more often than not complex endeavours with many things to consider [19]. So many, that it seems virtually impossible to perform a migration in a one-off project. Such intricate approaches that see migrations as complex endeavours are not sufficiently investigated.

Every migration contains aspects that are not considered but in hindsight seem that they should have been better thought through, leading to Microservices Bad Smells [24]. Balalaie et al. (2018), provide a valuable set of patterns that can guide a microservices migration initiative [2] and even though the patterns are very strong recommendations, some of them are not as trivial as they would be needed for practitioners to utilize them for a smooth migration. In addition, existing research presents practices with negative impact (aka anti-patterns) that are often used and undermine migration initiatives [25]. Many studies provide sufficient arguments on how to tackle problems that arise and how to technically perform a migration. However, all those lead to work for engineers that needs to be done and more often than not, the tasks to implement them are unknown to be planned accordingly. Also there is a gap of work that organizes rigorously and systematically aspects that describe precedent migrations [6].

The technologies and tools that implement microservices have grown over the years and got extensively applied [12]. Also, techniques to evaluate decomposition approaches are often not founded/evaluated on applications from industry, making problems appear in later stages of the development lifecycle, i.e. in production, when applied [6]. However, the focus is mainly on what stakeholders and developers could do differently and not what stakeholders and developers face during a migration. For example, migrating towards microservices entails challenges and activities that are not always in line with current best practices and these can be identified and investigated [5]. Hence, learning from organizations that migrated to microservices, can also help us understand the elements of a migration journey and raise awareness for them over to future migrations.

3   Methodology

Our research method is an interview study, based on techniques from grounded theory, with practitioners who have recently participated in a microservices migration project. We adopt such an inductive approach in order to better understand what developers go through during a migration and derive our theory from a comprehensive set of situational factors that migrations might entail. We conducted semi-structured interviews and the interview guide can be found in our replication package [17]. We omit interview transcripts from the replication package to preserve interviewee privacy and protect potential commercial interests of our interviewee's employers.

The interview analysis step of the study relies on techniques found in Grounded Theory (GT) [4], namely coding, memoing, sorting and constant comparison. Based on guidelines for GT in software engineering research, we cannot claim to use the classic GT method. Instead, we used an adaptation of constructivist GT as we had significant previous exposure to literature prior to the study [22], such that some of our themes align with both, previous research [2,12] as well as commonly identified processes [19]. When conducting the interviews, we used a semi-structured interview guide, which we constructed based on our research questions. However, we gave participants significant freedom to describe their own migration journeys in their own words.

In accordance to constructivist GT, we started with an initial research question that evolved throughout the study [22]. The initial research question was inspired both from practical experience and literature on the subject. At start, we targeted to address more generally the underlying elements of a microservices migration, but early on we needed to narrow the scope and focus specifically on the migration process. Then we further broke down the research question into multiple ones that could be addressed based on the analysis of the data. It is worth noting that this study is based on the re-analysis of data collected in a different MSA related study. Specifically, the other study does not focus on specifying the migration process, but on decision-making during microservices migrations [16]. Even though both studies rely on the same data, we conducted a new analysis for this work, based on a different portion of the data. The main methodological difference in this study is that saturation is observed retrospectively with the available data, rather than driving the termination of inviting more participants.

3.1   Participants

We relied on purposive sampling [3] and our personal network (e.g., through current and previous projects, colleagues, or students) to recruit interview participants that have a rich repertoire of experiences with microservice migrations. Furthermore, we used a snowballing approach, where we asked each interviewee to refer us further to other potential participants from their networks. This way we tackled the well-known challenge of recruiting a sufficient number of engineers for interview studies. The selection criteria for participants during the study were adjusted in order to include more experienced engineers along the way. We used an adapted saturation approach [4] in which we judged during data analysis that no new insights were appearing and therefore, there was no need to continue inviting more participants. For the selection of interviewees and case organizations, we used a set of acceptance criteria. Specifically, our interviewees are *(a)* software engineering professionals (not students) who *(b)* have participated (or were close observers) in a microservice migration project within their professional work. An overview of the participants is found in Table 1.

We have interviewed 19 professionals from 6 different countries (Cyprus, UAE, Germany, Romania, Sweden, The Netherlands), of which 18 were male and one female. Interviewers had on average 7.5 years of experience (ranging from 2 to 21) and they have worked at medium to large companies in twelve business domains. In addition, the migration cases are about systems delivered to external customers (e.g. Enterprise SaaS), in-house enterprise solutions for internal users and also Software Applications sold as a service (e.g. mobile app). Each interviewee worked in (at least) one case of microservices migration and we consider migrations from 16 different companies, as shown in Table 1.

3.2   Protocol

We conducted our interviews over a period of six months. Each interview took between 30 and 60 min. Due to the ongoing COVID-19 pandemic as well as geographical distance, interviews had to be carried out through video conferencing. Prior to each interview, participants were asked to sign a consent form, and consent to recording the interview. Further, participants were made aware that

Table 1. Interview participants and case organizations. Organizations size is reported in approximate numbers of full time employees. Experience is in years and values in brackets are on experience with microservices.

Organization	Org. size	Industry	Interview	Role	Experience (MSA)
Org1	50	Enterprise SaaS	I1	Full stack developer	2 (1)
Org2	4,000	Gaming	I2	Software Engineer	2 (2)
Org1	50	Enterprise Software	I3	Senior Team Leader	12 (2)
Org3	36,000	Banking Systems	I4	Software Engineer	2 (1)
Org4	9,000	Banking Software	I5	Software Engineer	19 (2)
Org1	50	Enterprise Software	I6	Software Engineer	2 (1)
Org5	3,000	Aviation Software	I7	Software Engineer	7 (2)
Org6	30,000	Telecommunications	I8	Software Developer	3 (3)
Org7	27,000	Enterprise Software	I9	Computer Scientist	5 (5)
Org8	200,000	Cloud Computing	I10	Principal Software Engineer	7 (4)
Org9	33,000	Marketing Analytics	I11	Software Engineer	6 (3)
Org10	150	Healthcare Software	I12	Data Engineer	6 (2)
Org11	83,000	Cloud Computing	I13	Senior Cloud Architect	10 (5)
Org12	50	Energy Software	I14	Software Engineer	4 (1.5)
Org12	50	Energy Software	I15	Software Architect	4 (4)
Org13	30	Logistics/Planning	I17	Co-founder	8 (5)
Org14	62,000	Logistics/Planning	I16	Software Architecture Consultant	13 (4)
Org15	25	Manufacturing	I18	CTO	10 (6)
Org16	1m	Manufacturing	I19	Enterprise Architect	21 (5)

they can drop out of the study at any point, which no interviewee made use of. We did not offer financial rewards to study participants.

3.3 Analysis

The analysis of the interviews is based on the constructivist variant of Grounded Theory and therefore, we applied initial, focused and theoretical coding on the transcribed interviews [4, 22]. After conducting every interview, it was transcribed and analyzed with initial coding. In initial coding we analyzed horizontally the data by fracturing them to find relevant statements. In focused coding, we aggregated and connected those excerpts into categories and themes, analyzing them vertically until achieving saturation. In theoretical coding we specified the relationships of the connected categories and integrated them into a cohesive theory, by conducting both horizontal and vertical analysis. Initial coding was conducted by the first author. All three authors collaborated in focused coding in three card sorting and memoing sessions lasting three to four hours each. All resulting findings are supported by statements from multiple participants. Finally, it is worth mentioning that literature played a supporting role to our analysis in order to enhance the validity of our findings. Existing literature helped us to understand more comprehensively the statements of software developers during the interviews in combination with the authors experiences and previous exposure to the topic. Also, in this analysis we took into account existing research guidelines on creating processes and taxonomies in Software Engineering [20].

4   Results

Our analysis of the 19 interviewees from 16 organizations that migrated towards microservices showcase that the migration journey takes place in an iterative process of change, until the 2 identified modes of change reach a final, stable state. These identified modes of change are, as presented in Fig. 1, *1) the long-term journey, architectural level of a migration* and *2) the short-term journey, on a system level.* The first mode is about the structural transition taking place in a migration. The second mode of change is on the evolution of the software system, as its artifacts change during a migration. In the identified modes of change, we identify 4 reoccurring thematic phases of activities, also shown in Fig. 1. The *phase of making design decisions* is about the design activities that take place at the start of a migration sprint (architectural or system-level). This phase is not to be confused with the architectural mode of a migration, since it only entails design activities on a narrow scope rather than architectural implementation. Then, *the phase of altering the system* is about the implementation activities that actively modify the software application, on the different modes of change. The *phase of setting up supporting artifacts* is a stage in the migration that the development and operations are configured in order to support effectively the new paradigm that microservices bring. Finally, *the phase of implementing additional technical artifacts* is about the development or modification of software or other artifacts that are needed along with microservices.

4.1   Architectural-Level Migration Journey

This level of the migration is comprised of the activities for the structural or architectural transition that take place in a migration, as shown in Fig. 2. These activities have a longer life-cycle, that takes a relatively large amount of time, and requires multiple things to be in place.

Make Design Decisions. The first identified activity in the studied migrations is to *clarify the business and technical drivers.* Clarifying the business and technical drivers is a step, usually used to align with all stakeholders. In all architectural migrations investigated, there was a large process of deliberation in which different stakeholders, with different concerns and interests had to exchange their views and align with each other. According to some highly experienced interviewees (I10, I13 and I17) this is the ideal phase to obtain a critical stance on microservices and consider if it is really a good fit for the overall objectives at hand. In fact, I17 described how missing this discussion at this stage made it costly later on to cancel the migration and revert towards a monolith once again. Also, I2 clarifies how MSA is not suitable for all types of systems.

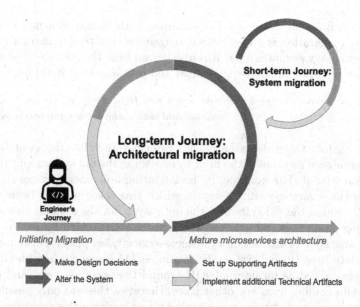

Fig. 1. The iterative nature of the migration journey along the different levels that constitute it.

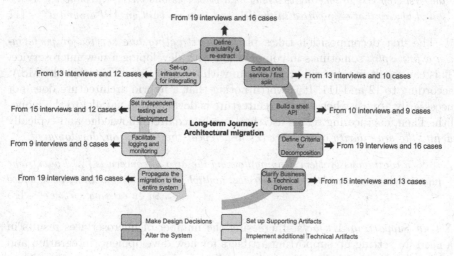

Fig. 2. The migration journey on an Architectural level, with its 9 activities

"it depends on the type of the product, the audience, time constraints. If you're saying to me that I should build now a system for a small company, I would build something monolithic. There's no serious reason to start building in microservices for that company." - I2

Once alignment among some stakeholders is achieved comes the activity of *defining the criteria for decomposition*. This step uses the input from stakeholders to define different goals. For example, both I5 and I8 mention how the microservice migration is driven from management that tries to market the company's technology as modern but it is also driven from the software development teams that try to eliminate dependencies and bottlenecks in development.

> *"It's a very loosely coupled structure and a new technology. So, we are trying to be updated and that's why we use microservices."* - I8

Alter the System Once the requirements are clear and the criteria are defined, most interviewees mentioned the need to managing the old system and the communication with it. For example, by investigating how microservices communicate with the legacy system. A way in which this takes place is by *building a shell API* around the old system or the data layer (for the systems that migrate by building an entirely new system from scratch - Org1 with I1, I3, I6). In this way, the first split or extraction of a microservice takes place. This enables the usage of data from the old system. For example, I11 (among others) built a middleware that acted as an internal API around the legacy system, and did not use any data coming from any other place. However, this was only possible with dedicating development time in maintaining and evolving this middleware.

> *"the first step was to take the back-end as a whole, as one piece [...] connect it with a linked library that is imported in the UI, and then we built an API around it."* - I11

The first decomposition takes place by *extracting one service or performing a first split*, sometimes in combination with developing a new microservice. This can result in a hybrid architecture with a small monolith within the MSA, according to I2 and I11. It is worth noting that a hybrid architecture does not necessarily appear when a new architecture is developed in parallel to the monolith. Then, engineering teams use their newly acquired knowledge and typically *define the granularity of the services and repeat the extraction/development.*

> *"is a continuous problem defining how big the area of concern is [...] I have some functionalities and are these one service, multiple services or something to be added in an existing service?"* - I15

Set up Supporting Artifacts. Increasing the number of microservices results in a need for setting up supporting artifacts for new development, integration and deployment issues that are surfacing with the adoption of microservices. Consequently, software development organizations *design and implement the infrastructure for integrating microservices*, that are either extracted from the monolith, or newly developed. This predisposes setting up CI and CD pipelines and writing scripts that will make the integration happen in a systemic way. Once the appropriate infrastructure is set, organizations are able to systematically extract existing or develop new microservices and re-define the granularity if needed. Consequently, this leads organizations to *facilitating independent and dynamic testing and deployment* for rolling-out new versions of the application. This includes setting up staging environments and processes, dynamic testing and delivery processes. Such processes include both automated structures but also more manual activities such as setting the communication among services.

> *"we have some automated testing [...], when everything is OK, the service is deployed on a staging Kubernetes cluster to be tested, and if everything is OK, it is promoted to production."* - I3

Implement Additional Technical Artifacts. At this stage our interviewees mention how they need to *facilitate logging and monitoring mechanisms.* Logging is perceived to be more crucial than for other architectures, as a lack of it leads to non-observable system behaviours. For example, both I1 and I2 described how their systems behaved unpredictably and had unknown bugs surfacing frequently, in initial migration attempts. In these attempts, a proportion of the code was reused without adding any logging. Hence, the systems became non-transparent making them hard to maintain. Finally, once the mechanisms are set for developing, testing and maintaining, the migration needs to be scaled and *propagated to the rest of the system.* Hence, the process is repeated in multiple places of the system and in lower levels of abstraction, until it reaches a mature stage of independent and decoupled services.

4.2 System-Level Migration Journey

On this level, we dive into how the system itself changes in time, as shown in the journey of Fig. 3 and based on the descriptions of the interview participants. This journey repeats multiple times in one complete iteration of the architectural journey. Our analysis reveals that activities in the architectural journey are on a too high level of abstraction and thus, they need to be complemented. The activities on the system-level are for operationalizing those of the architectural migration. The journey on a system-level is also separated in the four overarching phases.

Make Design Decisions and Alter the System. First, development teams start from understanding *the Business Logic,* which is the contextual information of the application and its purpose. Then, teams need to *prepare the Back-end for decomposition.* Due to the nature of the back-end and middleware, it is normally the starting point in building a shell API for example. This is often followed or takes place at parallel with splitting the *Data,* which is a central part in decomposing the monolith and migrating to microservices, according to the migrations investigated. Since relational databases are fundamentally structured around coupling, interviewees (e.g. I1, I2, I11) described how it comes in conflict with the fundamental principles of microservices and thus, a balance or trade-off was needed to be found there. Once the back-end and data layer are split, at least partially, organizations can start working with the *front-end.* The front-end comes later, due to its particularities with used frameworks and because its decomposition depends on the other parts of the application. Hence, the

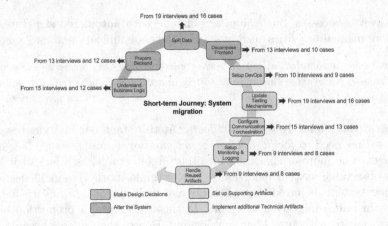

Fig. 3. The migration journey on a System-level with its 9 activities

front-end is often detached first from the rest of the application and at a later stage (potentially) decomposed.

> *"The front-end didn't get split (yet). It's doing one thing and there is high customization without it being overwhelming"* - I11

Set Up Supporting Artifacts. Many organizations indicated that when there are some microservices, the system grows and needs to be managed, considering all the new attributes of the introduced architecture. Hence, there is typically an alteration in *DevOps* practices. For example, this includes a difference in development in which engineers are no longer required to have a local version of the entire application on which they develop. Instead, small parts of the software - microservices - can be developed separately and then get deployed in a staging server, following a predefined process. This introduces some new practices, including the development and management of APIs and independent services. Furthermore, the *Testing mechanisms* are altered to support the distributed nature of the new architecture. Testing now takes place on different levels, starting from simple unit tests, to integration tests and to deployment tests.

> *"testing specific combinations of microservices is super hard to achieve [...] I know that we are doing a lot of manual work, individual tricky solutions and hacks to make our test frameworks do what we want to test this complexity."* - I18

Implement Additional Technical Artifacts. Moreover, there are additional technical artifacts that introduce an overhead in development, that are needed to support the new architecture. Once the application is decomposed, teams come across the need of developing *Communication and orchestration* between services. Many teams mention how a microservice-based architecture propagates the complexity of different pieces of software to the communication layer. Therefore, the way that microservices communicate with each other is in the end carefully designed. Also, as the amount of microservices grows, is typically required to develop a way of finding them in an inventory and orchestrating their execution. Furthermore, these additional technical artifacts include the development of different *Monitoring and Logging mechanisms*. Monitoring and Logging has a different nature in microservice-based Architectures, which needs to be designed accordingly. For example, interviewee I2 mentioned that putting proper exception handling to propagate errors correctly was not essential and entirely in place before. However, in microservices these practices are vital for being able to locate issues and bugs inside a complex network of microservices. Finally, more often than not, there are artifacts being reused from the old version of the system / architecture. Hence, there is a need to design the ways for *handling any reused artifacts*. This happens for example, using libraries and APIs around smaller monolithic parts within the microservices.

5 Discussion

Our results indicate the strong relationship and connection between the different modes of change and the phases of migration. The first mode is about the structural transition taking place in a migration. The second mode of change is on the evolution of the software system, as its artifacts change during a migration. Finally, all modes refers to the engineers' experiences in the transition to the new architecture. A common denominator across most investigated migration cases is that the migration project is more of an on-going and re-occurring project rather than a one-off execution of steps. For example, we showcase how before implementing change, there is a need of organizing the migration and designing how the system will change. Hence, architectural transition is important but only by itself it is a theoretical vision and not a practical change. Therefore, migrating the software architecture of the system is essentially taking place in the code and technical artifacts of the system. Thus, the system-level migration is the core element of change that continuously takes place across the journey. System-level migration is achieved by engineers that have to make it happen and their perspective is crucial, since it is not always easy to learn new technologies or changing their process.

Current research does not account for how the aforementioned levels of abstraction connect to each other and the long transformational journey that companies go through when migrating. Also, practitioners face practical difficulties when following existing approaches that are not always reported. On the one hand, the repetition is taking place in different parts of the system simultaneously on different teams. On the other hand, the repetition happens in increments or sprints from the same team, when evolving the same part of the system. For example, large organizations with predominantly monolith architectures have some teams with a relatively mature microservice-based architecture locally, on their part of the system. However, a central question on this level in most migrations is where the change should start from.

5.1   Changing Modes and the Reoccurring Phases of Migrations

Migration projects as continuous improvement initiatives: This study indicates the importance of the iterative and continuous nature of migrations. Specifically, we see that it is not a one-off project but a continuous endeavour that takes place in iterations. Many of the investigated software development teams that migrate do not consider the change of the system as a main value-adding project. Rather, they view the migration project as a necessary sideline activity and they focus on developing new features and value adding artifacts. Therefore, migrations are rather transformational and take place in parallel with other activities and thus, there is sometimes a pause and revisiting to the project. Furthermore, since it is such a complex and multidimensional endeavour, engineers need to keep in mind designing and developing for future updates and extensions.

Understanding the Progress of Migration Projects: One finding from our result is the importance of having visibility on the four phases of the migration and the different modes of migration. This helps the engineers migrating to have a positional awareness of the progress. As many changes take place in organizations during migrations, there are different modes of change. We see how for different levels of the migration we have a different pace. It is challenging to know if sufficient progress is made and to demonstrate it and placing the migration in one of the phases makes it possible. Also this can be used to anticipate work ahead and avoid repetition of work or taking wrong directions that would generate the need for a lot of work later on. For example, completely neglecting logging and exception handling might not be a good idea if it is anticipated to be an activity later on. Furthermore, this can bring awareness that using microservices is not a silver bullet and has some flaws that is good to plan for. The categorization on four different phases can help developers anticipate challenges timely and address them when they are relevant.

5.2   Implications for Engineering Teams

Diverse Skills Required: Based on our findings, engineers that started migrations had to educate themselves on the new technologies that microservices bring. This typically is taking place through the studying of Best Practices and available material regarding the technologies. Of course their goal was always to have a mature architecture that works in the ways that it is supposed to do. In addition, with microservices, concepts of individual service ownership are introduced to the engineering teams. Consequently, teams need to have more "T"-shaped abilities which means that more comprehensive and diverse skills are needed for each microservice. Such skills include developing different parts of the system, but also analysing business-wise the service, configuring tools and setting up the development or orchestration environments. Teams get in a position of designing the business and the software at the same time with development. Therefore, business-savvy programmers or programming-savvy Business Analysts and System Designers are needed in teams. This is often resolved by recruiting system architects or consulting services.

Shift of Complexity from Implementation to Configuration: However, one of the most important realizations of teams is the shift from traditional development/programming to workflow design and configuration. This entails the shift of complexity from implementation-level to a level of communication amongst services. Sometimes, the lack of being up to speed with the right skills, but also the growth of the microservices, lead to a discrepancy between the design or intended development processes and activities from the actual ones that the engineers do in reality. For example, even though there is the perception that there is strong decoupling in microservices, in reality there is sometimes a chain of microservices that leads to dependencies and coupling, but on a different level of abstraction. Hence, there is a difference between the intended and actual structures and processes.

5.3   Threats to Validity

We designed our research as a grounded theory study to empirically understand the phenomena taking place in migrations towards microservices. Our theory stems from empirical evidence and therefore, has a weight in its validity. However, some threats that are inherent to our chosen study methodology remain, which readers should take into consideration.

External Validity. Specifically, we cannot claim representativeness of our study demographics for the software industry in general, as the sampled population was mainly through our personal network and using a voluntary, opt-in procedure. To address and mitigate this threat, we selected interview participants that cover different sizes of companies, in different industries, and across different geographical regions.

Internal Validity. Furthermore, in terms of internal validity, an identified threat is that we are somewhat pre-exposed to existing research through our previous interest in the field. In addition, we also have practical experience and exposure to the extensive practitioner-focused guidance on how to conduct microservice migrations. This may have biased our interview design, and may have led that some parts of the migration journey and some challenges may have been given less prominence or judged as unimportant during analysis. For example, those not discussed in earlier work. Finally, a limitation of our study design is that we cannot claim that the identified journeys are the only way to successfully migrate towards microservices, but they are an aggregation of activities from many successful migrations.

6   Conclusion

Microservices migrations can be large projects, with many dimensions to consider and many challenges to overcome. The migration journey can be long and in this study we identify empirically what it entails. For example, there are many levels of abstraction that a migration takes place on. However, changes in all those levels of abstraction take place simultaneously during migrations. Hence, in this paper we aggregate the migration journey and challenges that typically arise in organizations that transitioned towards microservices. In this way, we provide a comprehensive guide of how to navigate between the migration journeys, based on the precedents of our interviewees' organizations. This journey entails both a large-scale process of change and a small-scale process of change. In addition, we address the gap of bridging high-level with comprehensive approaches that are on an abstraction level closer to the operational choices that organizations make during migrations.

The migration journey that companies go through when transitioning towards microservices is iterative in nature and takes place at 2 different modes of change. Each of the modes of change, namely on *1) architectural and 2) system-level* has its own sub-journey. Very importantly, these journeys are nested to each other. Each iteration in the architectural-level contains many iterations of the system-level. These modes of change entail activities, derived from the interviews, about the re-occurring phases of *1) Make design decisions, 2) Alter the system, 3) Set up supporting artifacts and 4) Implement additional technical artifacts*.

References

1. Balalaie, A., Heydarnoori, A., Jamshidi, P.: Microservices architecture enables DevOps: migration to a cloud-native architecture. IEEE Softw. **33**(3), 42–52 (2016)
2. Balalaie, A., Heydarnoori, A., Jamshidi, P., Tamburri, D.A., Lynn, T.: Microservices migration patterns. Softw. Pract. Exp. **48**(11), 2019–2042 (2018)
3. Baltes, S., Ralph, P.: Sampling in software engineering research: a critical review and guidelines. CoRR abs/2002.07764 (2020). https://arxiv.org/abs/2002.07764
4. Charmaz, K.: Constructing Grounded Theory. Sage (2014)
5. Di Francesco, P., Lago, P., Malavolta, I.: Migrating towards microservice architectures: an industrial survey. In: 2018 IEEE International Conference on Software Architecture (ICSA), pp. 29–2909 (2018)
6. Di Francesco, P., Lago, P., Malavolta, I.: Architecting with microservices: a systematic mapping study. J. Syst. Softw. **150**, 77–97 (2019)
7. Dragoni, N., et al.: Microservices: yesterday, today, and tomorrow. In: Mazzara, M., Meyer, B. (eds.) Present and Ulterior Software Engineering, pp. 195–216. Springer, Cham (2017). https://doi.org/10.1007/978-3-319-67425-4_12
8. Dragoni, N., Lanese, I., Larsen, S.T., Mazzara, M., Mustafin, R., Safina, L.: Microservices: how to make your application scale. In: Petrenko, A.K., Voronkov, A. (eds.) PSI 2017. LNCS, vol. 10742, pp. 95–104. Springer, Cham (2018). https://doi.org/10.1007/978-3-319-74313-4_8
9. Fritzsch, J., Bogner, J., Wagner, S., Zimmermann, A.: Microservices migration in industry: intentions, strategies, and challenges. In: 2019 IEEE International Conference on Software Maintenance and Evolution (ICSME), pp. 481–490 (2019)
10. Fritzsch, J., Bogner, J., Zimmermann, A., Wagner, S.: From monolith to microservices: a classification of refactoring approaches. In: Bruel, J.-M., Mazzara, M., Meyer, B. (eds.) DEVOPS 2018. LNCS, vol. 11350, pp. 128–141. Springer, Cham (2019). https://doi.org/10.1007/978-3-030-06019-0_10

11. Gysel, M., Kölbener, L., Giersche, W., Zimmermann, O.: Service cutter: a systematic approach to service decomposition. In: Aiello, M., Johnsen, E.B., Dustdar, S., Georgievski, I. (eds.) ESOCC 2016. LNCS, vol. 9846, pp. 185–200. Springer, Cham (2016). https://doi.org/10.1007/978-3-319-44482-6_12
12. Hassan, S., Bahsoon, R., Kazman, R.: Microservice transition and its granularity problem: a systematic mapping study. Softw. - Pract. Exp. **50**(9), 1651–1681 (2020)
13. Jamshidi, P., Pahl, C., Mendonça, N.C., Lewis, J., Tilkov, S.: Microservices: the journey so far and challenges ahead. IEEE Softw. **35**(3), 24–35 (2018)
14. Knoche, H., Hasselbring, W.: Using microservices for legacy software modernization. IEEE Softw. **35**(3), 44–49 (2018)
15. Lin, J., Lin, L.C., Huang, S.: Migrating web applications to clouds with microservice architectures. In: 2016 International Conference on Applied System Innovation, IEEE ICASI 2016. Institute of Electrical and Electronics Engineers Inc., August 2016
16. Michael Ayas, H., Leitner, P., Hebig, R.: Facing the giant: a grounded theory study of decision-making in microservices migrations (2021)
17. Michael Ayas, H., Leitner, P., Hebig, R.: Grounded theory on the microservices migration journey, April 2021. https://doi.org/10.5281/zenodo.4729781
18. Newman, S.: Building Microservices: Designing Fine-grained Systems. O'Reilly Media, Inc. (2015)
19. Newman, S.: Monolith to Microservices: Evolutionary Patterns to Transform Your Monolith. O'Reilly Media (2019)
20. Ralph, P.: Toward methodological guidelines for process theories and taxonomies in software engineering. IEEE Trans. Softw. Eng. **45**(7), 712–735 (2019)
21. Singleton, A.: The economics of microservices. IEEE Cloud Comput. **3**(5), 16–20 (2016)
22. Stol, K.J., Ralph, P., Fitzgerald, B.: Grounded theory in software engineering research: a critical review and guidelines. In: Proceedings - International Conference on Software Engineering, 14–22 May 2016, August 2015, pp. 120–131 (2016)
23. Taibi, D., Lenarduzzi, V., Pahl, C.: Processes, motivations, and issues for migrating to microservices architectures: an empirical investigation. IEEE Cloud Comput. **4**(5), 22–32 (2017)
24. Taibi, D., Lenarduzzi, V.: On the definition of microservice bad smells. IEEE Softw. **35**(3), 56–62 (2018)
25. Taibi, D., Lenarduzzi, V., Pahl, C., et al.: Microservices anti-patterns: a taxonomy. In: Bucchiarone, A. (ed.) Microservices, pp. 111–128. Springer, Cham (2020). https://doi.org/10.1007/978-3-030-31646-4_5
26. Thönes, J.: Microservices. IEEE Softw. **32**(1), 116 (2015)
27. Zimmermann, O.: Microservices tenets: agile approach to service development and deployment. Comput. Sci. - Res. Dev. **32**(3–4), 301–310 (2017)

Migrating from a Centralized Data Warehouse to a Decentralized Data Platform Architecture

Antti Loukiala[1](✉), Juha-Pekka Joutsenlahti[2], Mikko Raatikainen[3]⬤,
Tommi Mikkonen[3,4]⬤, and Timo Lehtonen[1]⬤

[1] Solita Ltd., Tampere, Finland
{antti.loukiala,timo.lehtonen}@solita.com
[2] TietoEVRY, Tampere, Finland
juha-pekka.joutsenlahti@tietoevry.com
[3] University of Helsinki, Helsinki, Finland
{mikko.raatikainen,tommi.mikkonen}@helsinki.fi
[4] University of Jyväskylä, Jyväskylä, Finland
tommi.j.mikkonen@jyu.fi

Abstract. To an increasing degree, data is a driving force for digitization, and hence also a key asset for numerous companies. In many businesses, various sources of data exist, which are isolated from one another in different domains, across a heterogeneous application landscape. Well-known centralized solution technologies, such as data warehouses and data lakes, exist to integrate data into one system, but they do not always scale well. Therefore, robust and decentralized ways to manage data can provide the companies with better value give companies a competitive edge over a single central repository. In this paper, we address why and when a monolithic data storage should be decentralized for improved scalability, and how to perform the decentralization. The paper is based on industrial experiences and the findings show empirically the potential of a distributed system as well as pinpoint the core pieces that are needed for its central management.

Keywords: Data warehousing · Data platform architecture · Distributed data management · Data decentralization

1   Introduction

Upon becoming the driving force for digitization, data is regarded as a central key asset by many companies. Used at an ever-increasing scale in decision making and applications, there is a constant demand for more data, at better quality and availability, and from a wider time horizon.

State of the practice technological solutions, such as data warehouse and data lake, have been introduced as a solution that integrates data from disparate sources into a central repository for analytic and reporting purposes. Thus, the

L. Ardito et al. (Eds.): PROFES 2021, LNCS 13126, pp. 36–48, 2021.
https://doi.org/10.1007/978-3-030-91452-3_3

solution can be considered as a central, monolithic solution that they are typically hard to scale [5]. Monolithic solutions tend to become hard to scale from the development point of view as multiple developers are working on the same code base making it hard to parallelize the work and in the larger systems code base can become very complex. Monolithic solutions are usually built around single technology that might not support all the use cases in an optimal way. There are also other complicating factors. In particular, central data warehouse teams require several special data management skills [1]. Furthermore, as the data warehouse is working with business domain-specific data, the team also requires deep domain knowledge.

The situation can be simplified with modern data engineering practices, including the use of version control, continuous integration and deployment, and metadata-driven data warehouse development, which automate many steps of data modelling, making the data available for consumption faster. Similarly, today's technologies typically do not create bottlenecks for data management – they usually scale well both vertically and horizontally. However, even with these improvements, integrating enterprise data, which may originate from numerous source systems, into a single model can lead to complex models that are hard to build, understand, use, and maintain. Moreover, the process of distilling data from the source to the final data warehouse model requires many, often time-consuming steps and wide technical expertise as well as deep domain knowledge. With this premise, centrally run data solutions even with the latest technology become easily a bottleneck for data management. A common way to scale is to bring in more expertise to the central team that is accountable for the solutions. This is not always feasible because the expertise required to build, improve and maintain these kinds of systems is very broad and hard to find in the labour market.

In contrast to data management, scaling centralised, monolithic applications have been addressed in software development, where sophisticated solutions have been introduced. For instance, large systems use distributed, service-oriented architectures, built using technologies, such as microservices, that also introduce other benefits as a side-effect. In addition, new innovations, such as the cloud, helps in scaling. However, while these technologies have been around for a while, data management related activities and operations have not seen a similar paradigm change.

This paper proposes decentralizing data management architecture, where different business functions take larger responsibility of exposing their data for general analytical use. The solution is based on experiences from a centralized data management architecture in a large Nordic manufacturing company where Solita[1], a Nordic midcap consultancy company, has been consulting on data related development. The Nordic manufacturing company has recently undergone a data decentralizing process, resulting in a decentralized data platform architecture. Our findings empirically show the potential of such architecture as well as indicate the core pieces that need central management.

---

[1] http://www.solita.com.

While we have developed the approach and the data platform architecture implementation independently, the recently introduced concept called *data mesh* is also used to refer to a similar decentralised approach to data management. The closest concrete data mesh-based approaches to ours, also building on designing a scalable data architecture, have been suggested by Zhamak Deghani [2] and ThoughtWorks [13]. However, to the best of our knowledge, neither one has reported uses in scientific literature. For the sake of simplicity, in this paper, we have retained our original terminology, as data mesh is such a new concept that several variations exist in its terminology.

The rest of the paper is structured as follows. In Sect. 2, we present the necessary background for the paper. In Sect. 3, we introduce the case context and its setup. In Sect. 4, we provide an insight into the drivers of the modernization process for the data architecture. In Sect. 5, which forms the core of the paper, we introduce the new data architecture in the case system. In Sect. 6, we discuss experiences gained in the process. In Sect. 7, we draw some final conclusions.

2   Background

Next, we introduce the key concepts of the paper. These include data warehousing, data lakes, data platform architecture, service-oriented architecture, and microservices. Each of these concepts is discussed in a dedicated subsection below.

2.1   Data Warehousing

Data warehousing [7] refers to building data storage used for reporting and analytics. A resulting data warehouse is a central repository of data extracted from different source systems. The data is integrated and remodelled to allows easy usage of data. Separating the analytical database in a data warehouse from the transactional databases used in daily operations allows one to apply heavy aggregations without compromising the operational work. Furthermore, a data warehouse typically stores the history of the operational data. In general, successful data warehousing requires an ecosystem of tools and capabilities to make this possible.

Data is typically published from the data warehouse in a form of a dimensional data model, which is a widely accepted way of modelling data for reporting and analytical usage. A dimensional data model creates a data presentation layer that simplifies the data access patterns.

To represent data from multiple sources in a common enterprise-wide format in a data warehouse, data is remodelled into a *canonical data model* for better accommodating the analytical needs. Forming a canonical model in a complex environment consisting of numerous sources is a complex task, because of contextual dependencies between domains. Therefore, in order to integrate data into a canonical data model requires heavy upfront data modelling, contextual mapping, and deep domain knowledge of the different data sources.

In order to make data warehouse development more efficient, highly specialized teams are formed that can deliver data for analytical applications. This often creates bottlenecks, as adding new data into the data warehouse as well as making new data assets available a huge amount of work.

2.2   Data Lakes

A *data lake* is a central repository of structured and unstructured data that can be of any format [12] unlike in a data warehouse, where a uniform data model is used. A data lake can speed up data availability because data is often stored in a raw format and the schema of data is defined at the read time allowing more flexible usage of data.

This form of storage is very suitable for data analytics and data science, as discoveries on the data assets can be made without the requirement of heavy data modelling upfront. A data lake also allows raw historical data storage at lower costs, taking off some of the burdens from a data warehouse based approach.

Modern big data tools allow easy usage of the data stored in a data lake, allowing even running SQL queries on the stored data, making it viable to store more curated and transformed data sets within it [8]. A data lake is separated from operational systems and therefore has little or no effect on source systems.

On the downside, even though a data lake allows more flexible access to data, a data lake is often built in a central manner creating similar bottlenecks as a data warehouse.

2.3   Data Platform Architecture

Modern usage of data in an organisation usually requires multiple different components to match all the needs. We use the term *data platform architecture* to refer to the architecture that defines how a data platform connects the different data sources to a bigger whole, enabling the use of data in a similar fashion one expects in a centralized approach. This includes fundamental structures, elements, and their relations to each other that are designed to match the strategic goals set by the company on data management.

Data platform architecture needs to fit the organisation and its strategic goals. Even though there is no single way of realizing a data platform architecture, a data platform is typically seen as a central service, maintained by a single team. Even in modern data platforms that are composed out of multiple functional elements, the platforms are very centrally built. Even though the platform approach can tackle demanding needs for diverse data analysis needs, a complex and large realization of centrally managed architecture suffers from an ability to scale.

The data platform architecture implementation we have composed is based on design principles from software design. The overall framework follows principles of service-oriented architecture, and microservices are used as the underlying implementation technique.

2.4   Service Oriented Architecture

Scaling large software development is not a new problem. In a *service-oriented architecture* (SOA), the software is separated into functions that provide services to other applications [10]. Every service in SOA is an independent, reusable, and discrete service that is decoupled from the other services and can be therefore developed and scaled independently [11]. A service is not tied to any technology but is a more abstract concept allowing each service to be built with the best technology available by a dedicated team. Even though the SOA has evolved and new even more distributed architectures have been introduced, the key to scaling remains in the distribution.

SOA integrates modular, distributed, and independent services [11]. The emphasis is on the communication and cooperation taking place usually over the network. An application programmable interface (API) is a central concept in SOA, as an API defines the communication interfaces. As with any distributed system, the definitions of used standards and technologies enable this communication to take place in the most convenient manner.

2.5   Microservice Architecture

Micro service architecture (MSA) [9] is an implementation technique that follows the ideals of SOA, but further emphasises the decentralized, distributed, and independent services. Much like the principles in SOA, modern MSAs are built using RESTful APIs that formalise the interfaces for communication between independent services. Such independent services provide scalability, flexibility, and reliability for agile development of business-centric systems [5]. Furthermore, self-contained systems with loose coupling enable continuous deployment according to customer's agile needs.

In MSA, each service is working on its dedicated business function and therefore should focus on that function solely [9]. This is somewhat opposite to forming a company-wide canonical data model, requiring heavy upfront investment and complex integration patterns. Instead, the focus in MSA is on the data and ontology of one business function alone. This approach is based on one of the core patterns of domain-driven design, called bounded context [3]: Large models are separated into explicit, internally consistent bounded contexts usually around a specific business function. This bounded context creates a place for ubiquitous language within its boundaries simplifying the data models.

The modularity of services adhering to MSA enables developing services independently of each other, thus supporting continuous software engineering [4] to take place. Modularity also allows each service to be technologically independent of each other, and hence the teams building the services can choose the best tools for the job they are performing. Each service can easily adapt to changes in demand by scaling human resources and technical resources, decoupled from other services. Legacy systems can be re-engineered incrementally by breaking parts of the legacy system functionality into individual services [6].

Finally, services can be monitored easily, in varying detail, depending on the needs and critically of the service in question.

Even though MSA has been around for a while in software development and used successfully as a way to scale applications, the architectural model of MSA has not been implemented in the field of data management. The data platform architecture is often designed to be a centralised system owned by a single team from IT.

3   Case Context and Challenges

We use a large Nordic manufacturing company as the case context in this study. The company operates in global markets. The company has several organizational units in different business domains and numerous partner companies in its business ecosystem. The operations are not limited to manufacturing but different post-sales services are also important.

Originally, the data management strategy of the company consisted of a central data warehouse as presented at top of Fig. 1. The data warehouse had been used for years and was running in a local data centre. An ETL (extract, transform, and load) tool was used to integrate data from multiple source systems into the data warehouse as well as re-model the data into dimensional data marts for reporting purposes. The central integration team provided a data bus, which was used wherever possible to support defining integration patterns.

The applications landscape based on data in the data warehouse was vast, including several hundreds of operational systems. The application landscape was also very heterogeneous in terms of age and technology. The development and operation models for the applications differed including in-house build applications, licensed off-the-self applications, and software-as-service applications from external vendors. Some of the applications were owned and operated by the company's partners. Applications were used in different business domains, linked to different business processes, and some used along with partners.

This legacy architecture had started to introduce several challenges for the business. With an old and heterogeneous application landscape, data from many of the operational source systems were not accessible for analytical or reporting use nor to the data warehouse. This was due to security reasons, performance issues, or networking limitations. As the data warehouse was in many cases the only way to access the data stored in the operational systems, the data warehouse was used for operational purposes as well analytical ones.

This central- and multi-role of the data warehouse kept increasing the number and complexity of requirements for the data warehouse as new data sets were requested constantly by different business domains for different purposes. Years of data warehouse development, when multiple operational systems were integrated into the central system, made the data model of the data warehouse very complex. Also the loading logic, as well as business logic, were hard to maintain. Bringing new data into the data warehouse had become cumbersome and error-prone delaying or even blocking the development of applications based on the data warehouse as well as breaking the existing reporting based on it.

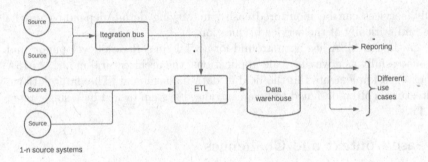

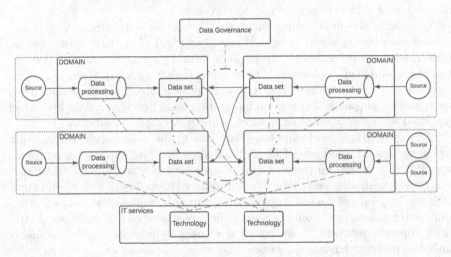

Fig. 1. Top: A high-level architecture of the existing centralized data management based on the data warehouse. Bottom: High-level architecture of our decentralized data platform.

Data management in charge of the data warehouse was limited in resources and had a hard time finding competent people to work with the ever-increasing complex context of the data warehouse. With the increasing amount of data loaded and modelled in the data warehouse, from multiple different business domains, caused a centralized team to become a bottleneck. Simply scaling around these central services and the central team of the data warehouse was not truly an option anymore.

4 Drivers of Modernization

The company had a high-level, strategic objective: take better advantage of data in its business operations that placed extra pressure and demand for the central data warehouse. The company was constantly looking into digitization and better usage of data. To guide this development, among the several principles were to be API and data-driven.

To make the data trapped in legacy applications available for wider analysis, the company started to modernize the legacy applications by building modern API facades on top of them about four years ago. The APIs simplified and even made possible the usage of the data from the legacy applications. In many cases, business domains, however, needed more data than what APIs provided. In particular, data from a longer time period was needed for analytics purposes in order to make better decisions based on the data. The data was used in many ways, often by data scientists who were able to create machine learning models, train artificial intelligence features in applications, and solve business-related analytical questions with data.

The departments of the company in different business domains were independent, empowered, and technologically savvy and the departments had accountability for their work. The departments were large enough to have their own developers, business process owners, solution owners, and other competencies related to the business domain they were working on.

The company had decided to make a technology transition from the in-house maintained infrastructure to a cloud-based infrastructure. The main cloud provider was chosen already two years ago, which created a very good foundation for a new data platform. To fully leverage the cloud, the data management team needed to reconsider what core functionalities it would provide to the company.

The cloud-transition decision was followed by a project to modernise the data warehouse infrastructure by moving the data into cloud-based solutions to better match the demand for scaling with increasing volume, variety, and velocity of data. To further support more flexible data usage, the design of a cloud-native data lake was introduced to create more direct access to the data for analytical purposes, as well as to support the data warehouse.

Since the organization had already elements of distributed application architecture by the means of MSA as a result of cloud transformation, it was proposed that the data management would be fitted into this same architectural model as well. The principle adopted from MSA was that by distributing the data management to the different departments much alike micro services distribute functionality, the central data management could focus more on core entities, connecting different departments, data governance, and providing required core services. In this data distribution, the departments would be in charge of the data assets they consume and produce as well as applications they built. This way the domain expertise would be placed naturally closer to the data assets they were dealing with. Departments would communicate with each other through curated data assets that were requested by the other departments.

A careful analysis of the technology offering being used at the time and adaptation of cloud services made it clear that also distributing the data platform to domains was technologically possible. Cloud offering supported the distribution and it was according to architectural principles.

5   New Data Architecture

A domain-oriented distributed data platform architecture (Fig. 1, bottom) was formed to overcome the scaling problems that the centralized data management was facing earlier with the data warehouse and lake. Using the same patterns that are fundamental to MSA allowed the data platform architecture to scale better. The domain oriented distributed data platform was implemented by distributing the data platform to different business domains and defining standardised interfaces for each domain to allow interaction between them. Each business domain was made responsible for the data assets they were in a relationship with as well as generating curated historised data assets for analytic usage. The business domains also had the freedom to develop data assets in a fashion most suitable for them as long as they adhered to defined core principles defined by the central data management team.

The decentralised approach allowed IT to move from building applications and data analytics into providing infrastructure, guidelines, standards, and services for the domain teams. The domain teams were provided with a cloud environment where they were able to readily build their applications and analytics, as well as create standardised data assets for general usage by leveraging services provided by IT. Distributing the data development was in line with the company's core principles. In many cases, the business domains had independent tech-savvy developers that made the transition of development to domains smooth.

Some of the central services were developed in parallel to the business domain data-intensive projects. A data lake was implemented in a distributed manner, where each domain team hosted their own analytical data in their own data store and, thus, formed distributed data storage. The team responsible for the data lake focused only on providing central data cataloging capabilities, metadata models, data standards as well as "getting started"-guides. A data warehouse renewal project was initiated to clean up the complexity of the existing data warehouse. The new data warehouse was to source the data from the new distributed data lake in order to form integrated data models for reports that were used company-wide. Consequently, the data warehouse was transformed from the central data repository to a single consumer of distributed data assets. Master data management was also used to form some data sets that were seen as key assets for the entire company. These data assets were shared through the data catalogue similarly to domain-oriented data assets. These traditional data management tools, data warehouse, data lake, and master data were distributed and seen as components of the distributed system.

The computing infrastructure was managed by the cloud providers, as they offered an excellent technological baseline for the distributed data platform architecture. Guidelines and standards were defined to make the data sets in the business domains discoverable as well as interoperable forming a base of the data governance practices. Central services included business domain agnostic services out of which among the most important was data catalogue. All the different data sets from business domains were registered to the central data catalogue with a very detailed data on-boarding process.

Business domains that had very little software development skills, struggled to get on board with the distributed data platform architecture. To help such teams getting started, the central data management team focused on bringing the basic setup for the teams easily available as well as generic infrastructure and code templates. The central data management team was able to guide different teams to use specific technologies by offering a set of development tools fast and easily but not limiting teams' liberties with the offerings. Templates were built so that they encouraged security and good development practices, giving a baseline on top of which the teams were able to build own extensions. Templates were generalized from different teams building their solutions. Later, a specialised team was dedicated to helping kick-start different business domains analytical data development to match the defined interfaces.

6 Experiences

The distributed data platform architecture described above removed many of the bottlenecks that traditional data management projects had faced from the central data warehouse and data lake. There were clear indications that having a cross-functional development team working in the business domain along with business stakeholders, allowed the teams to focus more clearly on business needs being able to respond more effectively and agile fashion. The business domains were no longer coupled with the central data warehouse or data lake and, therefore, the business domains were not heavily dependent on these centralized services and their schedules. With the introduction of the distributed data platform architecture idea, business domains used their own development teams to work on the business cases most relevant to them in the prioritised order.

The autonomous domain-oriented teams were able to work parallel to one another as the data platform architecture distributed the data. The domain teams were able to ingest raw data easily as they already had the source system and data knowledge in their control as well as business-subject matter experts in the team. Many of the domain teams worked in simple data assets composed out of source systems most relevant to them. With the data usually combined within the business domain, data models were kept simple and easy to manage.

Business domain data sets along with associated metadata were published in the central data catalogue service and in this way made known to the company internally. As the metadata contained key information about the data and some contact information, this sparked new interactions between the domains. The role of the data catalogues was key to making the distributed data platform work and to govern the publishing process. Data catalogue with well-defined metadata created the baseline for trust in the system and simplified the usage of the data. Data catalogue allowed different teams to connect to different data assets in an agile manner.

Table 1. Comparison between centralized and distributed data platform architecture.

Dimension	Centralized	Distributed
Competency location	Centralized single team	Cross functional domain teams
Technological choices	Single stack	Freedom of choice
Data Modeling	Top-to-Bottom	Bottom-up
Data governance	Centered around the team working on the model	Definition and monitoring of interface
Business & IT Alignment	IT focused	Business focused
Data ownership	IT owns the data and data lineage	Business owns the data and data lineage
Data application development	IT owns applications and the development	Business owns the applications and development

In many cases, the data was mainly needed by the business domain owning the data and there were only few teams that requested data from other business domains. In such cases, only the metadata was placed into the central data catalogue. The actual data was only released when requested. This just-in-time data releasing led to a more efficient and better-prioritised way of working.

Distributing the realization of data platform parts within the common data platform architecture to the business domains allowed the IT department to focus on enabling the business domain teams to build their data capabilities instead of building for them in IT. IT and data management were able to focus more on defining coherent, understandable, and usable unified data interfaces. Having the opportunity to review data assets that were to be published, allowed the data management team to maintain governance and quality of the system. As many of the teams were deep in digitalization, having their own development teams, the transition towards the distributed data platform was natural.

The distributed system required cross-functional teams to work on the issues. It should be noted that the company had adopted an API-driven mindset, which in turn had pushed the organisational structure towards the autonomous business domain-oriented cross-functional teams. This can be seen to have a large effect on the success of distributing the data management since data management knowledge was simply yet another factor that the teams needed to master. There were few domains that did not have development teams and had to set a development team up in order to work in a distributed manner. In many of these cases, the central IT was easily able to provide them with the infrastructure, templates, training, and even pioneering developers to get started.

7   Conclusions

Many larger companies are struggling to find a way to scale for the increasing demand for data in a centralized manner. Even though scaling by distribution has been seen as an effective way of working in many fields, there seems to be no dominant design at the moment. Rather, various proposals have been made, but from the industrial rather than the academic perspective.

In this paper, we have presented an industrial case on distributed data platform architecture. The principal contribution of the study is that centralized data platforms stop scaling at a certain point when organization domains are large, heterogeneous, and non-flexible by nature.

In the study, it was found out that distributed approach to data management provides features that enable complex enterprises' data platforms to scale (Table 1). This approach is based on two widely known and acknowledges principles – MSA and Domain-driven design. These principles adopted to data management and combined with agile autonomous cross-functional teams make rapid concurrent data development possible. On one hand, MSA enables data management to move from centralized solutions towards distributed information ecosystems. On the other hand, domain-driven design specifies distribution to domains and bounded contexts. Together, these two methodologies enable data platform development in clusters within each business domain without the limitations and restrictions of centralized data platform teams. Such a distributed approach to data management facilitates data quality and interoperability by orchestrating data and information management over domain-oriented teams. This enables data modelling without a canonical model and enables business domains to work independently.

Acknowledgement. This work is partly funded by Business Finland under grant agreement ITEA-2019-18022-IVVES and AIGA project.

References

1. Cohen, J., Dolan, B., Dunlap, M., Hellerstein, J.M., Welton, C.: Mad skills: new analysis practices for big data. Proc. VLDB Endow. **2**(2), 1481–1492 (2009)
2. Dehghani, Z.: How to move beyond a monolithic data lake to a distributed data mesh (2019). Martin Fowler's blog. https://martinfowler.com/articles/data-monolith-to-mesh.html
3. Evans, E.: Domain-Driven Design: Tackling Complexity in the Heart of Software. Addison-Wesley Professional, Boston (2003)
4. Fitzgerald, B., Stol, K.J.: Continuous software engineering: a roadmap and agenda. J. Syst. Softw. **123**, 176–189 (2017)
5. Hasselbring, W., Steinacker, G.: Microservice architectures for scalability, agility and reliability in e-commerce. In: 2017 IEEE International Conference on Software Architecture Workshops (ICSAW), pp. 243–246. IEEE (2017)
6. Kalske, M., Mäkitalo, N., Mikkonen, T.: Challenges when moving from monolith to microservice architecture. In: Garrigós, I., Wimmer, M. (eds.) ICWE 2017. LNCS, vol. 10544, pp. 32–47. Springer, Cham (2018). https://doi.org/10.1007/978-3-319-74433-9_3
7. Kimball, R., Ross, M.: The Data Warehouse Toolkit. Wiley Computer Publishing, New York (2002)

8. Miloslavskaya, N., Tolstoy, A.: Big data, fast data and data lake concepts. Procedia Comput. Sci. **88**, 300–305 (2016)

9. Nadareishvili, I., Mitra, R., McLarty, M., Amundsen, M.: Microservice Architecture: Aligning Principles, Practices, and Culture. O'Reilly Media, Inc., Sebastopol (2016)

10. Papazoglou, M.P., Traverso, P., Dustdar, S., Leymann, F.: Service-oriented computing: state of the art and research challenges. Computer **40**(11), 38–45 (2007)

11. Perrey, R., Lycett, M.: Service-oriented architecture. In: Proceedings of 2003 Symposium on Applications and the Internet Workshops, pp. 116–119. IEEE (2003)

12. Stein, B., Morrison, A.: The enterprise data lake: better integration and deeper analytics. PwC Technol. Forecast Rethink. Integr. **1**(1–9), 18 (2014)

13. ThoughtWorks: Data mesh (2020). https://www.thoughtworks.com/radar/techniques/data-mesh

How Do Agile Teams Manage Impediments?

Sven Theobald[✉] and Pascal Guckenbiehl

Fraunhofer IESE, Fraunhofer-Platz 1, 67663 Kaiserslautern, Germany
{sven.theobald,pascal.guckenbiehl}@iese.fraunhofer.de

Abstract. *Context:* Impediments are blockers that prevent teams from working efficiently and achieving their goals. They are central to the continuous improvement of agile teams. However, common agile methods like Scrum only provide limited guidance on how to handle impediments. Hence, agile teams develop individual ways of impediment management and would benefit from understanding overall aspects that need to be considered as well as from insights into the approaches of other practitioners. *Objective:* This study seeks to solidify and enhance the understanding of how agile teams identify, document, and resolve impediments in practice. *Method:* Based on an earlier interview study, an online survey was conducted that collected the experiences of 26 participants from the agile community. *Results:* The results provide a quantitative overview of the different ways teams identify, document, and finally track/resolve impediments. Based on this, the underlying impediment management process has been enriched and additional insights were gathered. *Conclusions:* The process and survey results are expected to aid practitioners in defining their own approaches for handling impediments and provide an overview of the various options found in practice.

Keywords: Agile · Impediment management · Impediment identification · Impediment documentation · Impediment resolution · Survey

1 Introduction

Agile development approaches are widely adopted in the software engineering community [1]. Improvement happens continuously, by inspecting and adapting the current process and making problems transparent along the way. The Agile Manifesto [2] states that "at regular intervals, the team reflects on how to become more effective, then tunes and adjusts its behavior accordingly". Scrum for example, as the most commonly used agile method [1], is based on transparency, inspection and adaptation [3]. The concept of impediments greatly supports such continuous process improvements. It be understood as a problem or blocker that slows down and sometimes even stops the progress of the team, therefore "impeding" the overall efficiency and productivity. In general, impediments may originate from within the team (e.g. through bad communication) or can be caused by dependencies on the external environment (e.g. other organizational parts).

Although managing impediments is essential for continuous improvement, there is not much (official) guidance for practitioners of agile methods. For instance, the well-known Scrum Guide [3] only mentions that the Scrum Master serves the team by causing

© Springer Nature Switzerland AG 2021
L. Ardito et al. (Eds.): PROFES 2021, LNCS 13126, pp. 49–65, 2021.
https://doi.org/10.1007/978-3-030-91452-3_4

the removal of impediments and that the Daily Scrum is used to identify them. Since Scrum only defines an essential framework, the details of how to handle impediments are intentionally left open. It might be due to such a lack of detailed information, that agile teams often use with varying implementations of frameworks [4] and especially individual approaches to impediment management.

Further, there is only little scientific research that explicitly tries to understand how agile teams manage impediments [6]. Such work could serve as valuable guidance on how to deal with impediments, especially when providing hands-on information embedded in a structured process. A better understanding of impediment management would aid Scrum practitioners as well as teams working with other methods such as Kanban and Extreme Programming or even scaled frameworks like SAFe and LeSS [5]. Agile Coaches, Scrum Masters and team members alike could benefit from best practices of the agile community, when dealing with impediments.

Thus, the goal of this paper is to further investigate impediment management in practice in order to outline important aspects that need to be considered, while also providing additional details on the varying implementations. The research is based on an interview study [6] and used the adapted interview guideline as survey questionnaire. With the help of 26 respondents in an online survey, the initial impediment management process was enriched with qualitative data. Users of agile approaches are encouraged to use the results to set up an impediment management process or evaluate and improve their existing one.

The remainder of this paper is structured as follows: Related work and background are presented in Sect. 2. The study design is described in Sect. 3, comprising research goals and questions, data collection and analysis, as well as the actual survey questionnaire. The structured results and possible threats to validity are presented in Sect. 4. Finally, a conclusion and ideas for future work are given in Sect. 5.

2   Related Work and Background

This section discusses the related work based on a short literature review, supplemented by an overview of non-scientific contributions regarding impediment management. Moreover, the background of this research is introduced through the results of a previous study on impediment management.

2.1   Related Work

Scientific Literature. For this short overview of the current state of research, recent papers dealing with impediments, especially in agile software development, were summarized. This may include the concept of waste in lean software development, since it can be quite similar to impediments, as the literature below suggests. It doesn't, however, extend to rather generic terms like "problem". For the time being, mainly sources revolving around software development have been considered because impediments originate and are therefore prevalent in this specific context. Further, work that focuses on obstacles to the agile transition has been excluded, as impediments (in the original referred to in this study) are first and foremost problems that occur within the daily business of teams. Sources already aggregated by the selected authors below (literature reviews) are not explicitly included either.

In general, impediment management seems to be a more recent research topic. The majority of related work has been written since the 2010s. Wiklund et al. [7] conducted a case study to understand which activities of the development process are responsible for most impediments. Power & Conboy [8] combined the already similar concepts of impediments and waste in agile software development and reinterpreted them as "impediments to flow". In addition, Power [9] further explained some techniques that may help to deal with impediments in a meaningful way. Larusdottir, Cajander & Simader [10] thematized a constant improvement process by conducting interviews that focused on whether activities generate value or do not. Later Carroll, O'Connor & Edison [11] aggregated essential related work and thus further enhanced the classification of impediments according to Power & Conboy. Alahyari, Gorscheck & Svensson [12] dealt in detail with waste, examining how the topic is generally perceived, including relevant types and ways to handle them in practice. Finally, Power [13] describes further studies that aim to validate existing types of impediments in his dissertation and derives a rather comprehensive framework for impediment management. For a more in-depth overview of the papers above, please see the preceding study [6].

Non-Scientific Literature. While the actual impediment management process was discussed rather marginally in the scientific context, it was given greater consideration by authors outside the research community. Perry [14] for instance explains what impediments are and provides information on how to discover, manage, and remove them. In addition, a catalog of supporting tools and techniques is given, as well as some insight into the use of gamification when dealing with impediments. Schenkel [15] also gives a definition and some examples of impediments and offers guidance regarding the responsibilities of Scrum Masters. He further discusses possibilities for documentation and provides recommendations for coping with challenges that may occur when dealing with impediments. Linders [16] describes what impediments are and why they should be handled at all. He further discusses impediments on the team level and beyond as well as some ideas on how to manage them effectively.

Summary & Contribution. Overall, the related work appears to be quite diverse. Scientific papers investigate impediments essentially through practical studies and literature reviews. They mostly agree on the similarity and relationship between the concepts of impediments and waste. However, the predominant focus lies on their categorization. Non-scientific literature on the other hand appears to be more interested in the way impediments are handled and managed, while still contributing to the understanding of the overall concept. Summing up, the various studies and guides all drive the exploration of possible manifestations of impediments, including promoting factors, general causes, and resulting effects of such issues. The related work seems to deal less with the actual management of impediments though. In particular, there is still only little (scientific) research on a comprehensive process for impediment management. This paper (together with the preceding study [6]) therefore aims to further fill this gap and provide insights for researchers and practitioners alike.

2.2 Background

As already mentioned, this research is based on and expands a previous qualitative study [6] that aimed to suggest a general impediment management process. It is broken down into three parts that build on one another and which, in principle, form a process for dealing with impediments from their first appearance to their resolution. Though, this primarily aims to provide an overview and raise awareness, so not every part and aspect is always mandatory and needs to be addressed. To facilitate understanding of the survey presented in this study, this process is shown in Fig. 1 and is briefly described below.

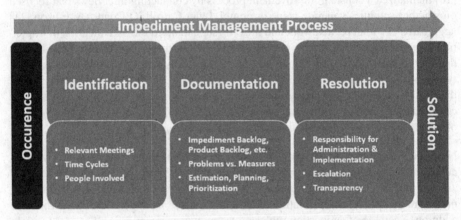

Fig. 1. Impediment management process (proposed by [6])

Identification. The first part focuses on the initial appearance of impediments and how they are recognized and addressed by the team afterwards. In detail, this refers to the overall opportunity, e.g., meetings in which problems can be identified, time intervals for doing so, and the people involved in the process.

Documentation. The second part is about recording identified impediments, more specifically about how this is done, if at all. This documentation of issues may happen via a dedicated impediment backlog or together with the product or sprint backlog items. It is also important whether the impediment itself is recorded or the measures to be taken to resolve it. The question then arises as to whether problems and especially measures are estimated and included in the sprint or handled independently. Finally, the possibility and form of prioritizing matters.

Resolution. The third and final part deals with resolving impediments. Initially, a distinction is to be made between taking responsibility for their administration (tracking the progress) and actually executing the measures for resolution. This also involves the process of escalation in case the team cannot find a solution to the problem on their own. Finally, this part also investigates the matter of transparency regarding the overall impediment management.

3   Study Design

This section provides an overview of the study design, starting with the research goals and respective research questions. In addition, some details regarding the data collection and analysis procedure are given and the central part of the survey questionnaire that was used is presented.

3.1   Research Goal and Questions

The goal of this research is to better understand the impediment management process of teams from the point of view of practitioners. The survey extends a former (qualitative) interview study on how agile teams manage impediments [6]. As part of this preceding research, an initial model of the impediment management process was proposed, which is briefly explained above. This survey aimed at validating and backing up said process through gathering quantitative data. The research questions therefore remain basically the same as before:

RQ1: How do teams identify impediments?
RQ2: How do teams document impediments?
RQ3: How do teams resolve impediments?

3.2   Data Collection and Analysis

Collection. The study was designed as a survey and executed via an online tool[1]. Therefore, data was collected through an online questionnaire (details on its structure follow below) that could be answered anonymously. The overall target group were practitioners who could report experiences regarding their team's impediment management. Compared to the previous interview study [6], which primarily focused on agile software development teams, the participants of this study may have any background. They also did not necessarily need to be in a purely agile team, e.g. through following Scrum or Extreme Programming with all its practices, as long as they were able to talk about the way their team deals with and manages impediments.

The study used a convenience sample. As the survey was designed in the context of the onsite research track of the XP 2020 conference, it was first distributed among conference participants. The survey link, together with a short summary and a video motivating the research endeavor, was made available via the conference website to all participants. Furthermore, the authors used the communication channels of the virtual conference to advertise the study. The survey was opened on June 7, 2020 and was then available to all participants during the time of the conference. It was then left open until July 22, 2020, although the last participant accessed the questionnaire on June 22, 2020. Additionally, a copy of the questionnaire was distributed via selected groups in the business networks LinkedIn and Xing. Those groups dealt with lean and agile software development, Scrum and even SAFe. The questionnaire was accessible between June

---

[1] www.limesurvey.org

29, 2020 and July 22, 2020. Table 1 shows the networks and the related groups to which an invitation was sent. In addition, the date of invitation as well as the number of group members at the date of invitation are shown.

Table 1. Distribution of the second survey

Network	Group name	# Group members	Invitation date
LinkedIn	Scrum Practitioners	121,295	06-29-2020
	Agile and Lean Software Development	168,173	06-29-2020
	Agile	67,646	06-29-2020
	Scaled Agile Framework	40,884	06-29-2020
	SCRUMstudy - #1 Group for Scrum and Agile	118,405	07-07-2020
Xing	SCRUM	13,957	07-01-2020
	Lean and Agile Software Development	2,928	07-01-2020
	Agile Talks	3,442	07-01-2020

Analysis. The data was automatically recorded in the survey tool and downloaded as an Excel file. Excel was used because it provides sufficient capabilities for analyzing the responses and creating diagrams. The analysis of aggregated data (from all sources) was conducted by one of the authors and reviewed by the other. During this process, incomplete responses that did not exceed the introductory questions (and therefore did not contribute to the research questions) were excluded. 17 out of 44 responses from the onsite research study were usable, as well as 9 out of 28 responses from the second survey. The remaining 26 datasets were evaluated by counting how many times the respective answer options were chosen and summarizing input of the open text fields. Particularly expressive results, as chosen by the authors, were visualized for better understanding. Finally, the results were described along the research questions.

3.3 Survey Questionnaire

As mentioned above, an online questionnaire was used to collect data. Since this study aims to expand the previous one, it was constructed based on the interview guideline used before (for detail information, please see preceding study [6]). These semi-structured used primarily open questions to gather qualitative information. This survey on the other hand comprises mostly closed questions and predefined answers, with the exception of free text fields for additional information and feedback. The questions revolve around the different phases and aspects of the underlying impediment management process. The resulting questionnaire can be seen in Table 2, divided into categories, questions and answers, as presented to the participants.

Table 2. Survey questionnaire

Category	Question	Answers
Intro & Context	What is your role?	< Scrum Master; Developer; Product Owner; Agile Coach/Consultant; Other: *free text* >
	How many years have you been working in your current role?	< *number* >
	How many employees work in your company?	< *number* >
	How many years is your team already working together?	< *number* >
	What type of product is your team working on?	< Software; Hardware; Other: *free text* >
	What agile practices is your team using?	< Scrum Master; Product Owner; Sprint Planning; Daily Standup; Sprint Review; Sprint Retrospective; Taskboard; Product Backlog; Other: *free text* >
	What dependencies or interfaces to other project/organizational parts exist? Please name some examples	< We have dependencies with other teams: *free text*; We depend on certain organizational functions (e.g. marketing, IT, operations, etc.): *free text*; We depend on customer input or input from other external stakeholders: *free text*; We have no dependencies: *free text*; Other: *free text* >
Identification (RQ1)	What do you understand as an impediment?	< Blockers that prevent progress towards the sprint goal; Improvement goals; Small problems that can be removed rather easily in short time; Larger problems that need a long time to be resolved; Other: *free text* >
	Which roles identify impediments?	< Scrum Master; Development Team; Product owner; Other: *free text* >
	What techniques do you use to identify impediments?	< *free text* >

(continued)

Table 2. (*continued*)

Category	Question	Answers
	In which situations do you identify impediments?	< Sprint Planning; Daily Standup; Continuously, e.g. conversation with Scrum Master; Sprint Review; Retrospective; Cross-team meetings; Other: *free text* >
	Do you have any other information regarding the identification of impediments?	< *free text* >
Documentation (RQ2)	Where do you document impediments? If possible, please specify why	< Impediments are documented in a separate backlog/list: *free text*; Impediments are documented in the taskboard or product backlog: *free text*; Impediments are documented in meeting protocols: *free text*; Impediments are not documented at all: *free text*; Other: *free text* >
	Which roles document impediments?	< Scrum Master: *free text*; Development Team: *free text*; Other: *free text* >
	How do you document impediments? If possible, please specify why	< We only document problems: *free text*; We only document possible solutions (action points): *free text*; We document both: *free text*; Other: *free text* >
	Are impediments estimated and considered in planning? If possible, please specify why	< Impediments are estimated: *free text*; Impediments are not estimated: *free text*; Impediments are considered in planning: *free text*; Impediments are not considered in planning: *free text*; Other: *free text* >
	Do you prioritize impediments?	< All existing impediments are prioritized: *free text*; Impediments are not prioritized: *free text*; Other: *free text* >
	Do you have any other information regarding the documentation of impediments?	< *free text* >

(continued)

Table 2. (*continued*)

Category	Question	Answers
Resolution (RQ3)	Which roles are responsible for tracking the progress of resolution?	< Scrum Master: *free text*; The whole development team: *free text*; the development team and the Scrum Master: *free text*; Individual developers: *free text*; Other: *free text* >
	Which roles are responsible for the actual resolution of impediments/implementation of measures?	< Scrum Master: *free text*; The whole development team: *free text*; the development team and the Scrum Master: *free text*; Individual developers: *free text*; Other: *free text* >
	How do you track impediments?	< *free text* >
	Are impediments escalated in case they cannot be solved? To where?	< *free text* >
	Do you have any other information regarding the tracking/resolution of impediments?	< *free text* >

4 Study Results

This chapter provides an overview of the demographics, followed by the results of the survey, presented along the research questions and thus following the phases of the impediment management process (identification, documentation, resolution).

4.1 Participant Demographics

This section is about context data and describes information regarding the participants themselves and their respective teams and companies.

Roles of Participants. Most of the study's participants reported occupying the role of either Agile Coach (n = 15) and/or Scrum Master (n = 11). Only a few claimed to be software developers (n = 2), while no one reported working as Product Owner (n = 0). Some of the respondents claimed to fulfill other roles than those suggested in the questionnaire (n = 6), such as change catalyst, business analyst, product manager, or a combination of different roles.

Years within this Role. The participants reported working in their respective roles for time spans ranging from 1–30 years, resulting in an average of about 7 years. However, the majority had spent between 1–10 years in the given role (n = 20), with an average of almost 5 years. Only few respondents claimed to have had their roles for 15, 20, or even 30 years (n = 3).

Number of Employees. The participants of this study came from companies of very different sizes, ranging from smaller businesses of up to 85 employees (n = 8) to medium-sized/large companies of 120–5,000 employees (n = 8) to very large corporations of 10,000–150,000 employees (n = 5). The average size of the respondents' companies was around 15,000 employees.

Number of Team Members. The size of most of the teams with (or in which) the participants were working was between 1–30 members (n = 18), with an average size of 9 team members. There were two exceptions though, with respondents reporting team sizes of 300 and 500 members.

Years of Team's Existence. The majority of the participants' teams had existed (in their current constellation) for about 2 months to 8 years (n = 19), resulting in an average of roughly 2.5 years. The exception was one respondent claiming that his team had already existed for 30 years.

Type of Product to Develop. Most participants reported working on software (n = 19), while only very few claimed to be working on hardware (n = 2). Furthermore, some described a different kind of product (n = 5), such as development tools, services, or games.

Agile Practices in Use. In general, the respondents were using different agile practices in various combinations. The most popular answers suggested in the questionnaire were Daily Standup (n = 21), Retrospective (n = 20), Product Backlog (n = 20), Sprint Planning (n = 19), Sprint Review (n = 17), Scrum Master (n = 16), Product Owner (n = 16), and Taskboard (n = 16). Some participants reported using other agile practices (n = 8), such as Backlog Refinement, Impediment Backlog, Dependency Board, Increment Planning, or Kanban.

Dependencies and Interfaces. All respondents described having dependencies in some form; no one reported having no dependencies at all. Participants reported dependencies on other teams (n = 15), dependencies on customer input or external stakeholders (n = 15), or dependencies on organizational functions (n = 12).

4.2   RQ1: Identification

Understanding of Impediments (Fig. 2). For the most part, the respondents understood impediments as blockers that prevent progress towards the sprint goal (n = 19), rather than overall improvement goals (n = 3). Furthermore, impediments were primarily seen as large problems that need a long time to be resolved (n = 15) and slightly less as small issues that can be removed rather easily (n = 11). Some of the participants (n = 6) understood impediments as all the above or generally as factors that slow down the team and prevent it from learning and providing value.

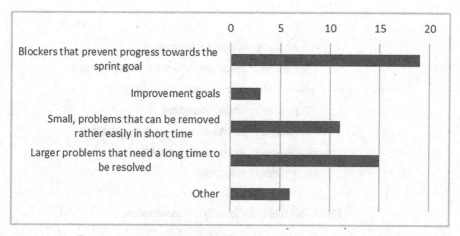

Fig. 2. Understanding of impediments

Roles that Identify Impediments. The respondents' answers regarding the act of identifying impediments resulted in an even distribution between Scrum Master (n = 19), development team (n = 19), and Product Owner (n = 16). In addition, some (n = 10) described all the above choices as well as other stakeholders and teams or, generally speaking, anyone involved.

Techniques for Identifying Impediments. The answers regarding certain techniques were quite extensive, although the participants did not necessarily specify concrete techniques. They described first and foremost basic agile meetings such as daily standups or retrospectives and possible facilitation techniques that come with them. However, the most important factors that lead to the identification of impediments seem to be the willingness for continuous improvement and reflection as well as effective communication at any given time. In addition, the guiding principle of "Inspect & Adapt" was mentioned.

Situations for Identifying Impediments (Fig. 3). In accordance with the previous question, the most relevant situations reported for impediment identification were continuous communication (n = 17), the daily standup (n = 17), and the retrospective (n = 7). Some also reported cross-team meetings (n = 10), sprint planning (n = 10), and reviews (n = 8) as relevant opportunities. A few participants (n = 5) explicitly mentioned that impediments can be identified basically anytime.

Further Information on Identification. Finally, some respondents reported that the identification of impediments relies on transparency, consensus, and trust within the team as well as efforts in cross-team communication, e.g., with clients. The inclusion of waste types may further aid in the process.

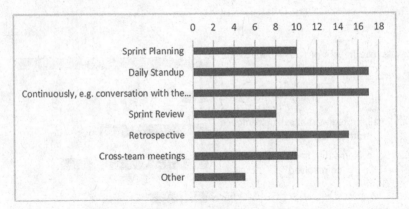

Fig. 3. Situations for identifying impediments

4.3 RQ2: Documentation

Artifacts for Documenting Impediments. The participants reported documenting impediments primarily in either the taskboard/product backlog (n = 11) or in a separate backlog (n = 10). The former can make sense in terms of linking impediments directly to the respective story they are blocking, while the latter seems useful to avoid unnecessary clutter and confusion. In both cases, JIRA was mentioned as the preferred tool. Also, a few respondents reported documenting impediments in meeting protocols (n = 2) or not documenting at all (n = 1), but rather addressing and fixing them right away or bringing them up again later otherwise.

Roles for Documenting Impediments. Based on the responses of the participants, the most important roles involved in the documentation of impediments are the Scrum Master (n = 14) as well as the development team (n = 11).

Ways for Documenting Impediments (Fig. 4). Most respondents claimed to document impediments in terms of underlying problems as well as possible solutions or action points (n = 10). This way, a root-cause analysis may be possible and together with a documentation of what worked and what did not, this can provide a jumpstart when dealing with similar impediments in the future. Some participants reported documenting problems only (n = 5), while none did so regarding solutions/action points (n = 0).

Estimation and Planning (Fig. 5). While the majority reported not estimating impediments (n = 13), a few respondents claimed to do so (n = 4). Reasons for avoiding estimation could be the difficulty of assessing the complexity/extent of an impediment; adding some extra points to the estimation of an affected story may be one way to do it despite this. Furthermore, this decision may be a matter of responsibility, e.g., a formal estimation does not seem useful when the development team does not take part in removing impediments anyway. Though the participants reported not estimating impediments for the most part, many did consider them in the Sprint Planning in some way (n = 10).

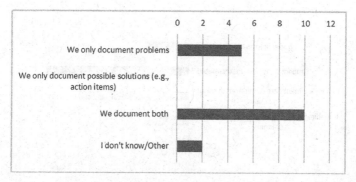

Fig. 4. Ways for documenting impediments

Only a few stated that they do not take them into account (n = 4). Considering impediments in the Sprint Planning without an actual estimation may be done by dedicating some buffer to impediments in general. Again, not including them here could be justified by the distribution of responsibility (see above).

Prioritization of Impediments. The responses regarding prioritization were quite balanced. Some participants reported prioritizing impediments at least roughly (n = 8), e.g., depending on factors like the extent of blocking, how they impact team morale, and how likely the situation is to change. Others claimed not to prioritize impediments (n = 7), e.g., as their small number makes it unnecessary. One respondent further claimed that this decision is a matter of definition. Impediments may be either fixed immediately or deferred; however, the latter would mean it is not a real impediment in the first place. Another respondent mentioned that this happens rather implicitly, by considering possible impediments in the prioritization of stories they are associated with (risk/value).

Further Information on Documentation. Some participants provided extra information regarding the way they document impediments. This includes the recommendation to revise documented issues regularly and maintain communication about them to push the resolution process forward. It was further mentioned that the long-term documentation and categorization of (similar) impediments and solutions may improve the overall process and therefore save time in the future.

4.4 RQ3: Resolution

Roles Responsible for Tracking Progress (Fig. 6). Most respondents reported that the Scrum Master and the development team share responsibility for tracking the progress of active impediments (n = 9). With this approach, it may also make sense to divide the responsibility between the team and the Scrum Master, depending on the nature of an impediment (technical vs. non-technical). Other participants described a clearer differentiation, with mainly the Scrum Master (n = 6) or sometimes the development team (n = 3) being fully responsible. In some cases, the tracking may more specifically be handled by individual developers (n = 2). Again, it was mentioned that this can vary depending on the given impediment.

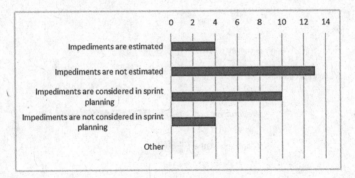

Fig. 5. Estimation and planning

Roles Responsible for Resolution (Fig. 6). The responsibility for the actual resolution was reported to be quite similar compared to the tracking of progress. Again, for the most part impediments are resolved in a joint effort of Scrum Master and development team (n = 9). Others described that either the development team (n = 4) or individual developers (n = 2) are responsible. The Scrum Master (n = 3) seems to be comparatively less involved and may further delegate responsibility to the developers while only acting as a guide and facilitator. In addition, the responsibility may generally fall on whoever is most suited to finding a solution and therefore depends on the impediment itself.

How to Track Impediments. Obviously, there are different approaches to tracking impediments, similar to the documentation. According to the respondents, these include the use of tools such as Jira and generally the use of some form of board or backlog for visibility, either digital or analog. Another important factor seems to be the regular (up to daily) inspection of progress.

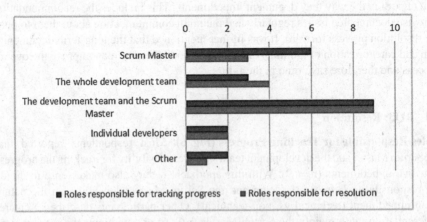

Fig. 6. Roles responsible for tracking progress and resolution

Escalation of Impediments. Almost all participants reported escalating impediments in case they cannot be solved within the team. This happens mostly vertically along a company's hierarchy and includes management positions from project to executive level. In some cases, it may also make sense to first escalate rather horizontally to other stakeholders who are involved and affected and may therefore provide help in resolving the issue at hand.

Further Information on Resolution. The respondents again highlighted the significance of visibility, regular inspection, and clarified responsibilities throughout the resolution process.

4.5 Threats to Validity

Similar to other surveys in the field of software engineering, the response rate was comparatively low. The distribution of the survey probably reached thousands of agile practitioners that potentially deal with impediments. However, it can't be said for sure due to the unclarity of response rate when dealing with business networks. It should therefore be mentioned that the rather small sample in this study most likely cannot represent the agile community as a whole. Further, the respondents were gathered from a broad international audience. Since this happened through sharing the survey and not by selecting certain individuals methodically, the origin of respondents remains mostly unknown. To ensure qualified answers nonetheless, the chosen conference and business networks had a strong thematic proximity to the topic at hand.

Another potential threat lies in the fact that most participants of the previous interview study were using Scrum, which led to an impediment management process (and finally an online questionnaire) that is strongly influenced by the Scrum terminology. However, the participants of this survey had the chance to give feedback in a free text field for every question, in case the set of predefined answers did not fit their own understanding or naming conventions. To make sure the questions were clear, understandable and thematically appropriate, the survey was reviewed and piloted by other researchers who are experienced with agile and empirical studies.

Finally, this research is based on a survey, as described above. Therefore, the answers given by the respondents can be subjective and a matter of understanding. What they really do may not necessarily coincide with what they claim to do. This should be kept in mind when interpreting the results.

5 Conclusion and Future Work

Conclusion. Many Agile teams use impediments for continuous process improvement. These blockers or obstacles to the team's productivity are commonly used to iteratively improve one's way of working. Agile methods like Scrum claim that the Scrum Master serves the team by causing the removal of impediments and that the Daily Scrum is used to identify. However, they do not provide (detailed) guidance regarding the systematical management of said impediments.

This study therefore investigated how agile teams manage impediments in practice. During an online survey with 26 participants, experiences were collected about how agile teams identify, document, and finally track/resolve impediments. The results described above enriched the underlying impediment management process proposed in the preceding study and backed it up with quantitative data. Summing up, this paper investigated the topic of impediments from the little-researched process perspective and offers further insights that can support and guide practitioners in reflecting and improving their current impediment management approach.

Future Work. Future research might address the benefits and drawbacks of certain approaches mentioned in previous work and by the participants of this survey. For instance, interviews could be conducted in order to better understand why one option might be more useful than another. For example, one team may choose to document only measures to resolve impediments, since they favor a very proactive approach with a short-term scope and their issues are rather easy to resolve. Another team however could decide to document primarily the problem itself, in order to comprehend the underlying root causes over time or because they are bound by dependencies lead to immediate solutions not always being apparent. A third team might then combine both approaches and therefore document both problems and measures, with the intention of examining the success of the latter by tracking back and checking the problems that made them necessary in the first. Thus, most practices used during impediment management can have benefits and drawbacks that make them more suitable in certain scenarios and contexts. Such an investigation of the rationale for using certain approaches would be of great importance for a comprehensive guide to impediment management that goes beyond the mere mentioning of possibilities, instead providing recommendations based on defined criteria. This could even be enhanced by gathering practical guidance on how to enact the different aspects of the impediment management by analyzing suitable templates, techniques or tools.

Acknowledgments. This research is funded by the German Ministry of Education and Research (BMBF) as part of a Software Campus project (01IS17047). We would like to thank all participants of our study, and Sonnhild Namingha for proofreading parts of this paper.

References

1. VersionOne, & Collabnet: 14th State of Agile Report (2020). https://explore.digital.ai/state-of-agile/14th-annual-state-of-agile-report. Accessed 10 July 2020
2. Manifesto for Agile Software Development (2020). www.agilemanifesto.org. Accessed 10 July 2020
3. Sutherland, J., Schwaber, K.: The Scrum Guide. The definitive guide to scrum: The rules of the game. Scrum.org (2013)
4. Diebold, P., Ostberg, J.P., Wagner, S., Zendler, U.: What do practitioners vary in using scrum? In: Lassenius, C., Dingsøyr, T., Paasivaara, M. (eds.) Agile Processes in Software Engineering and Extreme Programming. XP 2015. Lecture Notes in Business Information Processing, vol. 212, pp. 40–51. Springer, Cham (2015). https://doi.org/10.1007/978-3-319-18612-2_4

5. Theobald, S., Schmitt, A., Diebold, P.: Comparing scaling agile frameworks based on underlying practices. In: Hoda, R. (eds.) Agile Processes in Software Engineering and Extreme Programming – Workshops. XP 2019. Lecture Notes in Business Information Processing, vol. 364, pp. 88–96. Springer, Cham (2019). https://doi.org/10.1007/978-3-030-30126-2_11

6. Guckenbiehl, P., Theobald, S.: Impediment management of agile software development teams. In: Morisio, M., Torchiano, M., Jedlitschka, A. (eds.) PROFES 2020. LNCS, vol. 12562, pp. 53–68. Springer, Cham (2020). https://doi.org/10.1007/978-3-030-64148-1_4

7. Wiklund, K., et al.: Impediments in agile software development – an empirical investigation. In: Proceedings PROFES 2013, pp. 35–49. Paphos (2013)

8. Power, K., Conboy, K.: Impediments to flow – rethinking the lean concept of 'waste' in modern software development. In: LNBIP 179, pp. 203–207. Rome (2014)

9. Power, K.: Impediment impact diagrams – understanding the impact of impediments in agile teams and organizations. In: Proceedings Agile Conference 2014, pp. 41–51. Kissimmee (2014)

10. Lárusdóttir, M.K., Cajander, Å., Simader, M.: Continuous improvement in agile development practice. In: Sauer, S., Bogdan, C., Forbrig, P., Bernhaupt, R., Winckler, M. (eds.) HCSE 2014. LNCS, vol. 8742, pp. 57–72. Springer, Heidelberg (2014). https://doi.org/10.1007/978-3-662-44811-3_4

11. Carroll, N., O'Connor, M., Edison, H.: The identification and classification of impediments in software flow. In: Proceedings AMCIS 2018, pp. 1–10. New Orleans (2018)

12. Alahyari, H., Gorschek, T., Svensson, R.: An exploratory study of waste in software development organizations using agile or lean approaches – a multiple case study at 14 organizations. Inf. Softw. Technol. **105**, 78–94 (2018)

13. Power, K.: Improving Flow in Large Software Product Development Organizations – A Sensemaking and Complex Adaptive Systems Perspective. NUI Galway, Galway (2019)

14. Perry, T.L.: The Little Book of Impediments (2016). http://leanpub.com/ImpedimentsBook

15. Schenkel, M.: t2informatik GmbH: Impediment Guide (2018). https://t2informatik.de/downloads/impediment-guide/

16. Linders, B.: Problem? What Problem? Dealing Effectively with Impediments using Agile Thinking and Practices (2020). http://leanpub.com/agileimpediments

Keeping the Momentum: Driving Continuous Improvement After the Large-Scale Agile Transformation

Josefine Bowring[1,2]([✉]) and Maria Paasivaara[2,3]

[1] IT University of Copenhagen, Copenhagen, Denmark
[2] LUT University, Lahti, Finland
{josefine.bowring,maria.paasivaara}@lut.fi
[3] Aalto University, Helsinki, Finland

Abstract. The Scaled Agile Framework (SAFe) is currently the most popular framework to scale agile development to large projects and organisations. An organisational transformation to SAFe is usually driven by a Lean-Agile Centre of Excellence (LACE). What happens to the LACE after the initial transformation is over? How does the organisation keep improving? In this single-case study we investigated how the volunteer-driven LACE in a Nordic bank, Nordea, drives continuous improvement long after the organisation's transition to SAFe. We collected data by 10 semi-structured interviews and several observations. We found that the LACE at Nordea drives continuous improvements by working in a Scrum-like fashion: it uses Product Owners, maintains a backlog of improvement features, works in sub-teams to identify and solve issues, and meets once a week to coordinate and share between the sub-teams. The LACE consists of volunteers, which is an advantage as changes are identified and implemented by the same practitioners who experience the need for them. However, this volunteering model is not without challenges: the LACE lacks the formal mandate to implement the needed changes and other work takes priority for the participants.

Keywords: Scaled Agile Framework · Continuous improvement · Lean-Agile Centre of Excellence · LACE · Large scale agile

1 Introduction

Agile development is rising in popularity. With many companies adopting digital solutions to meet the rapidly changing needs of customers [10], even large organisations are shifting to agile methods to deliver value quickly and cost-efficiently [24]. The reported benefits of agile software development methods include increased flexibility, quality, and faster delivery speed [16]. Adopting agile in a large organisation is not an easy feat, and requires a significant change

Supported by Nordea.

in the culture of the organisation, which takes time, commitment, and customisation [5,7]. Several frameworks for scaling agile exist [27], the most popular of which is currently the Scaled Agile Framework (SAFe) [24]. In the 2020 annual State Of Agile Report [24], 35% of respondents reported using SAFe. The SAFe framework is extensive: it describes the required roles, processes, values and an implementation strategy for transitioning to using SAFe [22]. At the heart of this transition is the Lean-Agile Centre of Excellence (LACE), responsible for starting the behavioural and cultural transition across the organisation, and removing impediments for achieving these goals [22]. However, what happens to LACE after the initial transformation is over? How does the organisation keep improving? Continuous improvement is essential to agile, and one of the principles of the agile manifesto [1]. The agile transformation is often called a *journey* that does not end after the initial transformation is over, but will continue in the form of continuous improvement through self-inspection and reflection. The SAFe framework does not specify how the continuous improvements should be driven, who should be driving them, nor what exactly the role of LACE should be. The SAFe lists the typical responsibilities of LACE, which include also *"helping to establish relentless improvement"* [22]. In this study, we investigate how such a continuous improvement journey is driven by a LACE in an international Nordic bank, Nordea[1]. Their transformation to SAFe started in 2015, and the first LACE was installed as a part of the second wave. After reaching its transformation goals it dissolved, leaving an open gap for a central change-driving organ. In 2019, this space was taken up by a growing grassroots movement in the development organisation, reinstating the LACE and starting new improvement initiatives necessary to drive the organisation to a higher degree of organisational agility. Thus, the new LACE was formed as a relentless group of volunteers within the organisation insisting on a continuous change in the late state of transition. Without any given mandate, this volunteer-driven LACE is attracting change-hungry people, and raising new questions and opportunities surrounding the role and the boundaries of the LACE. In this paper, this nontraditional take on a LACE will be examined, described, and compared to its traditional LACE counterpart, change management theory, and empirical evidence in an attempt to describe this case-specific phenomenon and identify areas of improvement. The current research on large-scale agile has focused on the adoption of agile, the challenges faced and the benefits gained [5,19]. However, little research can be found on how "fully" transitioned agile companies keep continuously improving after the initial transition is over. With this paper we start filling in this research gap.

2   Background

2.1   Scaled Agile Framework (SAFe)

The Scaled Agile Framework (SAFe) is an extensive framework to scale agile practices to large organisations by expanding on existing team-focused method-

---

[1] https://www.nordea.com/en.

ologies and adding program- and portfolio layers to provide means to manage larger delivery organisations consisting of multiple agile teams. The framework provides definitions for various roles and details mechanisms to align and coordinate teams' efforts to develop solutions and maximise business value. On the team level, SAFe agile teams blend agile practices as they wish, typically using elements of Scrum, Kanban, and Extreme Programming [13]. In SAFe, teams use the roles, events, and artefacts of Scrum as defined in the Scrum Guide [23] to deliver working software in incremental, iterative cycles. Teams working on the same solution are organised in Agile Release Trains (ARTs), long-lived collaboration groups between teams and stakeholders [13]. Each ART coordinates development efforts through Product Increment (PI) Planning events.

When transitioning to SAFe, one element of the recommended SAFe Implementation road map is the LACE [22]. A LACE consists of a small team of dedicated, full-time change agents working to implement the SAFe Lean-Agile working methods. The LACE serves as a focal point for activities that power the organisation through the changes [13]. The responsibilities of a LACE according to Knaster and Leffingwell [13] include: 1) communicating the business need, urgency, and vision for change, 2) developing the implementation plan and managing the transformation backlog, 3) establishing the metrics, 4) conducting or sourcing training for all, 5) identifying value streams and helping define and launch ARTs, and 6) providing coaching and training. Knaster and Leffingwell [13] point out that a LACE is one of the key differentiators to look for when determining whether companies are fully committed to practising Lean-Agile. According to Knaster and Leffingwell a LACE often evolves into a long-term center for continuous improvement after the initial transition, as becoming a Lean-Agile enterprise is an ongoing journey rather than a destination. For smaller enterprises, a single LACE may be sufficient to support the development organisation, whereas larger organisations may consider either multiple, decentralised LACEs or a hub-and-spoke model where multiple LACEs are organised by a central hub [13].

2.2   Related Research

In their literature review on agile methodologies, Dingsøyr et al. [6] found that since the introduction of the Agile Manifesto [1] in 2001, significant amount of research has been done in the area of agile software development, while a clear rise in the number of studies took place after 2005. The majority of the studies concentrate on agile practices and methods [11], or attempt to further understand the agile concepts (e.g. [4,9]). While some progress has been made in these areas, agile software development is yet to find a common standard for the central challenge of combining research rigour with industrial relevance [11], as many important topics have not yet been fully explored. One topic requiring further research is large-scale agile and the different scaling frameworks [27] as their popularity in the industry keeps rising, but research is lacking behind [5].

Recently, several studies have pointed to *organisational culture change* as a challenge when scaling agile practices to large organisations [5,15,18,19]. Inspiration to solve this challenge may be found in change management and organisation theory. Chia [3] introduces the notion that organisations are constantly in a state of "becoming", to describe the continuous process of defining and redefining organisations as living and constantly changing entities. In this view, change is not an exception but a rule, and thus the approach to change in this view is more concerned with the large impact of small changes over time than changing quickly to a new state. Tsoukas and Chia [26] describe how microscopic change should have theoretical priority for organisational scientists: *"Such change occurs naturally, incrementally, and inexorably through "creep, "slippage" and "drift", as well as natural "spread""* [26]. Feldman [8] similarly argues that routines can be instrumental to continuous change in any organisation as long as humans are doing them because the embodied knowledge from routines is a process of organisational learning. In this view, change, as a constant and never-ending process, bears a resemblance to the *continuous inspection and adaptation* mechanisms agile methods emphasise as means to improve incrementally.

SAFe recommends a transition based on the 7-step process introduced by Kotter [14], a strategy for realising a stated vision by implementing deliberate changes by changing systems and structures supported by a powerful guiding coalition. If we compare the approaches to change of Kotter [14] and Chia and Tsoukas [3] to the change process ideal types introduced by Huy [12], the Kotter-inspired SAFe approach resembles what Huy describes as a *commanding intervention*: a direct, abrupt and rapid change strategy, with little attention to the organisation's internal capabilities or individual issues, driven by a small group of people typically from the top of the hierarchy, aided by external consultants [12]. The remaining intervention ideal types by Huy [12] are *engineering, teaching*, and *socializing*. Each type is compared in 3 temporal, and 8 non-temporal categories, identifying the underlying theories, change agents, and diagnostic models. The SAFe framework has turned out to be popular especially in the finance industry [21]. Experience reports on transformations to SAFe can be found from the SAFe website [22], while academic literature includes, e.g., case studies on transformations [20] and challenges faced [25] in the finance industry. However, to our knowledge no research exists specifically on one of the central elements of SAFe, the LACE. With this single-case study we start exploring the role and implementation of LACE in practice.

3   Research Method

3.1   Research Goals and Questions

As no other studies describing experiences on using LACE have been identified, this single, exploratory case-study [28] aims to investigate how LACE drives continuous improvement in a case organisation by answering the research questions:

1. How has the LACE changed over time?
2. How does the LACE work?
3. How does the LACE influence the organisation?
4. How can the LACE improve to inspire and facilitate change?

3.2   Case Organisation

Nordea is an international bank servicing household- and corporate customers with nearly 200 years of history. Nordea offers personal and corporate banking services such as transaction services, investment services, loans, mortgages, and asset management to customers via online and offline platforms in 20 countries, employing 28.000 people [17]. Nordea started the using agile around 2010 and their SAFe adoption journey started in 2015. Currently[2], the software development organisation operates over 100 ARTs with sites in several countries. Nordea's transformation to agile cascaded from country to country, supported by agile coaches and facilitated by external consultants.

3.3   Data Collection

Interviews: We chose semi-structured interviews as the main data collection method as we wanted to dive deep and explore a new topic [28]. Answering questions of *how* is a known strength of qualitative interviewing [2].

Table 1. Interviewees

LACE role	Role outside of LACE	Years in Nordea	Interview
Product Owner	Line-Manager	35	85 min
Product Owner	Line-Manager	7–8	60 min
Product Owner	Expert in Continuous Improvement	3	80 min
Active LACE Attendee	Scrum Master	N/A	60 min
Active LACE Attendee	Release Train Engineer	4	60 min
Active LACE Attendee	Agile Coach	5	60 min
Active LACE Attendee	Release Train Engineer	7	60 min
Active LACE Attendee	Release Train Engineer	9,5	60 min
Non-LACE Member	Product Manager	6,5	60 min
Non-LACE Member	Business Area Tech Lead	2,5	60 min

We interviewed ten persons as listed in Table 1. As the first interviewees we chose all *LACE Product Owners* due to their central role. The *LACE attendees* were invited to volunteer for the interviews to share their experiences of working in the LACE. To provide an outside perspective on how the LACE work impacts and is seen by other Nordea employees, we asked our Nordea contact persons to identify a few *non-LACE members* having some knowledge of LACE, but not participating in LACE work. Five volunteered LACE attendees and two non-LACE members were interviewed. We created interview guides for all three "roles". The questions common to all interviewees are listed in Table 2. The guides were kept flexible, using preliminary results of the previous interviews to

---

[2] in July 2021.

determine areas of interest worth adding to the following guides. The Product Owner interviews sparked more questions for the later groups, e.g., a Product Owner indicated LACE being empowering, which was added as a question for all attendees. In addition to the general questions, Product Owners were asked about the origins, the goals and the development of LACE, the backlog, and the LACE Product Owner role. The LACE attendees were asked about the LACE features they had been working on and the experienced challenges and successes. Additional interview questions can be found on Figshare[3]. All interviews were conducted online using Microsoft Teams or phone due to Covid-19 restrictions.

Table 2. General interview guide.

Theme	Question	RQ
Background	Work experience, education, previous roles	
Background	Role outside of LACE	1
Background	When did you join LACE, and what were you hoping to achieve?	1,2
Current work	How do you go about implementing this particular change?	3
Current work	Are there any backlog items you have had for a long time or cannot seem to solve?	2,3
History	What did you think about LACE before you joined?	3
History	Tell me about the achievements LACE has positively impacted the organisation in the past?	2,3
History	Have there been any transformation efforts you have had to give up on because it could not be done?	1,3,4
History	How has the backlog evolved over time?	2
History	How has the way you work in the LACE evolved over time?	2
Improvements	What is the biggest challenge the LACE is facing right now?	1,3,4
Improvements	Do you think you have the right resources to drive the transformation backlog?	3,4
Improvements	If you could change anything about the LACE for the better, what would it be?	4

Observations: As Brinkmann [2] notes, other data sources apart from interviews, such as observations, documents, and objects, are essential when researching social and cultural phenomena to get a complete picture of the object of interest. To understand how the LACE works is a partially observable process in the meetings between LACE attendees. Therefore, nine weekly LACE meetings of 30 min with 7–9 participants were observed during a period of two months. Additionally, three other meetings were observed: a one-hour feature sub-team

---

[3] https://doi.org/10.6084/m9.figshare.16729000.

weekly meeting, a one-hour LACE PI planning meeting that established the focus areas and OKRs for the next 3-month iteration, and a 40-min sub-team feature planning meeting during which 15 participants identified root causes of the observed challenge, planned feature scope and coordinated practical work. All observed meetings were conducted online in Microsoft Teams. The observer took detailed notes, e.g., regarding the current status of each discussed feature, and the challenges discussed.

3.4 Data Analysis and Validation

All interviews were transcribed and coded by the first author after reaching agreement of the coding labels with the second author. The relevance of interview segments and notes were marked to each research question, while RQ2 was split into multiple categories (goals, tools, and resources). To validate our findings, a Nordea representative, active in LACE, reviewed the article and gave a written consent for publication.[4]

4 Results

4.1 RQ1: How Has the LACE Changed over Time?

The First Nordea LACE: Nordea did not create a LACE in the early stages of the transition to SAFe, as suggested by the SAFe road map [22]. Instead, the LACE was established sometime after the initial SAFe transformation, as a part of the move to take the next step, referred to by one interviewee as part of the next wave - *Agile 2.0*. Another interviewee notes that the need to standardise work and run the same cadence across the entire development organisation gave rise to the first instance of the LACE. A third recalls that the LACE was known by a different name in the beginning, consisting of line managers especially from Agile Execution, Architecture, Product Ownership, and the Transformation Office. The improvement backlog, which agile coaches helped to carry out, was kept in this closed forum. Following a re-organisation, the first LACE group dissolved.

The New LACE: A new, less-centralised LACE rose around 2019, initiated by one of the current Product Owners. It was intended to be a community of practitioners consisting of volunteers who would contribute their experience, time, and knowledge to identify areas of improvement and remove systemic impediments. The LACE relies on goodwill to collaborate across teams and ARTs to improve the ways of working and promote organisational agility. Without official mandate or dedicated resources, the practitioners facing day-to-day struggles of agile development band together to gain support to solve them for the good of all. According to a LACE Product Owner the volunteer-based model was a deliberate choice to avoid resistance from the cost-conscious management team with

---

[4] Due to an active Non-Disclosure Agreement between the researchers and Nordea, all data used for this research project is protected from sharing.

an intention to prove the value of the LACE with results. However, this choice has its advantages and disadvantages. According the Product Owner, one such advantage is avoiding the closed group or *ivory tower* that the first instance of the LACE appeared to be, and that everyone wanting to improve the system has a chance to do so. However, a disadvantage is not having dedicated resources, such as a coach or coaches, to help implement the changes needed.

> "We were in a position at that point in time where we were cutting costs - cost-conscious. [...] And the plan was to show that the LACE can drive things, that it will, it can implement systemic changes. And then, from there, see if we could get an allocation to drive more. [...] And also, personally, I like the model where you engage people, and where everybody has a chance to be part of it, and it's not just the ones who are appointed to be part of the LACE."   — LACE Product Owner

Now that everyone was invited and encouraged to raise their issues, 20–30 people showing up with each their own agenda resulted in a scattered collection of small things with no sense of direction. According to a Product Owner, addressing them all was impossible with the limited capacity of the volunteers and no mandate to impose changes. With plenty of ideas for improvements but little concrete results, this "circle of friends" shrank. All three Product Owners find this time as a significant turning point for the newly re-instated LACE with much to prove. The third PO joined the LACE, leading to the realisation that the backlog of improvements lacked clear direction and was full of disorganised or abandoned ideas. The POs visualised every backlog item as a post-it, grouped them on a large office wall, and were overwhelmed by the amount of work it would take the LACE group to change everything described on the wall. Thus, the Product Owners concluded that a severe *clean-up of the backlog* was needed and a much more directed approach was essential to achieve a sense of focus for the upcoming work. Surprisingly, the backlog clean-up did not result in angry and overlooked LACE participants, as many had left the LACE behind.

4.2   RQ2: How Does the LACE Work?

Overall Goals: The Product Owners have defined the overall goals of the LACE to be: *1) relentless improvement, 2) cross-organisational scope,* and *3) increased customer focus.* At the heart of the LACE work lies continuous improvement for the organisation. The LACE seeks to attract people looking for a positive change for themselves and their colleagues and provides a place to find support and help each other to achieve the changes they want to see. This overarching theme came up repeatedly during the interview process, highlighting its importance. A Product Owner sees the LACE as an opportunity to experiment and solve complex problems in innovative ways, and expresses that other people may have felt compelled to join the LACE after being inspired by the passion the people in the LACE show for wanting to change and improve. A LACE attendee emphasises that it is the practitioners who are enabled to help themselves and implement their own solutions to the problems they face. Currently, there is no other way for the sub-units, such as a team or an ART, to take systemic issues forward. Thus, an explicit goal of the LACE is *making visible and attempting to implement cross-organisational improvement efforts at Nordea, which no sub-unit alone can easily solve*. All three LACE Product Owners highlight this over-arching goal emphasising that these changes should be achieved in collaboration across all units.

> "We are not interested in sub-optimising problems in some specific area only. And typically, there's not many problems, which are specific to some area only. [...] If there's no vehicle, these problems stay inside those silos, because there's no way to raise them up. So that's, of course, the way to provide this vehicle where you can raise and then what this vehicle tries to do is exactly, we talk about systemic issues."   — LACE Product Owner

Another focus point is a more *customer-centred approach to development*. A strong domain-focus combined with an extensive organisational structure that is still somewhat hierarchical and bureaucratic poses a significant barrier for a few members of the LACE working deliberately to increase the focus on one thing everyone in the organisation have in common: their customers. The interviewees that touch upon this subject recognise that this re-focusing from an inside-out to and outside-in perspective requires a significant change in the mind-set of their colleagues. An attendee speculates that the perceived product may not be the same for the IT development organisation, product development organisation, and the customer, while a Product Owner admits that attempting to change this mindset is bold, but something they are experimenting with and experience a great appetite for in the organisation, albeit not very broadly.

Improvement Features: When planning for the following PI, usually two large improvement items, *features*, and a number of smaller, more specific items are included. The number of features being worked on simultaneously is limited to the capacity of people working in the LACE at the given time, and as one Product Owner notes, the rest of the organisation also has a limited capacity to accept and adapt to the changes the LACE is working to implement. Currently, the most important features as identified by the Product Owners are: *"Clear Line of Sight"*, aiming to display the relations between smaller features and strategic projects, and *"Feature Lead Time"*, targeting shorter delivery times of development features by implementing a metrics dashboard. Additional ongoing LACE features include *"Lean Business Cases"*, a tool to clarify the expected value of features, and a *"Team Role-Card"*, describing the responsibilities of an agile development team to align expectations across the organisation.

Process: The interviewees report that the work process of the LACE resembles the process of an ART in SAFe. All LACE attendees share this common reference in their primary roles, making the overall process in the LACE incremental and easy to follow. The three LACE Product Owners from different line-organisations maintain a backlog of improvement features in collaboration with the LACE volunteers. The backlog items match the LACE Objective Key Results (OKR), quantitative metrics set by the Product Owners representing the vision for the LACE to move towards and measure their progress to stay on track moving in the same direction. New features should match these goals that are redefined and shared anew for each PI cycle. Using a 3-month increment for each PI, features are planned in a PI planning meeting, where a number of features are pulled into the PI according to the expected capacity of the LACE team. Since every LACE member is volunteering to work on LACE features on top of their regular role at Nordea, the expected capacity of LACE fluctuates, as some members may have a lot of work outside the LACE for some periods of time, and may be highly available for others. Due to this, the features pulled into the PI depend on the availability of the *"driver"*, the LACE member committed to drive the feature work. When a feature is moved from the backlog and the LACE work starts, the first step has been observed to be *identifying possible root causes* for the observed challenges. While the LACE participants may have some ideas for what is causing the challenge, it may be deemed necessary to contact more coworkers to grasp the extent and root of the issue and gain allies for the subsequent phases of the change work. The complex issues brought up in the LACE can be difficult to pinpoint and may have multiple causes and thus multiple ways to solve them. When the LACE sub-team working on the feature has examined all possibilities, a *hypothesis is formed*, and an *experiment is set up* to try to solve the problem. Rather than implementing the targeted improvement across the whole organisation, the LACE sub-team typically opts to experiment on a single team or an ART. If the results from the experiment show a positive impact and the hypothesis is validated, *communicating the effective method* of solving a challenging situation is recommended to a broader audience. The work to progress features happens in smaller *feature-specific sub-teams* that a specific person drives. The participants of these sub-teams are invited both from the inside and outside of LACE based on their expected input or interest in the specific feature. The LACE participants use their organisational network to invite persons of interest to work on features that impact them or who are otherwise instrumental to identify the root causes and get the change implemented. One Product Owner reflects that the LACE facilitates the process, but people having the hands-on experience find the best solutions, and thus collaboration is vital. Attendees report that working in small sub-teams is preferable, as too many people and too many opinions may prevent the team from finding consensus and taking action, and that the teams they had worked in were open, willing to collaborate and to do the work needed. The sub-teams meet on a regular basis, usually for one hour per week, to work on their feature, to set goals, to plan a course of action and to evaluate the results. The LACE meets *once per week for a 30-min online status meeting*, where an acting Scrum Master shares the LACE team's Jira Kanban board for the current PI and asks drivers for updates on features in progress. This role rotates among the LACE members. The drivers give short status updates about the progress since the last meeting and the planned actions for each feature. Attendance at these meetings is open to all and not mandatory. Drivers are asked to send a representative to provide an update if they cannot attend the meeting. According to one Product Owner, several different meeting types and lengths have been tried out, and this format has received the best response. According to several interviewees, the Kanban system helps the LACE group stay informed even though their availability to attend these status meetings varies over time. It provides an easy overview since the board is always accessible and Jira is used throughout the development organisation. During our observation period 7–9 persons participated in each weekly status meeting.

Volunteering: The LACE currently runs on an open, part-time, volunteer-based model, unlike the full-time LACE team described in SAFe [22]. Reflecting on the advantages and disadvantages of the volunteer model, one Product Owner points out that the LACE work can only continue as long as management allows LACE members to spend time working in it. If other initiatives are pushed the traditional power structures, requiring the organisation to respond quickly, the LACE will no longer be a priority. Several interviewees expressed a need for a full-time coordinating role within the LACE. All interviewees expressed that having "practitioners", i.e. persons working in other roles in the field, involved in the LACE as positive, and that every volunteer brings value to the LACE, no matter what their primary role or department is.

> *"I know how to drive and facilitate, but I need to bring in the needed people in order to get the right and the best solution out. So having this collaboration between the three different PO's I think we have managed to prove, that I mean, joining forces makes us even stronger."*   — LACE Product Owner

4.3   RQ3: How Does the LACE Influence the Organisation?

The LACE influences the rest of the organisation by including them in identifying and experimenting with solving *systemic issues*. As the LACE has no official mandate to impose changes to anyone in the organisation unwillingly, it relies on more subtle ways of influencing the peers to reach the goals.

Advisory Role: The bottom-up origins of the Nordea LACE and the official lack of mandate to make the high-level decisions is a well-known contradiction compared to the traditional SAFe-based LACE among the interviewees. Thus, currently the LACE's role is advisory. A LACE Product Owner comments that the LACE is empowering people to influence strategic decisions regardless of their role. However, only one LACE participant fully agrees when asked if the LACE is empowering. Instead, one says that empowerment comes from management and from business results. Another explains that in order to start making an impact, a broader audience is needed in LACE. Three of the interviewed LACE participants would like the LACE being given more support by higher management in order to have a more significant influence.

> *"We are missing some kind of mandate from the top, I'm talking about C-level management, to have such a LACE, which will provide the standards for all the business areas, because right now you can either follow the recommendations, [...], or you can do it in your own way, and no one will stop you [...] However, not having this mandate, it doesn't stop us to still implement Scrum, agile, Scaled SAFe, whatever we'll call that. Because the motivation, the beliefs, I think, it was proved through recent years that it's working."*   — LACE Attendee

Communicating the Achievements: One Product Owner and several LACE attendees bring attention to the challenge of broadly communicating the LACE results. The Product Owner's experience is that communicating the value of the changes is easier when the message comes from the same people that have experienced the results firsthand. A tool the LACE uses to raise awareness of the value being generated and the issues they are working with are *pilots*. Instead of deciding on the right path for a change straight away and putting a lot of work into implementing the changes broadly, many LACE projects start by experimenting on a smaller scale, in a team or a train. The purpose of the pilot is to get preliminary results and use those to gain traction and get people interested in the experiments and their results. For the purpose of inspiration and collectively sharing learning experiences, the LACE hosts a monthly business-line staff meeting, a *Huddle*, which is an opportunity to communicate the experiment results to a broad audience. One Product Owner sees the 15-minute time-slot available at the Huddle as a way to showcase the value of the features the LACE is working on. As this storytelling approach has yielded good results according to one Product Owner, piloting is a tool that is often used in the LACE not only to experiment to find the right solutions, but also as a way to communicate and accelerate the change to the rest of the organisation. One interviewee suggests marketing the LACE involvement in these pilots clearly to strengthen the presence of LACE in the minds of the larger organisation and to give momentum to the increasing influence of the LACE going forward.

> "You need to have some sort of a track record that you did something that you say, "Well, this is what we did, this is what we're good at and this is how you can benefit from that". And then you need to turn that into something that people want to carry on or get curious about. [...] And I think that's really something that you could advertise and have people ask questions about: "Okay, so how did this happen then?" and "What have you learned and where did the idea come from?". "Well, the idea came from, we have this group of people called LACE and we're actually developing more and more of those sorts of ideas"."   — LACE Attendee

4.4   RQ4: How Can the LACE Improve to Inspire and Facilitate Change?

Communicating the Achievements & Broader and Earlier Volunteering: Though the majority of interviewees agree that there is enough representation in the LACE currently to support a solid foundation to facilitate changes, expanding the LACE group by recruiting more colleagues is an ongoing improvement item on its own, that one sub-team has been working on. A LACE attendee comments that the network of LACE is extensive, which is an advantage, and that input comes from many different parts of Nordea. We observed that currently, the first three steps of transformation described by Kotter [14] *1: Establishing a Sense of Urgency, 2: Forming a Powerful Guiding Coalition, 3: Creating a Vision* are being done in a small group within the LACE. Establishing a sense of urgency can be seen as identifying features for the LACE backlog and relating them to the overall OKRs. A guiding coalition is formed based on interest within the LACE and the contacts in the network. The vision for change is created in a sub-team by forming hypotheses for how the situation could be improved. In the step four of the Kotter's model the rest of the organisation gets involved. Interviewees noted that communicating the vision for change and getting people outside of the LACE group on board with the changes is difficult at this point. For this reason, a LACE attendee suggested including the broader organisation earlier (e.g. at step one) and recruiting new colleagues based on interest and identification of a specific change feature. This LACE attendee suggested that the Nordea Intranet could be used to reach a broader audience, to both inform and include. The attendee emphasised the importance of people joining being aware that some work would be required to reach a solution, instead of simply complaining about the faced issue. This could make LACE more visible to the rest of the organisation. Another LACE attendee noted that to take the LACE to the next level, it would have to be so well-known that people in the organisation facing systemic issues would reach out to LACE, instead of the other way around, as they have previously heard about the work the LACE did.

> *"We believe that we are doing this for people, so we would like to change in order to make it a better place to work, easier to communicate and collaborate. [...] those people who are volunteering to be a part of this group, they have this drive, right, so they believe that it's not just about, you know, giving advice it's sometimes about, you know, getting your hands dirty and simply doing some activities."*
> — LACE Attendee

Introducing Retrospectives: The internal process of the LACE is a copy of that of an ART in the SAFe framework, that LACE repeats every three months. However, a participant pointed out the lack of retrospectives that aim to reflect on the current processes of an ART or a team to improve. While it is unclear why retrospectives are not currently organised in the LACE, it would be a familiar way to improve the ways of working in the LACE.

Splitting the Feature Size: LACE bases its process on the 3-month PI Planning cadence. Despite this, many features stay in progress for an extended period without much visible progress. At the weekly status meetings, it has been observed how many of the features stay in the same column in Jira for long periods, while the driver of the feature reports progresses nonetheless. One Product Owner explained that while LACE tries to break large features down into medium- and short-term targets, it is not always possible. Some items on the LACE's agenda are very large, ambitious transformations of culture and mindset such as reducing lead-time, thus, it is not surprising that the overall focus on reducing lead-time has been on the backlog for over a year, according to a LACE attendee. However, it is surprising is that this particular item has such a broad and unreachable goal. This feature seems to serve as a reminder of the transformational marathon the LACE is running. A LACE attendee points to this as the LACE's biggest challenge: usually, the large features the LACE is working on are difficult problems to solve, and suggests breaking the large efforts into smaller parts that are easier to tackle and progress is more visible.

"I think if that would be a much more bite-sized piece that we could actually imme-diately start working on and tackle, because we have a clear idea of what we're going to do, a clear idea of how to measure it, be actually Lean, then we can do it and move on to the next item. Right now, they kind of hang there in progress a little bit because they're too big and too ambiguous to really do something about them."
                                                                    — LACE Attendee

5   Discussion and Conclusions

The first Nordea LACE resembled what is described in the SAFe literature. It was dissolved after the initial transition goals were reached, but was re-invented by volunteers within the organisation as a way to facilitate continuous improvement efforts that were still relevant long after the transition. We found that the goals, resources and ways of working of this second installment were vastly different from the LACE described in the SAFe literature. With the long-term focus on continuous improvement within the agile space of Nordea, cross-collaboration and communication between units is highly valued and achieved by engaging volunteers in making change and compelling their peers in an advisory role. This way of working has the advantage that the practitioners engaged in the LACE work uses their network and experience to identify and implement wanted changes more easily, but a disadvantage of this is that their partial commitment may hinder progress and a lack of mandate to enforce change. We suggested the following improvements for the LACE internal processes and to increase influence to further their work: Working more closely with the traditional power structures in line-management, increasing the visibility of the LACE features by marketing them as such, involving more colleagues in change efforts by calling for help on specific changes, and conducting LACE-specific retrospectives.

While SAFe suggests a strategy resembling the *Commanding intervention* type identified by Huy [12], the Nordea LACE resembles the *Socializing inter-vention* type [12] in its democratic approach to change, empirical normative tactic, and participatory and experimental approach conducted in continuous work groups, relying more on organic and incremental spread of change simi-lar to the views of Tsoukas and Chia [26] than the top-down implementation of Kotter [14], on which SAFe bases its recommendation. This is likely due to the goal of the post-transition Nordea LACE differentiating significantly from the SAFe documentation LACE; As Huy notes, the Commanding type is likely effective at changing formal structures with fast improvements in the short-term [12], but for the purpose of long-term continuous improvement, the Socializing type appears to be working well for the Nordea LACE. However, this approach has been observed by the LACE Product Owners to have had some of the same limitations Huy foresaw: a splintered, anarchic organisation [12], a challenge which occurred when the LACE was highly popularised and lacked direction, and seemingly mitigated by an increased focus in the direction led by the three POs. Recognising that the results of this study may only be relevant for this particular context and not generalisable, this first study of one instance of a LACE documenting the experiences of participants may serve as an inspiration for other companies looking for ways to implement or improve a community-run organisation driving continuous improvements efforts from the bottom up. Currently, there is little research covering the continuous improvement elements that are at the heart of agile. The results of this case study open up the area of studying how continuous change can be institutionalised, organised, and work incrementally even long after a large-scale agile transition. Studying more cases in the future will enable researchers to compare different contexts and determine if there are common systemic issues present in mature large-scale agile set-ups. A limitation of this study is the small number of interviewees. Due to the limited resources, we were not able to interview as many non-LACE members nor former LACE members as we would have liked. This poses a potential threat to the validity of this study, as more views from the rest of the organisation, that the LACE is trying to influence, would have been a great addition to the empirical data.

We hope the positive experiences relayed in this paper of this alternative approach to a post-transition LACE may inspire other mature agile organisations to experiment with similar, volunteer-driven LACEs, as a means of facilitating continuous improvement efforts on an organisational level. It may also serve as grounds for more case-studies and comparison of the experiences from other post-transition LACEs attempting to keep the agile continuous improvement process going. We argue that the current body of organisation and change management theory present useful devices for doing so.

References

1. Beck, K., et al.: Agile Manifesto (2001). https://agilemanifesto.org/
2. Brinkmann, S.: Qualitative Interviewing: Understanding Qualitative Research. Oxford University Press, Oxford (2013)
3. Chia, R.: A 'Rhizomic' model of organizational change and transformation: perspective from a metaphysics of change. Br. J. Manag. **10**(3 SPEC. ISS.), 209–227 (1999). https://doi.org/10.1111/1467-8551.00128
4. Cohen, D., Lindvall, M., Costa, P.: An introduction to agile methods. In: Advances in Computers, vol. 62, pp. 1–66. Elsevier (2004). https://doi.org/10.1016/S0065-24 58(03)62001-2, https://linkinghub.elsevier.com/retrieve/pii/S0065245803620012
5. Dikert, K., Paasivaara, M., Lassenius, C.: Challenges and success factors for large-scale agile transformations: a systematic literature review. J. Syst. Softw. **119**, 87–108 (2016). https://doi.org/10.1016/j.jss.2016.06.013
6. Dingsøyr, T., Nerur, S., Balijepally, V., Moe, N.B.: A decade of agile methodologies: towards explaining agile software development. J. Syst. Softw. **85**(6), 1213–1221 (2012). https://doi.org/10.1016/j.jss.2012.02.033
7. Ebert, C., Paasivaara, M.: Scaling agile. IEEE Softw. **34**(6), 98–103 (2017). https://doi.org/10.1109/MS.2017.4121226
8. Feldman, M.S.: Organizational routines as a source of continuous change. Organ. Sci. **11**(6), 611–629 (2000). https://doi.org/10.1287/orsc.11.6.611.12529
9. Fernandes, J.M., Almeida, M.: Classification and comparison of agile methods. In: Proceedings - 7th International Conference on the Quality of Information and Communications Technology, QUATIC 2010, pp. 391–396 (2010). https://doi.org/10.1109/QUATIC.2010.71

10. Highsmith, J., Cockburn, A.: Agile software development: the business of innovation (2001). https://doi.org/10.1109/2.947100
11. Hoda, R., Kruchten, P., Noble, J., Marshall, S.: Agility in context. In: Proceedings of the ACM International Conference on Object Oriented Programming Systems Languages and Applications - OOPSLA 2010, p. 74. ACM Press, New York (2010). https://doi.org/10.1145/1869459.1869467, http://portal.acm.org/citation.cfm?doid=1869459.1869467
12. Huy, Q.N.: Time, temporal capability, and planned change. Acad. Manag. Rev. **26**(4), 601–623 (2001)
13. Knaster, R., Leffingwell, D.: SAFe 5.0 Distilled, 1st edn. Addison-Wesley Professional (2020). https://www.scaledagileframework.com/
14. Kotter, J.P.: Leading change: why transformation efforts fail. Harv. Bus. Rev. (1995). https://doi.org/10.4324/9780203964194-10
15. Laanti, M., Kettunen, P.: SAFe adoptions in Finland: a survey research. In: Hoda, R. (ed.) XP 2019. LNBIP, vol. 364, pp. 81–87. Springer, Cham (2019). https://doi.org/10.1007/978-3-030-30126-2_10
16. Leffingwell, D.: Scaling Software Agility: Best Practices for Large Enterprises. Addison-Wesley Professional, Boston (2007)
17. Nordea.com: Nordea homepage: Nordea at a glance. https://www.nordea.com/en/about-nordea/who-we-are/nordea-at-a-glance/
18. Pernstål, J., Feldt, R., Gorschek, T.: The lean gap: a review of lean approaches to large-scale software systems development. J. Syst. Softw. **86**(11), 2797–2821 (2013). https://doi.org/10.1016/j.jss.2013.06.035
19. Putta, A., Paasivaara, M., Lassenius, C., et al.: Benefits and challenges of adopting the scaled agile framework (SAFe): preliminary results from a multivocal literature review. In: Kuhrmann, M. (ed.) PROFES 2018. LNCS, vol. 11271, pp. 334–351. Springer, Cham (2018). https://doi.org/10.1007/978-3-030-03673-7_24
20. Putta, A., Paasivaara, M., Lassenius, C.: How are agile release trains formed in practice? A case study in a large financial corporation. In: Kruchten, P., Fraser, S., Coallier, F. (eds.) XP 2019. LNBIP, vol. 355, pp. 154–170. Springer, Cham (2019). https://doi.org/10.1007/978-3-030-19034-7_10
21. Putta, A., Uludağ, Ö., Paasivaara, M., Hong, S.-L.: Benefits and challenges of adopting SAFe - an empirical survey. In: Gregory, P., Lassenius, C., Wang, X., Kruchten, P. (eds.) XP 2021. LNBIP, vol. 419, pp. 172–187. Springer, Cham (2021). https://doi.org/10.1007/978-3-030-78098-2_11
22. Scaled Agile Inc.: Homepage: Scaled Agile Framework (2021). https://www.scaledagileframework.com/
23. Schwaber, K., Sutherland, J.: The Scrum Guide: The Definitive Guide to Scrum: The Rules of the Game (2020)
24. StateOfAgile: 14th annual State Of Agile Report. Annual Report for the STATE OF AGILE 14 (2020). https://explore.digital.ai/state-of-agile/14th-annual-state-of-agile-report
25. Nilsson Tengstrand, S., Tomaszewski, P., Borg, M., Jabangwe, R.: Challenges of adopting SAFe in the banking industry – a study two years after its introduction. In: Gregory, P., Lassenius, C., Wang, X., Kruchten, P. (eds.) XP 2021. LNBIP, vol. 419, pp. 157–171. Springer, Cham (2021). https://doi.org/10.1007/978-3-030-78098-2_10
26. Tsoukas, H., Chia, R.: On organizational becoming: rethinking organizational change. Organ. Sci. **13**(5), 567–582 (2002). https://doi.org/10.1287/orsc.13.5.567.7810

27. Uludağ, Ö., Putta, A., Paasivaara, M., Matthes, F.: Evolution of the agile scaling frameworks. In: Gregory, P., Lassenius, C., Wang, X., Kruchten, P. (eds.) XP 2021. LNBIP, vol. 419, pp. 123–139. Springer, Cham (2021). https://doi.org/10.1007/978-3-030-78098-2_8

28. Yin, R.K.: Case Study Research and Applications: Design and Methods, 6th edn. SAGE Publications, Los Angeles (2018)

Requirements

How Do Practitioners Interpret Conditionals in Requirements?

Jannik Fischbach[1]([✉]), Julian Frattini[2], Daniel Mendez[2,3],
Michael Unterkalmsteiner[2], Henning Femmer[1], and Andreas Vogelsang[4]

[1] Qualicen GmbH, Garching, Germany
{jannik.fischbach,henning.femmer}@qualicen.de
[2] Blekinge Institute of Technology, Karlskrona, Sweden
{julian.frattini,daniel.mendez,michael.unterkalmsteiner}@bth.se
[3] fortiss GmbH, Munich, Germany
mendez@fortiss.org
[4] University of Cologne, Cologne, Germany
vogelsang@cs.uni-koeln.de

Abstract. *Context*: Conditional statements like "If A and B then C" are core elements for describing software requirements. However, there are many ways to express such conditionals in natural language and also many ways how they can be interpreted. We hypothesize that conditional statements in requirements are a source of ambiguity, potentially affecting downstream activities such as test case generation negatively. *Objective*: Our goal is to understand how specific conditionals are interpreted by readers who work with requirements. *Method*: We conduct a descriptive survey with 104 RE practitioners and ask how they interpret 12 different conditional clauses. We map their interpretations to logical formulas written in Propositional (Temporal) Logic and discuss the implications. *Results*: The conditionals in our tested requirements were interpreted ambiguously. We found that practitioners disagree on whether an antecedent is only *sufficient* or also *necessary* for the consequent. Interestingly, the disagreement persists even when the system behavior is known to the practitioners. We also found that certain cue phrases are associated with specific interpretations. *Conclusion*: Conditionals in requirements are a source of ambiguity and there is not just one way to interpret them formally. This affects any analysis that builds upon formalized requirements (e.g., inconsistency checking, test-case generation). Our results may also influence guidelines for writing requirements.

Keywords: Logical interpretation · Requirements engineering · Descriptive survey · Formalization

1 Introduction

Context. Functional requirements often describe external system behavior by relating events to each other, e.g. "If the system detects an error (e_1), an error

© Springer Nature Switzerland AG 2021
L. Ardito et al. (Eds.): PROFES 2021, LNCS 13126, pp. 85–102, 2021.
https://doi.org/10.1007/978-3-030-91452-3_6

message shall be shown (e_2)" (REQ 1). Such conditional statements are prevalent in both traditional requirement documents [15] and agile requirement artifacts [14] alike. The interpretation of the semantics of conditionals affects all activities carried out on the basis of documented requirements such as manual reviews, implementation, or test case generations. Even more, a correct interpretation is absolutely essential for all automatic analyses of requirements that consider the semantics of sentences; for instance, automatic quality analysis like smell detection [11], test case derivation [14,17], and dependency detection [13]. In consequence, conditionals should always be associated with a formal meaning to automatically process them. However, determining a suitable formal interpretation is challenging because conditional statements in natural language tend to be ambiguous. Literally, REQ 1 from above may be interpreted as a logical implication $(e_1 \Rightarrow e_2)$, in which e_1 is a *sufficient* precondition for e_2. However, it is equally reasonable to assume that the error message shall not be shown if the error has not been detected (i.e., e_1 is a *sufficient* and also *necessary* condition for e_2). Furthermore, it is reasonable to assume that e_1 must occur *before* e_2. Both assumptions are not covered by an implication as it neglects temporal ordering. In contrast, the assumptions need to be expressed by temporal logic (e.g., LTL [21]). Existing guidelines for expressing requirements have different ways of interpreting conditionals; for instance, Mavin et al. [23] propose to interpret conditionals as a logical equivalence $(e_1 \Leftrightarrow e_2)$ to avoid ambiguity. We argue that the "correct" way of interpretation should not just be defined by the authors of a method, but rather from the view of practitioners. This requires an understanding how these interpret such conditionals. Otherwise, we choose a formalization that does not reflect how practitioners interpret conditional sentences, rendering downstream activities error-prone. That is, we would likely derive incomplete test cases or interpret dependencies between the requirements incorrectly.

Problem. We lack knowledge on how practitioners interpret conditional statements in requirements and how these interpretations should be formalized accordingly. Moreover, we are not aware of the factors that influence the logical interpretation of conditional clauses in requirements.

Contribution. In this paper, we report on a survey we conducted with 104 RE practitioners and determine how they interpret conditional clauses in requirements. The goal of our research is to provide empirical evidence for whether a common formal interpretation of conditionals in requirements exists. Key insights include, but are not limited to:

1. Conditionals in requirements are ambiguous. Practitioners disagreed on whether an antecedent is only *sufficient* or also *necessary* for a consequent.
2. We observed a statistically significant relation between the interpretation and certain context factors of practitioners (e.g., experience in RE, the way how a practitioner interacts with requirements, and the presence of domain knowledge). Interestingly, domain knowledge does not promote a consistent interpretation of conditionals.

3. The choice of certain cue phrase has an impact on the degree of ambiguity (e.g., "while" was less ambiguous than "if" or "when" w.r.t. temporal relationship).

Finally, we disclose all of our data as well as the survey protocol via a replication package at https://doi.org/10.5281/zenodo.5070235.

Related Work. Transforming NL requirements into verifiable LTL patterns [9] has received notable attention, as this formalization respects the temporal aspect of requirements and allows for an automatic assessment of requirements quality like ambiguity, consistency, or completeness [24]. However, most approaches are based on restricted natural language [20,27,31] and assume that a unanimously agreed upon formalization of NL requirements exist. We challenge this assumption by considering ambiguity in respect to conditional statements. Ambiguity in NL requirements itself has been explored in several studies so far. A general overview of the nature of ambiguity and its impact on the development process is provided by Gervasi and Zowghi [19]. De Bruijn et al. [4] investigates the effects of ambiguity on project success or failure. Berry and Kamsties [2] show that indefinite quantifiers can lead to misunderstandings. Winter et al. [29] show that negative phrasing of quantifiers is more ambiguous than affirmative phrasing. Femmer et al. [12] reveals that the use of passive voice leads to ambiguity in requirements. To the best of our knowledge, however, we are the first to study ambiguity induced by conditionals in requirements.

2 Fundamentals

To determine how to appropriately formalize interpretations by RE practitioners, we first need to understand how conditionals can be specified logically. We investigate the logical interpretations with respect to two dimensions: Necessity and Temporality. In this section, we demarcate both dimensions, and introduce suitable formal languages to the extent necessary in context of this paper.

Necessity. A conditional statement consists of two parts: the antecedent (in case of REQ 1: e_1) and the consequent (e_2). The relationship between an antecedent and consequent can be interpreted logically in two different ways. First, by means of an implication as $e_1 \Rightarrow e_2$, in which e_1 is a *sufficient* condition for e_2. Interpreting REQ 1 as an implication requires the system to display an error message if e_1 is true. However, it is not specified what the system should do if e_1 is false. The implication allows both the occurrence of e_2 and its absence if e_1 is false. In contrast, the relationship of antecedent and consequent can also be understood as a logical equivalence, where e_1 is both a *sufficient* and *necessary* condition for e_2. Interpreting REQ 1 as an equivalence requires the system to display an error message *if and only if* it detects an error. Consequently, if e_1 is false, then e_2 should also be false. The interpretation of conditionals as an implication or equivalence significantly influences further development activities. For example, a test designer who interprets conditionals rather as implication than equivalence might only add positive test cases to a test suite. This may lead to a misalignment of tests and requirements in case the business analyst actually intended to express an equivalence.

Temporality. The temporal relation between an antecedent and consequent can be interpreted in three different ways: (1) the consequent occurs simultaneous with the antecedent, (2) the consequent occurs immediately after the antecedent, and (3) the consequent occurs at some indefinite point after the antecedent. Propositional logic does not consider temporal ordering of events and is therefore not expressive enough to model temporal relationships. In contrast, we require linear temporal logic (LTL), which considers temporal ordering by defining the behavior σ of a system as an infinite sequence of states $\langle s_0, \cdots \rangle$, where s_n is a state of the system at "time" n [21]. Accordingly, requirements are understood as constraints on σ. The desired system behavior is defined as an LTL formula F, where next to the usual PL operators also temporal operators like $\Box$ (*always*), $\Diamond$ (*eventually*), and $\bigcirc$ (*next state*) are used. Since we will use these temporal operators in the course of the paper, we will present them here in more detail. To understand the LTL formulas, we assign a semantic meaning $[\![F]\!]$ to each syntactic object F. Formally, $[\![F]\!]$ is a boolean-valued function on σ. According to Lamport [21], $\sigma[\![F]\!]$ denotes the boolean value that formula F assigns to behavior σ, and that σ satisfies F if and only if $\sigma[\![F]\!]$ equals true (i.e., the system satisfies requirement F). We define $[\![\Box F]\!]$, $[\![\Diamond F]\!]$ and $[\![\bigcirc F]\!]$ in terms of $[\![F]\!]$ (see equations below). The expression $\langle s_0, \cdots \rangle [\![F]\!]$ asserts that F is true at "time" 0 of the behavior, while $\langle s_n, \cdots \rangle [\![F]\!]$ asserts that F is true at "time" n.

$$\forall n \in \mathbb{N} : \langle s_n, \cdots \rangle [\![\Box F]\!] \Rightarrow \forall m \in \mathbb{N}, m \geq n, \langle s_m, \cdots \rangle [\![F]\!] \tag{1}$$

$$\forall n \in \mathbb{N} : \langle s_n, \cdots \rangle [\![\Diamond F]\!] \Rightarrow \exists m \in \mathbb{N}, m > n, \langle s_m, \cdots \rangle [\![F]\!] \tag{2}$$

$$\forall n \in \mathbb{N} : \langle s_n, \cdots \rangle [\![\bigcirc F]\!] \Rightarrow \langle s_{n+1}, \cdots \rangle [\![F]\!] \tag{3}$$

Equation 1 asserts that F is true in all states of behavior σ. More specifically, $\Box F$ asserts that F is *always* true. The temporal operator $\Diamond$ can be interpreted as "it is not the case that F is always false" [21]. According to Eq. 2, a behavior σ satisfies $\Diamond F$ if and only if F is true at some state of σ. In other words, $\Diamond F$ asserts that F is *eventually* true. According to Eq. 3, $\bigcirc F$ asserts that F is true at the *next state* of behavior σ. In contrast to $\Diamond F$, $\bigcirc F$ requires that this state is not an arbitrary state of behavior σ, but rather the direct successor of state n. In conclusion, LTL can be used to incorporate temporal ordering into an implication $(F \Rightarrow G)$ in three ways:

1. G occurs simultaneous with F:
   $\Box(F \Rightarrow G)$, which can be interpreted as "any time F is true, G is also true".
2. G occurs immediately after F:
   $\Box(F \Rightarrow \bigcirc G)$, which can be interpreted as "G occurs after F terminated".
3. G occurs at some indefinite point after F:
   $\Box(F \Rightarrow \Diamond G)$, which can be interpreted as "any time F is true, G is also true or at a later state".

Formalization Matrix. To distinguish the logical interpretations and their formalization, we constructed a formalization matrix (see Fig. 1). It defines a conditional statement of F and G along the two dimensions (Necessity, and Temporality), each divided on a nominal scale (see Table 1). Each 2-tuple of characteristics can be mapped to an entry in the formalization matrix. For example, the LTL formula $\Box(F \Rightarrow \bigcirc G)$ formalizes a conditional statement, in which F is only *sufficient* and G occurs in the *next state*. Conditional statements that define F as both *sufficient* and *necessary* must be formalized with a further LTL formula: $\Box(\neg F \Rightarrow \neg(\Diamond G))$. This formula can be literally interpreted as "If F does not occur, then G does not occur either (not even *eventually*)".

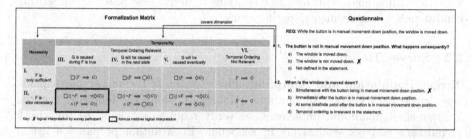

Fig. 1. Mapping between Questionnaire (right) and Formalization Matrix (left).

3 Study Design

To understand how practitioners interpret conditionals in requirements and how their interpretations should be formalized accordingly, we conducted a survey following the guidelines by Ciolkowski et al. [5].

3.1 Survey Definition

We aim to understand and (logically) formalize the interpretation of conditionals in requirements by RE practitioners in software development projects. The expected outcome of our survey is a better understanding of how practitioners logically interpret conditional clauses in requirements and which of the elements in our formalization matrix match their logical interpretations (see Fig. 1). We derived three research questions (RQ) from our survey goal.

- **RQ1:** How do practitioners logically interpret conditional clauses in requirements?
- **RQ2:** Which factors influence the logical interpretation of conditional clauses in requirements?
- **RQ3:** Which (if any) cue phrases promote (un)ambiguous interpretation?

RQ1 investigates how conditionals are interpreted by practitioners and how their interpretations should be formalized accordingly. RQ2 studies whether the logical interpretation of practitioners depends on certain factors. We focus on: 1) the role of the participant (e.g., writing requirements vs. reading and implementing requirements) and 2) the domain context of the requirement (i.e., does the requirement describe system behavior from a domain that is familiar to the participant, or does the requirement originate from an unknown domain?). RQ3 aims at the formulation of conditionals: Conditional clauses can be expressed by using different cue phrases (e.g., "if", "when"). We hypothesize that cue phrases impact the logical interpretation of practitioners. With RQ3, we want to identify cue phrases for which the interpretations are almost consistent, and cue phrases which are ambiguous. This insight enables us to derive best practices on writing conditionals in requirements specifications.

3.2   Survey Design

Target Population and Sampling. The selection of the survey participants was driven by a purposeful sampling strategy [1] along the following criteria: a) they elicit, maintain, implement, or verify requirements, and b) they work in industry and not exclusively in academia. Each author prepared a list of potential participants using their personal or second-degree contacts (convenience sampling [30]). From this list, the research team jointly selected suitable participants based on their adequacy for the study. To increase the sample size further, we asked each participant for other relevant contacts after the survey (snowball sampling). Our survey was started by 168 participants of which 104 completed the survey. All figures in this paper refer to the 104 participants that completed the survey. The majority of participants were non-native English speakers (94.2%). We received responses mainly from practitioners working in Germany (94.2%). The remaining 5.8% of survey completions originate from Croatia, Austria, Japan, Switzerland, United States, and China. The experience of the participants in RE and RE-related fields is equally distributed: 18.2% have less than 1 year experience, 26% between 1 and 3 years, 25% between 4 and 10 years, and 30.8% more than 10 years. The participants work for companies operating in 22 different domains. The majority of our participants is employed in the automotive (21%) and insurance/reinsurance (10.1%) industry. Over the past three years, our participants have worked in 18 different roles. Most frequently, they had roles as developers, project managers, requirements engineers/business analysts, or testers. 77.9% of the survey participants elicit requirements as part of their job. 59.6% verify whether requirements are met by a system. 46.2% read requirements and implement them. 45.2% maintain the quality of requirements.

Study Objects. To conduct the survey and answer the RQs, we used three data sets (DS), each from a different domain. DS1 contains conditionals from a requirements document describing the behavior of an automatic door in the automotive domain. We argue that all participants have an understanding of how an automatic car door is expected to work, so that all participants should have the required domain knowledge. DS2 contains conditionals from aerospace systems. We hypothesize that no or only few participants have deeper knowledge in this domain, making DS2 well suited for an analysis of the impact of domain knowledge on logical interpretations. DS3 contains abstract conditionals (e.g., If event A and event B, then event C). Thus, they are free from any domain-induced interpretation bias. To address RQ 3, we focused on four cue phrases in the conditionals: "if", "while", "after", and "when". To avoid researcher bias, we created the datasets extracting conditionals randomly from existing requirement documents used in practice. The conditionals in DS1 are taken from a requirements document written by Mercedes-Benz Passenger Car Development.[1] The conditionals contained in DS2 originate from three requirements documents published by NASA and one by ESA.[2] The conditionals in DS3 are syntactically identical to the conditionals in DS1, except that we replace the names of the events with abstract names. DS1–3 contain four conditionals each, resulting in a total of 12 study objects. Each cue phrase occurs exactly once in each DS.

Questionnaire Design. We chose an online questionnaire as our data collection instrument to gather quantitative data on our research questions. For the design, we followed the guidelines of Dillman et al. [8] to reduce common mistakes when setting up a questionnaire. Since our research goal is of descriptive nature, most questions are closed-ended. We designed three types of questions (Q) addressing the two dimensions and prepared a distinct set of responses (R), among which the participants can choose. Each of these responses can be mapped to a characteristic in the formalization matrix and thus allows us to determine which characteristic the practitioners interpret as being reflected by a conditional (see Fig. 1). We build the questionnaire for each study object (e.g., If F then G) according to a pre-defined template (see Fig. 2). The template is structured as follows: The first question (**Q1**) investigates the dimension of Necessity: if event G cannot occur without event F, then F is not only *sufficient*, but also necessary for G. We add "nevertheless" as a third response option (see R.1.1 in Fig. 2) to perform a sanity check on the answers of the respondents. We argue that interpreting that the consequent should occur although the antecedent does not occur indicates that the sentence has not been read carefully. The second question (**Q2**) covers the temporal ordering of the events. In this context, we explicitly ask for the three temporal relations *eventually*, *always* and *next state* described in Sect. 2. Should a participant perceive temporal ordering as irrelevant for the interpretation of a certain conditional, we can conclude that PL is sufficient for its formalization. We ask **Q1–2** for each of the 12 study objects, resulting in a total of 24 questions. To get an overview of the background of our respondents, we also integrated five demographic questions. In total, our final

---

[1] Thanks to Frank Houdek for sharing the document at NLP4RE'19 [7]: https://nlp4re.github.io/2019/uploads/demo-spec-automatic-door.pdf.

[2] We retrieved these documents from the data set published by Fischbach et al. [13]. We are referring to the documents: REQ-DOC-22, REQ-DOC-26, REQ-DOC-27 and REQ-DOC-30.

questionnaire consists of 29 questions and can be also found in our replication package.

Q1: F does not occur. What happens consequently?

- **R1.1**: G occurs nevertheless. (sanity check)
- **R1.2**: G does not occur. ($\rightarrow$ II)
- **R1.3**: Not defined in the statement. ($\rightarrow$ I)

Q2: When does G occur?

- **R2.1**: Simultaneously with F. ($\rightarrow$ III)
- **R2.2**: Immediately after F. ($\rightarrow$ IV)
- **R2.3**: At some indefinite point after F. ($\rightarrow$ V)
- **R2.3**: Temporal ordering is irrelevant in the statement. ($\rightarrow$ VI)

Fig. 2. Questionnaire template. The note after each answer option (e.g., $\rightarrow$ IV) indicates the matching characteristic in the formalization matrix (see Fig. 1). If a participant selects R1.2, for example, she implicitly interprets F as *necessary* for G. The notes were not included in the questionnaire.

3.3   Survey Implementation and Execution

We prepared an invitation letter to ask potential participants if they would like to join our survey. We incorporated all of our 29 questions into the survey tool Unipark [25]. To avoid bias in the survey data, we allow Unipark to randomize the order of the non-demographic questions. We opened the survey on Feb 01, 2021 and closed it after 15 days. We approached all eligible contacts from our prepared list either by e-mail or via Linkedin direct message. We also distributed the questionnaire via a mailing list in the RE focus group of the German Informatics Society (GI). As the traffic on our survey website decreased during the first week, we contacted all candidates again on Feb 08.

3.4   Survey Analysis

To answer the proposed research questions, we analyzed the gathered quantitative data as follows.

Analysis for RQ 1. We use heatmaps to visualize how the respondents logically interpret the individual study objects (see Fig. 3). Each cell in the heatmaps corresponds to a single 2-tuple. Based on the heatmaps, we analyse the logical interpretations of the participants and decide which formalization should be chosen for each study subject according to the most frequent 2-tuple.

Analysis for RQ 2. We focus on three factors (f_n) and investigate their impact on the logical interpretations of practitioners: (1) the experience in RE (f_1: **Experience**), (2) how the practitioners interact with requirements (elicit, maintain, verify,...) in their job (f_2: **Interaction**), and (3) the domain context of the conditional (f_3: **Domain**). To answer RQ 2, we examine the impact of f_1–f_3 on the dimensions described in Sect. 2. In our survey, we collected the dimensions for each sentence individually, resulting in 12 categorical variables per dimension (e.g., **nec$_{s1}$**, **nec$_{s2}$**, ... **nec$_{s12}$**). To get an insight across all sentences, we aggregated all 12 categorical variables per dimension to one variable (resulting in **Necessity**, and **Temporality**). This allows us to analyze, for example, whether the experience of the respondents has an impact on understanding an antecedent only as *sufficient* for a consequent or as both *sufficient* and *necessary*. In other words, does the perception of **Necessity** depend on **Experience**? As shown in Table 1, all five variables (3× factors and 2× dimensions) are categorical with a maximum of four levels. The majority is nominally scaled, while **Experience** follows an ordinal scale. The variable **Domain** was not gathered directly from the responses, but implicitly from our selection of the data sets. We thus add **Domain** as variable to our data set, using a categorical scale with three levels: domain knowledge is present (in case of DS1), domain knowledge is not present (DS2), and domain knowledge is not necessary (DS3). By introducing this new variable, we are able to investigate the relationship between domain knowledge and logical interpretations. We use the *chi-squared test of independence* (χ^2) to analyze the relationship between all variables. We run the test by using SPSS and test the following hypotheses (H_n):

for $f_n \in$ {**Experience**, **Interaction**, **Domain**} do
    for $v \in$ {**Necessity**, **Temporality**} do
        H$_0$: The interpretation of v is independent of f_n.
        H$_1$: The interpretation of v depends on f_n.
    end for
end for

We set the p-value at 0.05 as the threshold to reject the null hypothesis. To test our hypotheses, we need to calculate the contingency tables for each combination of f_n and dimension. The total number of survey answers per dimension is 1,248 (104 survey completions * 12 annotated sentences). Since we allow the respondents to specify multiple ways to interact with requirements (e.g., to both elicit and implement requirements), our survey data contains a multiple dichotomy set for **Interaction**. In other words, we created a separate variable for each of the selectable interaction ways (four in total for verify, maintain, elicit and implement). Each variable has two possible values (0 or 1), which indicate whether or not the response was selected by the participant. Therefore, we define a multiple response set in SPSS to create the contingency table for **Interaction**. The χ^2 test allows us to determine if there is enough evidence to conclude an association between two categorical variables. However, it does not indicate the strength of the relationship. To measure the association between our variables, we use Cramer's Phi ϕ [6] in case of two nominally scaled variables and Freeman's theta Θ [18] in case of one ordinally scaled and one nominally scaled variable. We calculate ϕ by using SPSS and Θ by using the R implementation "freeman-Theta". We interpret Θ according to the taxonomy of Vargha and Delaney [28]. For the interpretation of ϕ, we use the taxonomy of Cohen [6].

Analysis for RQ 3. A conventional way to measure ambiguity is by calculating the inter-rater agreement (e.g., Fleiss Kappa [16]). However, inter-rater agreement measures must be used carefully, as they have a number of well known shortcomings [10]. For example, the magnitude of the agreement values is not meaningful if there is a large gap between the number of annotated units and the number of involved raters. In our case, we examine only three units per cue phrase (i.e., "if" is only included in S2, S8 and S10), each of which was annotated by 104 raters. This discrepancy between the number of units and raters leads to a very small magnitude of the agreement values and distorts the impression of agreement. For example, if we calculate Fleiss Kappa regarding the dimension Temporality of sentences that contain the cue phrase "while", we obtain a value of 0.053. According to the taxonomy Landis and Koch [22], this would imply only a slight agreement between the raters. In fact, however, there is a substantial agreement among the raters that "while" indicates a simultaneous relationship. This can be demonstrated by the distribution of survey answers across the different Temporality levels (see Fig. 4). Thus, instead of reporting less meaningful inter-rater agreement measures, we provide histograms visualizing the distribution of ratings on the three investigated dimensions. We create the histograms for each set of study objects containing the same cue phrase. This allows us to analyze which cue phrase produced the highest/lowest agreement for a certain dimension.

Table 1. Overview of analyzed variables.

Name	Levels	Type	Scale
Experience	– less than 1 year – 1–3 years – 4–10 years – more than 10 years	categorical (single select)	ordinal
Interaction	– elicit – maintain – verify – implement	categorical (multiple select)	nominal
Domain	– domain knowledge present – domain knowledge not present – domain knowledge not necessary	categorical (single select)	nominal
Necessity	– nevertheless – only sufficient – also necessary	categorical (single select)	nominal
Temporality	– during – next state – eventually – temporal ordering not relevant	categorical (single select)	nominal

4 Results

RQ 1: How do practitioners logically interpret conditional clauses in requirements?

We first look at the total number of answers for each dimension across all data sets. Secondly, we analyze the distribution of ratings based on our constructed heatmaps (see Fig. 3).

Necessity. Our participants did not have a clear tendency whether an antecedent is only *sufficient* or also *necessary* for the consequent. Among the total of 1,248 answers, 2.1% correspond to the level "nevertheless", 46.9% to "also necessary", and 51% for "only sufficient". That means that more than half of the respondents stated that the conditional does not cover how the system is expected to work if the antecedent does not occur (i.e., the negative case is not specified).

Temporality. We found that time plays a major role in the interpretation of conditionals in requirements. Among the 1,248 answers, only 13% were "temporal ordering is irrelevant" for the interpretation. This indicates that conditionals in requirements require temporal logics for a suitable formalization. For some study objects, the exact temporal relationship between antecedent and consequent was ambiguous. For S3, 34 participants selected "during", 43 "next state", and 19 "eventually". Similarly, we observed divergent temporal interpretations for S2, S5, S7, S10, S11, and S12. In contrast, the respondents widely agreed on the temporal relationship of S1 (67 survey answers for "next state"), S4 (84 survey answers for "during"), S6 (73 survey answers for "during"), S8 (67 survey answers for "eventually") and S9 (83 survey answers for "eventually"). Across all study objects, 29.8% of survey answers were given for the level "during", 20.1% for "next state" and 37.1% for "eventually".

Agreement. Our heatmaps illustrate that there are only few study objects for which more than half of the respondents agreed on a 2-tuple (see Fig. 3). This trend is evident across all data sets. The presence or absence of domain knowledge does not seem to have an impact on a consistent interpretation. The greatest agreement was achieved in the case of S1 (48 survey answers for ⟨necessary, next state⟩), S6 (49 survey answers for ⟨necessary, during⟩), S8 (53 survey answers for ⟨sufficient, eventually⟩) and S9 (56 survey answers for ⟨sufficient, eventually⟩). However, for the majority of study objects, there was no clear agreement on a specific 2-tuple. For S5, two 2-tuples were selected equally often, and for S10, the two most frequent 2-tuples differed by only two survey answers.

Generally Valid Formalization? Mapping the most frequent 2-tuples in the heatmaps to our constructed formalization matrix reveals that all study objects can not be formalized in the same way. The most frequent 2-tuples for each study object yield the following six patterns:

1. ⟨necessary, next state⟩: S1, S3
2. ⟨necessary, irrelevant⟩: S2
3. ⟨necessary, during⟩: S6, S10, S11
4. ⟨necessary, eventually⟩: (S5)
5. ⟨sufficient, eventually⟩: (S5), S7, S8, S9
6. ⟨sufficient, during⟩: S4, S12

One sees immediately that it is not possible to derive a formalization for conditionals in general. Especially the temporal interpretations differed between the conditionals and the used cue phrases (see Fig. 4). However, it can be concluded that, except for S2, the interpretations of all study objects can be represented by LTL.

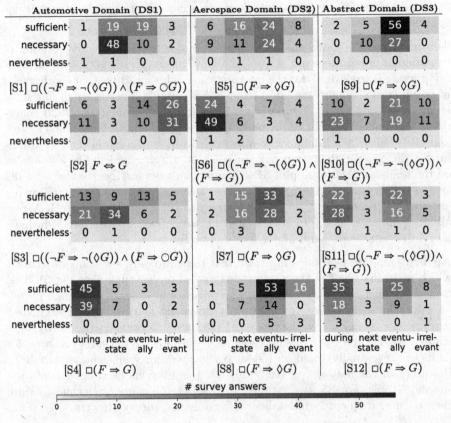

Fig. 3. Heatmaps visualizing the interpretations of the participants per study object $[S_n]$.

Table 2. Relationships between factors and interpretation.

Tested Relationship	Test Statistics			Measures	
	χ^2	df	p-value	ϕ	Θ
Experience and Necessity	2.384	6	0.881	–	–
Experience and Temporality	31.523	9	0.001	–	0.089
Interaction and Necessity	11.005	8	2.201	–	–
Interaction and Temporality	36.991	12	< 0.001	0.510	–
Domain and Necessity	22.310	4	< 0.001	0.134	–
Domain and Temporality	138.128	6	< 0.001	0.333	–

RQ 2: Which factors influence the logical interpretation of conditional clauses in requirements?

This section reports the results of our chi-square tests (see Table 2). In our contingency tables, no more than 20% of the expected counts are <5. Hence, we satisfy the assumption of enough observations per category for the chi-square test [32]. In the following, we explain the relationships where the chi-square test indicated a dependency between the logical interpretation and a factor.

The logical interpretation regarding Temporality depends on RE Experience. In the group with less than 1 year of experience, there is a tendency to perceive the temporal relationship between the events as "during" (36.4%). In the group of participants with 4–10 years of experience, most of the respondents rated the temporal relationship as "eventually" (41.3%). The χ^2 test reveals that the distribution of ratings differs between the experience levels. The calculated Θ value indicates that the strength of the relationship is low.

The logical interpretation regarding Temporality is dependent on how a practitioner interacts with requirements. Our contingency table reveals that the distribution of ratings differs between the interaction levels. Practitioners who implement requirements fluctuate mainly between "during" and "eventually", while they rarely selected the other two Temporality levels. A different pattern emerges for practitioners who maintain and verify requirements. Across all study objects, they choose the levels "during", "next state" and "eventually" equally often. A χ^2 test indicates a dependency between both variables. The calculated ϕ value indicates that the strength of the relationship is high.

The logical interpretation regarding Necessity is dependent on domain knowledge. The disagreement about whether an antecedent is only *sufficient* or also *necessary* holds regardless of domain knowledge. However, the trend differs between the data sets with respect to the Necessity levels. In the case of DS1 (domain knowledge assumed), more answers were given for "also necessary" (54.3%) than for "only sufficient" (45%). In contrast, more ratings were given for "only sufficient" in the case of DS2 (53.1%) and DS3 (55%). The slight difference in the distribution of the ratings regarding Necessity is supported by the χ^2 test. However, the strength of the relationships is low.

The logical interpretation regarding Temporality is dependent on domain knowledge. Our contingency table shows that the distribution of ratings regarding Temporality differs between the data sets. In the case of DS1, ratings were mainly given for "during" (32.9%) and "next state" (31.3%). In the case of the unknown domain (DS2), ratings were mainly assigned to "eventually" (46.2%), while only 20.7% were given to "next state" and 22.4% to "during". In DS3, where no domain knowledge is necessary for the understanding of the conditionals, most ratings were given to "during" (34.1%) and "eventually" (47.1%). A χ^2 test shows that there is a statistically significant dependency between both variables. According to the calculated ϕ value, the strength of the relationship is medium.

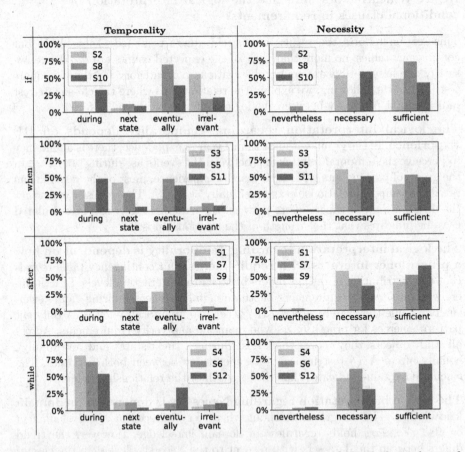

Fig. 4. Distribution of survey answers on the different variable levels for each set of study objects with the same cue phrase (e.g., S2, S8 and S10 include "if").

RQ 3: Which (if any) cue phrases promote (un)ambiguous interpretation?

The histograms in Fig. 4 show that the logical interpretation regarding Temporality depends on the cue phrase used to express a conditional. For study objects containing "while" (S4, S6 and S12), the respondents largely agreed that the consequent occurs simultaneously with the antecedent. In contrast, almost no respondent associated simultaneous events in the study objects with the cue phrase "after". Instead, the respondents vacillated between the temporal levels "next state" and "eventually". The largest disagreement, though, was found in the interpretations of the conditionals "if" or "when". Especially in the case of "when", there was no clear agreement across S3, S5 and S11 on whether antecedent and consequent are in a "during", "next state" or "eventually" temporal relationship. Regarding Necessity, we observe that the practitioners, irrespective of the used cue phrase, disagree whether the antecedent is only *sufficient* or also *necessary* for the consequent. We found one outlier in our histograms (S8), where an 80% agreement for the level "sufficient" could be achieved. For the remaining study objects, however, there is a balanced number of survey answers for both levels.

5 Threats to Validity

Internal Validity. The respondents may have misunderstood the questions resulting in poor quality or invalid answers. To minimize this threat, we followed the guidelines by Dillmann [8] in the creation of the questionnaire. In addition, we conducted a pilot phase to validate the questionnaire internally through discussions in the research team and externally through pilot survey runs. Selection bias is another threat. Although we have started with personal contacts to find participants, the sampling process has been extended by indirect contacts. As a result, selection bias has been reduced. Another possible threat is the selection of dimensions by which we formalize conditionals. The two dimensions, Temporality and Necessity, have been selected after extensive literature research and discussion among the authors. However, the completeness of dimensions can neither be proven nor rebutted. One threat that we were unable to control was the distribution of native speakers. Although one could argue that non-native speakers reading and writing English requirements are the standard case for most projects, and therefore, their interpretation is meaningful nevertheless, future research should validate the findings also with a dedicated group of native speakers. Another threat arises from our assumption that each participant has the necessary domain knowledge in case of DS1 but lacks it in case of DS2. To mitigate this threat, we analyzed the feedback received during our pilot study. In the case of DS1, almost no questions were raised, whereas in the case of DS2, many pilot users lacked knowledge about the described system behavior. This indicates that the respondents may have the necessary domain knowledge to interpret the conditionals described in DS1. Furthermore, the conditionals in DS1 are derived from the data set used in the tool competition at the NLP4RE workshop, which is claimed to be interpretable without specific domain knowledge.

External Validity. As in every survey, the limited sample size and sampling strategy do not provide the statistical basis to generalize the results of the study. However, we tried to involve RE practitioners working in different roles at companies from different domains to obtain a comprehensive picture of how conditionals are logically interpreted. We argue that our survey sample of 104 RE practitioners, who work in 22 different domains and of which a third have more than 10 years of experience in RE is sufficient for a first insight into the logical interpretation of conditionals.

Construct Validity. The questionnaire might not sufficiently cover our research questions limiting the availability of data that provides suitable answers to the research questions. To minimize this threat, we constructed a formalization matrix and designed our questionnaire according to the dimensions of the matrix to establish a distinct mapping between interpretation and suitable formalization.

6   Concluding Discussion and Outlook

Conditionals are common to specify desired system behavior. In this paper, we show that conditionals are interpreted ambiguously by RE practitioners. In particular, there is disagreement (1) about whether an antecedent is only *sufficient* or also *necessary* for a consequent, and (2) about the temporal occurrence of antecedent and consequent when different cue phrases (such as "when" or "if") are used. Thus, a generic formalization of conditionals will inevitably fail at least some practitioner's interpretation. We see two immediate implications in practice:

(1) Implications for automatic methods. Especially (if not limited) for automated test case generation, it is vital to understand which behavior is desired if the antecedent does not occur. The evidence presented in this paper refutes the prevailing assumption (cf. [13,23]) that antecedents can always be treated as *necessary* conditions. Hence, we propose that future methods should display the automatically generated positive and negative test cases to practitioners and explicitly verify: "Is the negative case of your conditional also valid?". This will foster the discussion within project teams about the expected system behavior and enables to resolve misunderstandings at an early stage.

(2) Implications for requirements authors. It should be incorporated into RE writing guidelines that it does matter which cue phrase is used for the formulation of a conditional. "While" is interpreted consistently, but "if" and "when" cause misunderstandings about the temporal interpretation of antecedent and consequent. This poses a problem especially in the implementation of requirements and eventually leads to discrepancies between actual and expected system behavior. Project teams should therefore agree early on how they want to interpret the different cue phrases to avoid ambiguities. Additionally, our findings provide empirical evidence for the claim by Berry et al. [3] and Rosadini et al. [26] that requirements authors should always specify the negative case (e.g., by using an else-statement) to prevent confusion about the necessity of antecedents.

Our observations open an avenue for further investigations. Among them, we believe that it is interesting to explore how other cue phrases (e.g. once, because, as soon as) are interpreted logically. It would furthermore be interesting to compare our results with the logical interpretation of requirements written in other languages.

References

1. Baltes, S., Ralph, P.: Sampling in software engineering research: a critical review and guidelines (2020)
2. Berry, D.M., Kamsties, E.: The syntactically dangerous all and plural in specifications. IEEE Softw. **22**(1), 55–57 (2005)
3. Berry, D.M., Krieger, M.M.: From contract drafting to software specification: Linguistic sources of ambiguity - a handbook version 1.0 (2000)
4. de Bruijn, F., Dekkers, H.L.: Ambiguity in natural language software requirements: a case study. In: Wieringa, R., Persson, A. (eds.) REFSQ 2010. LNCS, vol. 6182, pp. 233–247. Springer, Heidelberg (2010). https://doi.org/10.1007/978-3-642-14192-8_21
5. Ciolkowski, M., Laitenberger, O., Vegas, S., Biffl, S.: Practical experiences in the design and conduct of surveys in empirical software engineering. In: Conradi, R., Wang, A.I. (eds.) Empirical Methods and Studies in Software Engineering. LNCS, vol. 2765, pp. 104–128. Springer, Heidelberg (2003). https://doi.org/10.1007/978-3-540-45143-3_7
6. Cohen, J.: Statistical Power Analysis for the Behavioral Sciences. Academic Press, Cambridge (1988)
7. Dalpiaz, F., Ferrari, A., Franch, X., Palomares, C.: NLP tool showcase at NLP4RE. In: REFSQ (2019)
8. Dillman, D.A., Smyth, J.D., Christian, L.M.: Internet, Phone, Mail, and Mixed-Mode Surveys: The Tailored Design Method (2014)
9. Dwyer, M.B., Avrunin, G.S., Corbett, J.C.: Patterns in property specifications for finite-state verification. In: ICSE (1999)
10. Feinstein, A.R., Cicchetti, D.V.: High agreement but low Kappa: I. The problems of two paradoxes. J. Clin. Epidemiol. **43**, 543–549 (1990)
11. Femmer, H., Fernández, D.M., Wagner, S., Eder, S.: Rapid quality assurance with requirements smells. J. Syst. Softw. **123**, 190–213 (2017)
12. Femmer, H., Kučera, J., Vetrò, A.: On the impact of passive voice requirements on domain modelling. In: ESEM (2014)
13. Fischbach, J., Hauptmann, B., Konwitschny, L., Spies, D., Vogelsang, A.: Towards causality extraction from requirements. In: RE (2020)
14. Fischbach, J., Vogelsang, A., Spies, D., Wehrle, A., Junker, M., Freudenstein, D.: SPECMATE: automated creation of test cases from acceptance criteria. In: ICST (2020)
15. Fischbach, J., et al.: Automatic detection of causality in requirement artifacts: the CiRA approach. In: Dalpiaz, F., Spoletini, P. (eds.) REFSQ 2021. LNCS, vol. 12685, pp. 19–36. Springer, Cham (2021). https://doi.org/10.1007/978-3-030-73128-1_2

16. Fleiss, J.L., Levin, B., Paik, M.C.: The Measurement of Interrater Agreement (2003)
17. Frattini, J., Junker, M., Unterkalmsteiner, M., Mendez, D.: Automatic extraction of cause-effect-relations from requirements artifacts. In: ASE (2020)
18. Freeman, L.C.: Elementary Applied Statistics : For Students in Behavioral Science (1965)
19. Gervasi, V., Zowghi, D.: On the role of ambiguity in RE. In: Wieringa, R., Persson, A. (eds.) REFSQ 2010. LNCS, vol. 6182, pp. 248–254. Springer, Heidelberg (2010). https://doi.org/10.1007/978-3-642-14192-8_22
20. Ghosh, S., Elenius, D., Li, W., Lincoln, P., Shankar, N., Steiner, W.: Automatically extracting requirements specifications from natural language. arXiv preprint arXiv:1403.3142 (2014)
21. Lamport, L.: The temporal logic of actions. ACM Trans. Program. Lang. Syst. **16**, 872–923 (1994)
22. Landis, J.R., Koch, G.G.: The measurement of observer agreement for categorical data. Biometrics **33**, 159–174 (1977)
23. Mavin, A., Wilkinson, P., Harwood, A., Novak, M.: Easy approach to requirements syntax (ears). In: RE (2009)
24. Nikora, A.P., Balcom, G.: Automated identification of LTL patterns in natural language requirements. In: ISSRE (2009)
25. QuestBack AG: Unipark/enterprise feedback suite. https://www.unipark.com/
26. Rosadini, B., et al.: Using NLP to detect requirements defects: an industrial experience in the railway domain. In: Grünbacher, P., Perini, A. (eds.) REFSQ 2017. LNCS, vol. 10153, pp. 344–360. Springer, Cham (2017). https://doi.org/10.1007/978-3-319-54045-0_24
27. Giannakopoulou, D., Pressburger, T., Mavridou, A., Schumann, J.: Generation of formal requirements from structured natural language. In: Madhavji, N., Pasquale, L., Ferrari, A., Gnesi, S. (eds.) REFSQ 2020. LNCS, vol. 12045, pp. 19–35. Springer, Cham (2020). https://doi.org/10.1007/978-3-030-44429-7_2
28. Vargha, A., Delaney, H.D.: A critique and improvement of the CL common language effect size statistics of McGraw and Wong. J. Educ. Behav. Stat. **25**(2), 101–132 (2000)
29. Winter, K., Femmer, H., Vogelsang, A.: How do quantifiers affect the quality of requirements? In: REFSQ (2020)
30. Wohlin, C., Runeson, P., Höst, M., Ohlsson, M.C., Regnell, B., Wesslén, A.: Experimentation in Software Engineering (2012)
31. Yan, R., Cheng, C.H., Chai, Y.: Formal consistency checking over specifications in natural languages. In: DATE (2015)
32. Yates, D., Moore, D., McCabe, G.: The Practice of Statistics. W. H Freeman, New York (1999)

Situation- and Domain-Specific Composition and Enactment of Business Model Development Methods

Sebastian Gottschalk$^{(\boxtimes)}$, Enes Yigitbas, Alexander Nowosad, and Gregor Engels

Software Innovation Lab, Paderborn University, Paderborn, Germany
{sebastian.gottschalk,enes.yigitbas,gregor.engels}@uni-paderborn.de,
anowosad@mail.uni-paderborn.de

Abstract. Developing effective business models is a complex process for a company where several tasks (e.g., conduct customer interviews) need to be accomplished, and decisions (e.g., advertisement as a revenue stream) must be made. Here, domain experts can guide the choices of tasks and decisions with their knowledge. Nevertheless, this knowledge needs to match the situation of the company (e.g., financial resources) and the application domain of the product/service (e.g., mobile app) to reduce the risk of developing ineffective business models with low market penetration. This is not covered by one-size-fits-all development methods without tailoring before the enaction. Therefore, we conduct a design science study to create a situation-specific development approach for business models. Based on situational method engineering and our previous work in storing knowledge of methods and models in distinct repositories, this paper shows the situation-specific composition and enaction of business model development methods. First, the method engineer composes the development method out of both repositories based on the situational context. Second, the business developer enacts the method and develops the business model. We implement the approach in a tool and evaluate it with a industrial case study on mobile apps.

Keywords: Business model development · Situational Method Engineering · Lean development · Kanban boards · Canvas models

1 Introduction

The development of effective business models is an important but also challenging task for companies to stay competitive. One reason for that is that customers want more and more integrated solutions for their perceived needs instead of

This work was partially supported by the German Research Foundation (DFG) within the CRC "On-The-Fly Computing" (CRC 901, Project Number: 160364472SFB901) and the German Federal Ministry of Education and Research (BMBF) through Software Campus grant (Project Number: 01IS17046).

L. Ardito et al. (Eds.): PROFES 2021, LNCS 13126, pp. 103–118, 2021.
https://doi.org/10.1007/978-3-030-91452-3_7

single products [31]. Therefore, the business model can be even more important than the latest technology of the product [8]. Here, a study of CB Insights [7] in 2019 analyzed 101 bankrupt startups and concluded that 42% of them failed due to a missing market need. But also for established companies, the GE Innovation Barometer [14] in 2018 stated that 64% of the over 2000 business executives have the problem of developing effective business models for new ideas.

The development of business models is a complex and creative activity that consists of different phases (e.g., discover, develop, etc.) where multiple tasks (e.g., conduct customer interviews, analyze competitors, etc.) need to be accomplished [13]. Inside those tasks, communication and collaboration between different stakeholders (e.g., business developer, customer, etc.) often occur [10]. To support business model development, companies often rely on light visualization tools like kanban boards [18] for structuring the development process or canvas models [24] for structuring the information in different steps of the process. Due to the complexity of the process, there are several options for each process step, and as a consequence, a process with the wrong activities can lower the quality of the business model. Here, the guidance of a domain expert can support the development so that every stakeholder has the same needed understanding of the used methods on the kanban board and knowledge in the models [27]. In literature, different domain experts propose various methods to develop such business models in the form of development processes (e.g., [23]) and method repositories (e.g., [4]). Moreover, these experts provide knowledge in the form of taxonomies of possible (e.g., [19]) and patterns of successful (e.g., [12]) business models. However, the method should match the company's current situation (e.g., financial resources, target market size), and the information in the canvas models need to match the application domain (e.g., mobile app, social network) of the product/service of the company [28]. This, in turn, raises the chance of developing an effective business model for the company. Otherwise, the development of an ineffective business model can lead to poor market penetration of the product/service or even a company bankruptcy [26]. Although various business model development approaches have been proposed, they do not cover the step of tailoring the method to the current situation [17]. Tailoring by composing the method out of different method parts can include the situational context instead of a fixed one-size-fits-all development method for all contexts. Therefore our research question (RQ) is: *How to enable the situation-specific composition and enactment of business model development methods?*

To answer this question, we conduct a design science research (DSR) study [21] to develop an approach and a development tool. In our approach that supports non-experts in the development, the method engineer creates a method repository and models repository from the knowledge of different domain experts. We have already covered this in the past [16,17]. This paper aims to show the composition and enactment of the business model development method out of these repositories. While the method engineer should have high modeling capabilities based on Business Process Model and Notation (BPMN) for the method and feature models for the canvas during the composition, the business developer can stay with his lightweight structuring techniques of kanban boards and canvas models during the enaction. In comparison to existing methods for business model development, our approach focuses on the importance of the method engineer before the development. We implement the approach in an open-source tool and evaluate it based on a industrial case study of developing the business model for a local event platform. Our scientific contribution is the applied concept of situational method engineering to business model development while companies in practice are supported with a tool to develop their business models.

Concerning DSR, we structure the rest of the paper as follows: Sect. 2 covers the research background regarding business model development and situational method engineering. Section 3 provides insights into our DSR process. Section 4 shows the requirements of our solution divided into the provision of the method and knowledge repositories, the composition of the development method, and the enaction of the development method. Based on them, a concept is presented in Sect. 5 and implemented in Sect. 6. Section 7 evaluates the approach with a case study on developing a business model for a local event platform. Finally, Sect. 8 concludes the paper and gives an outlook on the next DSR cycle.

2 Background

2.1 Business Model Development

Business models can be defined as the rationale of how the organization creates, delivers, and captures value [24]. The development of business models is a complex task that often requires collaboration between different internal and external stakeholders [10]. To structure the complex process, some approaches like the BMI Magic Triangle [11] or the Cambridge Business Model Innovation Process [13] propose different phases (i.e., initiation, ideation, integration, implementation for [11]). Moreover, it is a crucial collaboration aspect to conduct experiments with the customers regularly to unfold their hidden needs [23]. Inside the different process activities, often light-weight visualization tools in the form of canvas models are used. Here, for example, the Value Proposition Canvas [25] summarizes the expected value proposition for a customer group, and the Business Model Canvas [24] visualizes the most important aspects of a business model. Moreover, the process can be supported with software-based Business model Development Tools (BMDTs). While the tools in practice mainly provide design support for business models based on the Business Model Canvas [30], there are also first approaches in research that integrate the knowledge of methods and models. For the methods, some approaches [9,32] propose ideas for BMDTs that provide software support for different phases (i.e., analysis, design, implementation, and management in [9]). For the models, some approaches provide the usage of domain-specific knowledge [5] or the usage of patterns [22] for the development of the models. However, none of these tools deeply integrate both knowledge sources and method composition prior to the enaction.

2.2 Situational Method Engineering

Situational Method Engineering (SME), with its origin in software development, aims to create a development method based on the situation of a specific project

[20]. For that, SME has the role of a method engineer who analyzes various methods and stores them in a method repository. After identifying the context of the project, the engineer composes a situation-specific development method out of the method base. This development method, in turn, is then enacted by the project manager to run his project. To structure the method base, a method can be divided into method fragments that are reusable atomic blocks that have a process (called work unit), a product (called work product), or a producer focus [6]. These method fragments are combined to method components that transform inputs of work products into outputs of work products and are tailored into methods. Besides their origin in software development, some approaches also cover the business aspects of the projects. Here, some approaches [3,15] cover business aspects as situational factors (i.e., customer, market characteristics, product characteristics, and stakeholder involvement in [3]) or use canvas models as work products (i.e., IoT Canvas in [15]). However, none of these approaches incorporates the whole development cycle of business models or uses an additional repository for the knowledge of the models.

3   Research Approach

This study uses design science research (DSR) to build an approach for the situation-specific development of business models. We use DSR because it focuses on the creation and incremental improvement of innovative artifacts based on existing theories. As method, we choose the DSR cycle of Kuchler and Vaishnavi [21] and based our research on the theories of opportunity creation [1] and boundary objects [29]. The opportunity creation theory states that businesses are co-created under high uncertainty [33]. Here, the development is an entrepreneurial process where companies create a business model based on their assumptions that need to be validated with the customers. Therefore, the process needs both parts of exploitation and exploration. The bounded object theory states the development is a heterogeneous task that requires the collaboration of different stakeholders with different knowledge [27]. Therefore, a common understanding between all stakeholders needs to be achieved. The process is shown in Fig. 1 and consists of two cycles with the five steps of taking *Awareness of [the] Problem*, making *Suggestion* for the solution, the *Development* of a corresponding artifact, the *Evaluation* of our solution, and the drawing of a *Conclusion*.

Based on both applied theories, in the *First Cycle*, we reviewed literature on business model development. Moreover, we conducted a systematic literature review on decision support systems for business model development. Based on that, we created conceptional parts for the situation-specific development of business models. For that, we used feature models to store the business model information of various business models. Out of this, a concrete business model for a single business model can be derived as an instance of the feature model. Moreover, we created a process to create and adapt those business models based on the conduction of experiments. Here, we evaluate the approach in a feasibility study with a tool implementation and the application of a usage scenario.

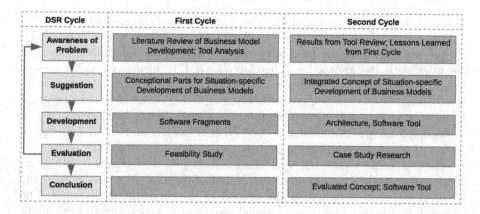

DSR Cycle	First Cycle	Second Cycle
Awareness of Problem	Literature Review of Business Model Development; Tool Analysis	Results from Tool Review; Lessons Learned from First Cycle
Suggestion	Conceptional Parts for Situation-specific Development of Business Models	Integrated Concept of Situation-specific Development of Business Models
Development	Software Fragments	Architecture, Software Tool
Evaluation	Feasibility Study	Case Study Research
Conclusion		Evaluated Concept; Software Tool

Fig. 1. Design science research process based on Kuechler and Vaishnavi [21]

In the *Second Cycle*, we took the lessons learned from the last cycle and the tool review to create an integrated concept of the approach. Here, we worked on the extensibility of the approach by concerning knowledge about methods and models from different domain experts. For that, we have used SME to derive a method repository with various methods to develop and validate business models for mobile applications [17]. Moreover, we have worked on an approach to consolidate the knowledge about business models from different real-world domain experts [16]. Based on both separate parts, we developed an integrated approach consisting of methods and models for the situation-specific development of business models. After implementing the tool and evaluating a case study on mobile apps, we concluded with an evaluated concept and a software tool.

4 Solution Requirements

At the beginning of our DSR study, we reviewed the literature regarding business model development and analyzed tools on decision support systems for business model development to get awareness of the challenges of software-based business model development. Out of this, we derived initial generic requirements that we refine to the current solution requirements. By considering the two stages of construction and development of a method from situational method engineering [20] and splitting up the provision from the method base from the construction of the method, we structure those requirements according to the topics of (R.1) Knowledge Provision of Methods and Models, (R.2) the Composition of the Development Method, and (R.3) the Enactment of the Development Method.

The requirement *(R.1) Knowledge Provision of Methods and Models* states that the solution should provide a variety of expert knowledge from which situation-specific development methods could be constructed. The usefulness of the approach profoundly relies on the usage of an appropriate method and corresponding models. Therefore, the solution needs a *(R.1.1) Storing of Expert Information* for different methods and models. Moreover, the approach depends on the situation of the company and the application domain of the product/service. As a consequence, the solution needs a *(R.1.2) Characterisation of Context* both for the company and the product/service. Visualization can help to simplify the work with the knowledge. Therefore, a *(R.1.3) Visual Representation of Knowledge* both for the methods and models is needed. Last, business model development is a continuous process where different stakeholders are involved in different process activities. Therefore, the solution needs to cover an *(R.1.4) Understandability of Knowledge* around all stakeholders and an *(R.1.5) Extensibility of Knowledge* during the process.

The requirement *(R.2) Composition of Development Method* states that the development method should be composed out of the expert knowledge from the methods and models by taking the context of the company into account. The approach highly relies on the situational factors of the company and the application domain of the product. Therefore, the solution should cover the explicit *(R.2.1) Identification of Context* before the composition of the development method. The composition of the method could be based on a huge amount of knowledge in the form of methods and models. As a consequence, the solution should provide *(R.2.2) Assistance in Method Composition* based on the context. The development of business models is a process under high uncertainty so that not all choices can be covered in advance. Therefore, the solution should allow a *(R.2.3) Generalization of Method Composition* to provide different business model development processes simultaneously and an *(R.2.4) Adaptation of Method Composition* that provides a runtime adaptation to a changing context.

The requirement *(R.3) Enactment of Development Method* states the development method should be enacted so that business models could be developed on top of the knowledge. The development of business models is a complex task that should be supported with a software tool. Therefore, the solution should provide *(R.3.1) Executebility of Method Enaction* to reduce the complexity. Business model development is a task with high uncertainties so that experts can not cover all knowledge in advance. As a consequence, the solution should cover *(R.3.2) Storing of Company Knowledge* so that the company can add internal methods and models. Moreover, the process is a complex task where different stakeholders are involved in different activities. Therefore, the solution should provide *(R.3.3) Traceability of Method Enaction* to reason all decisions in the past together with *(R.3.4) Stakeholder Involvement in Method Enaction* to allow the collaboration of different stakeholders in the activities.

5   Solution Concept

To address the solution requirements, we build our integrated approach for the situation-specific development of business models. An overview of the approach is shown in Fig. 2 which consists of the five roles of the *Meta-Method Engineer*, the *Method Engineer*, the *Domain Expert*, the *Business Developer*, and other *Stakeholders* together with the three stages of *(1) Knowledge Provision of Methods and Models*, *(2) Composition of Development Method* and *(3) Enactment of*

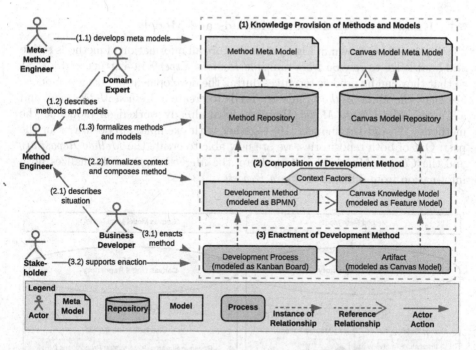

Fig. 2. Overview of the situation-specific business model development approach

Development Method. While we shortly describe each stage in the following, the respective subsections provide a more detailed explanation.

In the *(1) Provision of Methods and Knowledge Repository*, we provide general knowledge about methods to use and models to rely on within the business model development. For that, the *Meta-Method Engineer* needs first to create meta-models of how the methods and models should be structured *(1.1)*. After that, different *Domain Experts* explain their knowledge about methods and models to the *Method Engineer (1.2)*. The *Method Engineer*, in turn, formalizes the expert knowledge according to the meta-models to make them accessible during the composition of the method *(1.3)*. In the *(2) Composition of Development Method*, the development method is composed out of both repositories. Here, the *Business Developer* explains the current context in which the business model should be developed to the *Method Engineer (2.1)*. The *Method Engineer* formalizes this context as the situation of the method and the domain of the model. The engineer composes a situation-specific development method *(2.2)* consisting of the method itself as BPMN and the canvas knowledge models as feature models. In the *(3) Enactment of Development Method*, the composed method is enacted to develop the business model. Here, the *Business Developer* enacts the composed method *(3.1)* consisting of the development process as kanban board and the artifacts as canvas models. During this enaction, the development can be supported by other *Stakeholders (3.2)* (e.g., Designer).

5.1   Knowledge Provision of Methods and Models

The first stage, as shown in Fig. 3, aims to store all information of methods to use and knowledge to rely on from multiple *Domain Experts* in a structured format so that they can be used as resources during the development of business models. For that, the *Meta-Method Engineer* needs to create a *Method Meta Model* and a *Canvas Model Meta Model*. Here, we have already worked on modeling the methods [17] and the models [16] together with exemplary repositories in the past. Out of both repositories, we are now able to create the *Method Repository* and the *Canvas Model Repository*. Here, the *Method Engineer* formalizes both information from different *Domain Experts*.

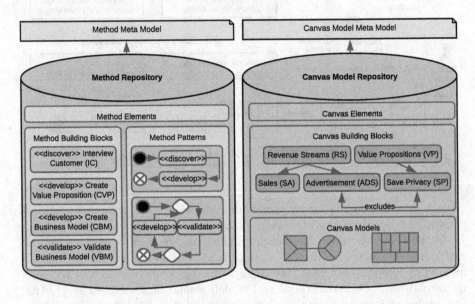

Fig. 3. Exemplary knowledge provision of methods and models

For that, we have developed repositories for the methods and the models *(R.1.1)*. Inside the *Method Repository*, we adapt the concept of situational method engineering [20] and have the *Method Elements*, the *Method Building Blocks*, and the *Method Patterns*. Here, *Method Elements* are atomic parts of a method that can be divided into the possible situational factors, different types of methods, performed tasks, involved stakeholders, created artifacts, and used tools. These elements are combined to *Method Building Blocks*, where each block can have different situational factors, a task, different types, the involved stakeholders, and tools that can transform input artifacts into output artifacts. These building blocks are structured according to *Method Patterns*, which are BPMN Process Parts with situational factors when they should be used *(R.1.2)*, and placeholders in which specific types of building blocks could be inserted. Inside the *Canvas Model Repository*, we adapt the concept of feature models [2]

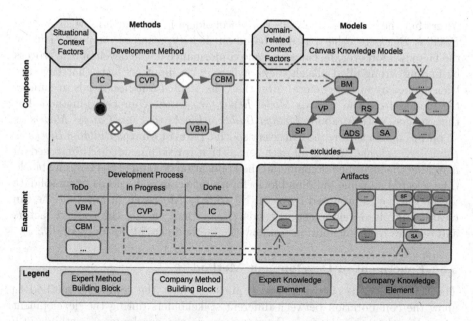

Fig. 4. Exemplary composition and enactment of development method

and have *Canvas Elements*, the *Canvas Building Blocks*, and the *Canvas Models*. Here, *Canvas Elements* are single chunks of knowledge that can be presented in a canvas model. Those elements are structured into a hierarchy within the *Canvas Building Blocks*. For the structuring, we use standard feature model relationships (e.g., requires, excludes) together with own relationships to save positive (e.g., supports) and negative (e.g., hurts) relationships between the elements. Moreover, we keep good practice patterns, and exemplary companies as instances of the building block together with an application domain of the block *(R.1.2)*. Last, we provide *Canvas Models* (e.g., Value Proposition Canvas) as representations to visualize the building blocks. We ensure the understandability with descriptions for all important knowledge *(R.1.3)* and extensibility with the support for different experts and linking all information to specific experts *(R.1.4)*.

5.2 Composition of Development Method

The second stage, as shown in Fig. 4, aims to use the context of the company to compose a business model development method. For that, the *Business Developer* describes the current context of the situation of the company and the application domain of the product/service to the *Method Engineer*. The *Method Engineer* formalizes this as situational factors of the *Method Repository* and a list of the domains from the *Canvas Model Repository* to compose the method.

The *Method Engineer* starts the composition of a BPMN process by choosing a *Method Pattern* from the *Method Repository* that is recommended to him by a matching of identified situational factors and the factors of the method *(R.2.1)*.

After that, he can iteratively fill the placeholders in the patterns with *Method Building Blocks* or other patterns based on their type and recommendations by the factors. Moreover, he can check the conformance of the development process by finding wrong-filled placeholders or flows with input artifacts that have not been defined as outputs before. After that, the *Method Engineer* needs to connect the models from the *Canvas Model Repository* to the composing method. For that, he gets notified about *Method Building Blocks* that use *Canvas Models* as an output artifact. Here, he can select specific parts of *Canvas Building Blocks* as *Canvas Knowledge Models* for each canvas that is recommended to him based on matching the identified domain and the application domain of the building block. If he selected multiple building blocks for a single canvas, he needs to consolidate the knowledge as proposed by us in [16] *(R.2.2)*. Moreover, at any time, he can create multiple development methods *(R.2.3)* and change the context factors and receives recommendations on how the method should be adapted *(R.2.4)*.

5.3   Enactment of Development Method

The third stage, as shown in Fig. 4, aims to enact the composed method to allow the collaboration between different stakeholders during the development steps. For that, the *Business Developer* enacts the development methods in a lightweight process engine to receive an executable process.

The process engine is based on a *Kanban Board* where the development steps out of the composed method are grouped into *todo*, *in progress*, and *done steps* (see Fig. 4) *(R.3.1)*. In every activity in progress, the *Business Developer* can communicate with all other *Stakeholders* that are mentioned in the definition of the corresponding *Method Building Block*. Moreover, if the building block is linked to a *Canvas Model*, the different stakeholders can collaborate on the specific canvas *(R.3.4)*. Here, the knowledge from the connected building blocks can be used as recommendations. The whole process with every step is traceable for all stakeholders so that every decision that has been made can be reasoned over time *(R.3.3)*. Moreover, the *Business Developer* can add his own method steps (e.g., a special type of interview) and canvas elements (e.g., a special type of advertisement) during the enaction to support flexible decision making *(R.3.2)*. Out of this process, the business model is developed over time.

6   Solution Implementation

Based on the solution concept, we provide an implementation of the so-called *Situational Business Model Developer*. Our tool supports all three proposed stages, is released as open-source[1] and can also be directly used in the web browser[2]. For that, the tool uses Angular to structure the web app, PouchDB to save all generated data in the web browser's storage, and BPMN.io to support the method representation. In the following, we explain the technical architecture and show the tool support.

---

[1] https://github.com/SebastianGTTS/situational-business-model-developer.
[2] http://sebastiangtts.github.io/situational-business-model-developer/.

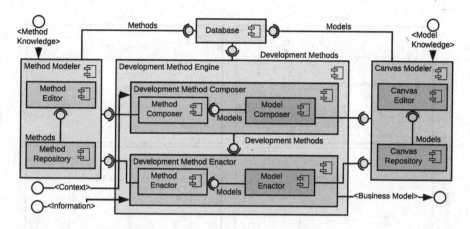

Fig. 5. Architecture of the *Situational Business Model Developer*

6.1   Architecture

The high-level architecture of our tool can be seen in Fig. 5. It consists of the *Database* of PouchDB to store the methods, models, and development methods together with the *Method Modeler*, the *Canvas Modeler*, and the *Development Method Engine*. The *Method Modeler* receives the *Method Knowledge* and stores it in the *Method Repository* by using the *Method Editor* and the BPMN.io Framework. The *Canvas Modeler* receives the *Model Knowledge* and stores it in the *Canvas Repository* by using the *Canvas Editor* and custom canvas boards. The *Development Method Engine* consists of the *Development Method Composer* and the *Development Method Enactor*. The *Development Method Composer* takes *Context* and composes a development method with the *Method Composer*, using BPMN structures from the *Method Modeler*, and the *Model Composer*, using consolidation and conflict detection algorithms from the *Canvas Modeler*. The *Development Method Enactor* takes *Information* about the development and enacts the method by using kanban boards in the *Method Enactor* and canvas models in the *Model Enactor* to output a *Business Model*.

6.2   Tool-Support

The screenshots of our tool can be seen in Fig. 6. While we have already covered the provision of knowledge of methods and models in previous work, we focus here on the composition and enactment of development methods. First, we have the composition of the development method, which is done by choosing the situational factors and modeling the BPMN process. Second, we have the linkage to the knowledge models, which is done by choosing the domain-related factors and merge the knowledge models. Third, we have the enactment of the development method based on the kanban board. Fourth, we have the usage of the linked models based on canvas model boards.

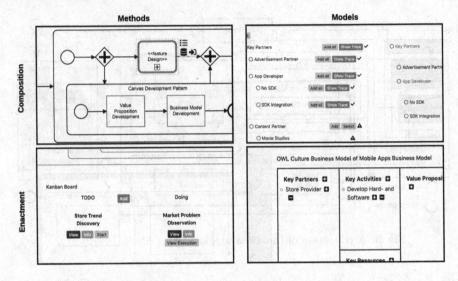

Fig. 6. Screenshots of the *Situational Business Model Developer*

7 Evaluation on Local Event Platform

To evaluate our approach, we conducted an industrial case study by developing a business model for a local event platform. For that, we explain our evaluation setting, provide execution of the study and analyze the results.

7.1 Evaluation Setting

Our aim is to investigate the integrated concept of situation-specific business model development to answer our stated research question. Here, we follow an explorative purpose to gather new insights for our third DSR cycle. For that, we provide the holistic case study of a single unit to develop a business model for OWL Live. The platform is created as part of an ongoing research project[3] and acts as a two-sided platform between event providers and event visitors. Here, the owner wants to use new data mining techniques to aggregate events from different providers together with natural language processing to provide an enhanced recommendation system to the visitors. To gather the corresponding data, we combine the direct method of customer interviews with indirect methods of a grey literature review together with an analysis of existing information.

7.2 Execution of the Study

During the conduction, we structure our procedure according to the three stages of Knowledge Provision of Methods and Models, the Composition of the Development Method, and the Enactment of the Development Method.

---

[3] Project Website: https://www.sicp.de/en/projekte/owlkultur-plattform.

The *Knowledge Provision of Methods and Models* has been made in previous research. Here, we have already created a method repository with various method elements, method building blocks, and method patterns based on a grey literature review on developing business models for mobile applications [17]. Moreover, for the canvas repository, we created existing canvas models of the Value Proposition Canvas (VPC) [25] and the Business Model Canvas (BMC) [24] together with a custom Feature Set Canvas (FSC) for storing possible features. While the knowledge of the BMC for the domain of mobile application, digital platforms, content aggregations, and social networks have been already created in [16], we created corresponding knowledge for the VPC and FSC.

In the *Composition of the Development Method*, we interviewed the project manager to gather the information about the current state of the platform (e.g., target customer), the situation of the project (e.g., margetSize:mass), and the application domain of the app (e.g., content aggregation). This, in turn, allowed us to tailor a customized development method based on the phases of discovery, analysis, design, develop and validation of a method pattern in [17]. Out of the situational factors, we suggested identifying the target audience in the *discovery* phase, followed by a market problem observation to understand current customer pains and a store trend analysis to find trending features. Here, especially trend analysis is often missed by other approaches. In the end, the results for the event provider should be validated with customer interviews and the event visitors with a social media survey. In the *analysis*, we suggested running a market potential analysis together with a competitor analysis inside and outside the app stores. In the *design*, the value proposition, the business model, and the feature set need to be developed. Here, we linked the underlying canvas model to the specific canvas knowledge models inside our model repository and consolidated the specific knowledge based on the given application domain. Moreover, based on the models, a competitive advantage analysis and prioritization of the features should be done. In the *development* phase, we suggested the development of a beta-version in front of the product development. During development, the interest of the customers could be enhanced by using inbound marketing. Last, in the *validation*, we suggested the ongoing interview of both customer groups.

During the *Enactment of the Development Method*, the first target audiences of event providers and event visitors were identified and refined (e.g., culture actors for event providers, early adopters for event visitors) based on the prior feasibility study and the interview. For the *discovery*, the feasibility study also covered the observation of the market problem. At the same time, in the store trend analysis, possible features (e.g., invitation mechanism, social media connection) were outlined. The interview of customers and conduction of social media surveys are longer scheduled ongoing tasks. During the *analysis*, various statistics are looked up for the market potential. Moreover, existing knowledge [16] for local competitors and event apps are used for both competitor analyses. In the *design*, two value propositions (i.e., event providers, event visitors) were developed together with three possible business models (i.e., content aggregator, ticket seller, sponsored platform). Moreover, the feature sets for these business models were modeled (e.g., pipeline component for content aggregator), and the competitive advantage was analyzed (e.g., travel time calculator). This competitor analysis was also the foundation for feature prioritization. All of the canvases were structured with the tool and supported by the existing expert knowledge. Based on those structures, a competitor analysis was done. Currently, in the *development*, the beta version of the app is developed, while the ongoing customer interviews and social media surveys should validate the different business models and feature sets. Moreover, inbound marketing (e.g., landing page, social media posts) is planned to ensure high traffic during the upcoming beta. Because of the ongoing development, the continuous *validation* phase has not been started.

7.3   Analysis of Results and Implications

To evaluate our approach, we conducted a case study on developing a business model for OWL Live. Here, the development is an ongoing task for what we presented our results for the first four phases. By conducting the case study, we investigate that our approach supports the development method with guidance in new tasks to do (e.g., inbound marketing) and possible decisions to be made (e.g., lock-in mechanism). Moreover, the approach is generalizable to allow the development of different business models from the same knowledge and traceable to reason all changes over time. Nevertheless, we found some limitations during the composition and enactment that we want to discuss and fix in the next DSR cycle. We divide those limitations into the Restrictions of Expert Knowledge, Complexity of the Tool, and the Conduction of Single Case Study.

For the *Restrictions of Expert Knowledge*, we currently have just a base of knowledge for methods and models that focuses on mobile applications and, in particular, on event apps. This, in turn, limits the applicability of the approach in other scenarios. Therefore, we want to extend the knowledge and focus on models and methods for digital platforms in the future. For the *Complexity of the Tool*, we currently focused on the applicability of all provided features and dismissed a user experience that is easy to understand. This, in turn, limits the usage of the tool by end-users. Therefore, we want to increase the usability of the approach so that end-users can use it without prior introductions. For the *Conduction of Single Case Study*, we currently have applied the approach to the case of a local event platform. This, in turn, limits the information if the approach can be easily transferred to other scenarios. Therefore, we want to validate the transferability by creating several scenarios in a user study.

8   Conclusion and Future Work

The development of business models is a challenging task that can be supported by the knowledge of methods and models from different domain experts. Here, the knowledge needs to match the company's situation and the application domain of the product/service. Using two cycles of DSR, we have developed a situation-specific business model development approach. We implemented the approach in an open-source tool and evaluated it by conducting a case study on a local event platform. Here, our results suggest that our approach supports business developers in developing business models by using the knowledge from existing methods and models. In the future, we will conduct a third DSR cycle to work on the extensibility of our approach and evaluate its usefulness in different scenarios. For that, we plan to modularize our concept so that single development steps (e.g., calculate business outcome) can be supported by different software modules. Moreover, we will evaluate our approach based on a user study in a lean development of mobile apps seminar where students have to develop business models for their apps over a more extended period.

References

1. Alvarez, S.A., Barney, J.B., Anderson, P.: Forming and exploiting opportunities: the implications of discovery and creation processes for entrepreneurial and organizational research. Organ. Sci. **24**(1), 301–317 (2013)
2. Apel, S., Batory, D., Kästner, C., Saake, G.: Feature-Oriented Software Product Lines. Springer, Heidelberg (2013). https://doi.org/10.1007/978-3-642-37521-7
3. Bekkers, W., van de Weerd, I., Brinkkemper, S., Mahieu, A.: The influence of situational factors in software product management: an empirical study. In: International Workshop on Software Product Management, pp. 41–48. IEEE (2008)
4. Bland, D.J., Osterwalder, A.: Testing Business Ideas. Wiley, Hoboken (2020)
5. Boßelmann, S., Margaria, T.: Guided business modeling and analysis for business professionals. In: Pfannstiel, M.A., Rasche, C. (eds.) Service Business Model Innovation in Healthcare and Hospital Management, pp. 195–211. Springer, Cham (2017). https://doi.org/10.1007/978-3-319-46412-1_11
6. Brinkkemper, S.: Method engineering: engineering of information systems development methods and tools. Inf. Softw. Technol. **38**(4), 275–280 (1996)
7. CB Information Services: CB Insights 2019: Top 20 Reasons Why Startups Fail. https://www.cbinsights.com/research/startup-failure-reasons-top/
8. Chesbrough, H.: Business model innovation: opportunities and barriers. Long Range Plan. **43**(2–3), 354–363 (2010)
9. Ebel, P., Bretschneider, U., Leimeister, J.M.: Leveraging virtual business model innovation: a framework for designing business model development tools. Inf. Syst. J. **26**(5), 519–550 (2016)
10. Eppler, M.J., Hoffmann, F., Bresciani, S.: New business models through collaborative idea generation. Int. J. Innov. Manag. **15**(06), 1323–1341 (2011)
11. Frankenberger, K., Weiblen, T., Csik, M., Gassmann, O.: The 4I-framework of business model innovation: a structured view on process phases and challenges. Int. J. Prod. Dev. **18**(3/4), 249 (2013)
12. Gassmann, O., Frankenberger, K., Csik, M.: The Business Model Navigator: 55 Models that Will Revolutionise Your Business. Pearson, Harlow (2014)
13. Geissdoerfer, M., Savaget, P., Evans, S.: The Cambridge business model innovation process. Procedia Manuf. **8**, 262–269 (2017)
14. General Electric Inc.: GE Global Innovation Barometer 2018. https://www.ge.com/reports/innovation-barometer-2018/
15. Giray, G., Tekinerdogan, B.: Situational method engineering for constructing internet of things development methods. In: Shishkov, B. (ed.) BMSD 2018. LNBIP, vol. 319, pp. 221–239. Springer, Cham (2018). https://doi.org/10.1007/978-3-319-94214-8_14

16. Gottschalk, S., Kirchhoff, J., Engels, G.: Extending business model development tools with consolidated expert knowledge. In: Shishkov, B. (ed.) BMSD 2021. LNBIP, vol. 422, pp. 3–21. Springer, Cham (2021). https://doi.org/10.1007/978-3-030-79976-2_1

17. Gottschalk, S., Yigitbas, E., Nowosad, A., Engels, G.: Situation-specific business model development methods for mobile app developers. In: Augusto, A., Gill, A., Nurcan, S., Reinhartz-Berger, I., Schmidt, R., Zdravkovic, J. (eds.) BPMDS/EMMSAD -2021. LNBIP, vol. 421, pp. 262–276. Springer, Cham (2021). https://doi.org/10.1007/978-3-030-79186-5_17

18. Gross, J., Mcinnis, K.: Kanban Made Simple: Demystifying and Applying Toyota's Legendary Manufacturing Process. AMACOM, New York (2003)

19. Hartmann, P.M., Zaki, M., Feldmann, N., Neely, A.: Capturing value from big data - a taxonomy of data-driven business models used by start-up firms. Int. J. Oper. Prod. Manag. **36**(10), 1382–1406 (2016)

20. Henderson-Sellers, B., Ralyté, J., Ågerfalk, P.J., Rossi, M.: Situational Method Engineering. Springer, Heidelberg (2014). https://doi.org/10.1007/978-3-642-41467-1

21. Kuechler, B., Vaishnavi, V.: On theory development in design science research: anatomy of a research project. Eur. J. Inf. Syst. **17**(5), 489–504 (2008)

22. Lüdeke-Freund, F., Bohnsack, R., Breuer, H., Massa, L.: Research on sustainable business model patterns: status quo, methodological issues, and a research agenda. In: Aagaard, A. (ed.) Sustainable Business Models. PSSBIAFE, pp. 25–60. Springer, Cham (2019). https://doi.org/10.1007/978-3-319-93275-0_2

23. McGrath, R.G.: Business models: a discovery driven approach. Long Range Plan. **43**, 247–261 (2010)

24. Osterwalder, A., Pigneur, Y.: Business Model Generation: A Handbook for Visionaries, Game Changers, and Challengers. Wiley, Hoboken (2010)

25. Osterwalder, A., Pigneur, Y., Bernarda, G., Smith, A., Papadakos, P.: Value Proposition Design: How to Create Products and Services Customers Want. Get Started With. Strategyzer Series. Wiley, Hoboken (2014)

26. Ries, E.: The Lean Startup: How Today's Entrepreneurs Use Continuous Innovation to Create Radically Successful Businesses. Crown Business, New York (2014)

27. Schwarz, J.S., Legner, C.: Business model tools at the boundary: exploring communities of practice and knowledge boundaries in business model innovation. Electron. Mark. **30**(3), 421–445 (2020)

28. Sosna, M., Trevinyo-Rodríguez, R.N., Velamuri, S.R.: Business model innovation through trial-and-error learning. Long Range Plan. **43**(2–3), 383–407 (2010)

29. Star, S.L., Griesemer, J.R.: Institutional ecology, 'translations' and boundary objects: amateurs and professionals in Berkeley's museum of vertebrate Zoology, 1907–39. Soc. Stud. Sci. **19**(3), 387–420 (1989)

30. Szopinski, D., Schoormann, T., John, T., Knackstedt, R., Kundisch, D.: Software tools for business model innovation: current state and future challenges. Electron. Mark. **60**(11), 2794 (2019)

31. Teece, D.J.: Business models, business strategy and innovation. Long Range Plan. **43**(2–3), 172–194 (2010)

32. Terrenghi, N., Schwarz, J., Legner, C., Eisert, U.: Business model management: current practices, required activities and IT support. In: Proceedings of the Conference on Wirtschaftsinformatik, pp. 972–986 (2017)

33. Vogel, P.: From venture idea to venture opportunity. Entrep. Theory Pract. **41**(6), 943–971 (2017)

Using a Data-Driven Context Model to Support the Elicitation of Context-Aware Functionalities – A Controlled Experiment

Rodrigo Falcão[1]([⊠])(iD), Marcus Trapp[1], Vaninha Vieira[2],
and Alberto Vianna Dias da Silva[3,4](iD)

[1] Fraunhofer Institute for Experimental Software Engineering IESE,
Kaiserslautern, Germany
rodrigo.falcao@iese.fraunhofer.de
[2] Institute of Computing, Federal University of Bahia, Salvador, Brazil
[3] Computer Science Graduate Program, Federal University of Bahia, Salvador, Brazil
[4] Federal Institute of Bahia, Salvador, Brazil

Abstract. Background: Context modeling to support the elicitation of context-aware functionalities has been overlooked due to its high complexity. To help overcome this, we have implemented a data-driven process that analyzes contextual data and generates data-driven context models. Objective: We aim at investigating to which extent a data-driven context model supports the identification of more complex contexts (i.e., contexts that combine several contextual elements) and unexpected context-aware functionalities. Method: We used a one factor with two treatments randomized design with 13 experienced software engineers. Given a specific system-supported user task, the participants were asked to come up with requirements that describe context-aware functionalities to improve the user task. Results: Use of the data-driven context model increased the average number of contextual elements used to describe requirements from 1.77 to 4.23. No participant from the control group was able to identify by themselves any of the contexts included in the model. All comparisons between groups had sufficient effect size and power. The participants regarded the data-driven context model as a useful tool to support the elicitation of context-aware functionalities. Conclusion: The data-driven context model has shown potential to support the identification of relevant contexts for given user tasks.

Keywords: Context awareness · Data-driven · Model · Requirements · Experiment

1 Introduction

Computers are part of everyday life and, in recent decades, have become increasingly ubiquitous. The number of software-based solutions that surround us constantly increases. Just to mention the mobile world, millions of apps are readily available in a market where competitors yearn to release new features to their users as fast as possible

This work has been partially supported by CNPq, Brazil.

L. Ardito et al. (Eds.): PROFES 2021, LNCS 13126, pp. 119–135, 2021.
https://doi.org/10.1007/978-3-030-91452-3_8

– but not just any feature. Ideally, competitors want to deliver *delightful* features, which amaze and capture their audience. These features fall into the category of unconscious requirements [16]; as such, they are hard to elicit.

Context-aware functionalities are perceived as a way to delight users (e.g., [7, 8, 15]). They consider context to produce a certain system behavior, typically a recommendation or an adaptation. These types of features can be mapped to Dey's definitions of the context-aware features "presentation" and "execution" [5], respectively. The elicitation of context-aware functionalities, in turn, demands context modeling, which involves an analysis of the relevance of contextual elements (CEs) (e.g., [4, 21]) and an analysis of combinations of CEs (e.g., [4, 10]) for a given user task (e.g., [5, 6]). According to practitioners, these are challenging steps and have been overlooked due to their high complexity: In a scenario with dozens of CEs, identifying which CEs influence a given user task, either individually or in combination with others, is time-consuming, non-intuitive, and error-prone [6].

Data-driven approaches have been named as promising to improve requirements engineering (RE) in general [14] and context modeling in particular [22]. Therefore, we formulate the following research question (RQ1): To which extent does a data-driven context model support the identification of more complex contexts and unexpected context-aware functionalities? We implemented a data-driven context modeling process to identify relevant contexts and create context models to support practitioners in the elicitation of context-aware functionalities. We used our implementation to generate a context model for the system-supported user task *"create a comment"* of DorfFunk[1], a communication app with characteristics of a social network that has approximately 25,000 active users. DorfFunk was developed and is maintained by Fraunhofer IESE. In this paper, we report on a controlled experiment carried out to verify to which extent the data-driven context model supports the identification of more complex contexts (i.e., contexts combining several CEs) and unexpected context-aware functionalities from contexts that, without the data-driven context model, would require more time to be identified.

This paper is organized according to the guidelines for reporting experiments in software engineering proposed by Jedlitschka et al. [12]. It is structured as follows: Sect. 2 discusses related work and summarizes the data-driven context modeling process; Sect. 3 contains the plan for the experiment; Sect. 4 describes the execution; Sect. 5 contains the analysis; Sect. 6 discusses the results; and Sect. 7 concludes the paper.

2   Background

Proposals for representing context models concerning RE are diverse; however, the challenge of identifying the relevant contexts remains high, independent of the chosen representation, especially when the context modeling activity is performed by humans. Alegre el al. [1], for example, surveyed existing RE modeling techniques for context-aware systems and mention no data-driven approach. Data-driven approaches have been used to improve context-aware systems, though: Saputri and Seok-Won [18] reviewed the use of machine-learning techniques (which are data-based approaches) in self-adaptive systems and found that in 41% of them, the purpose was to support modeling.

---

[1] https://www.digitale-doerfer.de/unsere-loesungen/dorffunk/.

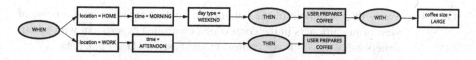

Fig. 1. Example of a data-driven context model.

Among these papers, only the work by Rodrigues et al. [17] is related to RE. In their work, data mining was employed to identify relevant contexts for dependable systems, which were later mapped manually to a contextual goal model [2]. Nonetheless, ad-hoc context modeling has been the state of the practice [6].

In our approach, we implemented a data-driven context modeling process introduced by Falcão [7] that creates context models to support the elicitation of context-aware functionalities. These models contain contexts that were found to influence a given user task. We define "context" as a set of instantiated CEs. For example, given a CE "time" and another CE "location", examples of contexts include "afternoon" (1 CE: Time), "home" (1 CE: Location), and "afternoon at home" (combination of 2 CEs: Time and location). The more CEs we have in a context, the more complex the context is. In the data-driven process, contextual data is collected from available sources based on the user task in focus, and then processed to generate a context model. The data collection is manual and the data processing (including the model generation) is automated. We classified the CEs as continuous or categorical, and used statistical methods to search for correlations among them. The outcomes were transferred to a diagram referred to as "data-driven context model", which is a directed acyclic graph with one root node. Each path from the root node towards a leaf describes how a context influences a user task of interest. Figure 1 shows an example. Consider that the user task is "Prepare a coffee". Each of the two paths contains a set of instantiated CEs (white boxes) that, together, were found to influence the task (e.g., "When location = WORK and time = AFTERNOON then user prepares coffee", i.e., the context "location = WORK and time = AFTERNOON" influences the user task "Prepare a coffee", according to the model).

3 Experiment Planning

3.1 Goals

From RQ1, we derived the following study goals using the GQM template [3]:

Goal 1   Increase the ability of practitioners to identify complex contexts to describe context-aware functionalities from the point of view of the researcher in the context of a controlled experiment with practitioners using a data-driven context model based on DorfFunk data.

Goal 2   Improve the efficiency of the identification of relevant contexts from the researcher's point of view in the context of a controlled experiment with practitioners using a data-driven context model based on DorfFunk data.

Goal 3   Improve the effectiveness of the identification of relevant contexts from the researcher's point of view in the context of a controlled experiment with practitioners using a data-driven context model based on DorfFunk data.

Goal 4   Verify the usefulness of the data-driven context model from the point of view of practitioners in the context of a controlled experiment with practitioners using a data-driven context model based on DorfFunk data.

3.2 Design

The controlled experiment had a one factor with two treatments randomized design [23]. The primary factor was the context modeling technique. The participants of the treatment group were assigned to the data-driven context model, whereas the participants of the control group received the list of available CEs.

3.3 Participants

In practice, elicitation of context-aware functionalities is an activity that can be performed by a large range of professionals, including requirements engineers, UX designers, software architects, and developers, among others [6]. Therefore, we generalized our population as *software engineers with experience in information systems*. No prior experience in context awareness was required. We drew a convenient (non-probabilistic) sample of it in the Information Systems Division at Fraunhofer IESE. We invited all 34 professionals in the division through a corporate email list. Participation was voluntary. In order to motivate the invitees, they were informed that in the experiment they would have the opportunity to learn about requirements elicitation of context-aware functionalities and to participate in a practical activity about it. The informed consent form was attached to the email. We had 21 volunteers, which was our initial sample size (it was later reduced to 13 participants due to a deviation in the execution – see Sect. 4.2).

3.4 Participants' Task

The participants were asked to create requirements in written form, in English, to describe context-aware functionalities for one given system-supported user task of the app DorfFunk. The control group participants were told that they were constrained to stick to the list of CEs they had received to elaborate the requirements, whereas the treatment group participants were asked to stick to using the data-driven context model to elaborate theirs. Note that for the treatment group participants, using the data-driven context model implied that they would be constrained by the same CEs available to the control group participants. All participants were informed that there was no minimum number of requirements they should create.

3.5 Hypotheses and Variables

– **H1: Use of the data-driven context model influences the ability of individuals to elaborate requirements with more complex contexts.** The contexts used in the requirements varied regarding the number of CEs they combined. We wanted to check whether the requirements elaborated by the treatment group participants were more (or less) complex, with complexity measured by the number of CEs combined to describe the context used in the requirement (see Goal 1). The independent variable was the context modeling technique (*ad-hoc* or data-driven), and the dependent variable was the number of CEs combined to describe the contexts of each requirement created by the individuals. The null and alternative hypotheses were formulated as follows: $H_{0_1} : \mu_{1\ control} = \mu_{1\ treatment}$ and $H_{1_1} : \mu_{1\ control} \neq \mu_{1\ treatment}$.

- **H2: Use of the data-driven context model influences the efficiency of individuals to identify the relevant contexts included in the data-driven context model.** We wanted to check whether the data-driven context model included relevant contexts that, within a limited amount of time, would not be found by the participants of either group (see Goal 2). The independent variable was the context modeling technique (*ad-hoc* or data-driven), and the dependent variable was the percentage of relevant data-driven contexts found by the individuals. The null and alternative hypotheses were formulated as follows: $H_{0_2} : \mu_{2\ control} = \mu_{2\ treatment}$ and $H_{1_2} : \mu_{2\ control} \neq \mu_{2\ treatment}$.

- **H3: Use of the data-driven context model influences the effectiveness of individuals to identify the relevant contexts included in the data-driven context model.** We wanted to verify whether the data-driven context model included relevant contexts that, within a limited amount of time, would be used more often by individuals of either group (see Goal 3). The null and alternative hypotheses were formulated as follows: $H_{0_3} : \mu_{3\ control} = \mu_{3\ treatment}$ and $H_{1_3} : \mu_{3\ control} \neq \mu_{3\ treatment}$.

- **H4: The data-driven context model is perceived by individuals as a useful instrument to support the elicitation of context-aware functionalities.** The data-driven context model is a new artifact aimed at improving the way individuals elicit context-aware functionalities. We wanted to verify how much the participants valued it (see Goal 4).

3.6 Experimental Materials

Informed consent: The informed consent form contained partial disclosure of the experiment in order to prevent undesirable change of behavior by the participants [23][2].
Briefing questionnaire: This contained three questions to characterize their professional experience. They were asked about the number of years of professional experience (less than 5 years, or 5 years or more), whether their professional experience included requirements elicitation (yes/no), and to which role most of their professional experience was related. **Instructions about the data-driven context model:** The treatment group participants received in advance a PDF file introducing the syntax and semantics of the data-driven context model they would use during execution of the experiment. **Introductory presentation:** A set of slides introducing the participants to the experiment was presented. The slides contained information about the concept of context awareness, examples of context-aware functionalities in well-known applications, a description of context modeling activities performed to support the elicitation of context-aware functionalities, and a presentation of the participants' task in the experiment. It included a video introducing the app DorfFunk, for which the participants were to create requirements. **Data-driven context model:** During the execution

---

[2] All materials are available at https://doi.org/10.5281/zenodo.5090748.

of the experiment, the treatment group participants received a PDF file containing the data-driven context model generated based on the analysis of contextual data of the app DorfFunk, with focus on a specific user task. **List of CEs:** During the execution of the experiment, the control group participants received a PDF file containing the list of CEs they could use to elaborate context-aware functionalities. There were 15 CEs. **Debriefing questionnaire:** Right after the participants had performed their task in the experiment, they were asked to answer a debriefing questionnaire about the experience. Three questions were posed to all participants: whether their task in the experiment was clearly explained; whether the time they had to participate was adequate; and whether they perceived their task as easy or not. They were also asked about how well they knew the app DorfFunk, because we regarded the amount of previous knowledge about the app as a possible confounding factor. The treatment group participants were asked additional questions about the data-driven context model they received to support the task. For this purpose, we employed the UTAUT (Unified Theory of Acceptance and Use of Technology [20]), tailoring the items to our case. **Requirements validation checklist:** We defined and used a checklist to guide the validation of the requirements generated by the participants in the analysis phase (see Sect. 5.2).

3.7 Procedure

The execution of the experiment was subdivided into three parts. In the first part, they were introduced to the concepts of context awareness, elicitation of context-aware features, and context modeling using the "introductory presentation". Then, they received a step-by-step introduction to the tool they would use to provide data during the execution of the experiment. At the end of the introduction, they were informed that the specific system-supported user task they should try to improve using context awareness was *"create a comment"*, and a story board illustrating the as-is situation of the system-supported user task was shown. The user task was revealed only at the end of the introduction in order to prevent the participants from thinking about possible context-aware functionalities in advance. In the second part, the participants had 30 min to perform their task (see Sect. 3.4). When the time was over, they were informed and proceeded to the last part, the debriefing questionnaire. At the end of the debriefing questionnaire, the control group participants were told that some participants received different artifacts to perform the task, and were given the opportunity to download these artifacts, namely the instructions about the data-driven context model and the data-driven context model. Due to the COVID-19 pandemic [24], all sessions were performed online via MS Teams[3]. In order to ensure that the same instructions would be provided to all participants across the sessions, the instructions were written down before and read at the time of the execution. After the completion of the questionnaire, they were asked to keep the participation confidential, since other participants would join different sessions in different date/times.

---

[3] https://www.microsoft.com/en-us/microsoft-teams/group-chat-software.

4 Execution

4.1 Preparation

Before the execution of the experiment, the participants were asked via email to answer the briefing questionnaire about their professional experience (see Sect. 3.6). The input was used to block participants before the randomization procedure. There were two blocks: those with less than 5 years of professional experience ($N = 6$), and those with 5 years or more of experience ($N = 15$). The other questions (experience with elicitation and major role) were not used to block the participants because they led to very small odd blocks in some cases, which would compromise the randomization. Within the blocks, the participants were randomly assigned to either the control group ($N = 11$) or the treatment group ($N = 10$). The treatment group participants received an email with a set of slides containing instructions about the data-driven context model, so they would know how to use it in the experiment. They were asked to read the material before the execution and to keep all information confidential.

Next, all participants were asked to provide their availability to participate in the experiment. Multiple time slots were offered over a period of two weeks. Based on their responses, we prepared and executed eight sessions between 18 and 27 May 2021.

4.2 Deviations

On the first day (18 May 18 2021), there were two sessions, with 9 participants ($p_1 - p_9$) in total, 5 of them belonging to the treatment group. At the end of the day, we performed a data validation to check the input provided by the participants. We noticed that the treatment group participants had apparently deviated from their task, as the results indicated that they did not use the data-driven context model as intended. Furthermore, there was a question to be answered in the debriefing questionnaire on a 5-point Likert-like rating scale about how clearly their task in the experiment was explained, and 60% of the treatment group participants did *not* agree that their task was clearly explained. In fact, one participant contacted the moderator via private chat during the execution to ask how they should use the data-driven context model. In addition to that, we had the chance to talk to one participant after the experiment and they confirmed that they did not quite understand how they should use the data-driven context model to perform their activity. For this reason, we changed the procedure of the experiment for the future treatment group participants: They would be explicitly introduced to the material "Instructions about the data-driven context model" (see Sect. 3.6), which they received before the experiment to read by themselves. For the control group participants, the procedure was not changed. In none of the remaining six sessions, participants from both groups took part, so we could change the procedure for the treatment group participants without having to reschedule sessions. As a consequence of the early data validation, where some participants were found to have misunderstood the task, the data collected should be considered invalid [23]. As we changed the instructions for the next treatment group participants, we also removed from the analysis all 5 subjects who had received the original instructions. Of these, 3 belonged to the less experienced block. The other 3 less experienced participants belonged to the control group, and were therefore also removed from the analysis; otherwise we would have had less experienced profession-als only in the control group. For that reason, we were left with 13 participants (p_4 who participated in the first session, and $p_{10} - p_{21}$ who participated in the later sessions), all of them professionals with 5 years or more of experience.

5 Analysis

We used quantitative methods to analyze the data. For the briefing and debriefing questionnaires, we used central tendency and data visualization measures. The con-texts used in each valid requirement were extracted. If these contexts contained any of those included in the data-driven context model, the corresponding contexts included in the models were classified as *relevant data-driven contexts*. Once the contexts were extracted, we were able to calculate the average number of CEs in the context of each group, as well as the effectiveness and efficiency of each participant in identifying the relevant data-driven contexts. We compared both groups using statistical tests and ver-ified the effect size using Hedges's g, a *d family* effect size measure recommended for small sample sizes [13].

5.1 Descriptive Statistics

Among the 13 participants, 12 (92.3%) reported that their professional experience included requirements elicitation. Figure 2a shows the participants' main professional role, organized by group. There was a prevalence of RE-related professionals (require-ments engineers, UX designers) in the treatment group. With respect to the participants' previous knowledge about the app DorfFunk, Fig. 2b shows that the control group par-ticipants were more familiar with it (more subjects were users of the app or even par-ticipated in the development team).

We asked the participants to rate their agreement with the statement "My task in this experiment was clearly explained". For this purpose, we used a 5-point Likert-like scale (Strongly disagree, Disagree, Neutral, Agree, and Strongly agree) and found that 11 participants (84.6%) strongly agreed and 2 (15.4%) agreed (*median = mode =* "Strongly agree"). Similarly, another statement was formulated with respect to the time the participants had to perform their task (see Fig. 2c). The mode and the median for the control group participants was "Strongly agree", whereas for the treatment group participants, both mode and median were "Neutral/Agree". Finally, a statement was formulated to get the participants' perception of the ease of their task. As can be seen in Fig. 2d, the mode and the median for both groups were "Neutral"; however, for the control group participants, the distribution of responses was spread wider, varying from "Strongly disagree" to "Strongly agree", whereas for the treatment group, it varied from "Disagree" to "Agree".

5.2 Data Set Preparation

The participants generated a total of 105 requirements; 55 (52.4%) came from the con-trol group and 50 (47.6%) from the treatment group. Before carrying out hypothesis

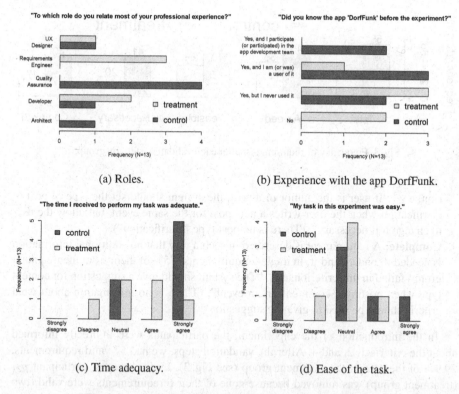

"To which role do you relate most of your professional experience?"

"Did you know the app 'DorfFunk' before the experiment?"

(a) Roles.

(b) Experience with the app DorfFunk.

"The time I received to perform my task was adequate."

"My task in this experiment was easy."

(c) Time adequacy.

(d) Ease of the task.

Fig. 2. Frequency of responses in the debriefing questionnaire.

testing, it was necessary to validate the requirements. As validation technique, we used a checklist with quality criteria for requirements as presented by Pohl and Rupp [16]. According to them, this technique improves the reproducibility of the validation. Our checklist covered the following quality criteria (derived from [16] and [11]), which were applied sequentially:

1. **Agreed:** A requirement should be directly related to the system-supported user task in focus. Moreover, it should describe a context-aware feature – in our case, either a recommendation or adaptation based on the context. In total, 24 requirements (58.3% of them from the treatment group) failed in this criterion, e.g., "The system should ask the user to turn on the notification of DorfFunk when the user is in the home network after 17:00" (no direct connection to the user task "Create a comment").

2. **Feasible:** A requirement should only use CEs available in the model; otherwise they would by technically unfeasible. In total, 5 requirements (80% of them from the treatment group) failed in this criterion, e.g., "User in the role of suggestion worker should have predefined answers based on *the content of the suggestion*." (The content of the suggestion was not available).

3. **Necessary:** A requirement must be currently applicable to the app DorfFunk. In total, 15 requirements (53.3% of them from the treatment group) failed in this crite-

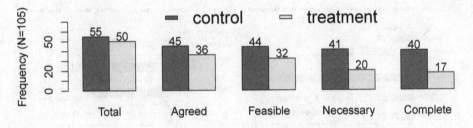

Fig. 3. Frequency of requirements after each validation step, by group.

rion, e.g., "If user is the author of a post, the system should set the type of post to clarification when the user writes a new post for the same event, but allow the user to change it if necessary". (There is no post type "clarification").

4. **Complete:** A requirement is described in such a way that no additional information is needed to understand it. In total, 4 requirements (75% of them from the treatment group) failed in this criterion, e.g., "The system should give a suggestion for content type when posting a comment on an event". (There is no information about what criteria should be used to give the suggestion).

In the introduction of the experiment, the participants were indirectly informed about the criteria 1, 2, and 4. After the validation steps, we had 57 valid requirements, 29.9% of them from the treatment group (see Fig. 3). In this process, participant p_{21} (treatment group) was removed because none of their 6 requirements were valid (two were not feasible and four were not necessary). The validation was performed by the first author, who is an experienced software engineer specializing in context awareness and with a broad understanding of the app DorfFunk. Whenever doubts came up concerning the criterion "necessary", the opinion of the product owner was heard. Next, we extracted the contexts of these 57 requirements and counted for each how many CEs were used to compose the context. Then we checked which of these contexts were included in the data-driven context model in order to define a list of relevant data-driven contexts according to the participants. The number of CEs used to describe contexts as well as the list of relevant data-driven contexts were used to support hypothesis testing. Due to space limitations, the raw data is not included here[4].

5.3 Hypothesis Testing

H1 ("more complex contexts"). The mean number of CEs that the control group participants used to describe their 40 contexts was $\mu_{1\ control} = 1.77$ ($SD = 0.80$, $min = 1$, $max = 5$, $median = 2$), whereas the mean from the treatment group (17 contexts) was $\mu_{1\ treatment} = 4.23$ ($SD = 0.97$, $min = 3$, $max = 5$, $median = 5$)[5]. We applied the Shapiro-Wilk normality test to the distributions and rejected the hypothesis of normality (control: $W = 0.73036$, $p - value = 3.183e - 07$; treatment:

---

[4] The anonymized raw data is available at https://doi.org/10.5281/zenodo.5090748.
[5] For H1, H2 and H3, we used $\alpha = 0.05$ as significance level and $\beta = 0.2$.

$W = 0.66011$, $p - value = 4.226e - 05$). Then we applied the non-parametric Wilcoxon rank sum test to compare the distributions and found that the difference between the means was significant ($p - value = 7.071e - 09$); consequently, H_{0_1} can be rejected. The effect size was large (Hedges's g = 2.84, 95% confidence interval: 2.06 to 3.62). We did a post-hoc power analysis and found power $1 - \beta = 0.9880658$; therefore, we can accept H_{1_1}. Conclusion: Individuals who had the model used more complex contexts ($\mu_{1\ treatment} > \mu_{1\ control}$) to elaborate their requirements.

H2 and H3 ("efficiency" and "effectiveness"). In total, 6 contexts included in the data-driven context model were used by participants to describe their context-aware functionalities. None of these contexts were found by participants of the control group, so $\mu_{2\ control} = \mu_{3\ control} = 0\%$. The efficiency and the effectiveness of the treatment group participants is shown in Table 1. The mean efficiency of the treatment group in identifying the relevant data-driven context was $\mu_{2\ treatment} = 36.6\%$ ($SD = 0.217$), whereas their effectiveness was $\mu_{3\ treatment} = 74.6\%$ ($SD = 0.347$). As we cannot assume normal distribution from the control group, we again used the Wilcoxon rank sum test to compare the differences and found that H_{0_2} and H_{0_3} were rejected ($p - value = 0.002033$ and $p - value = 0.001645$, respectively). In both cases, the effect size was large (efficiency: Hedges's g = 2.46, 95% confidence interval: 0.87 to 4.05; effectiveness: Hedges's g = 1.74, 95% confidence interval: 0.33 to 3.14). We did a post-hoc power analysis and found for efficiency power $1 - \beta = 0.9556588$, and for effectiveness power $1 - \beta = 0.7392546$; therefore, we can accept H_{1_2} and cannot accept H_{1_3}. Conclusion: Individuals who had the model were more efficient ($\mu_{3\ treatment} > \mu_{3\ control}$). No conclusion can be drawn about effectiveness.

H4 ("a useful instrument"). With respect to the usefulness of the data-driven context model, the participants provided their perception regarding 18 statements adapted from UTAUT [20], covering the following aspects: performance expectancy (PE, 3 questions), effort expectancy (EE, 4 questions), attitude toward using technology (AT, 4 questions), self-efficacy (SE, 4 questions), and anxiety (AX, 3 questions). We coded the answer options numerically (1 to 5). We reversed the code in item AT.1 of aspect AT, and in all items of aspect AX, for they were stated in a negative way. Figure 4 shows the distributions of the responses of each aspect.

Table 1. Efficiency and effectiveness of the treatment group participants.

Participant ID	Modeled contexts used	Total contexts used	Efficiency	Effectiveness
p16	1	3	16.7%	33.3%
p17	3	3	50%	100%
p18	1	1	16.7%	100%
p19	2	5	33.3%	40%
p20	4	4	66.6%	100%

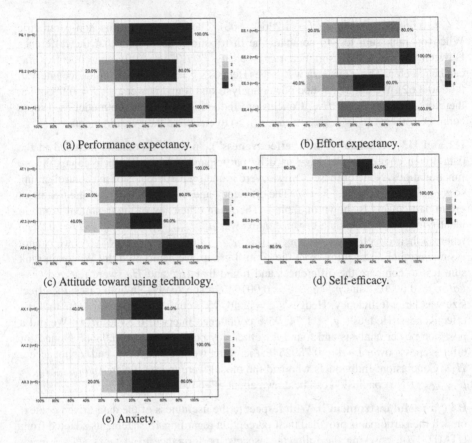

(a) Performance expectancy.   (b) Effort expectancy.

(c) Attitude toward using technology.   (d) Self-efficacy.

(e) Anxiety.

Fig. 4. Participants' assessment with respect to usefulness of model.

Table 2 shows the scores of each aspect and their reliability. The item scores were calculated based on the mean value of the participants' ratings; the aspect score was calculated as the mean of the item scores composing each aspect. To verify the reliability of the scores, we calculated their Cronbach's alpha, which was higher than 0.7 for PE, AT, SE, and AX, hence acceptable [9], whereas for EE it was not acceptable. Conclusion: Apart from the aspect Self-efficacy (SE), all aspects had high scores (> 0.4), meaning that the participants evaluated the model positively.

Table 2. The five investigated aspects of usefulness of the data-driven context model.

Aspect	Item	Item score	Aspect score	Cronbach's alpha
PE - Performance expectancy	PE.1	4.8	4.6	0.778
	PE.2	4.4		
	PE.3	4.6		
EE - Effort expectancy	EE.1	3.8	4.05	0.468
	EE.2	4.2		
	EE.3	3.8		
	EE.4	4.4		
AT - Attitude toward using technology	AT.1	5	4.34	0.804
	AT.2	4.2		
	AT.3	3.8		
	AT.4	4.4		
SE - Self-efficacy	SE.1	3.2	3.75	0.752
	SE.2	4.4		
	SE.3	4.4		
	SE.4	3		
AX - Anxiety	AX.1	3.8	4.2	0.903
	AX.2	4.6		
	AX.3	4.2		

6   Discussion

6.1   Evaluation of Results and Implications

The data-driven context model (and the process that creates it) is not about completeness: There is no claim suggesting that *all* relevant contexts for the user task in focus would be included in the model. Furthermore, these contexts were not said to be necessarily *better* than others. The point is that the data-driven context model is able to provide shortcuts in the solution space of a complex activity: context modeling. We confirmed in the experiment that, with its support, individuals were able to find some *unexpected* contexts – and to do so *faster*, for with unlimited time, we expect that individuals would eventually find these contexts anyway (which is a hypothesis to be investigated). As participants who used the data-driven context model were able to elaborate requirements with more complex contexts, we accepted H1. Our findings back the results of a previous empirical study performed by Falcão et al. [6], where they found that practitioners regard the analysis of combinations of CEs as a highly complex activity. We observed this in our experiment, as a significantly lower number of CEs were found in the contexts of the control group. In addition, this shows that the data-driven context model contained meaningful contexts with a larger number of CEs.

We measured the participants' efficiency and effectiveness in finding relevant data-driven context models included in the model. Although we had expected that the treatment group participants would perform better since they received the data-driven context model, we assumed that some of the contexts found in the data-driven context model would be "too obvious", and therefore participants of the control group would be able to identify them despite not having received the data-driven context model (and this expectation would be even higher if we knew in advance that the control group participants had better background knowledge about the app DorfFunk – see Sect. 5.1). For this reason, it was unexpected for us that not a single control group participant was able to identify by themselves any of the contexts included in the data-driven context model, which led to zero efficiency and zero effectiveness in identifying such contexts. It is worth noting that the result would be the same if we had considered all requirements generated by the control group before reducing the data set as presented in Sect. 5.2. Therefore, the treatment group participants were more efficient in finding relevant contexts included in the data-driven context model, which speaks (at least partially) in favor of the representation of the model and its content. We also found higher effectiveness, but without statistical power, which we believe was due to the sample size, since the effect size was large.

In fact, in all tests performed (H1, H2, and H3), the effect size can be considered large (according to Kampenes et al. [13]); however, for effectiveness (H3), it is worth noting that the 95% confidence interval ranged from small ($g \leq 0.376$) to large ($g \geq 1.002$) effect sizes, and we could not accept H_{1_3}. This may have been caused by participant p_{16}, who created 3 valid requirements, but 2 of them could not be directly mapped to the data-driven context model, even though they were clearly inspired by contexts presented in the model. This added to the practical utility of the model, but is not captured by the pragmatic evaluation we chose (e.g., in one case, p_{16} cleverly inverted a context described in the model to describe a context-aware functionality). In order to be consistent with our analysis procedure and give less room to subjectivity, we did not include such cases in the baseline of relevant data-driven contexts.

We generally found a positive trend towards acceptance of the data-driven context model in all aspects investigated, as can be seen in Fig. 4. One exception could be the aspect "self-efficacy", which had the lowest score. To a certain extent, it reflects our need to adjust the procedure after the first two sessions of the experiment (see Sect. 4.2), as we realized that the participants needed additional explicit instructions to understand how to use the data-driven context model. With respect to effort expectancy, the aspect whose reliability was not acceptable (see Sect. 5), we found the cause in item EE.1, which referred to how clear and understandable the usage of the data-driven context model would be. If EE.1 was removed, the aspect score would be 4.13 and the reliability would be acceptable (0.733).

Regarding RQ1, we conclude that the approach supports the identification of more complex contexts as well as unexpected functionalities. In a practical setting, we think the data-driven context model should be used to support creativity group sessions, providing individuals with triggers and input that can be copied as-is, combined, or transformed (the basic elements of creativity [19]) to generate new ideas – as happened, for example, with participant p_{16}. Working together, individuals will be in a better position to evaluate the meaning of contexts, judge their value, discard what is irrelevant, and leverage the shortcuts to insightful contexts provided by the model. Although, on the one hand, the automated process helps people identify some relevant contexts faster, on the other hand human participation remains a fundamental piece in the validation and in the creativity steps that follow context modeling. Moreover, we expected the outcomes to be more sound when contextual data is collected with context modeling in mind (in the experiment, we used available data for the sake of convenience) and when more CEs are included in the analysis, which is expected in a smart scenario [6,7].

6.2 Threats to Validity

Construct validity: *Mono-operation bias:* All participants performed the same task within the context of the same application, meaning that the results can reflect the particularities of the specific setting. *Confounding constructs or level of constructs*: The data-driven context model was created based on available CEs. A lower effect is expected, as fewer CEs were involved, whereas the results may be more pronounced, as more CEs were included in the analysis. *Restrict generalizability across constructs*: The process of generating the data-driven context model may have had an impact on the overall efficiency of the elicitation process. **Internal validity:** *Interaction with selections:* In the random assignment of participants to groups, those with major background experience in RE-related roles were concentrated in the treatment group, which may have benefited the group. On the other hand, the control group had participants with more prior knowledge about DorfFunk, which could also have been advantageous for the group. **External validity:** *Interaction between selection and treatment:* It is possible that the selection was not representative and the results are not generalizable, given the number of participants and the sample strategy. Moreover, if participants with particular expertise in the elicitation of context-aware functionalities had been involved, the outcomes might be different. However, such professionals belong to a hard-to-spot population [6]. **Conclusion validity:** *Reliability of measures:* The participants provided written requirements, and there was a manual activity to prepare the data set (see Sect. 5.2), extract contexts from the requirements, and count the number of CEs of each context. Mistakes in these manual steps, especially in the preparation of the data set, may have compromised the conclusions. *Experimental setting:* The experiment was performed in online sessions via the Internet. In such settings, it is harder to check the participants' compliance with the procedure, in particular to ensure that they focus exclusively on the activity during the experiment.

7 Conclusion and Future Work

Context modeling to support the elicitation of context-aware functionalities is a needed but rather overlooked activity due to its complexity, especially concerning the analysis of relevance and combinations of contextual elements. We implemented a semi-automated data-driven approach to analyze contextual data and generate context models that revealed relevant contexts that influence a given user task of interest. We used data from an app in use to create a data-driven context model. In this paper, we reported its evaluation in the context of a controlled experiment with experienced software engineers. The results showed that participants using the data-driven context model were able to describe requirements with more complex contexts, while participants without the context model were not able to identify any of the relevant contexts included in the model. Moreover, participants using the data-driven context model regarded it as a useful instrument to support the elicitation of context-aware functionalities. To the best of our knowledge, this paper contributes the first controlled experiment evaluating the usage of data-driven context modeling on the elicitation of context-aware functionalities.

A limitation of the data-driven approach is that it can only draw conclusions from existing data, and the universe of relevant combinations of CEs is much larger than what can be inferred via data analysis. Therefore, it must be clear that the data-driven context model reveals *some* relevant contexts, but never *all* of them. The data-driven context model anticipates the identification of relevant contexts for a given user task, meaning that part of the time-consuming work of analyzing relevant combinations can be skipped. Nonetheless, implementing the data-driven context modeling approach introduces effort as well; however, this is operational effort, which takes place in polynomial time, taking the list of CEs as input, whereas the analysis of relevant combinations is creative work requiring exponential time with the same input.

We want to run the experiment again with less experienced participants in order to check whether it can attenuate the experience factor in the elicitation of context-aware functionalities. We also consider it essential to generate the data-driven context model using a different application in order mitigate the mono-operation bias. Furthermore, we want to perform a case study where the participants would work together to create context-aware functionalities based on the data-driven context model. Finally, we plan to modify the data processor using different algorithms and evaluate which strategy reveals more relevant contexts – which might lead to a multi-strategy approach.

References

1. Alegre, U., Augusto, J.C., Clark, T.: Engineering context-aware systems and applications: a survey. JSS **117**, 55–83 (2016)
2. Ali, R., Dalpiaz, F., Giorgini, P.: A goal-based framework for contextual requirements modeling and analysis. Requirements Eng. **15**(4), 439–458 (2010)
3. Basili, V., Caldiera, G., Rombach, H.D.: The goal question metric approach. In: Encyclopedia of Software Engineering, pp. 528–532 (1994)
4. Bauer, C., Dey, A.K.: Considering context in the design of intelligent systems: current practices and suggestions for improvement. JSS **112**, 26–47 (2016)
5. Dey, A.K.: Understanding and using context. PUC **5**(1), 4–7 (2001). https://doi.org/10.1007/s007790170019
6. Falcão, R., Villela, K., Vieira, V., Trapp, M., Faria, I.: The practical role of context modeling in the elicitation of context-aware functionalities: a survey. In: RE 2021. IEEE (2021)
7. Falcão, R.: Improving the elicitation of delightful context-aware features: a data-based approach. In: RE 2017, pp. 562–567. IEEE (2017)
8. Google: Google Awareness API (2021). https://bit.ly/3wmoF56. Accessed 08 July 2021
9. Hair, J.F., Black, W., Babin, B., Anderson, R.: Multivariate Data Analysis. Pearson (2009)

10. Henricksen, K.: A framework for context-aware pervasive computing applications. Ph.D. thesis, The University of Queensland (2003)
11. ISO/IEC/IEEE 29148 - Systems and Software Engineering - Life cycle processes - Requirements engineering. Standard, ISO (2018)
12. Jedlitschka, A., Ciolkowski, M., Pfahl, D.: Reporting experiments in software engineering. In: Shull, F., Singer, J., Sjøberg, D.I.K. (eds.) Guide to Advanced Empirical Software Engineering, pp. 201–228. Springer, London (2008). https://doi.org/10.1007/978-1-84800-044-5_8
13. Kampenes, V.B., Dybå, T., Hannay, J.E., Sjøberg, D.I.: A systematic review of effect size in software engineering experiments. IST **49**(11–12), 1073–1086 (2007)
14. Maalej, W., Nayebi, M., Johann, T., Ruhe, G.: Toward data-driven requirements engineering. IEEE Softw. **33**(1), 48–54 (2016)
15. Olsson, T., Lagerstam, E., Kärkkäinen, T., Väänänen-Vainio-Mattila, K.: Expected user experience of mobile augmented reality services: a user study in the context of shopping centres. PUC **17**(2), 287–304 (2013). https://doi.org/10.1007/s00779-011-0494-x
16. Pohl, K., Rupp, C.: Requirements Engineering: Fundamentals, Principles, and Techniques, 2nd edn. Rocky Nook, San Rafael (2015)
17. Rodrigues, A., Rodrigues, G.N., Knauss, A., Ali, R., Andrade, H.: Enhancing context specifications for dependable adaptive systems: a data mining approach. IST **112**, 115–131 (2019)
18. Saputri, T., Lee, S.W.: The application of machine learning in self-adaptive systems: a systematic literature review. IEEE Access **8**, 205948–205967 (2020)
19. Trapp, M.: Creative people are great thieves with lousy dealers (2020). Proceedings http://ceur-ws.org ISSN 1613, 0073
20. Venkatesh, V., Morris, M.G., Davis, G.B., Davis, F.D.: User acceptance of information technology: Toward a unified view. MIS Q. **27**, 425–478 (2003)
21. Vieira, V., Tedesco, P., Salgado, A.C., Brézillon, P.: Investigating the specifics of contextual elements management: the CEManTIKA approach. In: Kokinov, B., Richardson, D.C., Roth-Berghofer, T.R., Vieu, L. (eds.) CONTEXT 2007. LNCS (LNAI), vol. 4635, pp. 493–506. Springer, Heidelberg (2007). https://doi.org/10.1007/978-3-540-74255-5_37
22. Villela, K., et al.: Towards ubiquitous RE: a perspective on requirements engineering in the era of digital transformation. In: RE 2018, pp. 205–216. IEEE (2018)
23. Wohlin, C., Runeson, P., Höst, M., Ohlsson, M.C., Regnell, B., Wesslén, A.: Experimentation in Software Engineering. Springer, Heidelberg (2012). https://doi.org/10.1007/978-3-642-29044-2
24. World Health Organization: COVID 19 - GLOBAL. https://bit.ly/3AI5RR0. Accessed 21 June 2021

A Transformation Model for Excelling in Product Roadmapping in Dynamic and Uncertain Market Environments

Stefan Trieflinger[1]([✉]), Jürgen Münch[1], Stefan Wagner[2], Dominic Lang[3], and Bastian Roling[4]

[1] Reutlingen University, Alteburgstraße 150, 72768 Reutlingen, Germany
`{stefan.trieflinger,juergen.muench}@reutlingen-university.de`
[2] University of Stuttgart, Universitätsstraße 38, 70569 Stuttgart, Germany
`stefan.wagner@iste.uni-stuttgart.de`
[3] Robert Bosch GmbH, Borsigstraße 24, 70469 Stuttgart, Germany
`Dominic.lang2@bosch.com`
[4] Viastore Software GmbH, Magirusstraße 13, 70469 Stuttgart, Germany
`b.roling@viastore.com`

Abstract. Context: Many companies are facing an increasingly dynamic and uncertain market environment, making traditional product roadmapping practices no longer sufficiently applicable. As a result, many companies need to adapt their product roadmapping practices for continuing to operate successfully in today's dynamic market environment. However, transforming product roadmapping practices is a difficult process for organizations. Existing literature offers little help on how to accomplish such a process. **Objective:** The objective of this paper is to present a product roadmap transformation approach for organizations to help them identify appropriate improvement actions for their roadmapping practices using an analysis of their current practices. **Method:** Based on an existing assessment procedure for evaluating product roadmapping practices, the first version of a product roadmap transformation approach was developed in workshops with company experts. The approach was then given to eleven practitioners and their perceptions of the approach were gathered through interviews. **Results:** The result of the study is a transformation approach consisting of a process describing what steps are necessary to adapt the currently applied product roadmapping practice to a dynamic and uncertain market environment. It also includes recommendations on how to select areas for improvement and two empirically based mapping tables. The interviews with the practitioners revealed that the product roadmap transformation approach was perceived as comprehensible, useful, and applicable. Nevertheless, we identified potential for improvements, such as a clearer presentation of some processes and the need for more improvement options in the mapping tables. In addition, minor usability issues were identified.

Keywords: Product roadmap · Product strategy · Transformation model · Agile development · Product management

© Springer Nature Switzerland AG 2021
L. Ardito et al. (Eds.): PROFES 2021, LNCS 13126, pp. 136–151, 2021.
https://doi.org/10.1007/978-3-030-91452-3_9

1   Introduction

For each company, it is crucial to provide a strategic direction, in which the product portfolio will be developed over time in order to achieve the corporate vision. For this purpose, product roadmaps are used in practice. Product roadmaps aim to provide an essential understanding, proximity, and some degree of certainty regarding the direction of the future product portfolio [1]. In general, roadmaps can take various forms, but the most common approach is the generic form proposed by EIRMA [2, 3]. This generic roadmap is a time-based chart, comprising several layers that typically include commercial and technological views. This approach enables to visualize the evolution of markets, products, and technologies to be explored, together with the linkage between the various perspectives [3]. In the context of software-intensive businesses, a product roadmap can be seen as a strategic communication tool and a statement of intent and direction. Consequently, a product roadmap should focus on the value it aims to deliver to its customer and the business [4]. Furthermore, a product roadmap aims to create alignment and a common understanding about the future direction to gather support and to be able to coordinate the effort among all stakeholders [5]. Due to increasing market dynamics, rapidly evolving technologies, and shifting user expectations, combined with the adoption of lean and agile practices it is becoming increasingly difficult for companies to plan ahead and predict which products, services, or features to develop, especially in the mid- and long-term [6]. A recent study [7] on the state of practice regarding product roadmapping revealed that most companies are using fixed-time- based charts that provide a forecast for specific products, features, or services (including concrete launch or deployment dates). However, this approach is too static and therefore not suitable for the operation in a dynamic and uncertain market environment [8]. As a result, companies are facing the challenge of deciding between breaking promises by permanently adjusting the roadmap or staying to a plan created months ago that seems increasingly outdated. Due to the mismatch between static product roadmaps and a dynamic and uncertain market environment, most companies have recognized that new approaches and procedures regarding the development and updating of product roadmaps are required. A typical first step in advancing product roadmapping capabilities is to assess the current state of product roadmapping practices in use. For this purpose, the product roadmap self-assessment tool called DEEP was developed by the authors in previous research [9]. The DEEP model enables practitioners to assess their current product roadmapping practice in order to identify improvement potentials. However, the DEEP model does not currently provide concrete measures that will lead to improvements in the product roadmapping practices currently in use and, consequently, to higher levels in the DEEP model. [9, 10]. This means that the derivation of proposals for improvement actions and changes based on the assessment performed is not yet included in DEEP. For this reason, in this article we propose an approach to transforming the product roadmap to the requirements of a dynamic and uncertain market environment. This transformation was built on the basis of the DEEP model and can thus be seen as an extension of our previous research. In more detail, practitioners can use this model to identify activities for improving their roadmapping practices based on their overall product roadmapping maturity determined with the DEEP model. The identified activities set the stage for achieving a higher maturity level according to DEEP.

2 Background and Related Work

2.1 Background

As mentioned above, the DEEP Product Roadmap Self-Assessment Tool developed in previous research served as the basis for developing the product roadmap transformation approach presented in this paper. The DEEP model was developed with the goal of providing practitioners with a tool to self-assess their organization's product roadmap capabilities. The model was especially developed for companies that operate in a dynamic and uncertain market environment. The model consists of nine dimensions, each comprising five stages. Each dimension describes a relevant aspect of product roadmapping such as "roadmap detailing", "reliability" or "confidence". Moreover each dimension is assigned to five stages, with each stage describing a common product roadmapping practice. In addition, each stage was assigned with scores that reflect their maturity. A company can perform a self-assessment by selecting the applicable stage for each dimension and summing up the corresponding score. After summing the scores for the nine selected dimensions, a company receives its overall maturity level for product roadmapping. A condensed presentation of the model is provided in Appendix A. Detailed information about the DEEP model as well as its validation can be found in Münch et al. [9, 10].

2.2 Related Work

Various papers can be found in the academic literature that address the maturity or maturity assessment of roadmapping practices as well as the improvement of such practices. Overall, the existing scientific literature provides only an abstract insight into how a company can evaluate its currently applied product roadmapping practices and how it can be systematically improved [11]. Moreover, to the best of our knowledge, a transformation model that provides detailed guidelines in order to adapt the currently applied product roadmapping practices to a dynamic and uncertain market environment does not exist. Moreover to the best of our knowledge, only the SAFe Implementation Roadmap [12] provided detailed guidelines to adapt the applied product roadmapping practices to a dynamic and uncertain market environment. It provides twelve steps to adapt a product roadmap to an agile environment. However, these steps, which include recommendations for actions, are not based on a company-specific assessment that focuses on all the details of the product roadmapping practices currently in use. Moreover Lombardo et al. [4] developed a so-called "Roadmap Health Assessment Checklist". The checklist includes 15 questions. The questions address various topics around product roadmapping including 1) focus on value, 2) embrace learning, 3) rally the organization about priorities, 3) get customers excited, and 4) avoid overpromising. The health check can be seen as a quick assessment that covers the main issues of product roadmapping. In contrast to the DEEP model, the checklist by Lombardo et al. [4] does not explicitly show various stages for each dimension and does not consider specific organizational aspects such as responsibility and ownership of the roadmap. In addition, the authors do not recommend any measures in order to improve the roadmapping practice, which is the focus of this paper. A comprehensive literature review on product roadmapping can be found in [11].

3   Research Approach

The research aims to help companies engaged in software-intensive business adapt their product roadmapping practices to the demands of a dynamic and uncertain market environment. In order to reach this objective, the authors defined the following research questions:

- **RQ1:** How can companies approach the transformation of their product roadmapping practice to a dynamic and uncertain market environment by using the DEEP product roadmap self-assessment tool?
- **RQ2:** How do practitioners perceive the product roadmap transformation approach?

The authors developed the product roadmap transformation approach by conducting expert workshops with three practitioners and two researchers. The authors selected the practitioners based on their practical experience with product roadmapping as well as their roles in the respective companies. The latter means that each of these participants is involved in the product roadmapping process in their respective company. In addition, each practitioner was also involved in the development of the DEEP model. In order to integrate different perspectives into the model development, we selected a heterogeneous set of practitioners to participate in the expert workshops. This means that those practitioners differ in their industry sectors within the software-intensive business and sizes of their respective companies. Table 1 gives an overview of the practitioners that participated in this workshop. We held three workshops on March 5th, 2021 (1,5 h), March 17th, 2021, (1 h), and March 30th,2021 (1,5 h). To give all participants, the opportunity to reflect on the results of the individual workshops, care was taken to ensure that there was sufficient time between the conduction of the various workshops. The same practitioners participated in all workshops. Due to the COVID-19 situation, the workshops were conducted online, and the tool Mural was used for documentation. In order to include the holistic product roadmap transformation approach, the conduction of the DEEP assessment was chosen as the start of our discussion. Then open discussions with the practitioners on what steps should be taken to reach a higher level with respect to the DEEP model were held.

Table 1. Practitioners that participated in the expert workshops (size classification: small <50, large >250).

Interviewee	Position	Experience	Company size by no. of employees
Participant 1	IT Coordinator	7 years	Large
Participant 2	Head of Product Management	8 years	Small
Participant 3	Product Owner	2 years	Medium

To answer RQ2, we provided the product roadmap transformation approach along with the DEEP model for practitioners to try without detailed explanations and instructions. The aim of this step was to validate the applicability and comprehensibility of the DEEP model. The practitioners who participated in the interviews were not involved in the development of the DEEP model and were using it for the first time. Specifically, practitioners were asked to first conduct a self-assessment using the DEEP model. Then, using the transformation model, they were asked to identify the dimension most in need of improvement. Finally, they were asked to use the mapping tables to identify appropriate actions to improve their roadmapping practices related to the previously identified dimension. This included assessing whether the measures received were useful from the practitioner's point of view. Afterwards, we interviewed each participant to identify potential for improvements (e.g., lack of clarity) of the product roadmap transformation approach. All interviews were conducted by the same researcher online. The average length of the interviews was 36 min with the range being between 27 min and 42 min. In order to focus and structure the interviews and to ensure thematic comparability, we developed an interview guide that consist of the following questions: 1) What do you think are the strengths and weaknesses of the model? 2) Which phrases did you find difficult to understand? 3) In your opinion, would the model help your company to adapt the current product roadmapping practice to a dynamic and uncertain market environment? In total, we recruited 11 experts who operate in a dynamic market environment (e.g., smart home). As with the expert workshops mentioned above the selection of the participants was based on their experience in product roadmapping and role in their company. For the search of suitable participants, we used our company network as well as the platform LinkedIn. Table 2 gives an overview of the practitioners who participated in the validation process of the transformation approach. In order to conduct an accurate data analysis, we took notes in each interview. We analysed these interview

Table 2. Participants of the interviews (size classification: small <50, large >250).

Interviewee	Position	Experience	Company size by no. of employees
Interviewee 1	Product Manager	5 years	Medium
Interviewee 2	Product Owner	3 years	Medium
Interviewee 3	Head of Product Management	7 years	Large
Interviewee 4	Software Engineer	6 years	Large
Interviewee 5	Product Manager	2, 5 years	Small
Interviewee 6	CEO	12 years	Large
Interviewee 7	Product Owner	6,5 years	Small
Interviewee 8	Product Manager	7 years	Medium
Interviewee 9	Head of Product Management	9 years	Medium
Interviewee 10	Sales Representative	3 years	Medium
Interviewee 11	Product Manager	3.5 years	Large

notes by extracting main responses, key statements, and key quotes. The results of the validation process can be found in Sect. 5. It should be noted that the product roadmap transformation approach presented in this paper is to be seen as the first version. This means that it will be refined based on practitioners' feedback (see Sect. 5) and evaluated in practice through further research.

4 Product Roadmap Transformation Approach

In the following, the product roadmap transformation approach that emerged from the expert workshops is outlined. The aim of the product roadmap transformation approach is to provide guidance and direction on what measures a company should take to adapt their currently applied product roadmapping practice to a dynamic and uncertain market environment. The product roadmap transformation approach is an extension of the DEEP model and consists of three parts: 1) a process that proposes steps in order to transform the currently applied product roadmapping practices to a dynamic and uncertain market environment, 2) recommendations on how to proceed in order to select a dimension in the DEEP model to be improved and 3) two mapping tables that provide the user of the transformation approach with measures that lead to an improvement of the previously selected dimension. Each of these parts is described in the following.

4.1 Process for the Product Roadmap Transformation

As mentioned above, the prerequisite for applying the transformation approach is to assess current roadmapping practices using the DEEP assessment model. As a result of applying the DEEP model, the user receives the overall product roadmap maturity level of their currently applied product roadmapping practice as well as a score for each dimension. In order to achieve a higher score in the DEEP model we propose a process to transform the product roadmap to the requirements of a dynamic and uncertain market environment. This means that the (often traditional) product roadmapping practices currently applied will be replaced by practices suitable for creating and operating a product roadmap in a dynamic and uncertain market environment. This process was built on the well-known principles of the Deming cycle for continuous improvement of processes and products and includes the individual steps "evaluate/analyse", "design", "realize", "operate" in an iterative way. The application of the whole process will take 4 to 12 weeks according to the experiences of the authors. The steps of the product roadmap transformation process are described in the following.

Analyze: Based on the results of the DEEP model, the first step of the product roadmap transformation process is to analyze which dimension of the DEEP model promises the most benefit when improved. It should be noted that the lowest-rated dimension does not necessarily have to be the highest priority for improvement. The reason for this is that this decision may also depend on the respective company context (e.g., market, industry), the company's goals, and the position of the person who is to plan and implement the improvements (e.g., product owner, member of the management team, head of product management).

Set Goals and Choose Measure: The phase "set goals and choose measure" includes the definition of a clear improvement objective as well as corresponding measures that contribute to the achievement of the defined objective. An example of an objective could be to improve the dimension "extent of alignment" from level 2 to level 4 by establishing a process that fosters alignment. Conceivable measures in this context could be 1) the development of a common product vision by conducting workshops with various stakeholders, 2) the review of this product vision by conducting customer interviews, and 3) the consolidation of the content of all existing and loosely coupled product roadmaps based on the previously created product vision. In order to define suitable measures for the set objective, the product roadmap transformation approach provides appropriate guidelines. With the help of two mapping tables (see detailed description below), measures can be identified that contribute to the improvement of the respective dimension. The transformation approach aims to rely as much as possible on existing empirical evidence. Care should be taken to define appropriate key results for each measure to be delivered at the end of the iteration. This helps to analyze to what extent the defined objective has been achieved.

Execute: This phase aims to implement the improvement actions identified in the previous phase as well as analyze their impact on the roadmapping process. In order to implement the identified measures, the authors suggest using an iterative process including the following steps: 1) plan (the preparation for the execution of the identified measures), 2) implementation (the conduction of the identified measures), 3) review (the analysis of the impact of the conducted measures) and 4) retrospective (i.e., the reflection of the approach, for instance with workshops or interviews). Example questions for a retrospective could be: what went well, what did not go so well, what actions need to be taken to improve the approach of improving the roadmapping practice? (Fig. 1)

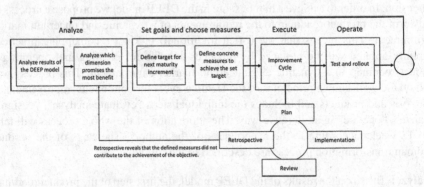

Fig. 1. Process of the product roadmap transformation

In the case that failures occur (e.g., the review or retrospective reveals that the defined measures did not contribute to the achievement of the objective) the authors recommend returning to the phase "analyze". The reason for this suggestion is that taking into consideration the learnings gained during the conduction of the process as well as changes in the frame conditions that have occurred during the time might lead to different decisions regarding which dimension should be in focus and which measures will most likely support them.

4.2 Procedure for Analyzing Which Dimension Promises the Most Benefit

An important step of the product roadmap transformation approach is to identify those dimensions that are most promising for improvement. This is done in the sub-step ("Analyse which dimension promises the most benefit for improvement) in the product roadmap transformation process described above (see Fig. 2). In the case that the assessment with the DEEP model results in the overall maturity levels 3, 4, or 5 (i.e., the respective level that a company has reached after summing up the points of the nine dimension), the authors recommend selecting one of the following dimensions: 1) roadmap items, 2) roadmap detailing, 3) product discovery, 4) confidence, 5) ownership, 6) responsibility, 7) extent of alignment or 8) prioritization. In contrast, if a company is on an overall maturity level 1 or 2, the authors suggest disregarding the two dimensions "prioritization" and "extent of alignment" (see Fig. 2). The reason why the dimension "prioritization" got excluded is that an essential success factor for an effective and efficient prioritization process for a dynamic and uncertain market environment is to understand the value that should be delivered to the customer and the business. If a user of the DEEP model selects a stage that considers the factor customer value (independent of the dimension) this leads to an overall maturity of level 3 or higher. Consequently, a company at level 1 or 2 does not include the customer value (which is crucial for the prioritization) in the roadmapping process and thus an improvement of the dimension prioritization within these levels is not advisable. The reason for excluding the dimension "extent of alignment" is that the product roadmap should be in a sufficiently mature state so that the stakeholders are able to align their activities with the roadmap. Therefore, the dimension alignment should not be considered until the product roadmap has reached a higher level of maturity.

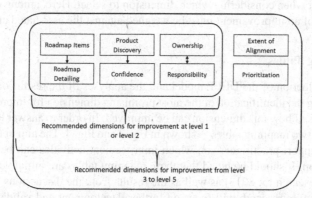

Fig. 2. Selection of the most beneficial dimension of the DEEP Model for improvement

Based on this pre-selection, the product roadmap transformation approach provides the following criteria as recommendations for the final determination of the dimensions to be improved:

- **Roadmap items and detailing of the roadmap:** The authors recommend considering improving the dimension "roadmap items" before improving the dimension "adequacy of item detailing based on the timeline (roadmap detailing)". The reason for this is that the usage of roadmap items of different granularity (such as products, themes, outcomes, epics) is likely to lead to a correlation between the timeline and the level of detailing of the roadmap items. It should be noted that ideally, the short-term planning consists only of roadmap items with high confidence.

- **Product discovery and confidence:** The authors recommend considering improving the dimension "product discovery" before improving the dimension "confidence". "Product discovery" is the ability of a company to identify and validate products or features before implementation. Examples of this are conducting customer interviews, customer focus groups or rapid prototyping. The relationship of the dimensions "product discovery" and "confidence" can be explained in the following way: the conduction of product discovery activities aims at reducing the uncertainty to a level that allows starting building a solution that provides value for the customers and/or the business. This includes that there is high confidence that the planned solutions will have a high impact on the customer and/or business goals. Therefore, conducting product discovery activities is likely to contribute to achieving confidence.

- **Ownership and responsibility:** The dimensions "ownership" and "responsibility" should be considered together. The dimension "ownership" describes who owns the roadmap (i.e., signs off and approves the roadmap), while the dimension "responsibility" answers the question of "who is responsible for defining the roadmap items and conducting the roadmapping process.

- **Role and authority of the "change agents":** The role and authority of those who are responsible for the transformation of the product roadmapping practice in an organization must be considered. The extent to which improvement is promising and the extent to which improvement can be influenced must be weighed here.

- **Company context and culture:** The corporate context and culture must also be taken into account when considering which dimension to select. Here, among other things, the impact of an improvement must be weighed against the associated effort.

4.3 Mapping Tables

After the conduction of the DEEP model and the analyses of the results of this assessment including the identification of the most promising dimension for improvement, the question arises of how this dimension can be improved. In order to answer this question, we developed two mapping tables as shown in Fig. 3 and Fig. 4. The aim of this mapping tables is to support practitioners on which improvement activities can be selected for each dimension. It should be noted that these mapping tables are initial versions based on previous research [5, 8, 13] as well as the results from the discussions in the expert workshops. Future research will focus on further development and validation of these mapping tables.

Goal Opportunity Map: The "Goal-Opportunity Map", as shown in Fig. 3, provides recommendations on how to improve a dimension of the DEEP model. For this purpose, the y-axis shows the dimensions of the DEEP model. In general, the improvement of a dimension of the DEEP model can be achieved by creating artifacts, implementing processes, or building capabilities that are essential for the operation in a dynamic and uncertain market environment but are still missing in the current product roadmapping process. Currently, the initial version of the "Goal-Opportunity Map" only lists artifacts (product vision, outcomes, ideas, hypotheses, and validated learnings) on the x-axis that are crucial for a successful product roadmapping in a dynamic and uncertain market environment. The artifacts were identified in the expert workshops.

Application of the Goal-Opportunity Map: The user can apply the "Goal-Opportunity Map" (see Fig. 3) by entering the previously identified dimension (see y-axis) to obtain an artifact (see x-axis) that is needed to improve the corresponding dimension. This is marked in Fig. 3 by the crosses that connect the dimensions and the artifacts. For example, the dimension "roadmap items" can be improved by developing the artifact product vision, while for the improvement of the dimension "product discovery" the formulation of hypotheses can lead to an improvement. Note that the "responsibility" and "ownership" dimensions have been omitted from this first version of the Goal-Opportunity Map, as they cannot be significantly improved by artifact generation. The reason for this is that the improvement of these dimensions depends very much on organizational aspects (such as the culture of the company) and less on the creation of artifacts. Therefore, the authors recommend using the assessment with the DEEP model as an eye-opener to discuss responsibility and ownership of the product roadmap with management (the decision of who is responsible and owns the product roadmap can usually only be changed by management). The application of the "Goal-Opportunity Map" does not provide an answer to the question of what activity must be performed to develop the artifacts on the y-axis. In order to answer this question, we developed a second map called Goal-Activity Map that is described in the following.

Dimension / Artifact	Product vision	Outcomes	Solution Ideas	Hypotheses	Validated Learnings
Roadmap items	X	X			X
Roadmap Detailing		X	X		
Product Discovery			X	X	X
Confidence			X	X	X
Prioritization	X	X			X
Alignment	X	X			

Fig. 3. Goal-Opportunity Map (excerpt)

Goal-Activity Map: The purpose of the "Goal-Activity Map" (see Fig. 4) is to propose concrete measures to develop the previously identified artifacts through the "Goal-Opportunity Map". For example, the creation of a product vision can be created by conducting a product vision workshop. Building prototypes or conducting one or more experiments can help to create validated learnings (e.g., results from experiments, insights).

Measure / Artifact	Product vision	Outcomes	Solution Ideas	Hypotheses	Validated Learnings
Product Vision Workshop	X				
Value Model		X			
Customer Interviews			X	X	
Prototyping				X	X
Experimentation					X

Fig. 4. Goal-Activity Map (excerpt)

The maps presented here are currently being completed as case studies in industry are conducted. The aim is to ensure that the recommendations contained in the tables are based on empirical experience and can be adapted to different contexts.

5 Perception of Practitioners

This section outlines the practitioner's perception of our approach including the feedback gathered during the interviews. As our proposed approach for adapting the product roadmap practice to a dynamic and uncertain market environment starts with the assessment of the currently applied product roadmapping practices, the DEEP model was also provided to the participants. This means that the practitioners first conducted a self-assessment using the DEEP model, followed by the application of the procedure to identify the most beneficial dimension for improvement as well as the use of the mapping tables to obtain suitable measures to improve the previously identified dimension.

Overall, our developed approach was perceived as comprehensible and applicable. For example, one participant mentioned: *"In my opinion, the whole approach is well structured and provides useful insights to adapt the currently applied product roadmapping practices." (product manager)* In particular, the focus of the approach on customer value was considered useful by the participants. One participant mentioned: *"What I particularly like about the model is that it addresses customer value. In our company, we don't think much about why a feature is being developed. I mean it is not always clearly understood what value the features deliver to the customer and how it contributes to our goals. Therefore, I think the focus on customer value is very useful." (Head of Product Management)* The start of the approach with an assessment of the currently applied product roadmapping practices was well received. In this context, one participant mentioned: *"In my opinion, it makes absolute sense to start the transformation process with an assessment of the company's current approach to product roadmapping. This enables to identify weaknesses in the current product roadmapping approach and communicate them clearly. Therefore, the assessment provides a good basis for further discussions, for example with the management." (Product Owner)* Another participant added: *"In our company, many people are not satisfied with the current product roadmapping approach. However, we struggle to identify a starting point for adapting the product roadmapping practices to a dynamic and uncertain market environment. Here, the discussions go round and round in circles and lead nowhere. Therefore, the DEEP model offers us a systematic way to determine the optimal starting point for the adaption of our product roadmap (Head of Product Management).* Moreover, the feedback of the participants provided comments for the improvement of specific dimensions of the DEEP model. Regarding the dimension "roadmap items", one participant did not understand the meaning of the used terms in the description of stage four. One participant asked: *"What is the difference between topics and themes?" (Software Engineer)* One participant pointed out that the term product vision should not be part of the dimension "roadmap items". *"In my opinion, a product vision is important for the development of a product strategy, but it is not an item on the product roadmap. Nevertheless, the product vision is important for a successful product roadmapping. For this reason, I would suggest separating the product vision into its own dimension." (Product Owner).* Furthermore, one participant indicates that an honest assessment through the DEEP model is the basis for the success of the subsequent procedure. *"In my view, the results of the DEEP model have a significant influence on the further process. This means that if the information in the DEEP model is incorrect, the subsequent steps will also be incorrectly defined. For this reason, I would invest as much capacity as possible to ensure that the DEEP Model has been applied truthfully. In other words, I would fill out the model with at least 10 participants from different departments and discuss deviations with all participants in a meeting." (Product Owner).*

Regarding the product roadmap transformation process, the process to select the most beneficial dimension for improvement, and the two mapping tables, the interviews showed that each participant understood how to apply them. Regarding the product roadmap transformation process one participant stated: *"In my opinion, the structure and functionality of the process were clear and understandable." (CEO)* Another participant mentioned: *"From the agile world and Scrum, the general structure of the process is familiar. Therefore, I had no problems understanding the application of the process." (Software Engineer)* Nevertheless, the interviews revealed some potential for the improvement of the product roadmap transformation process. In this context, two participants mentioned missing information when a process step was not fulfilled. *In the process I lack clear instructions on how to act if one or more measures do not contribute to the achievement of the defined goals. Should I first review the goal or keep the goal and define new measures?" (Product Manager)* In this context, *"it would be nice if the process would provide recommendations." (Product Manager)* Another participant commented: *"Let's assume that the improvement circle has been completed and the review and retrospective did not reveal any negative findings. But during the test phase in the phase "operate", I gain new insights that also include negative findings. Here, the process does not give any information about how I should behave. Would it make more sense to define new measures or start from the analysis?" (Product Owner)* Regarding the process we developed to select the most promising dimension for improvement, there was no ambiguity for the participants. In detail, each participant understood that in order to determine the most promising dimension a differentiation is made between levels 1 and 2 as well as levels 3, 4, and 5. The explanation why the two dimensions "prioritization" and "extent of alignment" should only be considered from level 3 onwards was also comprehensible to the participants. Finally, the structure and application of the two mapping tables did not pose any challenge to most participants. One participant mentioned: *"After I had conceptually identified a dimension that should be improved, I understood that this is the input for the first mapping table [i.e., the Goal-Opportunity*

Map]. Subsequently, I was able to determine without ambiguity the measure that is rec-ommended to improve the dimension I had chosen." (Head of Product Management) One participant had problems interpreting the crosses within the two mapping tables. *"When I first considered the mapping tables, it wasn't clear to me whether the crosses were a default or just an example. However, when I took a closer look at the structure and content of the mapping tables, I realized how it was meant." (Software Engineer)* Finally, three participants noted that while the proposed measures in the Goal-Activity Map are useful, they would like to have more measures to choose from. One participant mentioned: *"In my view, the measures in the second table are helpful. Nevertheless, I would like to see a wider choice for the creation of each artifact." (Product Manager)* Another participant adds: *"I would like to see more methods in the second table [i.e., the Goal Activity Map] that are less known within product management." (Product Manager).*

6   Threats to Validity

We use the framework according to Yin [14] as the basis for the discussion of the validity and trustworthiness of our study. Internal validity is not discussed with respect to the interviews since causal relationships were not examined in the study at hand. Since our study consists of developing the product roadmap transformation approach and conducting interviews, we describe the threats of validity according to these two parts.

6.1   Threats to Validity of the Development of the Transformation Approach

Construct Validity: A threat to the construct validity is that the participants in the expert workshops misunderstood the aim of developing the product roadmap transformation approach. For this reason, the goal and purpose of the expert workshop were explained to the participants in advance. In addition, technical terms were defined within the expert workshops. **Internal validity:** The expert opinions used to create the model may be incorrect or valid only in a context-specific manner. For this reason, several experts were consulted. **External validity:** The transformation approach was developed with the support of three practitioners operating in the software-intensive business. This limits the scope of the application of the transformation approach to companies that operating in such environments. **Reliability:** The reliability was supported by conducting the expert workshops in a systematic and repeatable manner involving two researchers and three practitioners. Therefore, a replication of the expert workshops and a reduction of researcher bias is supported.

6.2   Threats to Validity of the Interviews with Eleven Practitioners

Construct Validity: Similar to the expert workshops, the goal and purpose of the interviews were explained to the interviewees prior to the interviews. In addition, the way of data collection through interviews allowed for asking clarifying questions and avoiding misunderstandings. **External validity:** The external validity is restricted due to the limited number of participants and the fact that each participant is employed in a German company. Thus, the results are not directly transferable to other industry sectors. However, an analytical generalization may be possible for similar contexts. **Reliability:** The reported results are based on the personal perceptions of each participant. The participants may have provided answers that do not fully reflect the reality of their companies. This threat is mitigated by the fact that the participants had no apparent incentive to polish the truth. In addition, the researchers contacted the interviewees in case of any ambiguities or questions.

7 Summary and Future Work

In this study, the authors presented the first version of a product roadmap transformation approach. In addition, practitioners' perceptions of the approach were gathered by asking eleven practitioners to apply the approach in their respective company context. Afterwards, interviews with each participant have been conducted to gain feedback on the product roadmap transformation approach. Overall, the product roadmap transformation approach was perceived as comprehensible, useful, and applicable by the practitioners. Nevertheless, we identified potential for improvements, such as a clearer presentation of the steps of the product roadmap transformation process and the need for more content in the mapping tables. Practitioners can use the DEEP model in order to identify their current status of product roadmapping. Our approach to product roadmap transformation presented in this paper provides practitioners with a guide to identify improvement potentials of currently applied product roadmapping practices. This means identifying those parts of the currently applied roadmapping process that are not appropriate in the context of a dynamic and uncertain market environment. Based on this, practitioners can use our approach to systematically implement measures that will lead to an improvement in their product roadmapping. Identifying appropriate measures for this improvement can be done using the mapping tables we have developed. Future work is to refine and test the product roadmap transformation approach based on the feedback and perceptions we gathered with the interviews. In addition, we plan to incorporate further empirical findings on product roadmapping practices into the approach. This approach promises to help practitioners and companies to successfully manage the transfers to dealing with a more dynamic environment with many uncertainties by helping them change their roadmapping practices. In addition, the developed approach and its applications will indicate to researchers where research is needed, especially where empirical evidence is still lacking.

Appendix A. DEEP Product Roadmap Self-assessment Tool

PRODUCT ROADMAP MATURITY ASSESSMENT

DEEP Version 1.1

ROADMAP DETAILING
How adequate is your roadmap detailed with respect to the timeline?

1	3	8	15	20
Next steps are planned ad-hoc and there is only short-term planning	All tasks are planned and worked out in detail for short-, mid- and long-term	There is some correlation between time and level of detail but the detailing of the items is not done systematically	There is a clear correlation between time and level of detail. Timelier tasks are more detailed.	Short-term items are detailed, prioritized, estimated and validated. Mid-term items are under validation or being discovered. The long-term timeframe contains themes.

ROADMAP ITEMS
Which items are on your product roadmap?

1	3	10	12	20
Mainly products	Mainly products, features	Mainly business goals, products, features	Mainly customer and business goals, products, features and for the long-term timeframe topics (e.g., smart home)	Mainly product vision, customer and business goals, products, features and for the long-term timeframe themes (i.e., high-level customer needs)

RELIABILITY
How often do you adjust your product roadmap?

1	3	10	10	16
Permanent ad-hoc adjustments	Frequent ad-hoc adjustments	Mainly in regular review cycles (e.g., every 3 months)	Adjustments are mainly done reactively on demand.	Adjustments are mainly done proactively,

CONFIDENCE
How confident are you that the roadmap items have the expected impacts on goals?

1	4	7	10	14
The impacts are not considered.	The impacts are mainly estimated by experts.	The impacts are mainly determined based on data from the past (e.g., statistics)1	The impacts are partly validated.	The impacts are systematically validated.

DISCOVERY
How do you conduct product discovery?

1	2	4	8	10
No discovery activities. Typically a manager is defining the roadmap items.	Product roadmap items are mainly defined based on expert knowledge.	Product roadmap items are mainly defined based on customer requests.	Several discovery activities are conducted (e.g., user research) but they are not or only loosely integrated with delivery activities.	Close integration of discovery and delivery activities

PRIORITIZATION
How do you prioritize items?

1	2	3	3	8
First in, first out	Opinions determine priority.	Prioritization is based on the capability to deliver (e.g., low hanging fruits).	Prioritization is based on short-term benefit (e.g., shareholder value).	Prioritization is done with an established process and focuses on delivering value to customers and the business.

EXTENT OF ALIGNMENT
How do your align stakeholders?

1	1	2	3	6
No one or only one stakeholder such as high-level management has a product roadmap that is not communicated to others.	Several loosely connected product roadmaps for internal stakeholders exist.	Several loosely connected product roadmaps for internal and external stakeholders exist.	One central product roadmap exists for different internal and external stakeholders.	One central product roadmap exists that allows to derive different representations for different stakeholders. A process for achieving alignment is in place.

RESPONSIBILITY
Who is responsible for placing items on the roadmap?

1	2	2	3	3
Tools are used to decide if items are placed on the roadmap (e.g., decision matrix).	Management	Specific roles (e.g., portfolio manager)	Product management	Product management with cross-functional product teams in liaison with key stakeholders

OWNERSHIP
Who owns the product roadmap and is accountable?

1	2	3	4	3
No owner defined	Managers	Ownership is shared between multiple roles	Strategy or portfolio planning	Product management with cross-functional product teams

MATURITY
Please sum up the number of points for the fields you selected.

Total points: [ ]

Maturity level:	1	2	3	4	5
Score:	9 – 18 pts	10 – 30 pts	31 – 57 pts	58 – 83 pts	84 – 100 pts
Recommendation:	Complete reset of roadmapping practices		Incremental improvement of roadmapping practices		

CREATED BY: Jürgen Münch, Stefan Trieflinger, Dominic Lang

References

1. Kostoff, R.N., Schaller, R.: Science and technology roadmaps. IEEE Trans. Eng. Manag. **48**(2), 132–143 (2001)
2. Kameoka, A., Kuwahara, T., Li, M.: Integrated strategy development: an integrated roadmapping approach. In: PICMET 2003: Portland International Conference on Management of Engineering and Technology Management for Reshaping the World, pp. 370–379. Portland, OR, USA (2003)
3. Phaal, R., Farrukh, J.P.C., Probert, R.: Characterization of technology roadmaps: purpose and format. In: Portland International Conference on Management of Engineering and Technology. Proceedings, vol. 1: Book of Summaries (IEEE Cat. No. 01CH37199), pp. 367–374. IEEE (2001)
4. Lombardo, C.T., McCarthy, B., Ryan, E., Conners, M.: Product Roadmaps Relaunched - How to Set Direction While Embracing Uncertainty. O'Reilly Media, Inc., Gravenstein Highway North, Sebastopol, CA, USA (2017)
5. Trieflinger, S., Münch, J., Bogazköy, E., Eißöer, P., Schneider, J., Roling, B.: Product roadmap alignment – achieving the vision together: a grey literature review. In: Paasivaara, M., Kruchten, P. (eds.) Agile Processes in Software Engineering and Extreme Programming – Workshops. XP 2020. Lecture Notes in Business Information Processing, vol. 396, pp. 50–57. Springer, Cham (2020). https://doi.org/10.1007/978-3-030-58858-8_6
6. Münch, J., Trieflinger, S., Lang, D.: Why feature based roadmaps fail in rapidly changing markets: a qualitative survey. In: International Workshop on Software-intensive Business: Start-ups, Ecosystems and Platforms, pp. 202–218. CEUR-WS (2018)
7. Münch, J., Trieflinger, S., Lang, D.: What's hot in product roadmapping? Key practices and success factors. In: Franch, X., Männistö, T., Martínez-Fernández, S. (eds.) Product-Focused Software Process Improvement. PROFES 2019. LNCS, vol. 11915, pp. 401–417. Springer, Cham (2019). https://doi.org/10.1007/978-3-030-35333-9_29
8. Münch, J., Trieflinger, S., Bogazköy, E., Roling, B., Eißler, P.: Product roadmap formats for an uncertain future: a grey literature review. In: Euromicro Conference on Software Engineering and Advanced Applications (SEAA2020), pp. 284–291. IEEE (2020)
9. Münch, J., Trieflinger, S., Lang, D.: DEEP: the product roadmap maturity model: a method for assessing the product roadmapping capabilities of organizations. In: Proceedings of International Workshop on Software-Intensive Business: Start-ups, Platforms, and Ecosystems (SiBW2019), pp. 19–24. Conference Publishing Consulting, Passau (2019)
10. Münch, J., Trieflinger, S., Lang, D.: The product roadmap maturity model DEEP: validation of a method for assessing the product roadmap capabilities of organizations. In: Hyrynsalmi, S., Suoranta, M., Nguyen-Duc, A., Tyrväinen, P., Abrahamsson, P. (eds.) ICSOB 2019. LNBIP, vol. 370, pp. 97–113. Springer, Cham (2019). https://doi.org/10.1007/978-3-030-33742-1_9
11. Münch, J., Trieflinger, S., Lang, D.: Product roadmap -from vision to reality: a systematic literature review. In: Proceedings of the International Conference on Engineering, Technology and Innovation (ICE). IEEE (2019)
12. SAFe: SAFe Implementation Roadmap. https://www.scaledagileframework.com/implementation-roadmap/. Accessed 5 Oct 2021
13. Trieflinger, S., Münch, J., Knoop, V.: Facing the challenges with product roadmaps in uncertain markets: experience from industry. In: Proceedings of the International Conference on Engineering, Technology and Innovation (ICE), pp. 1–8. IEEE (2021)
14. Yin, R.K.: Case Study Research: Design and Methods, 5th edn. SAGE Publications Inc., London (2014)

Introducing Traceability in GitHub for Medical Software Development

Vlad Stirbu[1]([✉]) and Tommi Mikkonen[2,3]

[1] CompliancePal, Tampere, Finland
vlad.stirbu@compliancepal.eu
[2] University of Helsinki, Helsinki, Finland
[3] University of Jyväskylä, Jyväskylä, Finland
tommi.mikkonen@helsinki.fi, tommi.j.mikkonen@jyu.fi

Abstract. Assuring traceability from requirements to implementation is a key element when developing safety critical software systems. Traditionally, this traceability is ensured by a waterfall-like process, where phases follow each other, and tracing between different phases can be managed. However, new software development paradigms, such as continuous software engineering and DevOps, which encourage a steady stream of new features, committed by developers in a seemingly uncontrolled fashion in terms of former phasing, challenge this view. In this paper, we introduce our approach that adds traceability capabilities to GitHub, so that the developers can act like they normally do in GitHub context but produce the documentation needed by the regulatory purposes in the process.

Keywords: Traceability · Regulated software · Continuous software engineering · DevOps · GitHub

1 Introduction

Assuring traceability from requirements to implementation is a key element when developing safety critical software systems. Traditionally, this traceability is ensured by a waterfall-like process, where phases follow each other, and tracing between different phases can be managed with relative ease. To support this tracing, sophisticated software systems have been implemented, which take advantage of this phasing and help developers to focus on issues at hand in the current phase.

However, new software development paradigms, such as continuous software engineering [2] and DevOps [9], which encourage a steady stream of new features, committed by developers in a seemingly uncontrolled fashion in terms of former phasing, challenge this view. Instead of advancing in phases from specification to design to development in the same pace with all features, developers can select items from specification to work on, and eventually they commit new code back to the main codebase. This code is then automatically deployed to use, leaving

© Springer Nature Switzerland AG 2021
L. Ardito et al. (Eds.): PROFES 2021, LNCS 13126, pp. 152–164, 2021.
https://doi.org/10.1007/978-3-030-91452-3_10

virtually no trace between specification and the code, unless special actions are taken by the developers.

In this paper, we propose introducing traceability features to GitHub, the most popular site used by software developers. With these features, the developers can act like they normally do while developing software in GitHub context, but also produce the documentation needed by the regulators in the process. A prototype implementation has been built, following the ideas proposed in [11] as future work. The work has been carried out in medical context, but we trust that the same approach can be applied in other safety critical application domains covered by regulations. However, in the rest of this paper, we focus on the medical domain, as regulatory restrictions may vary across the domains.

The rest of this paper is structured as follows. In Sect. 2, we present the background and motivation of this work. In Sect. 3, we address the concept of design control, which is an essential part of designing software intensive medical products. In Sect. 4, we introduce the proposed approach, relying largely on GitHub concepts. In Sect. 5, we discuss our key observations and propose some directions for future work in connection with the proposed approach. Finally, we draw the conclusions in Sect. 6.

2 Background and Motivation

Medical device software development has unique needs. Its design, development, and manufacturing processes are strictly regulated. To comply with these regulations, there must be proper control mechanisms in place to ensure the end product's safety, reliability, and ability to meet user needs. These control mechanisms originate from the regulations' requirements, corresponding guidance documents, international standards, and national legislation. However, their plentiful existence is one of the reasons medical software is often considered a complex domain by developers.

In more detail, for every phase within the product lifecycle – design, development, manufacturing, risk management, maintenance, and post-market processes – certain standards must be followed for regulatory compliance. The set of applicable standards for software include general requirements for health software product safety (IEC 82304-1) [5], software life cycle process (IEC 62304 [3]), risk management process (ISO 14971 [7]), and usability engineering (IEC 62366-1 [4]). Furthermore, the manufacturers are expected to have a quality management system that must comply with further associated regulations – requirements of the Medical Device Quality Systems standard ISO 13485 [6] or its US counterpart, US FDA 21 CFR part 820. These standards form a minimum yet an overwhelming set of regulations to consider when developing medical devices with software.

To ensure compliance to the above standards, plan-driven methodologies have been the preferred way to develop products in regulated industries. Their cultural affinity with the language and format used by standards referred to above have made them the natural choice. However, the long feedback loops that characterize these methodologies are even longer in the high ceremony process required to comply with regulations. Furthermore, these practices are often somewhat distant from development activities that are used in non-regulated software development. Sometimes Application Lifecycle Management (ALM) tools, commonly used in regulated development, amplify this distance rather than helping to overcome it.

The situation becomes particularly complex when working with medical systems that consist of software only. The developers may have no experience at all in regulated activities, and, once the development activities are initiated, they should have adequate knowledge in regulation-related tasks as a part of the development. Although, the legally binding legislation texts and international standards describe the expected results, they do not describe how to achieve those results. Therefore, practical expertise is required to define the steps required to achieve the objectives [8]. To complicate matters further, many of the available ALM tools require that the developers invest time and effort to keep them in sync instead of relying on automation.

To deal with the situation, software developers – who are professionals in software development, not regulation – often resort to compliance over-engineering or adding extra effort to compliance-related activities to play it safe. This sometimes results in a view that compliance as the necessary evil that must be considered but has little practical relevance. Consequently, the compliance activities are often put aside while creating software and resurrected only when a new feature development task is completed. This resurrection often needs support from dedicated compliance personnel, which might not be fluent with the latest development methodologies.

The developers are not all wrong. The benefits of agile methods and continuous software engineering also apply to medical software. Still, using them in medical software development introduces the same concerns as with any technology – how to deal with legal and regulatory bindings in a new context [12]. This culminates in the context of continuous software development, where new releases can be made several times a day, but this is not leveraged because of regulatory constraints. Instead, the developers are stopped from deploying things until all the compliance and regulatory related processes are complete, breaking the natural flow of the development team.

To complicate matters further, regulatory affairs professionals have often practiced in environments where the medical devices always include hardware, and where they typically follow linear development model. Hence they might not have the skills and experience to operate in an agile software development environment, in particular when medical devices that only include software are considered.

3 Design Control in Software Intensive Medical Products

The concept of design control is a key element of a quality management system, which ensures that the manufacturer is able to deliver products that fulfill the user needs. The manufacturer is able to ensure, via systematic reviews, that

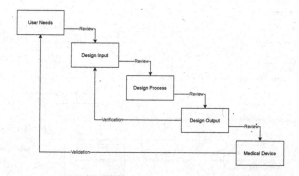

Fig. 1. Application of design controls to waterfall design process [1]

the identified user needs are transformed into actionable design inputs that can be used in a design process to obtain the design output, which serves as the medical device. Besides the reviews, the manufacturer needs to perform specific activities that ensures that the design output verifies the design input, and that the resulting medical device validates the user needs, as illustrated in Fig. 1.

For software intensive medical products the design control activities can be split into two layers, depicted in Fig. 2: the product and system development activities (IEC 82304 [5]), and the software development activities (IEC 62304 [3]). At the product level, the identified user needs are converted to system requirements that serve as design inputs for the software development process. During software development, the system requirements are transformed into high level software requirements that cover the software system and architectural concerns. Later on, the high level software requirements are further distilled into low level software requirements that serve as design input for implementation.

The resulting code, test cases and various other artifacts, such as architecture and detailed module design documentation, created during the software development activities, serve as the design outputs. The review of the artifacts and the automated test result provide an effective verification procedure at unit, integration and system level. Automated acceptance tests together with the result reports of clinical trials serve as the validation procedure. All these procedures ensure that the proper design controls have been applied during development, resulting in a medical product that meets the user needs.

The design control activities mentioned in IEC 82304 and IEC 62304 are intended to describe only the required activities and desired outcomes, but not the practical ways to achieve them. This approach gives the medical device manufacturers the leeway that allows them to customise their quality management system and software development methodology to reach the intended results. However, it is up to the manufacturers to ensure that the defined quality management system and methodology are compliant to the regulatory requirements.

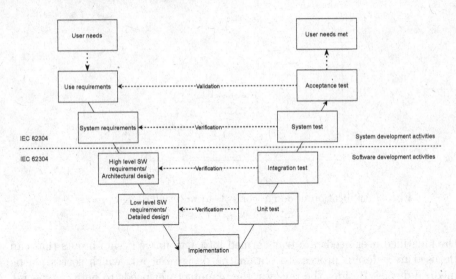

Fig. 2. System and software development design control activities

4 Proposed Approach

In the following, we describe our approach for implementing effective design controls and collect traceability artifacts using the GitHub native capabilities. First, we describe the information model used for implementing the traceability. We continue with an overview of the GitHub capabilities that serve as enablers of traceability infrastructure. Then, based on a prototype implementation, we describe how we mapped the information model into the GitHub context, and how we automated the traceability process using GitHub actions.

4.1 Traceability Information Model

To be effective for a software intensive product, the design controls and the traceability audit trail have to be applied to the concepts and tools that are used by the development team during their daily activities. In this context, a team developing medical product using an agile software development methodology and DevOps practices would be familiar with concepts like requirements that cover high level concepts such as user stories, or fine grained details of an implementation. They would be refining the user stories into implementation specifications during the iteration planning, would implement the requirements, and would integrate the product increment after the successful iteration review.

Our approach leverages this situation and builds an information model around *user needs*. The user needs are *refined* into system requirements, that are further *decomposed* into high level and low level software requirements. Each user need can validated by one or more acceptance *test case*. Similarly, a requirement can be verified using a relevant test suite at unit, integration or system level,

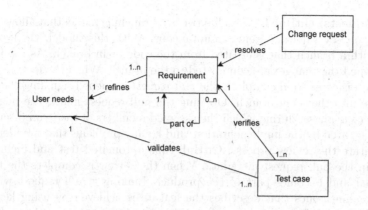

Fig. 3. Traceability information model

matching the corresponding requirement scope. The user needs, requirements and test cases serve as design inputs. The implementation of a requirement is modeled as a single *change request.* The change request bundles the code changes, configurations needed to build and run the iteration in scope, automated and manual test results, as well as design artifacts that describe the architecture and detailed implementation of a module. Together, the contents of the change request represents the design output. The change request becomes part of the product after it is verified in a formal review. The entities and the links between them convey in an effective manner the design control and the evidence in the form of an audit trail. The resulting traceability information model is depicted in Fig. 3.

4.2   Native GitHub Enablers

Over the years, GitHub has expanded their offerings with features beyond git. In the following, we provide a brief overview of the capabilities leveraged for design control and traceability in our prototype implementation.

Issues. Every GitHub hosted repository has an Issue section that enables teams to document and track the progress of requirements, specifications of work items, software bugs, feedback from users relevant for the scope of the software developed in the respective repository. An issue has a short title and a body that contains the detailed description using markdown[1]. The body can include *references* to other issues in the same or in a different repository. The references build semantic links between various issues, that can be traversed using the web user interface. Besides the title and the body that contains the description, the issue has associated metadata like *labels*, which allows categorization of issues, and *assignees*, which allows tracking who is performing the work.

---

[1] https://github.github.com/gfm/.

Pull Requests. GitHub flow is a lightweight branching model that allows teams to work on several work items simultaneous. With this model, the workflow starts with a branch that is created from the code main branch. As the feature is developed the changes are committed to the branch. When the feature implementation is considered complete, the *pull request* is opened signaling the intent to merge into the main branch. Opening the pull request marks the beginning of the *review* phase, during which the assigned members of the team discuss the changes created by the implementation, and fix any problems that are identified. To facilitate the review process, GitHub runs automated test and include the results in the pull request metadata. When the review is complete the feature is merged and becomes part of the product. Linking a pull request with the corresponding issues that describes the feature is achieved by using keywords followed by the reference in the pull request description, e.g. `resolves #10`.

Actions. GitHub makes easy to automate the software development workflows with *actions*. Although the actions are typically used for automating the building, testing and deploying steps of a software development process, they can be used for other purposes due to their ability to run custom jobs in response to any GitHub event, or even third party events. As such, actions are an effective way to extend the functionality of GitHub and enforce custom workflows, relieving team members from doing repetitive compliance related jobs that can be done better with automation.

4.3 Prototype Implementation

The prototype implementation relies on the GitHub native capabilities described above. The key features of the prototype are introduced below.

Mapping to GitHub Native Capabilities. As a first step in implementing the design controls and traceability audit trail, we need to map the information model to the capabilities available in GitHub. The use needs, the system and software requirements are implemented as issues labelled with the following labels: need, system requirement and software requirement. The issue creation in the correct format is facilitated by issue templates, which relieves the creator from the chores of ensuring that the issue structure (e.g. sections) and labels are fulfilled. The change requests are implemented with pull requests, while the structure of the pull request is enforced using the pull request template. The relations between issues are implemented using references. Finally, the test cases are described using Gherkin syntax[2] or Robot Framework[3]. The mapping is summarised in Table 1.

---

[2] https://cucumber.io/docs/gherkin/reference/.
[3] https://robotframework.org.

Table 1. Mapping traceability to GitHub native capabilities

Traceability	GitHub capability	Implementation
User need	Issue	User need template
System requirement	Issue	System requirement template
Software requirement	Issue	Software requirement template
Change request	Pull request	Pull request template
Relations	References	Reference to related concepts in issues and pull requests body
Test case	-	Gherkin or robot framework

```
## Issue section

Section description

---
partOf: #6

---
```

Listing 1: Issue body source with requirement relationship metadata

Conveying Parent Requirement Relationships. While GitHub is capable of encoding relationships between the issues, it lacks the ability to add semantics to the relationship. In our implementation, we decided to add the semantic information using the frontmatter, a YAML[4] formatted object that encodes issue

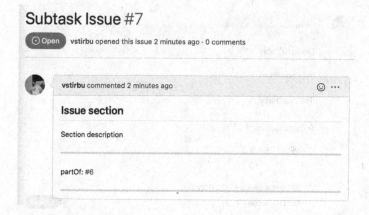

Fig. 4. GitHub rendering of an issue containing requirement relationship metadata

---

[4] https://yaml.org/spec/1.2/spec.html.

```
## Description

Issue description

## Traceability

### Related issues

- [ ] Subtask Issue (#7)
```

Listing 2: Issue body source with sub-requirements encoded as a checklist

metadata, typically located at the beginning or the end of the issue's description. The parent issue is indicated using `partOf` metadata. In the issue body presented in Listing 1, the parent of the issue is the issue #6 in the same repository. The issue is rendered by GitHub as seen in Fig. 4.

Visualizing Related Sub-requirements. To better visualize the issues that have been refined in sub-requirements, we are using the ability of GitHub to render markdown checklists. In Listing 2, we can see that the issue #7 defined earlier is listed as a related issue in its parent issue #6. We can also encode the status (e.g. open or closed), depending on the state of the corresponding checklist item. The GitHub rendering of this issue is depicted in Fig. 5.

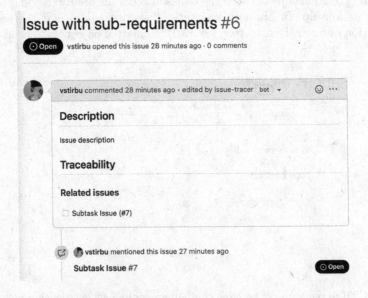

Fig. 5. GitHub rendering of an issue containing sub-requirements

```
@issue-7
Scenario: New test case
  Given initial state
  When the trigger
  Then resulting state
```

Listing 3: Test case described using Gherkin syntax

Linking Change Request with Requirements and Test Cases. GitHub has a built-in ability to link pull requests with issues using keywords such as `Resolves` followed by a reference to the corresponding issue. The capability goes further, as when an pull request is merged the linked issue is automatically closed. Our prototype implementation leverages this capability for building the traceability audit trail between the change request with the requirement resolved by it. In addition we construct relationships between the new test cases introduced by the pull request and the requirement. For example, the test case described in Listing 3, indicates that the new scenario tagged with `@issue-7` corresponds to requirement #7. The information is included an the *Traceability* section of the issue and rendered by GitHub as seen in Fig. 6.

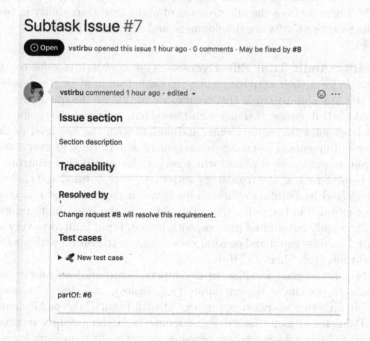

Fig. 6. GitHub rendering of an issue resolved by a change request and the associated test cases

Automation with GitHub Actions. GitHub user interface is able to render the descriptions of the issues, enabling the users to see the traceability information and traverse the link relations. However, crafting by hand the markdown according to the conventions used in this prototype implementation is laborious and prone to errors.

To overcome this obstacle, we have automated the process using GitHub actions. Our custom action reacts to *issue* and *pull_request* events as follows. When an issue event is triggered, the action inspects the body of the issue looking for parent relationship. If found, the action updates the parent issue with information about sub-requirements. Similarly, when the pull_request event is received, the action detects which issue the change resolves and updates the corresponding information about the test cases. When an issue is merged the status change is reflected in the issue by GitHub and out action updates the status in the parent requirement. As a result, the process of crafting the issue descriptions is performed mostly automated, leaving only two steps in which the user input is needed to indicate the parent relationship and the new issue.

5   Discussion

Based on the experiences with the prototype, we next consider two key goals of this work. These address the effectiveness of audit trail traceability in practice, and tooling issues of software development and regulatory activities.

Traceability Audit Trail Effectiveness. Our approach enables compliance officers to perform their activities using the same tool used by the development team. They are able to track the decomposition of the design inputs in form of labelled GitHub issues, starting with the system requirements, going through the high level software requirements, and ending with the low level or detailed software requirements. The change management is performed at every level during the pull request review phase, which serves also as a design control. During the pull request review, the regulatory activities are performed and the evidence trail is collected by building relationships between requirements, test cases and artifacts contained in the pull request, according to the traceability information model. The highly automated process, with human input limited to very specific procedures, enables rapid and continuous software certification without the need of special tools (e.g. Sherlock [10]).

Lightweight formats familiar to developers like markdown, serve as effective means to document design inputs (e.g. issues), and design outputs (e.g. software architecture and design augmented with PlantUML[5] or Mermaid[6] diagrams). Being text-based, these design documents can be properly version either directly into GitHub, as is the case of issues, or in the git repository for all other documents. Additionally, keeping the design documents close to the code and

---

[5] https://plantuml.com.
[6] https://mermaid-js.github.io/mermaid/.

performing the change management activities in a single step (e.g. pull request review) ensures that the documentation is properly maintained, following the software development pace.

Common Tooling for Software Development and Regulatory Activities. Traditionally, ALM tools address product lifecycle management, covering governance, development, and maintenance. These include management, software architecture, programming, testing, maintenance, change management, integration, project management, and release management. However, as already mentioned, these often require manual interventions from developers, and a waterfall-like approach favored by compliance officers is often prescribed in them as the advocated process. Hence, a divide between software developers and compliance officers emerges.

Distributed teams, sophisticated version management systems, and increasing use of real-time collaboration have given rise to the practice of integrated application lifecycle management, or integrated ALM, where all the tools and tools' users are synchronized with each other throughout the application development stages. The proposed tool falls to this category, building on these capabilities that are immediately available in GitHub and on an extensions that support tracing the artifacts needed for compliance reasons. This in essence integrates regulatory activities in the continuous software engineering pipeline. This in particular concerns pull requests, which are the way to introduce changes to software, but which can also be used as means to manage compliance with respect to changes in code.

The proposed implementation is at present only at prototype stage. However, although the approach looks rough comparing with the much more polished ALM tools, it has several benefits that can be associated with the use of state-of-the-art software engineering tools and associated ecosystems. These include (i) leveraging a large 3rd party DevOps tools ecosystem, which includes numerous beneficial tools and subsystems that are available either in open source or as hosted services; (ii) the solid GitHub APIs, which are used in numerous GitHub projects; and (iii) close integration with popular development environments such as Visual Studio Code[7].

Limitations and Future Work. The effective use of the proposed approach requires a level of familiarity with GitHub and related the DevOps ecosystem. Although this should be the case for experienced software-intensive organizations, traditional medical device manufacturers and compliance professionals may find it difficult to switch from an integrated document oriented compliance process to one where the documentation is managed as code and the authoring tools are not word processors or spreadsheet applications. Better authoring tools and simpler ways of navigating the GitHub user interface for non-programmers would simplify the adoption process and make this way of working more accessible.

---

[7] https://code.visualstudio.com.

6   Conclusions

Developing regulated software is often considered as an activity that is complicated by compliance related aspects, such as traceability and risk management. For many organizations, this has meant using waterfall-like development approaches, where the sequential phases help in managing traceability. However, such approach in essence eliminates the opportunity to use agile or continuous software engineering methods.

To improve the situation, in this paper we have described our approach that expands the GitHub functionality with traceability from requirements to implementation, a key element when developing safety critical software systems. Our prototype implementation demonstrates that GitHub serves as an effective design control mechanism, allowing regulatory professionals to conduct their regulatory activities alongside software developers.

Acknowledgements. The authors would like to thank Business Finland and the members of the AHMED (Agile and Holistic MEdical software Development) consortium for their contribution in preparing this paper.

References

1. FDA - Center for Devices and Radiological Health: Design Control Guidance for Medical Device Manufacturers (1997)
2. Fitzgerald, B., Stol, K.J.: Continuous software engineering: a roadmap and agenda. J. Syst. Softw. **123**, 176–189 (2017)
3. International Electrotechnical Commission: IEC 62304:2006/A1:2015. Medical device software - Software life-cycle processes (2015)
4. International Electrotechnical Commission: IEC 62366-1:2015. Medical devices - Part 1: Application of usability engineering to medical devices (2015)
5. International Electrotechnical Commission: IEC 82304-1:2016. Health software - Part 1: General requirements for product safety (2016)
6. International Organization for Standardization: ISO 13485:2016. Medical devices - Quality management systems - Requirements for regulatory purposes (2016)
7. International Organization for Standardization: ISO 14971:2019. Medical devices - Application of risk management to medical devices (2019)
8. Laukkarinen, T., Kuusinen, K., Mikkonen, T.: DevOps in regulated software development: case medical devices. In: 2017 IEEE/ACM 39th International Conference on Software Engineering: New Ideas and Emerging Technologies Results Track (ICSE-NIER), pp. 15–18. IEEE (2017)
9. Lwakatare, L.E., et al.: DevOps in practice: a multiple case study of five companies. Inf. Softw. Technol. **114**, 217–230 (2019)
10. Santos, J.C.S., Shokri, A., Mirakhorli, M.: Towards automated evidence generation for rapid and continuous software certification. In: 2020 IEEE International Symposium on Software Reliability Engineering Workshops (ISSREW), pp. 287–294 (2020)
11. Stirbu, V., Mikkonen, T.: CompliancePal: a tool for supporting practical agile and regulatory-compliant development of medical software. In: 2020 IEEE International Conference on Software Architecture Companion (ICSA-C), pp. 151–158. IEEE (2020)
12. Wagner, D.R.: The keepers of the gates: intellectual property, antitrust, and the regulatory implications of systems technology. Hastings LJ **51**, 1073 (1999)

Human Factors

A Preliminary Investigation on the Relationships Between Personality Traits and Team Climate in a Smart-Working Development Context

Rita Francese[1], Vincent Milione[1], Giuseppe Scanniello[2]([envelope]) [iD],
and Genoveffa Tortora[1]

[1] University of Salerno, Fisciano, Italy
{francese,tortora}@unisa.it, v.milione3@studenti.unisa.it
[2] University of Basilicata, Potenza, Italy
giuseppe.scanniello@unibas.it

Abstract. Developers collaborating with collective efforts in large-scale distributed software typically have different personalities that might play a central role in software development and in team climate. In this paper, we have investigated if personality traits are related to the perceived team climate of software developers (Computer Science master students) in a smart-working development context. In particular, we conducted a preliminary study with 53 master students of a Computer Science course conducting a project work during the Covid-19 pandemic. Participants were grouped into 19 distributed teams. We analyzed the correlation between personality traits and team climate factors and created a predictive model for Task Orientation using these correlations. Results suggest that the Extroversion personality trait (characteristic of social and easy-going people) is statistically significant. We also observed a (weak) positive correlation with considered team climate factors.

Keywords: Team climate · Personality trait · Distributed development · Smart-working · Empirical study · Covid-19

1 Introduction

Personality traits are responsible for the individual's preferences, opinions, attitudes, values, and behaviors and contribute in distinguishing each individual from the others. The Software Engineering (SE) research has been investigating the impact of personality on the quality and performance of a software project since 1960 [15,16,24]. Software project results are influenced by the work style of each team member who often has a different background [17]. Team members have to work together to accomplish a specific task, often while being face-to-face [14]. During the Covid-19 pandemic period, cooperation has been mainly conducted remotely, by using both asynchronous distributed development tools

© Springer Nature Switzerland AG 2021
L. Ardito et al. (Eds.): PROFES 2021, LNCS 13126, pp. 167–182, 2021.
https://doi.org/10.1007/978-3-030-91452-3_11

and synchronous video calls. Meetings have been regularly conducted to discuss the evolution of the project and to increase the collaboration among team members, thus enhancing *team climate*.[1] The Team Climate influences not only the personal relationships within the team and the team members' satisfaction, but it also affects the project result in terms of quality and performance.

In the literature, there is a growing interest in the team's climate, the individual's personality, and the relationships between productivity and team members' satisfaction [2,7,21,23]. Many studies are focused on how different kinds of team climate, such as for innovation or safety may derive specific results of the workgroup outcomes (*e.g.*, oriented toward innovativeness or accident avoidance). To obtain such a result, a shared team climate has to be perceived by the team members and measured in a reliable way [4]. Although the interest of the SE community on team's climate there is a lack of studies in the context of smartworking, *i.e.*, a work arrangement in which employees do not commute to a central place of work, such as an office building. As mentioned, such a kind of work has gained in popularity during the years in software projects and obtained a further boost during the Covid-19 pandemic.

In this paper, we present the results of a correlation study—conducted during the Covid-19 pandemic—aiming at improving our body of knowledge on the personality traits and the team climate relationships in a distributed smartworking development context when developers are Computer Science students. The participants in the study were 53 master students (graduate students) in Computer Science at the University of Salerno. They were grouped into 19 teams, each of them aiming at conducting a multi-platform project in distance fashion.

The main contributions of the research presented in this paper can be summarized as follows:

- the correlation between personality traits and team climate factors in a distributed smart-working context have been empirically analyzed from the point-of-view of Computer Science master students;
- a regression model for predicting Task Orientation from Extroversion has been defined.

The remainder of the paper is organized as follows. In Sect. 2, we present background and discuss related work. In Sect. 3, we present the adopted research methodology. Results of the study are reported in Sect. 4. The threats to validity and possible implications for our results are discussed in Sect. 5 and Sect. 6, respectively. We conclude the paper with final remarks and future direction for our research in Sect. 7.

2 Background

In this section, we first introduce the adopted personality and team climate models, then we discuss related work referring to the SE studies on the relationships between personality and team climate.

---

[1] Team climate refers to a shared perception among the team members of the team's work procedures, practices, and members' behaviors [25].

2.1   Big Five Model and Associated Instruments

Several models have been proposed to describe personality traits. In this paper, we adopt the *Big Five Model* [11], a well-known taxonomy of personality traits. It was originally proposed in 1961. The Big Five Model identifies 5 major personality traits described in a broad dimension.

- *Openness to experience* indicates how strong the individual's imagination, aesthetic sensitivity, and adventurousness are. High scores on this trait are normally interpreted as the individual being intellectual, creative, and curious; on the other hand, those who score low tend to be close-mind and conservative.
- *Conscientiousness* expresses an individual's achievement orientation and control over their impulses. Conscious individuals tend to be good and well-organized workers capable of planning and completing tasks perfectly and efficiently. Individuals with low scores in conscientiousness are typically impulsive and unorganized, less bound by rules.
- *Extroversion* indicates how individuals may be friendly, approachable, talkative, and active. Individuals who score high on this trait tend to be sociable, stimulated by others, and easy-going. Whereas low scores indicate the individual may be more reserved and solitary.
- *Agreeableness* represents how cooperative, trusting, or empathetic an individual may be. Agreeable individuals tend to be kind in nature, sympathetic, cooperative, and trust others more. Disagreeable individuals, instead, tend to be suspicious and antagonistic, uncompromising, or unconcerned with other individuals' needs.
- *Neuroticism* is the measure of the individual's emotional instability. Highly neurotic individuals tend more likely to be anxious and insecure. Less neurotic individuals tend to appear stable and calm.

For assessing personalty most SE studies (*e.g.*, [6,20]) adopted the freely available International Personality Item Pool (IPIP) [12], as it gives free sets of items and psychometric scales based on the Big Five Model framework. Among the many questionnaires based on IPIP, we selected IPIP-NEO-120. It is made up of 120 items. Each item is rated by the submitter using a Likert scale varying from 1 (highly inaccurate) to 5 (highly accurate).

2.2   Team Climate Research in Software Engineering

Team climate may be defined as team member's shared perceptions of the team's work procedures, practices, and member behaviours [1]. To work together effectively, it is very relevant to get a positive group climate based on personal relations [27]. The concept of team climate is complex and has been decomposed into different dimensions. The Team Climate Inventory (TCI) [25,26] aims at assessing the team climate perception. It is largely adopted in SE for assessing the team climate. It has been used for evaluating team performance [18], satisfaction of the team members [2] and software quality [1]. Team climate is commonly assessed by using the Team Climate Inventory (TCI), a questionnaire proposed by Anderson and West [4]. It is based on the following four factors:

- *Vision* shows how clear, attainable, and valued objectives are to the individual and across the team.
- *Participation Safety* measures the participation levels of members in decision-making processes and the psychological safety perceived when members would share new or improved methods.
- *Support for Innovation* measures how much the team supports the ideas of using new technologies so accepting the risks of using new and unfamiliar technologies.
- *Task Orientation* measures the team's commitment to achieving the highest performance in their work.

The most adopted variant consists of 38 questions and was proposed by Anderson and West [4] in 1998. A five-point Likert scale from 1 to 5 (from little extent to great extent) is adopted to evaluate each item. Each factor is then calculated by computing the average of all its related items.

2.3   Related Work

Many SE studies focus on team composition and team members' personalities, but only a few of them concern team climate. For example, Gomez and Acuna [13] conducted a quasi-experiment to assess whether developers' personality affects team climate. They measure personality traits with the NEO-FFI Test [9] and the TCI questionnaire. Participants were 105 Computer Science students. Results suggested that the Extroversion personality factor has an influence on software quality and no relation with team satisfaction.

Soomro *et al.* [22] conducted a survey with 36 IT employees concerning the relationship between personality traits, team climate, and performance. They adopted IPIP-NEO personality and TCI tests for assessing the personality traits and team climate perception, and the performance by following the approach proposed in [8]. Extroversion was significantly related to both team climate and team performance.

Soomro *et al.* [21] performed a Systematic Literature Review (SLR) on the research studies in SE investigating the relationships between personality traits and team climate and performances. Their results revealed that at that date of the execution of such SLR, there was no significant research on the relationships between personality and team climate.

Acuna *et al.* [2] investigated the effect of personality and team climate on product quality and satisfaction in software development teams. Results were aggregated from a twice replicated quasi-experiment and revealed that there exists a positive relationship between all four climate factors and satisfaction. Also, individuals with higher Agreeableness personality factor have the highest satisfaction levels, while both Extroversion personality and Participative Safety and Task Orientation climate perceptions are positively correlated to software product quality.

Shameem *et al.* [18] proposed a framework aiming at associating personality traits with team climate factors. The authors asserted that conscious and extroverted team members have a positive influence on the team climate and may get effective team performance. Only a discussion is conducted, without the support of empirical investigations.

Vishnubhotla *et al.* [23] studied the relationships between the five-factor model personality traits and the factors related to team climate within the context of Agile teams working in a Telecom company. Participants were 43 software professionals. Their results revealed that the Agreeableness personality trait has a significant positive relationship with the perceived level of team climate. The authors also defined regression models for predicting team climate factors from Agreeableness.

User studies in the context of (distributed) smart-working are lacking. We conducted the study presented in this paper to better understand personality-team climate relationships in a distributed smart-working development environment due to the current pandemic context. We also provided a linear regression model for predicting Task Orientation.

3   Study Design and Planning

3.1   Goal

Many software companies, in their software development process, use remote cooperation among team members, for example, both asynchronously by using distributed development tools and synchronous by video calls. This was why we were interested in studying the relationships between personality traits and team climate when members work in a smart-working context. Therefore, the goal of our study, using Goal-Question-Metric (GQM) [5], can be defined as follows:

> *Analyze* personality traits and team climate *for the purpose of* understanding their perception and correlation *with respect to* the development of multi-platform applications for smart devices *from the viewpoint of* the developer *in the context of* distributed smart-working development teams composed of Computer Science students.

3.2   Participants

The participants were 53 students of a master degree (*i.e.,* graduate) in Computer Science at the University of Salerno. Students were enrolled in the Enterprise Mobile Application Development (EMAD) course for the a.y. 2020/2021. This course was delivered in Italian Language. The students enrolled in the EMAD course were 23.06 years old on average ($\sigma = 1.24$), 3 were female (6%), and the remaining were male (94%). Students were grouped into 19 teams according to their preferences; 15 teams were composed of three members and 4 by two. All the students had web programming experience (average score of object-oriented programming, web programming, and database courses was higher than

24/30) and, before the EMAD course, they did not know React Native, NodeJS, and Firebase, namely the technologies presented in that course.

As a laboratory activity of the EMAD course, the students were asked to accomplish a software project in groups. Each course project consisted of the development of a multi-platform application for smart devices with both front-end and back-end. The teams were asked to develop the front-end by using React Native, while the back-end with NodeJS or serverless technology, like Firebase. We asked the participants to use Microsoft Teams for F2F meetings and Github for distributed version control and source code management. Although we did not impose any restriction on the communication language, the communication took place in Italian. The development lasted from the beginning of October 2020 to the end of February 2021. The participation in our study was voluntary and all the students of the EMAD course took part to it.

3.3   Data Collection

The course started on September 15th 2020. After one week, the lecture of the course (one of the authors) sent an email to each student asking if they would like to participate in our study. If she was willing to participate, she first filled in a consensus form, and then she filled in the IPIP-NEO-120 questionnaire. Both in the email and survey we stated the purposes of our research and assured students that their data would be used only for research purposes and treated anonymously. To alleviate any possible concerns, we guaranteed anonymity to each participant and assured that none other than members of the research group would have access to the data collected. All 53 students complied with these terms and submitted the first survey. Each survey was tagged with a unique id (such as M1, M2...). The participants had to fill in the IPIP-NEO-120 questionnaire by October 15th. All 53 students submitted the TCI questionnaire by February 15th 2021. Participants filled in a consensus form. Following the approach adopted by [23], the IPIP-NEO-120 answers of all members were entered by one of the authors into an online version of the IPIP-NEO questionnaire,[2] which compares the given responses with responses given by individuals of similar age and gender. These numerical scores are in percentile form. The individual reports give further information as it classifies the given scores as low, average, or high.

3.4   Data Analysis Procedure

We used the R statistical environment[3] to perform our data analysis according to the following steps:

---

[2] Dr. John A. Johnson, Professor of Psychology, Penn State University, Short Form for the IPIP-NEO (International Personality Item Pool Representation of the NEO PI-R®), https://bit.ly/3nHo8tK.

[3] https://cran.r-project.org.

- **Descriptive analysis.** We show the data distribution of the two question-naires by using boxplots. We also report descriptive statistics, *i.e.,* median, mean, and standard deviation, and Coefficient of Variation (CV). CV is a dimensionless measure defined as the ratio of the standard deviation and the mean. It represents the variability in relation to the mean of the population. It is useful to perform a relative comparison of two measurements with different units of measure.
- **Data Aggregation.** To analyze overall team view it is needed to aggregate the scores of individual subjects. The aggregation of individual data is only justified if there is consensus among team members, which must be measured using some form of inter-rater agreement. To this aim, generally, the ICC(1) index is computed. This requires that the ICC(1) index be over 0.20. ICC is based on the assumption that data are normally distributed.
- **Correlation analysis.** We decided to perform correlation analysis to mea-sure the relationships between personality traits and team climate factors. We planned to use the Pearson correlation test. To apply this kind of analysis, we verified the normality of data by using the Shapiro-Wilk test [19] on the TCI and personality trait scores by setting a 95% confidence interval ($\alpha = 0.05$). A p-value smaller than α allows us to reject the null hypothesis and to conclude that the distribution is not normal. In this case, we exploited the Spearman non-parametric test by fixing α equals to 0.05 as for all the other statistical tests used in our data analysis. Thus, to reject the null hypothesis–samples are uncorrelated) the $p - value$ must be less than 0.05. When either the Pearson correlation test or the Spearman non-parametric test allowed us to reject the null hypothesis that samples are uncorrelated, we further studied that significant correlation. As for the meaning of the correlation, we consider the interpretation provided in Table 1, *e.g.,* if the correlation value is in the interval $[0.20, 0.39]$ the correlation is then considered weak and positive.
- **Regression analysis.** By following the approach adopted by [23], we used linear regression for assessing whether some personality trait variables explain some team climate factors. Linear regression may be performed when specific requirements are held. Samples have to be normally distributed, check per-formed during the correlation analysis. The relationship between the inde-pendent and dependent variables to be linear. The linearity assumption may be tested by examining the scatter plots. We also verified the normality of the residual errors by using the Shapiro-Wilk normality test on the residuals, requiring $p - value \geq 0.05$. The absence of auto-correlation was verified by using the Durbin-Watson test, passed for results in the $[1.5, 2.5]$ range. The homoscedasticity in our residuals was tested with the Breusch-Pagan test, passing for $p - value \geq 0.05$.

4   Results

In this section, we present the results of our data analysis.

Table 1. Correlation Intervals

Correlation intervals	Strength of the correlation
0.00 to 0.19 (−0.19 to 0)	Very weak positive (negative)
0.20 to 0.39 (−0.39 to −0.20)	Weak positive (negative)
0.40 to 0.69 (−0.69 to −0.40)	Moderate positive (negative)
0.70 to 0.89 (−0.89 to −0.70)	Strong positive (negative)
0.90 to 1 (−1 to −0.90)	very Strong positive (negative)

4.1 Descriptive Analysis

In Table 2, we report the descriptive statistics to the answers to the IPIP-NEO questionnaire according to the five personality traits: Openness, Extroversion, Agreeableness, Conscientiousness, and Neuroticism. The answers to this questionnaire are graphically summarized by the boxplots shown in Fig. 1. In these boxplots, we also show three thresholds, so delimiting the scores for personality traits as: low, average, and high. For example, a score is average if it is in between 30 and 70. All the medians reported in Table 2 and shown in the boxes in Fig. 1 are in the average area and the highest median value is for Agreeableness (65). This is a relevant aspect for team working: it represents the tendency to be altruistic, kind, trustworthy, and cooperative. Also, Conscientiousness has a high median (61). This factor denotes that team members generally are careful and diligent. As for Neuroticism, which is a negative quality, the medial value is equal to 50. The lower median value can be observed for Openness, which means that team members tend to be less creative, imaginative, and adventurous.

Table 2. Distribution of personality traits' scores.

Personality trait	Mean	Median	Std. Dev.	CV
Openness	39.15	37	21.99	56%
Extroversion	52.43	50	24.35	37%
Agreeableness	60.92	65	26.08	43%
Conscientiousness	60.42	61	22.50	37%
Neuroticism	46.26	50	25.09	54%

In Table 2, we report also the values of the Coefficient of Variation (CV) for each personality trait. Openness is the personality trait with the greatest CV value (56%). This means that Openness has the biggest dispersion around the mean. Neuroticism has also a relatively high CV (54%). CV values less than 50% can be observed for the other traits. In addition, for Conscientiousness and Agreeableness high mean values can be observed. Therefore, we can safely assume that most of the participants are cooperative and kind, due to the high

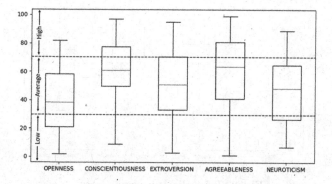

Fig. 1. Personality trait scores.

Agreeableness (average value is equal to 60.92) , and also well organized and determined, (average value for Conscientiousness is equal to 60.42).

The team climate score statistics are reported in Table 3, while we graphically summarize the distributions of the values for Vision, Participation Safety, Support for Innovation, and Task Orientation by the box-plots shown in Fig. 2. These boxplots show that the distributions are negatively skewed for Support for Innovation, Vision, and Participation Safety. As for Participation Safety, 50% of the scores is over 4.63 and CV = 14.75%. This denotes that the values are concentrated around the mean. All the distributions are characterized by a low dispersion around the mean and a few outliers can be observed for Vision and Participation Safety (Fig. 2). The medians of Vision and Participation Safety were amongst the highest. However, median scores for the other two traits can be considered high as well. Descriptive statistics suggest that most team members had a clear vision of the team objectives and were able to safely participate in the team decisions.

We also computed the Individual Perceived Team Climate (IPTC) [23]. A person's IPTC is computed by averaging his overall scores of the four team climate factors. We show in Fig. 3 the distribution of all the IPTC values in corresponding teams. We can observe that the Individual Perceived Team Climate scores of the teams is higher than 3, except for team 3, where one of the members scored 2.56.

Table 3. Distribution of team climate scores.

Team climate trait	Mean	Median	Std. Dev.	CV
Vision	4.12	4.36	0.72	17.39%
Participation Safety	4.38	4.63	0.65	14.75%
Support for Innovation	4.12	4.13	0,69	16.75%
Task Orientation	3.79	3.78	0.51	13.43%

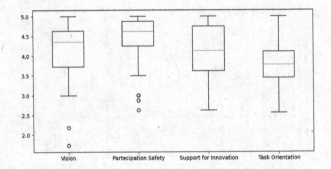

Fig. 2. Team climate overall scores.

4.2 Normality Test Results

The application of the Shapiro-Wilk test to the personality trait values revealed that only Extroversion ($p-value = 0.248$) was normally distributed, while Conscientiousness ($p-value = 0.041$), Agreeableness ($p-value = 0.032$), Neuroticism ($p-value = 0.014$) and Openness to Experience ($p-value = 0.020$) were not. In the case of team climate factors, only the values for Task Orientation ($p-value = 0.657$) were normally distributed.

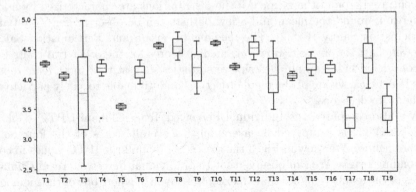

Fig. 3. IPTC team scores.

4.3 Correlation Analysis

In this section, we present the results of correlation analysis.

In Table 4, we show in bold the correlations having $p-value$ less than 0.05 (*i.e.*, statistically significant) for which the correlation—between Personality Traits and Perceived Team Climate—is significant and can be analyzed. On the basis of the results shown in Sect. 4.3, we used the Spearman non-parametric

Table 4. p-value correlation matrix for personality traits and team climate factors.

	Vision	Task orientation	Support for innovation	Participation safety
Extroversion	**0.029**	**0.001**	**0.016**	**0.00031**
Agreeableness	0.7	0.99	0.48	0.15
Conscientiousness	0.16	0.97	0.96	0.38
Neuroticism	0.21	0.28	0.26	0.16
Openness	0,71	0.72	0.37	0.94

test in all the cases with the only exception of Extroversion/Task Orientation, where we adopted the Pearson correlation test.

Concerning the correlation between Extroversion and Vision, the correlation result is $R = 0.3$. This denotes a weak positive correlation. This means that the increase in value of one of the variables generally corresponds to the increase of the other. Thus, extroverted individuals have in general a better clarity of the team objectives.

The correlation results for Extroversion and Task Orientation is depicted in Fig. 4. Also in this case, a (weak) positive correlation is shown ($R = 0.37$). This means that in general extroverted individuals are inclined to maximize the quality of task performance.

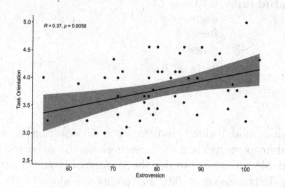

Fig. 4. Extroversion - task orientation.

Extroversion is also related to Support for Innovation by a (weak) significant positive correlation ($R = 0.33$). This means that extroverted individuals are also creative and promote new ideas.

Extroverted individuals seems also actively involved in group interactions with interpersonal and non-threatening relationships and favor a non-judgemental climate (Participation Safety) with $R = 0.48$. The correlation between Extroversion and Participation Safety can be considered moderate positive.

4.4   Regression Analysis

In this section, we study the contribution of Extroversion on Task Orientation, namely the only team climate factor that satisfied the normality assumption required to apply the linear regression analysis. In Table 5, we report the results of the test of the assumptions required to apply regression analysis. As shown, all the three assumptions are satisfied.

Table 5. Tests for validating regression assumptions.

Predictive model	Shapiro-Wilk	Durbin-Watson	Breush
Extroversion-Task Orientation	p-value = 0.6063	1.76439	0.8294

Table 6. Regression model description for predicting task orientation.

	Estimate	Stand. Error	t-value	p-value
Intercept	2.476705	0.461988	5.361	Signif level 0.00
Extroversion	0.016316	0.005671	2.877	Signif level 0.01
Residual Standard Error	0.4769 on 51 degrees of freedom			
R-squared	0.1396			
F-statistic	8.278 on 1 and 51 DF			Signif level 0.05

The regression model that predicts Task Orientation is summarized in Table 6. The intercept value is 2.48. It represents the expected value of Task Orientation variable when we consider the average of Extroversion computed on all the samples. Extroversion = 0.02 represents the slope of the line in Fig. 4. It means that when Extroversion increases by 1 the average score of Task Orientation increases by 0.02. R-squared is the percentage of the response variable variation that is explained by a linear model. In this case, R-squared is 13.96%. This means that 13.96% of Task Orientation is due to the Extroversion value. The percent error measures how close a value measured by the model is to a true value. It is given by the ratio between the residual standard error (0.477) and the expected value of Task Orientation variable (the intercept equal to 2.477), which is 19.25%. $p-values < 0.01$ for intercept and slope. This means that both individual variables are significant. Besides, $p-values < 0.05$ for F-statistic. We can conclude that R-squared is not equal to zero, and the correlation between the model and dependent variable is statistically significant.

5   Threats to Validity

In this section, we discuss the main threats that could affect the validity of the results of this study.

Internal Validity. Correlation studies prove associations, they do not demonstrate causation [3]. Therefore, this study can just prove that a correlation between some personality traits and team climate factors exists (as the defined research question asked). We also defined a regression model between a personality trait and a team climate factor. Also, the difference among the projects each team had to accomplish may be a threat that may influence the team climate.

Construct Validity. We considered a single variable for each construct studied in the study. Concerning social threats, we tried to prevent evaluation apprehension by informing participants that their data were anonymized and used in aggregated form. To mitigate the threat of violated assumptions of statistical tests, in case of not normally distributed data we adopted the Spearman's correlation test which does not require data normality. The strength of the associations between the variables in the case of Spearman's or Pearson's correlation index (*i.e.*, R) is the index itself, so any issue that affects the ability to draw the correct conclusion seems to have been handled. To deal with this threat we plan to replicate the study in different contexts with a larger number of participants.

Conclusion Validity. Two standard questionnaires were adopted to measure personality traits and team climate perception (Reliability of measures). Both the questionnaires are largely adopted in the literature. Nevertheless, participants may not have answered sincerely or carefully to the statements of both the questionnaires. To try to limit this threat we informed the participants in the study that their data were anonymized and that they could freely leave the study when they want.

External Validity. The study we conducted could not be generalized to the universe of the distributed smart-working development projects. Participants were master students. But they may be more skilled in the multi-platform technologies adopted for performing the software application because these are relatively new. They were in the second year of their master degree in Computer Science and coming to work soon. This may mitigate this threat. The number of developers and the number of teams might be considered limited. Each team is composed of at most three participants. This might threaten the validity of the results since teams in real projects could include a larger number of members.

6   Implications

Extrovert individuals like to deal with others and interact and communicate easily. The results of our study revealed that Extroversion has a positive correlation on all the team climate factors in our context (Computer Science students - Smart-working development). This factor may be particularly relevant in the case of smart-working, because greater Extroversion may be needed when F2F contact is missing. It is also worth mentioning that it seems that Extroversion is related to software quality [2], and also with both team climate and team performance variables [22]. Vishnubhotla *et al.* [23] in the context of a Telecom company determined Agreeableness as related to team climate factors, no relationship was found for Extroversion. The researcher may be interested in determining the considered relationships to different kinds of users (*e.g.*, smart-working professionals) or specific development processes (*e.g.*, Agile context). In that respect, our results pose the basis for future research.

In the defined regression model Extroversion explained the 13.96% of Task Orientation. The judgment of the R-squared value depends on the context: in a quantitative environment these results may be modest, but in a social science context many variables intervene. Thus, low values as 10% may be accepted for studies in the field of arts, humanities, and social sciences because human behavior is difficult to predict [10]. This point may interest for the researcher: she may improve our results by considering a different and wider sample where TCI data are normally distributed and try to improve our model or get other prediction models for the other team climate factors. It is important to point out that this study is correlational, so no causal inference can be made (for example, we cannot say that adding an extrovert to the team will raise the climate level).

In our study, we cannot aggregate the data of the team climate and personality traits factors because data were not normally distributed. But we can consider the scores of the project works produced by the teams according to the teacher evaluation that assessed participation, system complexity, technological difficulty, usability, and presentation, with a score ranging from 1 to 5 and weight 25% of the total score for each factor. Results revealed that T3 obtained the worst score (score = 1), while T19 and T17 scored 2. The T3 team members had several discussions and the project risked being abandoned, see Fig. 3. The teacher intervention was required to solve the conflicts. This gives us the idea that different climate visions among the team members may be related to performances, but it is only an idea that should be better investigated.

7   Conclusion

In this paper, we presented the results of a preliminary investigation aiming at studying the relationships between personality traits and team climate in a distributed smart-working development context. Two largely adopted standard questionnaires were used for collecting data about the perceptions of 53 Computer Science students grouped in 19 teams. Results of the correlation analysis revealed that extrovert, out-going individuals in the current pandemic context when performing remote distributed work the Extroversion personality trait seems to be related to team climate. We also defined a regression model for predicting task Orientation scores by using the Extroversion personality trait. The value of our research concerns the improvement of our body of knowledge in the context of personality traits and team climate in a smart-working distributed development context.

To deal with external validity threats, we plan to replicate our study with a greater number of participants. Also, a different kind of them (*e.g.*, students vs. practitioners) could provide a better basis for the generalization of the results. We also plan to replicate our study when the Covid-19 pandemic will be concluded. We are going to execute replications—as similar as possible to the study presented in this paper—with the goal of showing differences in the results (original experiment vs. replications) and plan future work to understand the role of the Covid-19 pandemic on team climate. Future work will be also devoted to study the relationships with productivity and other project metrics as well as product software metrics.

References

1. Acuña, S.T., Gómez, M., Juristo, N.: Towards understanding the relationship between team climate and software quality-a quasi-experimental study. Empir. Softw. Eng. **13**(4), 401–434 (2008). https://doi.org/10.1007/s10664-008-9074-8
2. Acuña, S.T., Gómez, M.N., Hannay, J.E., Juristo, N., Pfahl, D.: Are team personality and climate related to satisfaction and software quality? Aggregating results from a twice replicated experiment. Inf. Softw. Technol. **57**, 141–156 (2015)
3. Aldrich, J.: Correlations genuine and spurious in Pearson and Yule. Stat. Sci. **10**(4), 364–376 (1995). http://www.jstor.org/stable/2246135
4. Anderson, N.R., West, M.A.: Measuring climate for work group innovation: development and validation of the team climate inventory. J. Organ. Behav.: Int. J. Ind. Occup. Organ. Psychol. Behav. **19**(3), 235–258 (1998)
5. Basili, V.R., Rombach, H.D.: The tame project: towards improvement-oriented software environments. IEEE Trans. Softw. Eng. **14**(6), 758–773 (1988)
6. Calefato, F., Iaffaldano, G., Lanubile, F., Vasilescu, B.: On developers' personality in large-scale distributed projects: the case of the apache ecosystem. In: Proceedings of the 13th International Conference on Global Software Engineering. ICGSE '18, pp. 92–101. Association for Computing Machinery, New York (2018). https://doi.org/10.1145/3196369.3196372
7. Caulo, M., Francese, R., Scanniello, G., Tortora, G.: Relationships between personality traits and productivity in a multi-platform development context. In: Chitchyan, R., Li, J., Weber, B., Yue, T. (eds.) EASE 2021: Evaluation and Assessment in Software Engineering, Trondheim, Norway, 21–24 June 2021, pp. 70–79. ACM (2021)
8. Chen, J., Qiu, G., Yuan, L., Zhang, L., Lu, G.: Assessing teamwork performance in software engineering education: a case in a software engineering undergraduate course. In: 2011 18th Asia-Pacific Software Engineering Conference, pp. 17–24 (2011). https://doi.org/10.1109/APSEC.2011.50
9. Costa, P.T., McCrae, R.R., Pando, A.C., Pamos, A., Cubero, N.S., Aranda, M.D.A.: Inventario de Personalidad Neo Revisado (NEO PI-R); Inventario Neo Reducido de Cinco Factores (NEO-FFI): manual profesional. Tea (2008)
10. Falk, R.F., Miller, N.B.: A primer for soft modeling. University of Akron Press (1992)
11. Goldberg, L.R.: The structure of phenotypic personality traits. Am. Psychol. **48**(1), 26 (1993)
12. Goldberg, L.R., et al.: The international personality item pool and the future of public-domain personality measures. J. Res. Pers. **40**(1), 84–96 (2006)

13. Gómez, M.N., Acuña, S.T.: A replicated quasi-experimental study on the influence of personality and team climate in software development. Empir. Softw. Eng. **19**(2), 343–377 (2014). https://doi.org/10.1007/s10664-013-9265-9

14. Jones, M.C., Harrison, A.W.: Is project team performance: an empirical assessment. Inf. Manag. **31**(2), 57–65 (1996). https://doi.org/10.1016/S0378-7206(96)01068-3. https://www.sciencedirect.com/science/article/pii/S0378720696010683

15. Lee, J.M., Shneiderman, B.: Personality and programming: time-sharing vs. batch preference. In: Proceedings of the 1978 Annual Conference, vol. 2, pp. 561–569 (1978)

16. McCrae, R.R., Costa, P.T., Jr.: Reinterpreting the Myers-Briggs type indicator from the perspective of the five-factor model of personality. J. Pers. **57**(1), 17–40 (1989)

17. Perry, D.E., Siy, H.P., Votta, L.G.: Parallel changes in large-scale software development: an observational case study. ACM Trans. Softw. Eng. Methodol. (TOSEM) **10**(3), 308–337 (2001)

18. Shameem, M., Kumar, C., Chandra, B.: A proposed framework for effective software team performance: a mapping study between the team members' personality and team climate. In: 2017 International Conference on Computing, Communication and Automation (ICCCA), pp. 912–917. IEEE (2017)

19. Shapiro, S.S., Wilk, M.B.: An analysis of variance test for normality (complete samples). Biometrika **52**(3/4), 591–611 (1965)

20. Smith, E.K., Bird, C., Zimmermann, T.: Beliefs, practices, and personalities of software engineers: a survey in a large software company. In: Proceedings of the 9th International Workshop on Cooperative and Human Aspects of Software Engineering, pp. 15–18 (2016)

21. Soomro, A.B., Salleh, N., Mendes, E., Grundy, J., Burch, G., Nordin, A.: The effect of software engineers' personality traits on team climate and performance: a systematic literature review. Inf. Softw. Technol. **73**, 52–65 (2016)

22. Soomro, A.B., Salleh, N., Nordin, A.: How personality traits are interrelated with team climate and team performance in software engineering? a preliminary study. In: 2015 9th Malaysian Software Engineering Conference (MySEC), pp. 259–265. IEEE (2015)

23. Vishnubhotla, S.D., Mendes, E., Lundberg, L.: Investigating the relationship between personalities and agile team climate of software professionals in a telecom company. Inf. Softw. Technol. **126**, 106335 (2020)

24. Weinberg, G.M.: The psychology of computer programming, vol. 29. Van Nostrand Reinhold New York (1971)

25. West, M.A.: The social psychology of innovation in groups (1990)

26. West, M.A., Altink, W.M.: Innovation at work: individual, group, organizational, and socio-historical perspectives. Eur. J. Work Organ. Psy. **5**(1), 3–11 (1996)

27. Zander, A.F.: Making Groups Effective. Jossey-Bass, Hoboken (1994)

Searching for Bellwether Developers for Cross-Personalized Defect Prediction

Sousuke Amasaki[1]([⊠])[iD], Hirohisa Aman[2][iD], and Tomoyuki Yokogawa[1][iD]

[1] Okayama Prefectural University, 111 Kuboki, Soja 719-1197, Japan
{amasaki,t-yokoga}@cse.oka-pu.ac.jp
[2] Center for Information Technology, Ehime University, Matsuyama 790-8577, Japan
aman@ehime-u.ac.jp

Abstract. Context: Recent progress in the use of commit data for software defect prediction has driven research on personalized defect prediction. An idea applying one personalized model to another developer came in for seeking an alternative model predicting better than one's own model. A question arose whether such exemplary developer (bellwether) existed as observed in traditional defect prediction. Objective: To investigate whether bellwether developers existed and how they behaved. Method: Experiments were conducted on 9 OSS projects. Models based on active developers in a project were compared with each other to seek bellwethers, whose models beaten models of the other active developers. Their performance was evaluated with new unseen data from the other active developers and the remaining non-active developers. Results: Bellwether developers were identified in all nine projects. Their performance on new unseen data from the other active developers was not higher than models learned by those developers. The bellwether was only a practical choice for the non-active developers. Conclusion: Bellwethers were a useful prediction model for the non-active developers but not for the other active developers.

Keywords: Personalized defect prediction · Transfer learning · Bellwether effect

1 Introduction

Software defect prediction (SDP) is an active research area in software engineering. Traditionally it uses static code metrics from source files to represent characteristics of modules like classes. Machine learning approaches are often used to train prediction models with pairs of the metrics and historical records of bugs identified. Tremendous prediction approaches have still been proposed so far.

A recent study [10] coined just-in-time software defect prediction (JIT SDP) that utilizes a change in a version control system as a unit of prediction. JIT SDP extracts metrics such as the number of adding lines from a commit and trains a prediction model to specify bug-inducing commits. An immediate and

L. Ardito et al. (Eds.): PROFES 2021, LNCS 13126, pp. 183–198, 2021.
https://doi.org/10.1007/978-3-030-91452-3_12

finer prediction when a developer makes a commit is an advantage of JIT SDP. It also bring another advantage that prediction models can utilize developer-related information such as experience on a system in addition to code-related metrics. For those reasons, JIT SDP has been a popular research topic [7,12, 21,22]. The feature of JIT SDP implies that prediction models can be trained with the commit records of an individual developer. *Personalized software defect prediction* focuses on developer's personal data to train and predict the fault proneness of changes [8]. It was expected to improve the prediction performance focusing on and capturing developers' unique characteristics.

A common issue, regardless of a unit of software defect prediction, is a small amount of data available for training prediction models. The shortage of training data might result in poor performance or abandonment of using software defect prediction in practice. *Cross-project defect prediction* tackles this issue by using data outside a project for training prediction models. Many CPDP approaches have also been proposed so far [5,6,23]. Most of those studies had assumed the traditional software defect prediction that used static code metrics. Recent studies have also tried to improve JIT SDP in the context of CPDP [2,9,18,24]. One of the topics on CPDP is what kind of cross-project data is to be chosen for training among multiple cross-projects. Some studies assumed a single project and did not care about it or combined them into a single one. Other studies proposed selection approaches among the cross-projects [4,5,25].

Krishna et al. [11] proposed a *bellwether method* for the cross-project selection issue. They defined the bellwether method that searches for an exemplar project from a set of projects worked by developers in a community and applies it to all future data generated by that community. The authors then demonstrated with OSS projects that such exemplar projects were found and effective for predicting faulty modules of the other projects. A question arose here whether seeking an exemplary developer was beneficial in the context of cross-personalized software defect prediction. Many contributors to OSS projects are non-active developers and make a small number of commits in a short term. No personalized defect prediction model can be built for them. If an exemplar developer exists, it would be helpful to predict the fault-proneness of their commits. On the one hand, bellwether candidates, who are active developers making commits enough to train personalized prediction models, had worked on the same project together. On the other hand, they are very different from each other [17]. Therefore, an exemplar developer was expected to be found as well as an exemplar project.

In this paper, for cross-personalized software defect prediction, we set out to search for bellwether developers. Through empirical experiments, we addressed the following research questions:

RQ$_1$ How often bellwethers exist among active developers in a project?

RQ$_2$ How are the bellwethers effective for predicting faults made by the other active developers in a project?

RQ$_3$ How are the bellwethers effective for predicting faults made by the rest of the developers in a project?

To answer these research questions, we applied the bellwether method to developers of 9 OSS projects. Bellwethers found were used to train personalized software defect prediction models and applied to unseen commit data of the other active developers. Personalized software defect prediction models by the active developers, including the bellwethers, were also compared with each other regarding the prediction performance on the commit data made by the rest of the developers.

The rest of this paper was organized as follows: Sect. 2 describes past studies related to personalized software defect prediction and bellwethers. Section 3 explains the methodology we adopted. Section 4 shows the experiment results with figures and tables and answers the research questions. Section 5 discusses the threats to the validity of our experiments. Section 6 provides a summary of this paper.

2   Related Work

Software defect prediction (SDP) aims to prioritize software modules regarding the fault-proneness for efficient software quality assurance activities. Different granularity levels, such as function and file, have been considered in past studies. As software version control systems had been prevalent, SDP at change-level (often called just-in-time (JIT) SDP [10]) got popular in software engineering research. An advantage of JIT SDP is that a faulty change can be attributed to a developer as changes are recorded with the information of the authors. Another advantage is that developers' characteristics can be utilized for prediction in addition to code changes.

Building JIT SDP for each developer was promising as the relationships between developer characteristics and faults were also revealed. For instance, Schröter et al. [17] reported that the defect density by developers was very different from each other. Rahman et al. [16] also showed that an author's specialized experience in the target file is more important than general experience. Jiang et al. [8] constructed a personalized defect prediction approach based on characteristic vectors of code changes. They also created another model that combines personal data and the other developers' change data with different weights. Furthermore, they created a meta classifier that uses a general prediction model and the above models. Empirical experiments with OSS projects showed the proposed models were better than the general prediction model. Xia et al. [20] proposed a personalized defect prediction approach that combines a personalized prediction model and other developers' models with a multi-objective genetic algorithm. Empirical experiments with the same data as [8] showed better prediction performance. These personalized defect prediction approaches utilized other developer's data to improve the prediction performance.

Cross-project defect prediction is a research topic that uses data from outside of a target to overcome the small amount of dataset obtained. Many CPDP approaches have also been proposed so far [5,6,23]. Combining defect prediction models based on other projects was also studied as CPDP [15]. Therefore, the personalized defect prediction approaches in the above can be considered as cross-personalized defect prediction approaches. Cross-personalized defect prediction has not been studied well yet, and it seems a promising research topic.

Krishna et al. proposed a cross-project defect prediction approach based on the bellwether effect [11]. Their bellwether method searches for an exemplar project and applies it to all future data generated by that community. This approach is so simple that a part of developers in a project is simply specified as bellwethers. We thus focused on this approach first to see whether the bellwether effect was observed in the context of cross-personalized defect prediction.

3   Methodology

3.1   Bellwethers Approach

According to [11], we defined the following two operators for seeking bellwether developers in a project:

- GENERATE: Check if the project has bellwether developers using historical commit data as follows.
  1. For all pairs of developers from a project $D_i, D_j \in P$, predict the fault-proneness of historical commits of D_j using a prediction model learned with past commits of D_i
  2. Specify a bellwether developer if any D_i made the most accurate prediction in a majority of $D_j \in P$
- APPLY: Predict the fault-proneness of new commit data using the prediction model learned on the past commit data of the bellwether developer.

GENERATE operator is a process to find a bellwether developer. Each developer model was applied to each training data of the other developer models. The most accurate prediction was specified using a statistical method described in Sect. 3.4.

APPLY operator is a process to validate whether a bellwether can really make a good prediction on future commit data. As the bellwether was defined in the context of cross-personalized defect prediction, the prediction was made on the commit data of the other developers only.

Finally, we omitted MONITOR operator defined in [11] as we set aside only one testing commit data set from each developer. Such chronological evaluation needed to be conducted in future work.

3.2   Datasets

We used commit datasets collected from 9 OSS projects[1] in a past study [1]. The nine datasets were available through a replication package[2]. Table 1 describes the

---

[1] Originally ten datasets were provided but one (JGroups) was removed because only one active developer remained after preprocessing described in this section.

[2] http://doi.org/10.5281/zenodo.2594681.

definitions of change metrics in the datasets. The change metrics consist of 14 metrics of 5 dimensions defined in [10].

The datasets had no author information, and commits were linked to authors through UNIX timestamps recorded in the datasets and the commits of their corresponding git repositories. Commits with the same timestamp were all removed as it was impossible to connect those commits and their authors. The datasets contained cases having negative values in metrics that should have recorded counting numbers. We also removed suspicious cases that had zero values, meaning nothing committed.

In general, not a few OSS developers made a small number of commits, not enough to build personalized defect prediction models. We thus needed to identify *active developers* who had commits enough to build a personalized defect prediction model (i.e., training data) and to validate the model (i.e., testing data) using a git repository and a bug-fixing history. GENERATE and APPLY operators required older commits for training and newer commits for testing, respectively. Commit data of each developer were thus separated into two parts according to their timestamps. Training data and testing data had to have enough faulty and non-faulty commits. To this end, we decided to select developers having at least 20 faulty commits and 20 non-faulty commits in training data and having at least 10 faulty commits and 10 non-faulty commits in testing data. A separation was found as follows: Commits of an author were aligned chronologically, and then a separator moved from the latest commit to the previous one until the above condition was satisfied. Note that the separations did not assure that the training data of active developers had the same number of commits.

Table 2 shows statistics of the original datasets, the number of selected commits, and the number of active developers identified. These numbers were varied among the datasets, and it was suitable for evaluation. Note that the commit data of *non-active developers* were also set aside to address RQ3.

3.3 Prediction

We followed the prediction approach in [11]. Random Forests were employed to predict the fault-proneness of commits. SMOTE [3], a well-known over-sampling technique, was also used to mitigate the issue caused by the imbalance of class labels. We followed to use these two techniques for prediction. We used SMOTE of imblearn package as SMOTE and RandomForestClassifer of scikit-learn package as Random Forests. No parameter optimization was applied. As randomness came in due to SMOTE, the model construction and prediction were repeated 40 times.

3.4 Performance Evaluation

This study adopted distance from perfect classification (ED) [13] as well as [11]. The ED measures the distance between a pair of Pd (recall) and Pf (false alarm) and the ideal point on the ROC (1, 0), weighted by cost function θ as follows.

Table 1. Changes measures

Dimension	Name	Definition
Diffusion	NS	Number of modified subsystems
	ND	Number of modified directories
	NF	Number of modified files
	Entropy	Distribution of modified code across each file
Size	LA	Lines of code added
	LD	Lines of code deleted
	LT	Lines of code in a file before the change
Purpose	FIX	Whether or not the change is defect fix
History	NDEV	The number of developers that changed the modified files
	AGE	The mean time interval between the last and the current change
	NUC	The number of unique changes to the modified files
Experience	EXP	Developer experience
	REXP	Recent developer experience
	SEXP	Developer experience on a subsystem

Table 2. Statistics of datasets

Project name	Period	# commits	# selected commits	# developers
Brackets	12/2011-12/2017	17, 311	8, 038	24
Broadleaf	11/2008-12/2017	14, 911	9, 430	14
Camel	03/2007-12/2017	30, 517	25, 645	17
Fabric8	12/2011-12/2017	13, 004	9, 135	10
Neutron	12/2010-12/2017	17, 311	4, 119	21
Nova	08/2010-01/2018	48, 938	15, 393	67
NPM	09/2009-11/2017	7, 893	6, 579	4
Spring-Integration	11/2007-01/2018	8, 692	7, 025	8
Tomcat	03/2006-12/2017	18, 877	1, 7908	9

$$Pd = \frac{TP}{FN + TP}$$

$$Pf = \frac{FP}{TN + FP}$$

$$ED = \sqrt{\theta \cdot (1 - Pd)^2 + (1 - \theta) \cdot Pf^2}$$

where TP, FN, FP, TN represent true positive, false negative, false positive, and true negative, respectively. The smaller the ED, the better the personalized prediction model. θ was set to 0.6 as well as [11].

The Scott-Knott test [14] was used to statistically compare the performance of methods on each dataset. This test makes some clusters, each of which consists of homogeneous personalized software defect prediction models regarding their prediction performance. A cluster with the highest performance holds treatments that are clearly better than the others while the performance of those treatments is equivalent.

4   Results

4.1   RQ1: Is There a Bellwether Developer in a Project?

Approach: To address RQ1, we first plotted the prediction performance of active developers in boxplots to see how they were similar to and different from each other. Then, GENERATE operator defined in Sect. 3.1 was applied to those active developers to obtain a bellwether. As we occasionally found no statistical difference among some developers while they were significantly better than the others, we grouped them as *a flock of bellwethers*, which held bellwether developers with the same prediction performance. The sizes of flocks were observed to see whether they were a majority of the active developers or not.

Results: Figure 1 shows the performance variations among developers. Each subfigure in Fig. 1 corresponds to each project and shows boxplots of EDs of developers on the training data of other active developers. Developer names were anonymized in the subfigures. The boxplots were ordered according to the median ED performance. The left-most developer provided the best prediction model while the right-most developer did not. We observed trends of the performance distributions as follows:

Brackets: Figure 1(a) shows the median prediction performance varied between 0.32 to 0.71. A trend was gently upward from the left side to the right side. No chasm was found between any adjacent developers except for the right two developers.

Broadleaf: Figure 1(b) shows the median prediction performance varied between 0.36 to 0.76. A trend was gently upward, and a chasm was found on the right side.

Camel: Figure 1(c) shows the median prediction performance varied between 0.32 to 0.66. Some left-side developers looked similarly. Their performance was not different from each other. The performance of the others got worsen steadily.

Fabric: Figure 1(d) shows the median prediction performance varied between 0.32 to 0.71. The left two developers were apparently better than the others. The others formed a gentle slope with no apparent chasm.

Neutron: Figure 1(e) shows the median prediction performance varied between 0.31 to 0.54. They formed a gentle slope, and some developers did not look different from each other. The performance of the others got worsen steadily.

Table 3. The number of bellwether developers found in a project

Project	# of bellwethers
brackets	1
broadleaf	1
camel	3
fabric	2
neutron	6
nova	41
npm	1
spring-integration	3
tomcat	1

Nova: Figure 1(f) shows the median prediction performance varied between 0.36 to 0.73. They formed a gentle slope, and not a few developers did not look different from each other. No clear chasm was not appeared except for the rightmost developer.

Npm: Figure 1(g) shows the median prediction performance varied between 0.5 to 0.64. The range was narrow, but the boxes were thin. The left-most developer thus looked significantly better than the others.

Spring-integration: Figure 1(h) shows the median prediction performance varied between 0.32 to 0.65. The left three developers looked significantly better than the others. No clear chasm did not appear among the others.

Tomcat: Figure 1(i) shows the median prediction performance varied between 0.32 to 0.68. The left-most developer was apparently better than the others. No clear chasm did not appear among the others.

These observations shared some characteristics. The median performance values among developers got changed constantly from the left side to the right side. Steep changes were occasionally observed to figure out the best and the worst prediction models. The ranges of prediction performance were not so different among projects. The median performance varied between 0.3 to 0.8 approximately. Some projects showed narrower ranges to suggest a group of personalized defect prediction models of equivalent performance. However, the best models often made significantly better predictions.

Table 3 shows the number of bellwether developers found as a result of the Scott-Knott test. A single bellwether was found in four out of the nine projects. A flock of bellwether developers was specified in the other projects. Figure 1 visually supported these results.

An interesting observation was that the number of bellwethers was not necessarily relevant to the number of active developers shown in Table 2. For instance, Brackets had a single bellwether developer while Neutron specified six bellwethers though they had a similar number of active developers. From this point

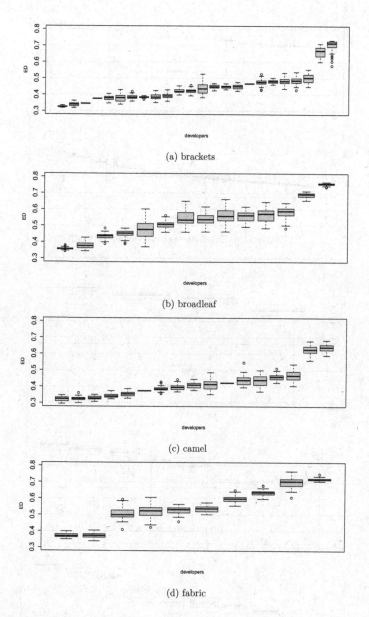

(a) brackets

(b) broadleaf

(c) camel

(d) fabric

Fig. 1. Performance distributions among developers in terms of ED

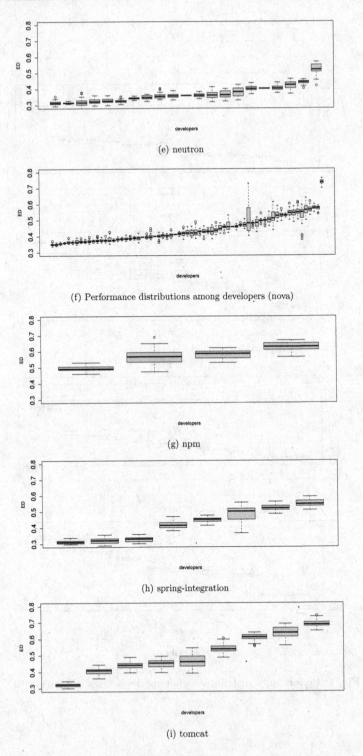

(e) neutron

(f) Performance distributions among developers (nova)

(g) npm

(h) spring-integration

(i) tomcat

Fig. 1. (*continued*)

of view, Neutron and Nova projects were different from the other projects. They had more than half the number of active developers in a project. The difference seemed due to the homogeneity of development activities among active developers.

Answer to RQ1: Four out of the nine projects had a bellwether developer. The rest of the projects formed a flock of bellwethers. The number of active developers might not be related to the number of bellwethers. The homogeneity of the active developers might cause the difference.

4.2 RQ2: How Are the Bellwethers Effective for Predicting Faults Made by the Other Active Developers in a Project?

Approach: This research question asked whether a bellwether model could replace models of other active developers that were applied to their own commits. To address RQ2, we applied the APPLY operator shown in Sect. 3.1. We evaluated the prediction performance of the bellwethers as follows:

1. Prepare local models, each of which was learned on training data of each the other active developers
2. Predict the testing commit data using the local model corresponding to the active developer of the testing data
3. Predict the same commit data provided from the other active developers using each of the bellwether models
4. Compare the result from the bellwether and each result from the local models using the Scott-Knott test
5. Make a decision on the prediction performance of the bellwethers.

We decided that a bellwether was "effective" if the bellwether made predictions significantly better than or equivalent to all the local models. A bellwether was decided as "ineffective" if the bellwether made predictions worse than all the local models. Otherwise, we decided that it was marginal. That is, the bellwether was better than some local models but worse than other local models.

Results: Table 4 shows the number of bellwether models that were decided as effective, marginal, or ineffective. We found that only one bellwether developer of NPM project made significantly better predictions than all the local models. Also, no bellwether developer was decided as ineffective. Most of the bellwether developers were decided as marginal. This result implied that active developers in the investigated projects were so diverse that bellwether developers were not effective nor ineffective. Therefore, bellwether developers were not useful to support other active developers in defect prediction. It can also be said that bellwether models might be a help for some active developers. However, it was unknown who was to be an appropriate recipient. A practical recommendation was to use their own local models.

Table 4. The performance of bellwether models in comparison to local models

Project	Effective/Marginal/Ineffective
brackets	0/1/0
broadleaf	0/1/0
camel	0/3/0
fabric	1/1/0
neutron	0/6/0
nova	0/41/0
npm	1/0/0
spring-integration	1/2/0
tomcat	0/1/0

Answer to RQ2: The bellwether developers identified in RQ1 were not useful to support other active developers in defect prediction. Using local models would be a practical choice.

4.3   RQ3: Do the Bellwether Developers Also Predict Faulty Commits of the Others Than the Bellwether Candidates?

Approach: To address RQ3, we compared the performance of personalized prediction models learned with training commit data of the active developers, including bellwethers. These prediction models were applied to commit data of the non-active developers defined in Sect. 3.2. Then, the prediction results were supplied to the Scott-Knott test to see whether bellwethers in RQ1 kept their places. The purpose is to observe changes between the rankings shown in RQ1 and those on the non-active developers. Therefore, we also adopted Spearman's ρ to see how the rankings in RQ1 changed.

Results: Table 5 shows the results of the comparisons. The second column denotes values of Spearman's ρ. The bold figures mean the correlation was statistically significant at $\alpha = 0.05$. All the coefficients were high. As the insignificance of NPM project seemed due to a small number of active developers ($n = 4$), we could say the trends observed in Fig. 1 were preserved well. The third column shows whether bellwethers in RQ1 were still a bellwether here. All the bellwethers kept their positions in four out of the nine projects, namely, Broadleaf, Fabric, NPM, and Tomcat projects. For these projects, the bellwether developers were useful to predict the fault-proneness of the non-active developers. In Brackets and Camel projects, the bellwethers were no longer the best choice for defect prediction for the non-active developers. The fourth column of Table 5 shows to which ranks those bellwethers moved. They kept second or third places

Table 5. The performance of bellwethers in comparison to the bellwether candidates on the others data

Project	Spearman's ρ	# of keep/drop	New ranks of the drops
brackets	**0.83**	0/1	2
broadleaf	**0.81**	1/0	—
camel	**0.81**	0/3	2, 2, 3
fabric	**0.89**	2/0	—
neutron	**0.69**	1/5	2, 3, 3, 5, 5
nova	**0.74**	34/7	2, 3, 3, 3, 3, 4, 4
npm	0.63	1/0	—
spring-integration	**0.87**	1/2	3, 4
tomcat	**0.97**	1/0	—

and thus were practically better choices among more than ten active developers. The same logic went to the rest of the projects. Neutron, Nova, and Spring-integration projects had both types of bellwethers, but they totally kept better places.

> **Answer to RQ3:** The bellwether developers identified in RQ1 were useful to support non-active developers in defect prediction. They were not necessarily the best choice but practical choices among their many active developers.

5   Threats to Validity

Our study suffered from some threats to validity that were often observed in data-oriented software engineering research. First, we relied on commit data from a past study. Commits and bugs of the data were linked with Commit Guru[3]. Therefore, some class of defects might miss due to a limitation of this tool. The change measures shown in Table 1 are popular but recent studies (e.g., [19]) proposed new measures to improve the predictive performance. These factors might affect our conclusions. Furthermore, these data had no information regarding developers who committed as described in Sect. 3.2. We thus linked developers and commits based on timestamps and dropped off not a few commit data, as shown in Table 2. These automatic processes might miss correct links and find incorrect links. Its accuracy affected our experiment results.

Second, our study divided commits of each developer into training data and testing data chronologically but did not set the same separation among developers. Some commits were thus predicted using commits made in the future.

---

[3] http://commit.guru.

Furthermore, we might miss the effects of chronological proximity between commits. Experiments in a chronological online situation are desirable in future work.

Finally, the results in our study were limited to the projects investigated. Experiments on different projects might lead to different conclusions such as the absence of bellwether developer. We think this threat to external validity was slightly mitigated as OSS projects were different in size, active developers, and so on.

6   Conclusion

This study investigated the existence and performance of bellwether developers for cross-personalized defect prediction. The first experiment revealed that bellwether developers existed in all the nine projects we investigated. Their personalized defect prediction models achieved better performance on training data of personalized defect prediction models of the other active developers in a project. However, the second experiment showed that these personalized defect prediction models were rarely the best choice for new unseen commit data made by the active developers. We then found that the bellwethers were practical choices for non-active developers to predict the fault-proneness of their commits.

In future work, we will conduct experiments under chronological online situations, which is a more realistic setting for developers. The setting will enable us to analyze what time an active developer gets and step down a bellwether developer, for example. Also, comparisons to other cross-personalized defect prediction approaches are an interesting topic for improving prediction performance.

Acknowledgment. This work was partially supported by JSPS KAKENHI Grant #18K11246, #21K11831, #21K11833, and Wesco Scientific Promotion Foundation.

References

1. Cabral, G.G., Minku, L.L., Shihab, E., Mujahid, S.: Class imbalance evolution and verification latency in just-in-time software defect prediction. In: 2019 IEEE/ACM 41st International Conference on Software Engineering (ICSE), pp. 666–676 (2019). https://doi.org/10.1109/ICSE.2019.00076
2. Catolino, G., Di Nucci, D., Ferrucci, F.: Cross-project just-in-time bug prediction for mobile apps: An empirical assessment. In: 2019 IEEE/ACM 6th International Conference on Mobile Software Engineering and Systems (MOBILESoft), pp. 99–110 (2019). https://doi.org/10.1109/MOBILESoft.2019.00023
3. Chawla, N.V., Bowyer, K.W., Hall, L.O., Kegelmeyer, W.P.: SMOTE: synthetic minority over-sampling technique. J. Artif. Intell. Res. **16**, 321–357 (2002)
4. He, Z., Peters, F., Menzies, T., Yang, Y.: Learning from open-source projects: an empirical study on defect prediction. In: Proceedings of ESEM 2013, pp. 45–54. IEEE (2013)
5. Herbold, S.: Training data selection for cross-project defect prediction. In: Proceedings of PROMISE '13, pp. 6:1–6:10. ACM (2013)

6. Hosseini, S., Turhan, B., Gunarathna, D.: A systematic literature review and meta-analysis on cross project defect prediction. IEEE Trans. Softw. Eng. **45**(2), 111–147 (2019)
7. Jahanshahi, H., Jothimani, D., Başar, A., Cevik, M.: Does chronology matter in JIT defect prediction? A partial replication study. In: Proceedings of the Fifteenth International Conference on Predictive Models and Data Analytics in Software Engineering, pp. 90–99 (2019). https://doi.org/10.1145/3345629.3351449
8. Jiang, T., Tan, L., Kim, S.: Personalized defect prediction. In: Proceedings of International Conference on Automated Software Engineering, pp. 279–289 (2013)
9. Kamei, Y., Fukushima, T., McIntosh, S., Yamashita, K., Ubayashi, N., Hassan, A.E.: Studying just-in-time defect prediction using cross-project models. Empir. Softw. Eng. **21**(6), 2072–2106 (2016). https://doi.org/10.1007/s10664-015-9400-x
10. Kamei, Y., et al.: A large-scale empirical study of just-in-time quality assurance. IEEE Trans. Softw. Eng. **39**(6), 757–773 (2013). https://doi.org/10.1109/TSE.2012.70
11. Krishna, R., Menzies, T., Fu, W.: Too much automation? The bellwether effect and its implications for transfer learning. In: Proceedings of International Conference on Automated Software Engineering, pp. 122–131 (2016)
12. Li, W., Zhang, W., Jia, X., Huang, Z.: Effort-aware semi-supervised just-in-time defect prediction. Inf. Softw. Technol. **126**, 106364 (2020). https://doi.org/10.1016/j.infsof.2020.106364
13. Ma, Y., Cukic, B.: Adequate and precise evaluation of quality models in software engineering studies. In: Proceedings of International Workshop on Predictor Models in Software Engineering, p. 9 (2007)
14. Mittas, N., Angelis, L.: Ranking and clustering software cost estimation models through a multiple comparisons algorithm. IEEE Trans. Softw. Eng. **39**(4), 537–551 (2013)
15. Panichella, A., Oliveto, R., De Lucia, A.: Cross-project defect prediction models: L'Union fait la force. In: Proceedings of CSMR-WCRE '14, pp. 164–173. IEEE (2014)
16. Rahman, F., Devanbu, P.: Ownership, experience and defects: a fine-grained study of authorship. In: Proceedings of International Conference on Software Engineering, pp. 491–500 (2011)
17. Schröter, A., Zimmermann, T., Premraj, R., Zeller, A.: Where do bugs come from? SIGSOFT Softw. Eng. Notes **31**(6), 1–2 (2006)
18. Tabassum, S., Minku, L.L., Feng, D., Cabral, G.G., Song, L.: An investigation of cross-project learning in online just-in-time software defect prediction. In: Proceedings of International Conference on Software Engineering, New York, NY, USA, pp. 554–565 (2020). https://doi.org/10.1145/3377811.3380403
19. Trautsch, A., Herbold, S., Grabowski, J.: Static source code metrics and static analysis warnings for fine-grained just-in-time defect prediction. In: 2020 IEEE International Conference on Software Maintenance and Evolution (ICSME), pp. 127–138 (2020)
20. Xia, X., Lo, D., Wang, X., Yang, X.: Collective personalized change classification with multiobjective search. IEEE Trans. Reliab. **65**(4), 1810–1829 (2016)
21. Yang, X., Lo, D., Xia, X., Sun, J.: TLEL: a two-layer ensemble learning approach for just-in-time defect prediction. Inf. Softw. Technol. **87**, 206–220 (2017)
22. Yang, Y., et al.: Effort-aware just-in-time defect prediction: simple unsupervised models could be better than supervised models. In: Proceedings of the 2016 24th ACM SIGSOFT International Symposium on Foundations of Software Engineering, pp. 157–168 (2016)

23. Zhou, Y., et al.: How far we have progressed in the journey? An examination of cross-project defect prediction. ACM Trans. Softw. Eng. Methodol. **27**(1), 1–51 (2018)

24. Zhu, K., Zhang, N., Ying, S., Zhu, D.: Within-project and cross-project just-in-time defect prediction based on denoising autoencoder and convolutional neural network. IET Softw. **14**(3), 185–195 (2020). https://doi.org/10.1049/iet-sen.2019.0278

25. Zimmermann, T., Nagappan, N., Gall, H., Giger, E., Murphy, B.: Cross-project defect prediction: a large scale experiment on data vs. domain vs. process. In: Proceedings of ESEC/FSE '09, pp. 91–100. ACM (2009)

Using Machine Learning to Recognise Novice and Expert Programmers

Chi Hong Lee[✉] and Tracy Hall[✉]

Lancaster University, Lancaster LA1 4YW, UK
gabriel@gabrielchl.dev, tracy.hall@lancaster.ac.uk

Abstract. Understanding and recognising the difference between novice and expert programmers could be beneficial in a wide range of scenarios, such as to screen programming job applicants. In this paper, we explore the identification of code author attributes to enable novice/expert differentiation via machine learning models. Our iteratively developed model is based on data from HackerRank, a competitive programming website. Multiple experiments were carried using 10-fold cross-validation. Our final model performed well by differentiating novice coders from expert coders with 71.3% accuracy.

Keywords: Code · Authorship analysis · Novice programmers · Expert programmers

1 Introduction

Agrawal et al.'s study [1] suggests that grouping strong students with weaker students could improve student achievement overall. Lui et al.'s study [8] shows that in programming courses, identifying and isolating weak students to apply a different teaching method could lead to higher performance in the examination and improve confidence in programming. In contrast, companies hiring programmers have been shown to exclude exceptional candidates where students' grade point average was used to pre-screen or filter candidates [5]. The ability to distinguish experienced programmers from novices could allow companies to gain insight into candidates quickly and accurately, improving their hiring process.

Code stylometry is the study of code authorship or related analysis through feature identification in code. Many research studies have been conducted in this field, with at least 57 publications published between 1957 and 2020 related to this topic [7]. Most previous research focuses on attributing the author of a piece of code, very few previous studies classify features of the code author, such as coding experience. The main aim of this paper is to explore the use of code stylometry with machine learning to classify coding experience. Our three main Research Questions are:

RQ1. Can programmers' experience levels be classified using features from their code?

© Springer Nature Switzerland AG 2021
L. Ardito et al. (Eds.): PROFES 2021, LNCS 13126, pp. 199–206, 2021.
https://doi.org/10.1007/978-3-030-91452-3_13

RQ2. What code features improve the performance of a machine learning model to predict programmer experience?
RQ3. Which modelling techniques achieve the best classification performance for programmer experience?

A prediction model was developed using data from novice and expert programmers. Data was crawled from HackerRank[1], a competitive programming or programming interview preparation site. Different configurations to fetch such data and features to extract were experimented with to optimize model performance. Our final model achieves 71.3% accuracy for correctly classifying expert and novice programmers.

2   Related Work

Halstead [6] proposed a set of metrics to evaluate a piece of code that measures the complexity of the code, which is heavily affected by the algorithms used in the code. Halstead's Metrics were reported to have a strong correlation with student performance on computer programming courses [4]. Oman and Cook's work [9] on code authorship attribution used a set of 16 metrics. These metrics identified features in code comments and formatting and were inspired by techniques used for English literature authorship analysis. Oman and Cook [9] were able to categorize most code by author accurately by applying cluster analysis. Spafford and Weeber [10] analyzed code left in a computer system by a hacker, to establish his or her identity. The proposed features for source code or binary code files including:

- Language (The programming language used)
- Formatting (e.g. Number of statements per line, etc.)
- Special features (Such as code specific for certain compilers to read)
- Comments (Consistency, frequency and length)
- Variable names (e.g. naming styles of local temporary variables)
- Language features (e.g. use of for loops versus while loops, etc.)
- Scoping (Global versus local identifiers, scope of helper functions)
- Errors
- Other metrics (Halstead metrics, McCabe metrics, etc.)

Burrows and Tahaghoghi [3] explored the use of n-grams for code authorship analysis. Using 1,640 files from 100 authors, Burrows and Tahaghoghi achieved a 67.01% accuracy. Wisse and Veenman [11] combined 10 traditional structural, style and layout features with 4 different n-gram metrics to reach a 91.4% accuracy with 10 authors and 85% accuracy with 45 authors. Bhattathiripad [2] proposes different types of metrics, programming blunders, to be used to evaluate code. Bhattathiripad points out that most explored code features focus on the general coding styles or algorithmic choices of the whole piece of code, Bhattathiripad explores the use of programming blunders to identify code authorship. Examples of programming blunders include unused variables, unused imported libraries, or a section of code that never gets executed.

---

[1] https://www.hackerrank.com/.

3   Methodology

3.1   Dataset

We chose HackerRank as the data source for this project as code samples are in a one-file script format and it is possible to attribute the author's experience level. HackerRank is a company that provides programmer hiring solutions to technology companies by using their coding test systems. Their website provides coding test practice questions, with over 7 million programmers using the website in 2020. All submitted code is visible to the public, along with the programmer's profile, with some programmers also providing a link to their LinkedIn profile. We used programmers' LinkedIn profiles for insight into levels of experience.

In this paper, we have defined a novice programmer as one that received programming training, but has not had any work experience, including part-time work or internships. We have defined an expert programmer as someone who has had full-time programming-related work experience. With this definition, developers with marginal experience, lying between novice and professional, is eliminated as we believe this would help develop a more accurate model. This binary rather than continuous classification was chosen due to the limitation in the size of the data set. However, in reality, a programmer's expertise is not binary. The classifications were made by manually analyzing information on the programmer's LinkedIn profile. For all experiments, the same 199 code samples were used (1 for each author). Where 91 samples were classified as novice and 108 as expert.

3.2   Features

Initially, we selected 15 features (base feature set) to extract from the data set. These features are similar to those used in previous studies [9,10] and include: 1) number of lines of code 2) ratio of empty lines to all lines 3) average length of lines 4–7) number and average length of line comments and block comments respectively 8–9) number and average length of the names of variables 10–15) number of if, for, do, while, switch and cast statements. These features are simple to extract and have been previously shown, by Oman and Cook [9], to reliably attribute code to authors.

3.3   Machine Learning Models

Ten machine learning algorithms, shown in Table 1, were selected to be trained and tested for all experiments. A wide range of different types of algorithms is used, such as linear models, neural networks and decision trees. This was done to identify the best model in experiments as well as which models generally do better with the data set.

The models are built using the 10-fold cross-validation technique, and predictive performance is measured using accuracy, F1 and Matthews Correlation Coefficient (MCC).

Table 1. Models used in experiments

Initial Used	Full Name
LR	Logistic Regression
LDA	Linear Discriminant Analysis
KNN	K-neighbours
CART	Decision Tree
NB	Gaussian Naive Bayes
SVM Lin	Support Vector Classification (with linear kernel)
SVM Pol	Support Vector Classification (with polynomial kernel)
SVM/SVM RBF	Support Vector Classification (with radial basis function kernel)
MLP	Multi-layer Perceptron
RF	Random Forest

4   Results

This section presents the key experiments performed with a full list of experiments provided in the Appendix. We describe how we iteratively evolved the models via a series of experiments in order to gain improved predictive performance. Note that all experiments were conducted based on the same dataset as described in previous sections.

A replication package is available on the repository on GitHub.[2]

4.1   Exp0: First Experiment

This experiment was performed to establish a baseline against which subsequent experiments are compared. Using all unmodified 199 code samples, and the initial set of features listed in the previous section, the average accuracy achieved by all 10 models was 0.605, where the top 5 averaged at 0.643.

Exp1: Base Model, Code Cleaning. Following experiment 0, we looked into the code samples and the values of the extracted features. We noticed that in each code sample, there is a section, referred to as general code, that is identical in each file, such as the code which prints the function result out to standard output for evaluation, this code is provided by HackerRank in their code template. We proceeded to perform experiment 0 again but with all general code removed. This resulted in an average accuracy of 0.627 (3.67% increase), and 0.662 in the top 5 models (2.96% increase). We have decided that the set of modified files with general code removed will be used in all future experiments.

Exp2: Halstead Metrics. This set of experiments is done aiming to compare the model accuracy using data with and without Halstead metrics (volume, difficulty and effort value). In experiment 2.1, only Halstead metrics' values were

---

[2] https://github.com/gabrielchl/novice-expert-dev-classifier-replication-package.

extracted from the code samples. The models had an average accuracy of 0.548, and 0.570 in the top 5 models. In experiment 2.2, we combined the Halstead metrics with the set of features used in experiments 0 and 1. This increased the average model accuracy to 0.601, and 0.639 for the top 5 models, but these accuracy values were still lower than those from previous experiments.

Exp3: Cyclomatic Complexity. In this experiment, we included cyclomatic complexity as one of the features to extract from the code samples. The models had an average accuracy of 0.630, where the top 5 averaged at 0.670. The inclusion of cyclomatic complexity resulted in a slight increase in accuracy.

Exp4: Style Features. two new style-related features were included in this experiment, cond_space_ratio and bracket_line_ratio. cond_space_ratio is the ratio of cases where a space is absent before the opening bracket (e.g. "if(") of a condition to where the space is present (e.g. "if ("). bracket_line_ratio is the ratio of cases where curly brackets are placed on the currently (e.g. ") {") to placed on a new line (e.g. ")<line break>{"). The average accuracy of all models was 0.623, where the top 5 reached 0.669. The top 5 models with style features performed slightly better than the top 5 models from the base experiment.

Exp5: Normalization. In this set of experiments, normalization techniques were applied to the dataset. In experiment 5.1, a min-max scaler was applied, resulting in a 0.646 and 0.667 accuracy in all models and the top 5 respectively. A standard scaler was applied in experiment 5.2, resulting in a 0.650 average accuracy across all models and 0.683 in the top 5 models. Applying the standard scaler resulted in a 3.67% and 6.89% improvement in the average accuracy value for all models and the top 5 models.

Exp6: Final Model. Learning from the results of all previous experiments, a final experiment was conducted. This experiment used the same dataset as the previous experiments, with general code removed. Features-wise, Halstead metrics were not included, while the cyclomatic complexity value and style features were included. Standard scaler was also applied to the dataset values. With this configuration, the final set of models achieved a 0.653 average accuracy and 0.678 in the top 5 models. The best model, logistic regression, reached an accuracy of 0.713. The models' accuracy, f1 and MCC values are shown in Fig. 1. The coefficients found in the best performing model is shown in Fig. 2.

5 Ethical Concerns

Given that the application is designed to give corporations the ability to determine one's programming experience by analyzing their code, ethical concerns may arise regarding related issues.

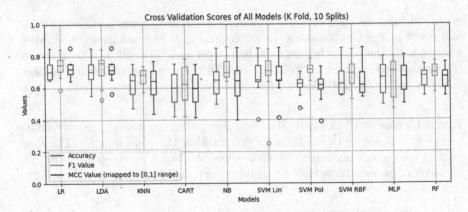

Fig. 1. Cross validation scores of all models in experiment 6

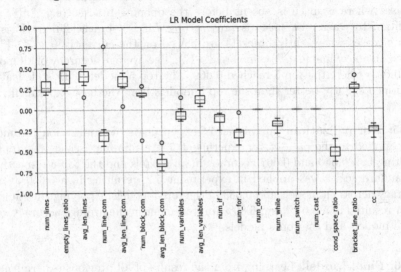

Fig. 2. Coefficients found in the final logistic regression model

The preselection of job application candidates would be the biggest concern of all concerns. While it is understood that such pre-selection methods are not always accurate and causes the loss of talents or results in hiring candidates who are not suitable for the job, it could be arguable that these methods help save time for both the company and the candidates, making the entire application process more efficient.

The main concern is if the pre-selection method is fair. As the model was trained using a dataset, biases could be existing in the dataset and be carried over to the final model during the training model. These biases could be due to the bias in the data source itself, or by human-induced, or systematic bias during the collection of data. These biases could damage the reliability of the model, as well as its fairness as it could give an advantage or disadvantage to a group of people whose code exhibits features picked up by the model but non-related to their development experience.

The model developed in this project is not ready for real-life deployment. Not only does it have low accuracy, but it was not thoroughly studied as well, such as to establish the fact that whether there are biases in the model. Before these concerns are investigated and addressed, such a system should not be deployed.

6   Conclusion

6.1   Review of the Research Questions

RQ1. Can Programmers' Experience Levels Be Classified Using Features from Their Code? A logistic regression model was trained using 199 code samples, achieving 71.3% accuracy.

RQ2. What Code Features Improve the Performance of a Machine Learning Model to Predict Programmer Experience? From the final model's coefficient values, the top 5 features influencing the classification are as follows: Average length of block comments, ratio of bracket without to with a space before it, ratio of empty lines to all lines, average length of lines, and the average length of comments.

RQ3. Which Modelling Techniques Achieve the Best Classification Performance for Programmer Experience? Comparing the results of all experiments, logistic regression performed best in the final, as well as most, experiments.

6.2   Further Work

A More General and Larger Data Set. The current data set is very specific and focused as it helps narrow the scope of this paper. However, the data set must be more generalized for real-world use, such that different types of code could be analyzed. Besides, a larger data set could further benefit the model's accuracy.

Experiments on Features and Models. Most of the features used in this paper were focused on syntactic features, such that they are easily extracted. More experiments could be carried on more complex features, such as n-grams and more abstract syntax tree features, as well as to test different combinations of those features against the accuracy of the models. Furthermore, while the set of models selected for this study is rather diverse, further work could be done to experiment with different configurations of those models, or to test new models, in an attempt to reach better results. More work could also be done on the final model, where the correlation found between features and the classification could be further studied, as well as to test the model in extreme cases and against possible biases.

References

1. Agrawal, R., Golshan, B., Terzi, E.: Grouping students in educational settings. In: Proceedings of the 20th ACM SIGKDD International Conference on Knowledge Discovery and Data Mining - KDD 2014 (2014). https://doi.org/10.1145/2623330. 2623748
2. Bhattathiripad, P.V.: Software piracy forensics: a proposal for incorporating dead codes and other programming blunders as important evidence in afc test. In: 2012 IEEE 36th Annual Computer Software and Applications Conference Workshops (July 2012). https://doi.org/10.1109/compsacw.2012.46
3. Burrows, S., Tahaghoghi, S.: Source code authorship attribution using n-grams (January 2007)
4. Castellanos, H., Restrepo-Calle, F., Gonzalez, F.A., Echeverry, J.J.R.: Understanding the relationships between self-regulated learning and students source code in a computer programming course. In: 2017 IEEE Frontiers in Education Conference (FIE) (October 2017). https://doi.org/10.1109/fie.2017.8190467
5. Clark, J.G., Walz, D.B., Wynekoop, J.L.: Identifying exceptional application software developers: a comparison of students and professionals. Commun. Assoc. Inf. Syst. **11**, 8 (2003). https://doi.org/10.17705/1cais.01108
6. Halstead, M.H.: Elements of Software Science (Operating and programming systems series). Elsevier Science Inc. (May 1977)
7. Kalgutkar, V., Kaur, R., Gonzalez, H., Stakhanova, N., Matyukhina, A.: Code authorship attribution. ACM Comput. Surv. **52**, 1–36 (2019). https://doi.org/10. 1145/3292577
8. Lui, A.K., Kwan, R., Poon, M., Cheung, Y.H.Y.: Saving weak programming students. ACM SIGCSE Bull. **36**, 72 (2004). https://doi.org/10.1145/1024338. 1024376
9. Oman, P.W., Cook, C.R.: Programming style authorship analysis. In: Proceedings of the Seventeenth Annual ACM Conference on Computer Science : Computing trends in the 1990's Computing trends in the 1990's - CSC 1989 (1989). https:// doi.org/10.1145/75427.75469
10. Spafford, E.H., Weeber, S.A.: Software forensics: can we track code to its authors? Comput. Secur. **12**, 585–595 (1993). https://doi.org/10.1016/0167-4048(93)90055-a
11. Wisse, W., Veenman, C.: Scripting dna: identifying the javascript programmer. Digit. Investig. **15**, 61–71 (2015). https://doi.org/10.1016/j.diin.2015.09.001

Is Knowledge the Key? An Experiment on Debiasing Architectural Decision-Making - a Pilot Study

Klara Borowa[✉][iD], Robert Dwornik, and Andrzej Zalewski[iD]

Institute of Control and Computation Engineering, Warsaw University of Technology, Warsaw, Poland
klara.borowa@pw.edu.pl

Abstract. The impact of cognitive biases on architectural decision-making has been proven by previous research. In this work, we endeavour to create a debiasing treatment that would minimise the impact of cognitive biases on architectural decision-making. We conducted a pilot study on two groups of students, to investigate whether a simple debiasing presentation reporting on the influences of cognitive biases, can provide a debiasing effect. The preliminary results show that this kind of treatment is ineffective. Through analysing our results, we propose a set of modifications that could result in a better effect.

Keywords: Cognitive biases · Software architecture · Architectural decision-making · Debiasing

1 Introduction

The occurrence of cognitive biases is inherent to the human mind, and as such, can influence all individuals taking part in the software development process [10]: developers [3], architects [14], designers [9], testers [2].

In particular, cognitive biases have been proven to distort architectural decision-making [18] by influencing software architects' reasoning [14]. This influence can be particularly strong, since every systems architecture is actually a set of design decisions [6] made by individuals. Thorough education about cognitive biases turned out to significantly improve software effort estimation [12], which is severely afflicted by cognitive biases [5]. Similarly, in this work we examine, *(RQ) whether educating software architects about cognitive biases can provide a beneficial debiasing effect, which increases the rationality of decision-making.*

In order to answer this question, we designed an experiment and ran a pilot study on two groups of students. The preliminary findings show that educating engineers about the possible impact of cognitive biases is not sufficient to mitigate the influence of cognitive biases on design decisions.

Therefore, more advanced debiasing techniques are needed. We analysed how exactly cognitive biases influenced various elements of the conversation (arguments, counterarguments, and general conversation). Based on that, we proposed additional debiasing techniques that can be used in order to create a more

© Springer Nature Switzerland AG 2021
L. Ardito et al. (Eds.): PROFES 2021, LNCS 13126, pp. 207–214, 2021.
https://doi.org/10.1007/978-3-030-91452-3_14

effective debiasing treatment. We plan to perform a modified version of this experiment, on a larger sample, in the near future. Our long time objective is to develop effective, debiasing techniques for architectural decision-making.

2   Related Work

The concept of cognitive biases was introduced by Tversky and Kahneman in their work about Representativeness, Availability and Anchoring biases [17]. Cognitive biases are a by-product of the dual nature of the human mind – intuitive (known as System 1) and rational (known as System 2) [7]. When the logic-based reasoning of System 2 is not applied to the initial decisions of System 1, we can say that the decision was biased.

Software architecture, defined as set of design decisions [6], is influenced by various human factors [16]. One of these factors are cognitive biases [18]. Their influence on architectural decision-making has been shown as significant in recent research [8,14,18,19]. When no debiasing interventions are applied, the consequences of such biased decisions can be severe – for example resulting in taking on harmful Architectural Technical Debt [1].

In the domain of architecture decision-making, various debiasing techniques were proposed [1,18]. The use of techniques that prompt designers to reflect on their decisions, have turned out to be effective in improving the quality of the reasoning behind design decisions [15].

Debiasing, by educating software developers about the existence of cognitive biases and their influences, has recently been proven to work as a powerful tool in the realm of software effort estimation [12]. The effectiveness of this approach to debiasing architectural decision making, has not yet been empirically tested.

3   Study Design

3.1   Bias Selection

Based on the cognitive biases researched previously in relation to software development [10], as well as biases shown previously as influencing software architecture [1,18,19], we selected three cognitive biases as the subject of the experiment:

1. Anchoring – when an individual over-relies on a particular solution, estimate, information or item, usually, the first one that they discovered or came up with [17].
2. Optimism bias – when baseless, overly positive estimates, assumptions and attributions are made [11].
3. Confirmation bias – the tendency to avoid the search for information that may contradict one's beliefs [13].

3.2 Data Acquisition

In order to obtain the data for our study, we took part in four meetings with two groups of students that were working on a group project during their coursework. The meetings were conducted online through the MS Teams platform. Both groups were supposed to plan, design and implement a system as a part of their course. The topic for the project was at their discretion, with the only hard requirement being the use of Kubernetes in their solution.

In the case of one of the groups, we prepared a presentation during which we explained the concept of cognitive biases, and how they can influence architectural decision-making. We explicitly explained the three researched cognitive biases and gave examples of their possible influence on the students' project. We did not mention anything about cognitive biases or debiasing to the second group.

The meetings proceeded as follows:

1. We asked the participants for their consent to record the meeting and to use their data for the purpose of our research.
2. In the case of the debiased group (Team 2), we showed them our presentation about cognitive biases in architectural decision-making. We did not perform this action with the other group (Team 1).
3. The meeting continued naturally, without our participation, although a researcher was present and made notes when necessary.

We also asked the participants to fill in a small survey to obtain basic statistical data about them.

3.3 Data Analysis

The recordings from the meetings were transcribed. In order to identify the cognitive biases, and their influence on decision-making, we defined a coding scheme presented in Table 1. The codes were applied to indicate the occurrence of the researched biases, as well as the arguments for and against the discussed architectural decisions.

The first and second author coded the transcripts independently. Then, they used the negotiated coding [4] method to discuss and correct the coding until they reached a full consensus.

Subsequently, we counted the number of occurrences of each code, and analysed the fragments of the meetings that were found to have been influenced by cognitive biases.

3.4 Participants

We recorded four meetings with two different groups of students that were working on their Master's degrees in Computer Science at Warsaw University of Technology. The students grouped themselves into teams depending on their own preferences and had to choose a team leader. The teams consisted of five

Table 1. Coding scheme

Code category	Code	Definition
Bias – Anchoring	KOT	Putting too much emphasis on the first piece of information or idea that was heard/proposed/invented.
Bias – Optimism	OPT	Naive faith that the unpleasant consequences of our decisions will not happen. Typical statements include: "It will somehow be." "No need to think about possible problems.", "Let's just start coding, it will be fine."
Bias – Confirmation	POT	Not accepting and not seeking information that is inconsistent with our current beliefs.
Arguments for the decision	ARG	An argument that was in favour of choosing a particular solution.
Arguments against the decision	PARG	A counterargument, against choosing a particular solution

members each. Most of the students (with a single exception) had prior professional experience in software development. More detailed information on the students is presented in Table 2.

Table 2. Participant data

Age	Gender	Has professional experience?	Job position	Experience [years]	Team No
23	M	Yes	Data Engineer	1	1 (not debiased)
24	M	Yes	Software Developer	2.5	1 (not debiased)
23	M	Yes	Software Developer - intern	0.1	1 (not debiased)
24	M	Yes	Cloud/DevOps	3	1 (not debiased)
23	M	Yes	Systems Engineer	2	1 (not debiased)
24	M	Yes	Java Developer	1.5	2 (debiased)
24	M	Yes	Full Stack Developer	2	2 (debiased)
24	M	Yes	Java Developer	2	2 (debiased)
23	F	Yes	Sales Analyst	1	2 (debiased)
25	M	No	No professional experience	0	2 (debiased)

4 Results

Using the coding scheme presented in Table 1, we obtained the following information:

- The percentage of biased arguments in statements for or against certain architectural decisions (see Fig. 1).
- How many arguments for and against certain architectural decisions were made during the meeting (see Fig. 2).
- How many of these arguments and counterarguments, were influenced by cognitive biases (see Fig. 3).

– How many cognitive biases were present in statements not related to architectural decisions (see Fig. 3).

Figure 1, which presents the percentage of biased arguments used during the meetings, shows that Team 1 (non-debiased) used more rational arguments than Team 2 (debiased). This means that the debiasing treatment – simply informing the participants about the existence of cognitive biases – was ineffective.

Figure 2 shows that there was a significant difference between the amount of arguments and counterarguments in the discussions. Teams were less likely to discuss the drawbacks of their decisions than their positive aspects.

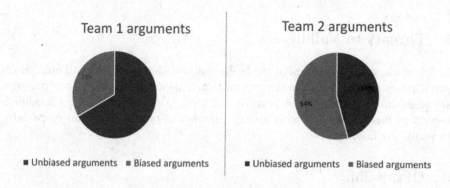

Fig. 1. Biased arguments

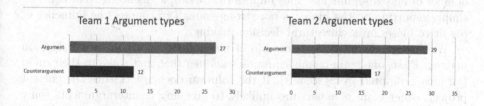

Fig. 2. Argument count

Figure 3 illustrates the number of biased statements, as well as the ratio between the researched biases depending on statement type.

In the case of both teams, most cognitive biases were present in statements not related to architectural decision-making. In this type of discussion, confirmation bias and optimism bias were the most prevalent. This was usually due to the teams' need to reassure themselves that their course of action was correct.

In both teams, most of the biased arguments were influenced by the anchoring bias. This means that both teams considered an array of solutions that came to their minds first, without any additional argumentation on why the specific solution is correct. When it comes to counterarguments, against specific architectural solutions, confirmation bias was prevalent in both teams. This was usually due to the teams' unwillingness to change a previously made decision.

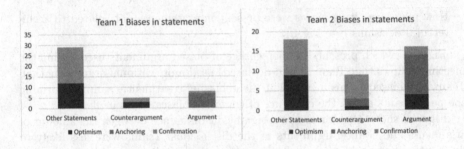

Fig. 3. Biases in statements

5   Threats to Validity

In this work, we describe a pilot study. Its main weakness is the small number of participants that took part in the experiment. This means that all of our findings are preliminary and cannot be perceived as final. We plan to perform a modified version of this experiment with a larger number of teams, to obtain more data to verify our findings.

6   Discussion

The team that was not debiased by our presentation used a significantly lower number of biased arguments. This implies that a simple debiasing treatment, by simply reporting on the biases is not strong enough to counter the influence of cognitive biases on architectural decision-making.

We discovered the typical scenario of bias-influenced architectural decision making. First, one team member proposes an idea that first came to their mind (an idea prompted by System 1). If the solution does not disturb the current project, other team members are unlikely to give any counterarguments (only around half of the arguments used were counterarguments) as they are already anchored on the initial proposition. If the solution requires changes to previously made decisions, other team members (due to confirmation bias), are likely to give biased counterarguments to avoid changes. Additionally, the whole atmosphere of the conversation is heavily influenced by the confirmation bias and optimism bias, making the team unlikely to notice any errors in their decision-making.

With these findings in mind, we propose (Sect. 7) a set of modifications to our debiasing approach.

7   Research Outlook

Since the pilot study showed that a simple debiasing treatment does not help to overcome the biases, we plan to extend and repeat this experiment with the following modifications:

- Since the most biased arguments in favour of a solution were influenced by anchoring, and participants were overall less likely to use counterarguments – we propose that the person presenting a solution, should also present at least one drawback.
- Since most biased counterarguments were influenced by confirmation bias, due to the teams' reluctance to change a previously made decision – we propose that one of the team members should monitor the discussion and point out the occurrence of such a biased argumentation.
- Since optimism bias and confirmation bias influenced the overall atmosphere of the meetings - we propose that, at the end of the meeting, after making the initial decisions, teams should explicitly list their drawbacks. Then, if the need arises, decisions should be changed accordingly.
- We will add an additional code to the coding scheme - "decision". Which will mean the decision that was ultimately made during the meeting. This will enable us to count how many rational and biased arguments were made in favour of the decisions that were eventually chosen.
- Instead of a simple debiasing presentation, we will hold a longer debiasing workshop. During this workshop, we will do more than simply inform the participants about the influence of cognitive biases on architectural decision-making. The participants will also be taught, through a series of practical exercises, how to apply our debiasing techniques.
- The next experiment will be performed on a significantly bigger sample of participants.

8 Conclusion

The preliminary results (see Sect. 4) show that a simple presentation about cognitive biases and their possible influence on architectural decision-making is not an effective debiasing method. At the same time the pilot study revealed crucial information about how biases influenced the arguments for and against certain decisions. This made it possible to develop a series of modifications to our debiasing approach (as presented in Sect. 7) in order to reshape the entire experiment.

References

1. Borowa, K., Zalewski, A., Kijas, S.: The influence of cognitive biases on architectural technical debt. In: International Conference on Software Architecture (ICSA) (2021)
2. Çalikli, G., Bener, A.B.: Influence of confirmation biases of developers on software quality: an empirical study. Softw. Qual. J. **21**(2), 377–416 (2013). https://doi.org/10.1007/s11219-012-9180-0
3. Chattopadhyay, S., et al.: A tale from the trenches: cognitive biases and software development. In: International Conference on Software Engineering (ICSE), pp. 654–665 (2020). https://doi.org/10.1145/3377811.3380330

4. Garrison, D.R., Cleveland-Innes, M., Koole, M., Kappelman, J.: Revisiting methodological issues in transcript analysis: negotiated coding and reliability. Internet High. Educ. **9**(1), 1–8 (2006). https://doi.org/10.1016/j.iheduc.2005.11.001

5. Halkjelsvik, T., Jørgensen, M.: Time Predictions: Understanding and Avoiding Unrealism in Project Planning and Everyday Life. Springer Nature, Heidelberg (2018)

6. Jansen, A., Bosch, J.: Software architecture as a set of architectural design decisions. In: Proceedings - 5th Working IEEE/IFIP Conference on Software Architecture, WICSA 2005, vol. 2005, pp. 109–120 (2005). https://doi.org/10.1109/WICSA.2005.61

7. Kahneman, D.: Thinking, Fast and Slow. Macmillan, New York City (2011)

8. Manjunath, A., Bhat, M., Shumaiev, K., Biesdorf, A., Matthes, F.: Decision making and cognitive biases in designing software architectures. In: Proceedings - 2018 IEEE 15th International Conference on Software Architecture Companion, ICSA-C 2018, pp. 52–55 (2018). https://doi.org/10.1109/ICSA-C.2018.00022

9. Mohanani, R., Ralph, P., Shreeve, B.: Requirements fixation. In: International Conference on Software Engineering (ICSE), pp. 895–906 (2014). https://doi.org/10.1145/2568225.2568235

10. Mohanani, R., Salman, I., Turhan, B., Rodriguez, P., Ralph, P.: Cognitive biases in software engineering: a systematic mapping study. IEEE Trans. Softw. Eng. **5589**(c) (2018). https://doi.org/10.1109/TSE.2018.2877759

11. Ralph, P.: Toward a theory of debiasing software development. In: Wrycza, S. (ed.) SIGSAND/PLAIS 2011. LNBIP, vol. 93, pp. 92–105. Springer, Heidelberg (2011). https://doi.org/10.1007/978-3-642-25676-9_8

12. Shepperd, M., Mair, C., Jørgensen, M.: An experimental evaluation of a debiasing intervention for professional software developers. In: Proceedings of the 33rd Annual ACM Symposium on Applied Computing (2018). https://doi.org/10.1145/3167132.3167293, http://arxiv.org/abs/1804.03919

13. Stacy, W., Macmillan, J.: Cognitive bias in software engineering. Commun. ACM **38**(6), 57–63 (1995). https://doi.org/10.1145/203241.203256

14. Tang, A.: Software designers, are you biased? In: Proceedings - International Conference on Software Engineering (January 2011), pp. 1–8 (2011). https://doi.org/10.1145/1988676.1988678

15. Tang, A., Bex, F., Schriek, C., van der Werf, J.M.E.: Improving software design reasoning-a reminder card approach. J. Syst. Softw. **144**(April 2017), 22–40 (2018). https://doi.org/10.1016/j.jss.2018.05.019

16. Tang, A., Razavian, M., Paech, B., Hesse, T.M.: Human aspects in software architecture decision making: a literature review. In: Proceedings - 2017 IEEE International Conference on Software Architecture, ICSA 2017, pp. 107–116 (2017). https://doi.org/10.1109/ICSA.2017.15

17. Tversky, A., Kahneman, D.: Judgment under uncertainty: heuristics and biases. Science **185**(4157), 1124–1131 (1974)

18. van Vliet, H., Tang, A.: Decision making in software architecture. J. Syst. Softw. **117**, 638–644 (2016). https://doi.org/10.1016/j.jss.2016.01.017

19. Zalewski, A., Borowa, K., Ratkowski, A.: On cognitive biases in architecture decision making. In: Lopes, A., de Lemos, R. (eds.) ECSA 2017. LNCS, vol. 10475, pp. 123–137. Springer, Cham (2017). https://doi.org/10.1007/978-3-319-65831-5_9

Communicating Cybersecurity Vulnerability Information: A Producer-Acquirer Case Study

Martin Hell[1(✉)] and Martin Höst[2]

[1] Department of Electrical and Information Technology, Lund University,
Lund, Sweden
martin.hell@eit.lth.se
[2] Department of Computer Science, Lund University, Lund, Sweden
martin.host@cs.lth.se

Abstract. The increase in both the use of open-source software (OSS) and the number of new vulnerabilities reported in this software constitutes an increased threat to businesses, people, and our society. To mitigate this threat, vulnerability information must be efficiently handled in organizations. In addition, where e.g., IoT devices are integrated into systems, such information must be disseminated from producers, who are implementing patches and new firmware, to acquirers who are responsible for maintaining the systems. We conduct an exploratory case study with one producer of IoT devices and one acquirer of the same devices, where the acquirer integrates the devices into larger systems. Through this two-sided case study, we describe company roles, internal and inter-company communication, and the decisions that need to be made with regard to cybersecurity vulnerabilities. We also identify and discuss both challenges and opportunities for improvements, from the point of view of both the producer and acquirer.

Keywords: Cybersecurity · Open-source software · Case study · Vulnerabilities · IoT

1 Introduction

The use of open-source software (OSS) is increasing and a recent GitHub report shows that for e.g., JavaScript, 94% of active repositories use OSS, with a median number of 10 direct and 683 indirect (or transitive) dependencies [5].

Recently, cybersecurity has made headlines across a range of media. The number of reported vulnerabilities is increasing and cyber attacks are becoming more sophisticated, even with nation-states as the identified attackers [6]. During 2020, the number of new vulnerabilities reported by the National Vulnerability Database (NVD) was more than 18k. This can be compared to the 4–8k annually reported vulnerabilities during 2005–2016 [9].

© Springer Nature Switzerland AG 2021
L. Ardito et al. (Eds.): PROFES 2021, LNCS 13126, pp. 215–230, 2021.
https://doi.org/10.1007/978-3-030-91452-3_15

The combined increase in the use of OSS and the increase in newly found vulnerabilities puts the industry at higher risk than ever. Indeed, OSS vulnerabilities can potentially be exploited in all devices, products, and services that are using those components, though admittedly, just having the component does not necessarily mean that you are using the vulnerable part [11]. Still, as reported by IBM, scanning for and exploiting vulnerabilities was the top attack vector during 2020, with 35% of all incidents. This is an increase from 30% in 2019 and by that taking over the first position of common attack vectors from phishing [14].

This higher risk raises the bar for how the industry should work with identifying and patching vulnerabilities. However, the producer of devices that are responsible for developing the patches is often not the same as those responsible for maintaining the devices, e.g., installing the new firmware. Moreover, in case of a breach, it is the acquirer that is responsible towards the end customers in the role of delivering and maintaining the system. Thus, in the ecosystem of producers and acquirers, information regarding vulnerabilities and patches needs to be efficiently communicated, such that devices can be immediately updated, reducing the time of exposure [10].

Serror et al. [15] analyze the security aspects of Industrial IoT system ("Industry 4.0") and identify patch management as one important area. Especially for long-lived components procedures for identifying patches are important and for systems with a large number of devices automatic updates are important. There are some attempts to support organizations in vulnerability management through systems for supporting identification, evaluation, and remediation of vulnerabilities [1,2]. To our best knowledge the main focus in research on vulnerability management has been on systems and systems developed by a single organization. There is still a need to understand how communication of vulnerability information between organizations take place, and how the complete processes of managing vulnerabilities can be supported.

Outside the area of vulnerability management there is some research on information sharing between companies. Corallo et al. discusses "Value Networks" and conducts an interview study in an aerospace collaboration with several companies [3]. The focus is on innovation networks, i.e., advanced R&D projects with several partners. They conclude that different activities need different management approaches. Du et al. derive a model for analysing information sharing in supply chains based on game theory [4]. The focus is on supply chains with two parties, and the focus is more on the amount on information sharing rather than the content of the shared information. These aspects are related, but there is still a need to first investigate the actual practices of sharing information about vulnerabilities between organizations and to understand that, before, e.g., more advanced models are built.

The overall goal of this case study is to understand how considerations regarding vulnerabilities in third-party components arise, are communicated, and are assessed within and between a producer and an acquirer. Specifically, through interviews with one producer and one acquirer, we aim to answer the following research questions.

- **RQ1:** What roles and responsibilities can be identified?
- **RQ2:** How is vulnerability information communicated within and between the respective organizations?
- **RQ3:** What decisions must be made and what information is used?
- **RQ4:** What challenges and opportunities can be identified, both within organizations and in the communication between them.

RQ1 is seen as a prerequisite for understanding the organizational context and to adequately understand the result of RQ2. Similarly, RQ3 is used to better understand the challenges and opportunities in RQ4. Based on this, we provide insight into how vulnerabilities in IoT devices are handled on both sides of this producer-acquirer chain, and how they are communicated between the two companies. This insight also allows us to understand what challenges and opportunities there are for improving the handling and the communication of vulnerabilities.

The paper is outlined as follows. In Sect. 2 we explain the methodology used in our case study, including the involved companies and questions. We also discuss the validity of the research. In Sect. 3 we give the results, relating to the research questions above. We summarize and discuss the identified challenges and opportunities in Sect. 4 and we conclude the paper in Sect. 5.

2 Methodology

The research was conducted as a case study with two companies, a producer and an acquirer. Referring to the case study classifications given in [12,13], we conduct an exploratory case study, meaning that we aim to find out what is happening and seek new insights for the situation where there are questions or issues regarding cybersecurity vulnerabilities. The study is qualitative as it is based on interviews with the involved companies and with a flexible design allowing us to adapt interviews based on the answers from both current and previous interviews. The overall methodology is depicted in Fig. 1. Each company had a company lead for the case study. They had coordinating roles for their respective organization. This coordination included identifying the most suitable people to interview, initiating contact with the interviewees, and continuously discussing the results or possible misconceptions.

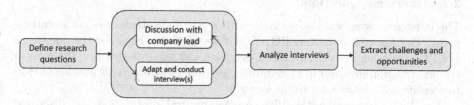

Fig. 1. Overall methodology

Table 1. Participants at companies

Company	Role	Nbr
Producer	Product Specialist	1
Producer	Software Security Group (SSG)	1
Producer	Release Group	1
Producer	First-Line Support	1
Acquirer	Support team technician	2
Acquirer	Head of Support Team	1
Acquirer	Product Owner	1

2.1 Involved Companies

The study focuses on two companies, for confidentiality reasons hereafter called the *producer* and the *acquirer*.

The producer produces and sells products in the area of IoT, primarily in the high-end segment and with a focus on a global B2B market. The IoT units can be seen as embedded systems with hardware and software. The software consists of a combination of in-house developed code and OSS. The organization has a history of more than 30 years, has today more than 1000 employees, and is a leading provider in the high-end segment.

The acquirer has a long tradition of providing high-security systems. It was founded more than 80 years ago and has more than 100 000 employees worldwide. The company has several business units and is active in a wide variety of domains. One core business is to integrate IoT products into larger systems and in turn, being a provider of these systems. The organizational part used in this study provides IoT systems, using products from the producer (among others). The integration of IoT into systems has not been in focus until the last few years. Thus, this specific business is rather new to the company, but knowledge from integrating high-security systems has been transferred also to this business.

Our case study was performed through interviews with representatives from both the producer and the acquirer. The role and affiliation of the interviewees are summarized in Table 1.

2.2 Interview Questions

The interviews were semi-structured, with a set of questions used as a starting point. The research questions RQ1-RQ4 were used as a basis for the questions. For RQ1 (roles and responsibilities), everyone was asked to describe the roles in the organization involved in vulnerability-related questions. This also allowed us to identify additional roles to interview.

For RQ2, we started out with an assumed natural information flow, discussed with and verified by the company leads in the respective organization. The information flow is divided into five steps. In the first three steps, we consider how questions regarding vulnerabilities

1. arise in the acquirers' organization,
2. are communicated to the producer, and
3. are communicated to and from the answering role within the producer's organization.

Once the producer has reached an answer to the question, this answer is returned to the acquirer. The parts related to the answer are divided into

4. how the answer is communicated back to the acquirer, and
5. how the answer is communicated within the acquiring organization.

The sequence of events starts at (1) in case the question is sent to the producer, but it can also be initiated at (4) in case of publishing advisories or if the producer pre-emptively contacts the acquirer with information.

For the acquirer, this was from the point of view of questions only targeting this particular producer, but for the producer, the scope was vulnerability-related questions from all their customers. In addition to the information flow, we also aimed to understand who is making the decisions, and what information was used to make decisions (RQ3). These questions were integrated with (3) and (4) above for the producer, and (5) for the acquirer, as this became a natural part of the interviews. The final part of the interviews was devoted to identifying possible improvements to the different parts of this process (RQ4). Improvements are here defined as initiatives or modifications that could make this process either easier for the involved people, more efficient for the organization, or more accurate in terms of providing answers to questions.

Since the interviewees had different roles in the information chain, the focus of the questions varied somewhat. Understanding the overall information and role structure was our first objective, achieved together with the company leads (and verified during interviews). Then, the interview focus could be tailored for that role in the information chain.

A last thing to note is that the interviews were also adopted to allow us to verify claims and descriptions from previous interviews.

2.3 Validity

The validity of the research has been considered during the planning through a number of measures.

- *Prolonged involvement* means that the research is not conducted in isolation, meaning that there is a trust between parties. In this case, the study was conducted in a setting with a longer cooperation, and the coordinators have cooperated with the researchers in other studies.
- *Triangulation* was mainly achieved in the interviews by repeating questions and checking results with several roles in the two organizations.
- *Peer debriefing* means that a group of researchers were involved and thereby the risk of bias from one researcher is avoided. In this case, both authors were involved in discussions and interpretation of the results.

- *Member checking* means that, e.g., participants in the study review and reflect on the results. In this case, especially the coordinators were involved during the study e.g. available to answer questions about results and helping out to interpret results.
- *Audit trail* means keeping track of all data in a systematic way. In this study, notes were taken from all interviews, and the analysis was based on these notes. The researcher that took the notes was the main person in the analysis which solves the main problems of interpreting notes from someone else.

Based on the methodology and these measures our view is that the main validity problem is external validity. Care must be taken when generalizing the results, but we believe that the findings can still serve as input to further studies.

3   Results

In this section, we present the results from our interviews. Each subsection corresponds to one of the research questions presented in Sect. 1.

3.1   Roles and Responsibilities

The acquirer has responsibility for the actual products and their integration into the operating environments. Attacks taking advantage of vulnerabilities in the products will in the end affect their customers so vulnerability information is essential for securing customers' environments and assets. Vulnerabilities are typically handled by updating or patching the firmware. Since this can be associated with large costs it is important to understand the impact of the vulnerabilities. Recall that the acquirer organizational part in focus in this study manages units at their customers' sites. We have identified the following roles and responsibilities within this organizational part for handling vulnerabilities.

- The *support team* is centralized in one country and provides a "managed by" solution to the production teams. It consists of approximately 20 people, including both technicians, management, and sales. The support team introduces new functionality and is responsible for identifying and prioritizing new vulnerabilities found in the products. They are not in contact with the actual customer sites.
- Each country has one *production team*, offering the integrated system to end customers. When new vulnerabilities are discovered, they are responsible for communicating with their customers, and also to deploy new firmware to the individual units.
- The *product owner* defines the requirements for the "managed by" product. This role does not take an active part in the process and is not part of the actual decision regarding vulnerabilities.

The producer, being a provider of high-end products, is working with security in a structured way. The organization takes inspiration from the BSIMM maturity model [7], with a core software security group that has close contact with development teams. Much effort is put into raising awareness throughout the organizations using so-called satellites, people with interest in security that can help to disseminate knowledge and information to their respective teams. For vulnerabilities in third-party components specifically, we identify the following roles and responsibilities.

- *First line support* receives security-related questions from customers. Here we also include key account managers, though these are formally part of the sales organizations. First-line support either answers the questions directly or forward them to a product specialist, while the key account manager opens a support issue with first-line support in order to make sure that all questions pass their organization and expertise.
- The *product specialists* have deep knowledge about the products and take an active part in product development and sprint planning. They have thus direct contact with developers. They are responsible for answering questions that can not be immediately answered by first-line support.
- The *development teams* are responsible for integrating OSS components. Individual developers are also responsible for keeping track of the OSS components and monitoring new updates, features, and vulnerabilities.
- The *software security group* (SSG) develops and leads the security initiatives throughout the company. They are experts in the technical details surrounding vulnerabilities. They are responsible for conducting the triage of new vulnerabilities, i.e., understanding the exploitability and impact of vulnerabilities in the context of the products and their operating environment.
- The *release team* is responsible for making new firmware releases in case of newly discovered vulnerabilities require immediate patching. New firmware can be released the same day if needed, provided that the developers have implemented the patch. The main bottleneck is often to identify which devices need new firmware.

These roles were agreed upon by all participants in this study.

3.2   Communication Within and Between Producer and Acquirer

How Questions Arise Within the Acquirer's Organization. Product and software security is the responsibility of the support team. The roles and the communication paths for security vulnerabilities are depicted in Fig. 2. Note that the different production teams typically do not communicate with each other at all. While questions potentially could arise directly from customers, through the production team, and to the support team, this has so far not happened. Since the customer purchases a solution, they typically assume that vulnerabilities are handled by the acquirer. A similar assumption is made by the production team, namely that since the support team is responsible for security, those issues are handled by them. The support team has two main sources of vulnerability-related information that can lead to questions escalating to the producer.

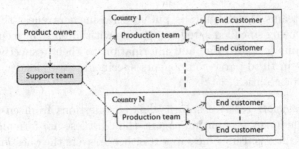

Fig. 2. Virtually all vulnerability related questions stems from and are handled by the support team.

- *Externally produced information material.* This mainly includes forum discussions, news articles, and research articles.
- *Internally produced information material.* This material is dominated by reports from vulnerability scans.

Of these two, the latter is most common. The support team regularly scans the network, searching for units and possible vulnerabilities in these. This is done on a weekly basis for central parts of the systems, but for other parts, it is much less regular. Finding information from externally produced material is much less formalized. Searches are at best done on an ad-hoc basis, and most information reaches the teams due to wide media coverage.

How Questions are Communicated to the Producer. During the interviews, both the producer and acquirer were asked about how, what, and to/from whom questions were communicated. A summary of the answers is given in Table 2. Note that the producer referred to questions from all its customers, not only the specific acquirer in this study.

An interesting observation is that the producer organization often does not know the role or background of the one asking. First-line support, receiving the original question, had the impression that it was not security experts, but mostly junior with little or no security training.

> "It is very rare that the question comes from someone with deep cybersecurity knowledge or even someone in the cybersecurity business. It is rather someone that just got the task to run a network scan on the equipment."

Since the actual role is unclear, this information is not propagated in the organization together with the question. This is a limiting factor since the technical level of the response can then not be aligned with the person asking the question. While the SSG expressed some concerns about this in the interview, the product specialists never experienced any actual problems related to this. Answers were always accepted as is.

The producer observed that a very common event is that (information from) a report from vulnerability scanning is sent to the producer, with the goal of

Table 2. A summary of how vulnerability related questions are communicated to the producer, both from the producer and acquirer's point of view.

Questions	Answers
Who is asking the question?	**Producer:** Not clear, but seems to not be security experts
	Acquirer: Support technicians (through a web portal) or head of support team (to key account manager). The latter is most common
Who is the question directed towards?	**Producer:** First line support gets basically all questions, but sometimes through the key account manager
	Acquirer: Key account manager directly, or using support portal in which case recipient is unknown
What question medium is used?	**Producer:** Always through a webform, ending up in the CRM. A support email address is not even provided
	Acquirer: Mostly through a web form but sometimes phone calls to key account manager
What do the customers want to know?	**Producer:** One or more of "Do you know about this vulnerability?", "How did you handle it?", "Is it fixed?", "Can we protect us in ways other than patching?"
	Acquirer: Are we affected by this vulnerability?
How is the question posed?	**Producer:** By submitting a list of CVE numbers or vulnerability scanning results
	Acquirer: If they are affected by a specific vulnerability, referring to a vulnerability scan or CVE number
How often do you get/ask questions about vulnerabilities?	**Producer:** 1–2 per month for first-line support in one country, 3 per week to PS (from all first-line support units), 1 per month to SSG
	Acquirer: Several times per year, but not as often as once per month

understanding to which extent deployed units are vulnerable. The information can be in the form of a report or a screenshot from the scanner, with the accompanying question "We seem to have these vulnerabilities, is it true and how do we fix it?"

This description fits very well with how this was actually done at the acquirer side, with regular network scans to identify problems and vulnerabilities.

All questions are directed to first-line support. This is the main channel for customer support. Customers send their questions through the online helpdesk portal, while some have a direct connection to a key account manager and send their questions directly to them, either by phone or by email. For security-related questions, the key account manager must always open an issue with first-line support such that these questions go through them. This is nowadays strictly enforced due to historical events where bypassing first-line support resulted in delays and misinformation.

Not only do many questions arise from vulnerability scans, but the results of these scans are often directly referenced in the question. Many customers use consultants for security and penetration testing, which results in a list of potential vulnerabilities. Since the customers do not have the expertise to interpret and validate the results of such scans, and it is not clear if the products are really affected, such scans escalate to questions directly to the producer.

For one first-line support country, the number of vulnerability-related questions are in the order of a few per month. This amounts to a very small proportion of the total number of questions (<1%), but it was still evident that the numbers have increased over the last few years.

On very rare occasions, the customer asks for a meeting with the R&D department. This can happen when they are afraid that the problem is serious, and they require firsthand and immediate information on how to take action.

Communication to Answering Role Within Producer's Organization. The communication inside the producer's organization is depicted in Fig. 3. As noted in Sect. 3.2, questions are directed to first-line support, or possibly to the key account manager who in turn forwards it to first-line support. Sometimes, first-line support can answer directly, but if this is not the case, security-related questions are re-directed to the product specialists, since the questions are related to the products. It was estimated that 70% of all questions were answered directly by first-line support, and 30% propagated further. For these 70%, it was almost always the case that an old firmware version was used and the solution was to update to the newest firmware.

Upon reaching the product specialist, these can sometimes answer the question directly. This primarily happens if the question has been asked before, or if the answer can be found from previous security-related discussions. A quick search in the email inbox can often answer this. Otherwise, if the question is related to a CVE identifier, then the NVD database is used to find more information. This database includes a short description of the vulnerability, a severity score (CVSS), information on vulnerable and non-vulnerable versions, and links to further information about the vulnerability. While it has been shown that this information is not always accurate [8], it can still provide enough information to answer the question, e.g., in which version the vulnerability was patched. The product specialist then contacts the development team to see when the software was patched. Questions stemming from external media are often related to new vulnerabilities, which are not patched in deployed releases. The product specialist works closely with the development teams and takes part in sprint planning and prioritization of tickets. Thus, they have a direct connection to finding out when software is patched.

It should be noted that the time of patching is not the same as releasing a new firmware. The answer the product specialist is really looking for is when the new release appears, not when it was patched on the main branch. This is controlled by a release team, which communicates closely with the developers and the product specialist in case there are severe vulnerabilities that must be fixed. If needed a new secure firmware can be released within a day. However, in most cases, this team is not aware of the fact that the new release includes particular vulnerability fixes. The release notes, which include vulnerability information, are written by the product specialist.

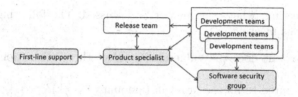

Fig. 3. First-line support, product specialists, and the software security group handle vulnerability related questions. Development teams implement patches and the release team compiles the new firmware.

The software security group is sometimes involved in the process. This is typically when the vulnerabilities require additional effort for "triaging" and to understand their potential impact. Some technical details of a vulnerability can often be very involved, in which case the product specialist can not answer directly. SSG is the last resort for answering questions. At this stage, the product specialist has refined the question, from the result of a vulnerability scan to a more direct question related to a CVE. For a CVE, the SSG performs a triage process, which is further discussed in Sect. 3.3. SSG has no communication with first-line support at all.

Communication Back to Acquirer. When an answer has been found to an explicit question, it is communicated back to the acquirer through email, or specifically in the CRM which results in an email to the registered address. Communication is always through first-line support. If the question escalated all the way to SSG, then it is returned to first-line support through the product specialist.

Some questions are implicitly answered by release notes and advisories. Release notes describe what has been changed for a specific release and which vulnerabilities, if any, have been solved. The advisory is a specific document, often relating to one or a few vulnerabilities of particular importance. The document can provide information on both workarounds and/or which firmware release to upgrade to. Advisories can be a result of questions, but can also be initiated directly from the producer's organization as a pre-emptive measure, acknowledging that many customers will benefit from this information. The release notes are written by the product specialist.

A third possibility is that the key account manager directly contacts the acquirer. This is often the case for important vulnerabilities, where the producer quickly wants to disseminate the information to the largest customers. This is an example of communication originating on the producer's side, i.e., starting with step (4) as given in Sect. 2.2.

How Answers are Communicated Within the Acquiring Organization. Answers are returned to the support team via email. This email initiates an immediate meeting, where the answer is discussed. The following aspects are discussed at this meeting.

- To which extent does the vulnerability affect the organization and its customers?
- What is required to fix the problem (amount of work)?
- Can the support team fix this or is production team involvement needed?
- How urgent is it?
- What preparation is needed by the support team?

Based on this information, the head of the support team contacts the affected production teams, who in turn are responsible for upgrading the firmware to a non-vulnerable version. There is no follow-up that the new firmware has actually been installed, mostly because there are no technical tools for doing this. Thus, this can be seen as a one-way communication of the information from the support team to the production teams.

3.3 Decision and Information

To answer the question if a customer's product is vulnerable to a given vulnerability, several pieces of information are needed

- Product information. This includes the type of product(s) and the firmware version(s) used.
- Vulnerability information. This includes which versions of the software are vulnerable and which are not.

As the majority of vulnerability-related questions are posed in the form of a vulnerability scan report, such reports typically include the vulnerability identifier. Most often the model identifier is also included when the question is sent, but it happens that a follow-up question is needed to identify this.

Knowing the product and model, first-line support looks at the release notes which very often enumerate which vulnerabilities have been remedied in a specific firmware. Most of the time the vulnerability is listed in release notes and the answer to upgrade and to which firmware version can be delivered promptly. First-line support has a Service-Level Agreement (SLA) with a defined number of hours for answering questions, but vulnerability-related issues are prioritized and the answer is often returned within a few hours depending on the issue queue and office hours. Handling a specific vulnerability-related question is often finished in around 30 min upon opening the issue.

Further vulnerability information is typically found in NVD. First-line support does not go this far in their analysis, but this is a primary information source for the product specialist. Together with the development teams, this information can reveal which firmware releases could be vulnerable.

Having a vulnerable version does not equal being vulnerable. Additional work on understanding vulnerabilities is performed by SSG in a vulnerability triage process. This process includes looking at the base CVSS score for a vulnerability and understand how it affects the products. Sometimes high severity vulnerabilities turn out to be of very low or no severity in the product. This is e.g., the case if the vulnerable part of a component is not even used by the product. Other times, but less often, low severity vulnerabilities turn out to be of higher severity in the product. One example could be if availability impact is low, but considered of very high importance to the product. A full severity analysis can however not be performed since the SSG only knows how the software is used in the product, but not how the product is used in an actual system.

The acquirer instead has the information needed to decide if they are actually vulnerable. As one example, in the systems that they manage, the devices are typically not reachable from the public Internet but resides on their own networks. This can dramatically affect the exploitability of the vulnerability and how to prioritize an update. Such contextualized information is not known to the producer. It is clear that the information gathering and decisions are here very centralized to the support team.

3.4   Identified Challenges and Opportunities

In this section, we discuss challenges and opportunities that were identified in our interviews.

From the Producer's Point of View. As noted in Sect. 3.2, the vulnerability scanning performed by the acquirer is often used as a basis for questions. They wish to better understand if they are vulnerable. At the same time, the producer also performs similar vulnerability scanning of their products. Using results from these scans could be used to more efficiently answer such questions, but a process to leverage this has not been defined.

The escalation of questions from first-line support, to the product specialist, and finally to SSG heavily relies on either searching in email correspondence or using the collective memory of the product specialists. Both the product specialist and the SSG representative identified this as a possible area of improvement.

> "This system could break when the company grows or with growing employee turnover."

A better approach would be to document relevant information. Moreover, the vast majority of vulnerabilities are already known to the SSG or to developers, being responsible for that OSS, so the information flow can be made more efficient by documenting this analysis and vulnerability information.

A possible improvement for first-line support would be to have more security training. They do have access to a set of training videos, but many questions come in as scanning reports, and one suggestion was to let the people working in first-line support do such scanning themselves, just to get an idea of how they work and the information they provide. Submitted reports sometimes lead to a bit of "panic" and with more understanding, they could carry out their investigation with more confidence. There is currently one person with security training and OSCP certification, who often becomes the go-to person for all these issues.

From the Acquirer's Point of View. Though vulnerability scans against deployed products are performed on a regular basis, there is no structured work for security vulnerabilities. This includes monitoring information sources for faster identification of potential vulnerabilities. At the same time, there is much trust in the producer's ability to fix vulnerabilities and it is convenient to leave this responsibility to the producer. There are also no recorded events of when things have gone wrong. Still, there is a perceived need to have a more structured approach to security and vulnerabilities. To this extent, the information provided by the producer, both in release notes and in answers to direct questions is often not enough to make informed decisions.

4 Discussion and Analysis

Based on the results in Sect. 3, we summarize a set of challenges and opportunities that have been identified.

Challenge: *Scattered knowledge*
There is little or no centralization of knowledge regarding vulnerabilities within the producer's organization. The knowledge is built and disseminated by different parts of the organization, while at the same time being information that needs to be communicated quickly in order to protect the managed systems from attacks. While having a well-defined process for handling vulnerability-related questions from customers, this decentralization of knowledge could have a negative effect on efficiency and accuracy in case there is a higher turnover of employees in the future.

Challenge: *Role-targeted security training*
Though first-line support answers a majority of vulnerability-related questions, they lack security training, and in particular training targeting the actual questions that they receive. This lowers their confidence when it comes to these types of questions.

Challenge: *Strong reliance on the producer*
The acquirer is strongly reliant on the producer providing firmware updates and timely information. Much information regarding vulnerabilities in devices is provided through release notes. With many devices and models, it is hard to track the newly released firmware and understand which needs to be applied urgently and which can wait until regular maintenance.

Opportunity: *Leverage internal scan information*
Re-using and centralizing information from internal scans can increase the understanding of customers' challenges. Since there is in-house scanning of firmware already in place, transferring this knowledge to first-line support seems to be a

cost-efficient way of increasing efficiency, accuracy, and confidence in answering questions.

Opportunity: *Register for Release Notes.* Release notes are linked to a specific firmware, and the firmware is only applicable to a set of device types and models. Allowing the acquirer to subscribe to release notes for certain devices and models can help them to more efficiently identify if the vulnerability applies to them or not. This need was described by the acquirer, and based on the fact that many answers are found by first-line support consulting the release notes, this could potentially also reduce the number of support cases.

The fact that the answer often is not enough to make decisions is reasonable. Indeed, the producer has no knowledge of the environment in which the products are operating. Vulnerability information is often generic, and it is up to the affected party to determine to which extent the vulnerability can be exploited. Only to some extent, this can be done by the triage at the producer's side since they know how the software is used in the product. This is also evident in the severity score given to vulnerabilities (CVSS), where the worst-case scenario is assumed when determining the base score. The environmental CVSS score is instead defined for adjusting the severity level for the operating environment. This highlights the need for security expertise throughout the supply chain.

5 Conclusion

We conducted a case study to better understand how vulnerability-related questions are handled by a producer and an acquirer of IoT devices. We describe both how such questions are handled in the respective company and how the information is communicated between them. The study is motivated by the fact that the use of OSS is increasing and that new vulnerabilities are discovered and reported to public databases at an increasing rate. Having an efficient process for identifying, analyzing, and communicating information regarding firmware upgrades is essential to mitigate an increased cybersecurity threat. Our study revealed a set of challenges and opportunities that can be considered to facilitate improved processes. While these are identified based on the involved companies' needs and procedures, we believe that they can also be considered by other companies to improve their cybersecurity. For future work, it would be valuable to better understand if, how and why vulnerability-related information fundamentally differs from other types of time-critical information that need to be communicated within or between organizations. Such an understanding could allow us to identify optimizations, both from a technical, but also from an organizational perspective.

Acknowledgements. This research was funded in part by the Swedish Government Agency for Innovation Systems (Vinnova), grant 2018-03965, and in part by the Swedish Foundation for Strategic Research, grant RIT17-0035.

References

1. Aldea, M., Gheorghică, D., Croitoru, V.: Software vulnerabilities integrated management system. In: Proceedings 13th International Conference on Communications (COMM), pp. 97–102 (2020)
2. Cobleigh, A., Hell, M., Karlsson, L., Reimer, O., Sönnerup, J., Wisenhoff, D.: Identifying, prioritizing and evaluating vulnerabilities in third party code. In: 2018 IEEE 22nd International Enterprise Distributed Object Computing Workshop (EDOCW), pp. 208–211 (2018)
3. Corallo, A., Lazoi, M.: Value network collaborations for innovations in an aerospace company. In: Proceedings IEEE International Technology Management Conference (ICE) (2010)
4. Du, Z.T., Xie, X.Z.: Research on construction strategy of enterprise information sharing in supply chain. In: Proceedings International Conference of Information Science and Management Engineering (ISME), pp. 49–53 (2010)
5. GitHub: The 2020 state of the octoverse (2020). https://octoverse.github.com
6. Mansfield-Devine, S.: Nation-state attacks: the escalating menace. Netw. Secur. **2020**(12), 12–17 (2020)
7. Migues, S., Steven, J., Ware, M.: Building security in maturity model - version 11 (2021). https://www.bsimm.com
8. Nguyen, V.H., Massacci, F.: The (un)reliability of NVD vulnerable versions data: an empirical experiment on Google Chrome vulnerabilities. In: Proceedings 8th ACM SIGSAC Symposium on Information, Computer and Communications Security, pp. 493–498 (2013)
9. NIST: National vulnerability database (2021). https://nvd.nist.gov/
10. Olsson, T., Hell, M., Höst, M., Franke, U., Borg, M.: Sharing of vulnerability information among companies - a survey of Swedish companies. In: Proceedings Euromicro Conference on Software Engineering and Advanced Applications (SEAA), pp. 284–291 (2019). https://doi.org/10.1109/SEAA.2019.00051
11. Ponta, S.E., Plate, H., Sabetta, A.: Beyond metadata: code-centric and usage-based analysis of known vulnerabilities in open-source software. In: Proceedings IEEE International Conference on Software Maintenance and Evolution (ICSME) (2018)
12. Robson, C.: Real World Research: A Resource for Social Scientists and Practisioner-Researchers. Blackwell (2002)
13. Runeson, P., Höst, M., Rainer, A., Regnell, B.: Case Study Research in Software Engineering - Guidelines and Examples. Wiley (2012)
14. IBM Security: X-force threat intelligence index 2021 (2021). https://www.ibm.com/se-en/security/data-breach/threat-intelligence
15. Serror, M., Hack, S., Henze, M., Schuba, M., Wehrle, K.: Challenges and opportunities in securing the industrial internet of things. IEEE Trans. Ind. Inf. **17**(5), 2985–2996 (2021). https://doi.org/10.1109/TII.2020.3023507

Software Quality

Analyzing SAFe Practices with Respect to Quality Requirements: Findings from a Qualitative Study

Wasim Alsaqaf[1]([⊠]), Maya Daneva[1]([⊠]), Preethu Rose Anish[2]([⊠]),
and Roel Wieringa[1]([⊠])

[1] School of Computer Science, University of Twente, Enschede, The Netherlands
{w.h.a.alsaqaf,m.daneva,r.j.wieringa}@utwente.nl
[2] Tata Research Development and Design Center, TCS, Pune, India
preethu.rose@tcs.com

Abstract. Quality Requirements (QRs) pose challenges in many agile large-scale distributed projects. Often, project organizations counter these challenges by borrowing some heavyweight practices, e.g. adding more documentation. At the same time, agile methodologists proposed a few scaled agile frameworks to specifically serve agile organizations working on large and distributed systems. Little is known about the extent to which these proposals address QRs and the specific ways in which this happens. Moreover, evidence regarding the practical implementation of these frameworks with respect to QRs is scarce. Our paper makes a step towards narrowing this gap of knowledge. Using an exploratory research process, we analyze one well-documented framework, namely the Scaled Agile Framework (SAFe). We first analyzed the elements of SAFe as they were described in the methodological book of SAFe to identify the possible remedies to the QRs challenges reported in previous work. We then conducted a qualitative interview-based study to understand the practices that SAFe practitioners actually use to mitigate those QRs challenges. Our documentary analysis of SAFe resulted in identifying 25 SAFe elements that could (at least partially) mitigate one or more of the reported QRs challenges. Nine of those SAFe elements were reported in our interview-based study by SAFe practitioners as remedy for some of the reported QRs challenges. While practitioners attempted to use the recommended SAFe strategies for QRs, they often changed them in their own ways, or altogether resorted to heavyweight practices that the case study organizations knew from previously done non-SAFe projects.

Keywords: Agile scaled framework · SAFe · Quality requirements · Requirements engineering · Documentary analysis · Empirical research · Qualitative interview-based study

1 Introduction

The necessity of reacting quickly to the rapidly changing market, pushes large organizations to believe that the success stories of agile methods' application in the context they

© Springer Nature Switzerland AG 2021
L. Ardito et al. (Eds.): PROFES 2021, LNCS 13126, pp. 233–248, 2021.
https://doi.org/10.1007/978-3-030-91452-3_16

originally were designed for (e.g. small co-located teams) can be successfully repeated in large-scale distributed context. However, the transferability of experiences made in the original context to the realities of large-scale distributed contexts is far from flawless [1–4]. Although several agile scaled frameworks have been proposed by agile practitioners to guide the application of agile methods in large-scale distributed context (e.g. Scaled Agile Framework (SAFe) [5], Large-Scale Scrum (LeSS) [6], Scrum@Scale (S@S) [7]) relatively little research is published about these frameworks' effectiveness in practice, especially on an enterprise scale [2, 8]. Moreover, as per a 2018 review [3], large-scale agile enterprises adopting these frameworks report a broad range of technical and enterprise-level challenges due to resistance to change, shifts in the ways of thinking of hierarchies of requirements, lack of transparency, and lack of knowledge on proper integration of agile and non-agile ways of working. Our current paper is dedicated to one specific type of requirements challenges in large-scale agile delivery, namely those pertaining to quality requirements (QRs), such as security and usability. The paper builds upon an earlier study [9] in which the authors found that often, enterprises counter QRs challenges by borrowing some heavyweight practices, e.g. creating new artefacts (security or usability stories) or roles (e.g. security officer, UX team), and then adding these practices to their agile delivery cycle. Therein [9], is also stated that the introduction of these heavyweight practices unexpectedly brought with them new problems. But do agile scaled frameworks propose a remedy to QRs challenges in large-scale agile? If so, is the remedy effective in practice? As we found no publication answering these questions, we initiated an exploratory qualitative research process to understand and evaluate the agile methodologists' proposals for treating QRs challenges. For the purpose of our research we chose for inclusion those scaled agile frameworks deemed 'most popular' according to the 14th annual state-of-agile report issued by market observing firms [10]. As already said, the present work rests on a previously published exploratory study [9] that found 15 QRs challenges and 9 practices that agile practitioners currently use to cope with the identified challenges. We note that these findings [9] came out of an interview-based research with practitioners in enterprises committed to agile project delivery. However, these 9 practices were not collected in relation to any existing prescriptive or descriptive agile scale framework such as LeSS [6] nor agile method such as Scrum [11]. Given this background, in the present research we aim to explore those agile practices that are suggested by the most popular published agile scaled frameworks and that could help mitigate the QRs challenges which were identified in the previous work [9].

The present paper reports our results of analyzing one specific scaled framework, namely, SAFe 5.0 [5]. Our ongoing research also includes some other frameworks, however these are out of scope in this paper. In this paper, we set out to answer the following research question: *What are the agile practices suggested by SAFe that could mitigate the effect of the QRs challenges identified in [9]?* This question is decomposed in three sub-questions:

RQ1: Which SAFe elements described in the SAFe methodological textbook and related literature could possibly mitigate the QRs challenges defined in [9]?
RQ2: Do SAFe practitioners experience the QRs challenges identified in [9]?
RQ3: If yes, then which SAFe elements do they utilize to mitigate these challenges?

Using (i) a documentary research process [12] that takes as input the SAFe methodological textbook [5] and its related literature, and (ii) a qualitative exploratory interviews with practitioners from agile organizations [13], we analyzed the practices that the SAFe methodologists [5] proposed to use in large projects. In what follows, we first give a background information and describe related work (Sect. 2). Thereafter we describe our research process and provide definitions of the most important concepts (Sect. 3 and 4). We then present and discuss our results (Sect. 5 and 6) and the threats of validity (Sect. 7). We conclude in Sect. 8.

2 Background and Related Works

The question of how large-scale frameworks (such as SAFe [5] and LeSS [6]) treat RE problems in general, and QRs problems in particular, has become an area of active research relatively recently. A 2017 systematic literature review [14] found that while QR challenges are documented in empirical studies, relatively few solutions to them have been demonstrated to work consistently well. An empirical follow-up case study research of Alsaqaf et al. [9] indicated nine solution practices that practitioners resort to in large-scale agile projects. However (as mentioned in the Introduction), these solution practices were not traceable to any particular methodological guidelines linked to large-scale framework, be it SAFe, LeSS or S@S. Next, in 2016–2020, Kasauli et al. [15] carried out a large-scale research initiative on RE challenges and practices in large-scale agile system development. Moyon et al. [16] extends SAFe with the S^2C-SAFe framework to achieve security compliance in large-scale agile context. To the best of our knowledge, the empirical articles (e.g. [15, 16]) of these authors are among the very few who particularly focused on SAFe and LeSS in order to derive potential solutions to RE challenges. Kasauli et al. [15] also indicated that despite one might find potential solution elements in the popular large-scale frameworks and their methodological guidelines, for very few of these elements there is empirical evidence to work as assumed. Furthermore, Beecham et al. [17] examined how two scaled frameworks – SAFe and DAD [18], address software development risks in global projects, where requirements risks formed a major category. Using two longitudinal case studies implementing each framework, the authors conclude in regard to the requirements risks that these "are addressed well by both methods". However, the authors also elaborate that requirements risks are not in fact eliminated; only the impact of these risks could be reduced. We make the note however that the addressed risks refer to scope, project goals and conflicting requirements in general, and not particularly to QRs challenges.

Most recently, other researchers examined how large-scale agile project (that had adopted large-scale frameworks, e.g. SAFe) cope with specific types of QRs, such as security compliance requirements and privacy requirements [19]. The authors of [19] developed and evaluated approaches to each of these requirements that are meant to complement SAFe. The specificity of these approaches however makes it hard to generalize across solutions to other types of QRs.

3 Research Method

This study is part of an exploratory research initiative in which we analyze the practices described by well-known agile scaled frameworks from practitioner's perspective, in order to understand the extent to which these practices mitigate the impact of the QR's challenges identified in [9]. To achieve our goal we chose to develop a two-step qualitative research design [13]. This is suitable in cases in which researchers first use documentary analysis techniques for examining texts (e.g. guidelines, policies, proceedings) in order to develop sensitivity of the aspects of the phenomenon under study and to come up with assumptions about what is supposed to happen in real-world situations, and then use qualitative exploratory techniques (c.g. in-depth interviews) to understand what actually happens in the real-world context and how much this deviates from what is supposed to happen. We adopted this approach because it fits our research context and also because it has demonstrated its viability in an earlier study [17] in a context similar to ours. We designed the following research process including the following steps: **Step 1** explains our reasoning for including certain frameworks. This is described in Sect. 3.1. **Step 2** is concerned with examining the applicability of the selected agile scaled frameworks' practices – as described by the authors of each framework in their respective methodological textbook with guidelines and their repository of related documents (appendices, templates, cases) –, in mitigating the QRs challenges found in our previously published study [9]. This step is described in Sect. 3.2. It performs a documentary analysis grounded on the methodological guidelines of Appleton and Cowley [12]. The outcome of this step is a list of assumptions that agile methodologists have about how to treat QRs in large-scale projects. **Step 3** is described in Sect. 3.3 and it investigates the practices of the selected agile scaled frameworks as utilized in real life by practitioners in real-world organizations, to empirically examine their application in mitigating the identified QR's challenges (as per the perceptions and the experiences of those working in the field). As this paper is focused on one framework only (SAFe [5]), it in turn reports on Steps 2 and 3 as executed in the context of analyzing this specific framework. We describe the steps of our process in the next sub-sections.

3.1 Selecting Agile Scaled Framework

Over the years, the community of agile practitioners proposed more than 30 scaled agile frameworks [20]. Portman [20] classified those into two categories: (1) *enterprise-targeted* frameworks (e.g. SAFe [5], LeSS [6], S@S [7]) aiming to deliver complex enterprise-level products whereby the collaboration between distributed teams is essential, and (2) *web-scale-targeted* frameworks (e.g. Spotify [21], Scaled Agile Lean Development (ScALeD)[1]) aiming to support a company's IT-department in maintaining existing applications, whereby the dependencies between distributed teams are minimalized. In this paper, we focus on the first category—"enterprise-targeted frameworks"–because these frameworks match our research interest, namely the distributed and large-scale systems development context. Furthermore, for the purpose of our research initiative, we limit our selection of frameworks to those that are the most used according to the

---

[1] http://scaledprinciples.org/.

14th annual state-of-agile report of market observers [10]. This source [10] indicates the "enterprise-targeted framework" SAFe [5] as the most popular across large organizations today. While our research initiative will include more frameworks (e.g. LeSS, and S@S), in this paper we focus solely on the agile practices of SAFe [5]. However, our choice for SAFe [5] does not imply that we prefer or recommend SAFe. The other frameworks will be investigated in our follow-up research.

3.2 Uncovering the Assumptions in SAFe About Engineering the QRs

The information about SAFe provided on its official website https://www.scaledagilef ramework.com/ as well as in its official textbook 'SAFe 5.0 Distilled Achieving Business Agility with the Scaled Agile Framework' [5], was taken as input into our documentary analysis. The objective of this stage of the research process was to answer RQ1. The first two researchers analyzed the SAFe practices by first reading and re-reading the textbook [5] and the text resources in the website to identify those SAFe elements that could be considered potential candidate strategies to cope with the QR challenges identified in [9]. For clarity, we list these QRs challenges in Table 1, where the first column shows the categories of the challenges as reported in [9] and the second column reports the specific challenges of each respective category in the first column.

Table 1. The QR challenges as reported in [9].

Category	Challenges
1. Teams coordination and communication challenges	Late detection of QRs infeasibility
	Hidden assumptions in inter-team collaboration
	Uneven teams maturity
	Suboptimal inter-team organization
2. Quality assurance challenges	Inadequate QRs test specification
	Lack of cost-effective real integration test
	Lengthy QRs acceptance checklist
	Sporadic adherence to quality guidelines
3. QRs elicitation challenges	Overlooking sources of QRs
	Lack of QRs visibility
	Ambiguous QRs communication process
4. Conceptual challenges of QRs	Unclear conceptual definition of QRs
	Confusion about QR's specification approaches
5. Architecture challenges	Unmanaged architecture changes
	Misunderstanding the architecture drivers

Our documentary analysis proceeded as follows: In a first round, the two researchers worked independently to come up with a list of SAFe elements for which the SAFe textbook [5] gives explicit or implicit information that the respective practice helps with QRs. In a second round the researchers got together and have discussed their identified practices of SAFe based on an argumentative discussion [22] and Conklin's dialog mapping technique for qualitative data structuring [23], in order to examine each practice's fitness in mitigating the QRs challenges reported in [9]. The goal was to reach a shared rationally-supported hypothetical mapping [23] between each SAFe element and one or more QR challenges. The result of this step was a list of assumptions indicating to us those SAFe practices that could possibly mitigate the QR challenges in Table 1. These assumptions mean theoretical mappings (we adopt the term from Beecham et al. [17]) and in Step 3, we want to complement them with real-world insights from an exploratory interview study, in order to compare and contrast our findings from theory (i.e. the SAFe textbook) and practice. We provide more details on our analytical activity and results in Sect. 5.1.

3.3 Understanding How Real-World SAFe Projects Resolve QRs Challenges

As indicated earlier, at this point of our research process, we wanted to know if practitioners in real-world organizations experiences the QRs challenges and if so, how did they mitigate their effects (RQ2 and RQ3). Toward this end, we performed a qualitative exploratory study in the context of real world large-scale distributed agile projects in two different organizations, labeled as **O1** and **O2**. Both were selected purposefully based on their size and their rich experience with SAFe implementation. The first (O1) is a large Dutch government organization with about six years of SAFe experience. O1 has about 30000 employees spread over the whole country, however the IT department is located in one big building in one city. The agile teams of the IT department are distributed within this building. The software delivered by O1 is used by both individuals and companies to manage their taxes and allowances and is subject to strict legal regulations. The SAFe variant that O1 implemented is Portfolio SAFe [5] (it is explained more in detail in the next section). The second organization (O2) is an Indian large multinational consulting company with approximately 100000 employees. O2 is one of the biggest IT companies in the world. It operates in more than hundred locations across several countries. O2 is CMMI level 5 certified and has worked with SAFe since the introduction of SAFe in 2011. The agile teams of O2 are distributed across different locations and countries. The SAFe variant they implemented is Large Solution [5]. As already stated, by doing this interview based we aimed to answer RQ2 and RQ3. To collect the data, we conducted nine semi-structured, open- ended, in-depth interviews according to the guidelines of Boyce and Neale [24]. We chose the qualitative interview-based case study approach, because our desired depth of understanding could not be achieved meaningfully through the use of survey questionnaires and closed questions. As per Benbasat et al. [25], employing such a research method is a particularly suitable to research situations in which researchers study socially constructed processes in systems development projects and seek to achieve as good as possible grasp of reality. The selection of participants was based on the following criteria: (1) they all have at least 3 years of experience in SAFe and at least 10 years of IT experience, (2) they all had exposure to tasks related to the engineering of QRs, (3) they all were willingness to participate. They were drawn purposefully from the professional circle of the first and the third authors. As we were striving for a variety of roles to cover various perspectives, we included participants employed in different jobs (See Table 2). Four of the participants are from O1 and their interviews took place in the Netherlands, with the first author as the interviewer. The other participants are from O2 and the interviews took place in India, with the third author as the interviewer. The participants' roles in SAFe and their experience are described in Table 2. All interviews were in English and took around one hour. Our interview process included the following: (i) we asked each interviewee to choose a SAFe project in which he/she was actively involved in and in which QRs played a significant role, (ii) we showed the list of the reported QRs challenges [9] and asked the participant to indicate which ones he/she observed in his/her experiences in that SAFe project, and finally (iii) we asked which SAFe elements has each participant used to cope with the experienced QRs challenges. A list with the identified QRs challenges [9] was sent to all participants before the interview, in order to give them the chance to understand the challenges correctly.

Table 2. The participants in our interview-based study.

Participant ID	Organization	Role	Years of experience in IT
P1	O2	Technical lead	12
P2	O2	Agile coach	30
P3	O2	Solution architect	14
P4	O2	Agile coach	20
P5	O2	Project manager	13
P6	O1	Agile coach	15
P7	O1	IT manager	24
P8	O1	Product manager	10
P9	O1	IT manager	18

The interviews were audio-recorded and then thereafter transcribed by a professional company to avoid biases. The first two researchers read the transcripts separately and established a mapping between the by practitioners used SAFe elements and the QRs challenges they mitigate. Using coding [26] and Conklin's dialog mapping technique for qualitative data structuring [23], these researchers sorted out the qualitative data and mapped the participants' answers against the QRs challenges in Table 1. The results of this analytical activity are reported in Sect. 5.2. However, before that, we present the SAFe framework [5] as this is important for understanding the context of our research.

4   Scaled Agile Framework (SAFe)

SAFe is described by its authors [5] as a set of principles, practices and guidance that can be used by enterprises to deliver small solutions as well as complex systems in an agile way. It is a configurable framework with four variants as described below:

Essential Safe (ES) is the smallest SAFe configuration (between 50–150 practitioners) and the fundamental building block for all other SAFe configurations. The so-called agile release train (ART) is the fundamental concept of ES. It is a team of 5–12 agile teams where each team is a cross-functional group of 5–11 practitioners. Furthermore, ES consists of two levels, namely (1) team level that contains artefacts, events and processes an agile team needs to do in order to deliver value and (2) program level which contains all artifacts, events and processes needed to coordinate the work between the agile teams at the team level. The agile teams apply several agile practices (e.g. Scrum, Extreme Programming, Kanban) to deliver their part of the solution within a sprint. ART is further responsible for planning, committing, and deploying all the work together within a Program Increment (PI) (typically between 8 and 12 weeks). Scrum of Scrums is used to coordinate the dependencies between the different agile teams.

Large Solution SAFe (LSS) is a SAFe configuration for delivering large and complex systems without the need for portfolio and strategy alignment. In essence, LSS is an ES with additional roles (e.g. Solution train, Solution train engineer), and practices (e.g. Solution engineering, Solution management). The so-called solution train (ST) is the basis of LSS which coordinates the work of multiple ARTs by using Scrum of Scrums to deliver a complex system within a shared PI. As already said, O2 uses LSS.

Portfolio SAFe (PS) is concerned with managing value streams by aligning value streams to ARTs. Values are defined as Epics and managed by an Epic owner through the so-called portfolio kanban system. Value streams are the activities needed by an enterprise to deliver end-to-end customers' value. As stated earlier, O1 uses PS.

Full Safe (FS) is the complete SAFe configuration consisting of all previous configurations, which is used in large enterprises to align portfolios to very large solutions. We note that FS, while leveraging the elements of all three configurations, does not add any new elements.

5   Results

5.1   SAFe Elements Assumed Mitigate the QRs Challenges Defined in [9]

This section summarizes our findings in regard to RQ1. We found that SAFe as presented in [5] does recognize the importance of QRs. In fact, QRs are explicitly mentioned in all SAFe configurations. SAFe treats QRs as constraints on the backlog items or as restrictions on the software design and not as independent backlog items. In Tables 3, 4, 5 and 6, we present the results of our documentary analysis. These tables show, respectively, those elements – i.e. roles, artifacts, events, practices – of all four SAFe configurations which are supposed to influence the engineering of QRs, according to the SAFe textbook [5] and the documents at the official SAFe website. In each of these tables, column 1 represents the identified SAFe element which our analysis found to be a good candidate solution to use for coping with the QRs challenges from Table 1. The second column of each table shows the SAFe configuration in which the identified SAFe element is utilized (i.e. Essential SAFe (ES), Large Solution SAFe (LSS) and Portfolio SAFe (PS)). Finally, the third column gives a short description of the respective SAFe element. A dash "-" in a cell means that SAFe doesn't mention a value for that particular element in corresponding column. We note that elements which are related to Scrum [11] (e.g. sprint, sprint review) are not taken into consideration in our analysis for two reasons: 1) they are not specific to SAFe which is the subject of this study, 2) Scrum is originally designed for a small, single, co-located teams [3] while our focus is large-scale distributed agile teams.

Table 3. The identified SAFe roles that could help cope with QRs challenges

Roles	SAFe configuration	Description
Product management	ES	A team who is responsible for the program backlog
Solution management	LSS	A team who is responsible for the Solution backlog
Lean portfolio management	PS	A team who is responsible for the portfolio backlog
Epic owner	PS	The owner of an epic from the portfolio backlog that gets implemented
System engineer	ES	An individual who is responsible for defining and communicating the technical requirements where QRs might be part of within the ART
Solution engineer	LSS	An individual who is responsible for defining and communicating the technical requirements where QRs might be part of within the ST
Agile release train (ART)	ES	A team of agile team created around values which coordinate the activity of those teams to deliver customer values
Solution train (ST)	LSS	A SAFe construction to organize the work of multiple ARTs in order of delivering complex systems

Table 4. The identified SAFe artifacts that could help cope with QRs challenges

Artifacts	SAFe configuration	Description
Program backlog	ES	A repository of all features that need to be broken down to teams user stories
Solution backlog	LSS	A repository of all (supportive) activities needed to enable the implementation of other activities
Portfolio backlog	PS	A repository of the most abstract epics
Solution intent	LSS	A repository of all knowledges and requirements of the solution to be implemented
Enabler	ES, LSS, PS	It is e.g. epic, feature of user story needed for extending the architecture to meet certain requirements

As indicated in Sect. 3, we note that Full SAFe includes all other SAFe configurations (e.g. ES, PS and LSS) and does not describe any unique specific element which only exists when implementing the Full SAFe. That explains why we did not identify specific Full SAFe elements in Tables 3, 4, 5 and 6. After identifying the SAFe elements that could mitigate the QRs challenges identified in [9], the first two researchers mapped these elements (in Tables 3, 4, 5 and 6) to the reported categories of the challenges by using Conklin's dialog mapping technique for qualitative data structuring [23]. Table 7 summarizes this mapping. The first column of Table 7 shows the reported challenges, while the second column shows those SAFe elements that could be used to mitigate the related challenge in the first column. A dash "–" in the second column means that SAFe does not explicitly specify a particular element (e.g. artifact, role, event, practice) that could mitigate the reported QR challenge in the first column. SAFe describes elements of four types – i.e. artifacts, roles, events, practices – that could (at least partially) mitigate the QRs challenges reported in [9]. E.g., the different backlogs of the different SAFe configurations (e.g. Program backlog, Solution backlog) in combination with the Solution intent artifact could be used to eliminate confusions about conceptual definitions of QRs. SAFe however treats QRs in an unambiguous way as constraints on the product backlog items (PBIs) and not as independent PBIs. Besides, SAFe introduces several roles, namely: System engineer and Solution engineer, both possibly helping mitigate architectural challenges e.g. "Unmanaged architecture changes" and "Misunderstanding the architecture drivers" (see Table 1). However, we did not find appropriate SAFe elements that could mitigate the following two QRs challenges: "Lengthy QRs acceptance checklist", "Confusion about QR's specification approaches". We discuss this further in our Discussion section.

Table 5. The identified SAFe events that could help cope with QRs challenges

Events	SAFe configuration	Description
Program Increment (PI) planning	ES	It is a two to three whole day planning session where all agile teams of an ART come together to obtain a shared understanding of the business and fill in their own backlogs by breaking down the program backlog items including QRs. It is analog to Sprint planning
Inspect and adapt (I&A)	ES, LSS	At the end of each PI, the teams of an ART come together to inspect the delivered product, quality and de development process. It is analog to sprint review and retrospective
Scrum of Scrums (SoS)	ES	Representatives of all teams of an ART gather ate least once weekly for 30–60 min to discuss teams progress and dependencies
PO sync	ES	A 30–60 min weekly meeting for all POs and product management of all agile teams to discuss PI objectives, product features and scope
Pre and post PI planning (PPPI)	LSS	Two events of two whole days occurs before and after de PI planning to coordinate and follow-up work of various ARTs in relation to the Solution train
Portfolio sync	PS	It is a monthly event for the Lean Portfolio Management to discus epics implementation, addressing dependencies and removing impediments
Innovation and planning iteration (IPI)	ES	An iteration following the last iteration of an increment. It is used to experiment, inspect test results and plan possible technical changes

Table 6. The identified SAFe practices that could help cope with QRs challenges

Practices	SAFe configuration	Description
Set-based design (SBD)	LSS	A practice of delaying a definitive design decision as long as possible until all possible options are verified and validated
Model-Based Systems Engineering (MBSE)	LSS	A model-centric approach to define, design and document complex systems
Economic framework	PS	A set of decision guidelines that should be used to evaluate the feasibility of QRs
Architectural runway	LSS	The existing code, infrastructure and architectural guidelines to help teams enabling the implementation of near-term features
Quadrant 4	–	Agile test matrix that explains which tests should be performed by which way (e.g. manual, automated) to validate QRs

Table 7. Mapping SAFe elements to QR challenges

QR challenges [9]	SAFe elements
Late detection of QRs infeasibility	SoS, Program backlog, Solution backlog. Portfolio backlog. Solution intent. PO sync, Portfolio sync, PPPI, PI planning
Hidden assumptions in inter-team collaboration	SoS, ARTs, STs, PI planning, IPI
Uneven teams maturity	Economic framework, Architectural runway, I&A, IPI
Suboptimal inter-team organization	ARTs
Inadequate QRs test specification	MBSE
Lack of cost-effective real integration test	Quadrant 4
Lengthy QRs acceptance checklist	–
Sporadic adherence to quality guidelines	Economic framework, I&A, SoS
Overlooking sources of QRs	Product management, Solution management, Lean Portfolio Management, Epic owner, System engineer, Solution engineer, Solution intent, PO sync
Lack of QRs visibility	System engineer, Solution engineer
Ambiguous QRs communication process	System engineer, Solution engineer, SoS, ARTs, STs
Unclear conceptual definition of QRs	SoS, Program backlog, Solution backlog. Portfolio backlog. Solution intent
Confusion about QR's specification approaches	–
Unmanaged architecture changes	System engineer, Solution engineer, Architectural runway, SBD, Enablers
Misunderstanding the architecture drivers	System engineer, Solution engineer, Architectural runway, SBD, MBSE, Enablers

5.2 Answers to RQ2 and RQ3

This section summarizes our answers to RQ2 (Do the SAFe practitioners experience the QRs challenges identified in [9]?) and RQ3 (If yes which SAFe practices they utilize to mitigate these challenges?) The answers came out of our qualitative analysis of the data in our interview-based study. We note that not all challenges were observable by all participating practitioners. For each of them, we analyzed the challenges this practitioner experienced and the way SAFe practices were used to confront the challenges (as per this practitioner's experience). Using coding [26] and concept-mapping practices [23], the first two researchers mapped SAFe elements identified by the practitioners to the challenges reported in [9]. Table 8 summarizes this mapping. The first column of the table shows the reported categories and their related challenges, while the second column shows the SAFe elements used by the practitioners to mitigate the related challenge in the first column. A dash "–" in the second column means that no remedy has been identified by the practitioners.

Table 8. Mapping SAFe elements used by practitioners to mitigate their QR challenges

QR challenges [9]	SAFe elements
Late detection of QRs infeasibility	–
Hidden assumptions in inter-team collaboration	SoS
Uneven teams maturity	Architectural runway
Suboptimal inter-team organization	ARTs, Component teams
Inadequate QRs test specification	Team architects, Automated test
Lack of cost-effective real integration test	–
Lengthy QRs acceptance checklist	References to external documents
Sporadic adherence to quality guidelines	Automated tools
Overlooking sources of QRs	–
Lack of QRs visibility	Business owner, PO, Product management
Ambiguous QRs communication process	PI planning, SoS, Architectural runway, ARTs
Unclear conceptual definition of QRs	–
Confusion about QR's specification approaches	DoD, Product backlog, A generic ART's DoD
Unmanaged architecture changes	Team architects, Solution architect, Enablers, Architectural runway
Misunderstanding the architecture drivers	Enterprise architect, Solution architect, Enablers, Architectural runway

In the experience of our participants, there are several remedies to the identified QRs challenges. E.g., for the challenge "Ambiguous QRs communication process", the practitioners used PI planning, SoS, and Architectural runway to cope with it. In contrast, for other challenges (e.g. "Unclear conceptual definition of QRs") the practitioners did not identify any SAFe remedy. Moreover, even when practitioners belong to same organization, they had different views on some challenges. E.g., a practitioner from O2 did not perceive "Lengthy QRs acceptance checklist" as a challenge while another practitioner of the same organization recognized this challenge: *"If they put QRs in the DoD, it will be a challenge for developers. We do not put them in DoD"*. A practitioner from O1 recognized this challenge as well: *"In the Definition of Done we reference to QRs"*. The practitioners had different views as well regarding the challenge "Unclear conceptual definition of QRs". In their experiences, some of them treated QRs as PBIs: *"Performance is important for us, we described it as user stories"*, *"We treat both functional requirements and QRs as user stories"*. Other practitioners considered QRs as constraints on the PBIs and specified them in both the acceptance criteria and in the DoD *"Performance, it comes back in the acceptance criteria".* These practitioners in fact were aligned with the methodological source of SAFe [5] which states to treat QRs as constraints on PBIs and advices to specify them in both the acceptance criteria and in the DoD of the PBIs. For the challenge *"Late detection of QRs infeasibility"*, the practitioners did not identify any remedy. In fact, they accepted the invisibility of the QR as a consequence of complex system development *"You are building a complex software and you find out that it is in practice slightly different than you had thought. I think it doesn't matter at all what method you use, whether it is SAFe, Scrum or waterfall, you just run into that and you have to deal with that".*

Another practitioner explained that the *"Lack of cost-effective real integration test"* is difficult to mitigate: *"It is difficult to simulate complex production environment to obtain a reasonable integration test results."* Finally, we found that in the collective experience of our practitioners, there was no remedy for the challenge "Overlooking sources of QRs" as well. As a practitioner from O1 reported: *"Within our organization we have more than six hundred systems that communicate with each other. Each of each has its own stakeholders. It is almost impossible to have an overview of all stakeholders".*

6   Discussion

Table 7 maps the SAFe elements we (i.e. the authors) identified as remedy to the QRs challenges reported in [9], while Table 8 maps those SAFe elements actively used by practitioners to mitigate the QRs challenges. We compared both tables and noticed the contrast between the remedies assumed in the literature of SAFe and the remedies reported by the practitioners. E.g., we have identified Quadrant 4 and Economic framework as possible remedies for, respectively *"Lack of cost-effective real integration test"* and *"Sporadic adherence to quality guidelines"*. However, no participant has mentioned those SAFe elements as possible remedies for any of the reported challenges in [9], despite the use of the Portfolio SAFe configuration by their organization (O1) or the Large Solution SAFe configuration (O2). We think that this discrepancy can be explained by the fact that the implementation of SAFe in real life differs from its theory. In line with this thought, practitioners reported the use of different non- SAFe elements: *"We have a preparation team which is not a SAFe-construct. It consists of information managers who prepare the work for the agile teams. Those managers were not willing to anticipate in agile teams so we created a team for them to keep calmness". "We are fan of silo's, so we have a lot of architect's flavor e.g. a business process architect, a process architect and an IT architect".* The tendency of introducing non-SAFe elements into what was supposed to be SAFe, in the experience of our practitioners, was traceable to the *"long and consistent waterfall experience"* of our case study organizations in large-scale systems delivery projects. As one of our case study organizations was a CMM5-certified, their adoption of SAFe happened in a highly disciplined environment in which SAFe co-exists with metrics, measurement procedures, progress tracking practices and milestone-compliance practices. For this reason, it seems logical that if practitioners see a QR problem they might be open to resort to a heavyweight practice that they knew to work well from their pre-agile professional experience. Moreover, one could argue that our interviewees experienced QRs challenges because the SAFe remedies were not implemented with the due discipline and commitment, e.g. some practices might have been too much *"free-styled"*, which means being used in an idiosyncratic way. While this might well be possible, we think that for a large-scale organization it might not be realistic to assume a strict SAFe implementation as per the SAFe textbook [5]. More research is needed to substantiate this.

Furthermore, we found that despite the fact that our case study organizations did employ some SAFe elements in their coping strategies for QRs, no practitioner indicated that this was done in a cost-effective way. This let us think that it might be possible that SAFe and more heavyweight methods could both be comparably expensive approaches. This seems unsurprising, knowing that dealing with QRs represents an expensive part of any large-scale project [15]. Next, we found that SAFe [5] treats QRs as constraints on the backlog items or as restrictions on the software design. This observation agrees with the treatment of QRs in heavyweight life cycle models (e.g. [27, 28]) where QRs are operationalized into functional requirements and architecture design choices. Next, it's worthwhile noting that our practitioners experienced SAFe as a complex framework. A practitioner from O1 explains *"SAFe is very precisely defined, almost a work instruction. It is a complex framework, have you seen how big is the SAFe book in comparison to other agile scaled frameworks' books?."* This reflection is in line with observations of [29, 30] regarding the SAFe's complexity.

Finally, we found that SAFe integrated different elements that could be recognized as heavyweight non-agile elements such as Model-Based Systems Engineering. This finding is in line with [9]. The authors of [9] reported that heavyweight practices often get integrated in organizations' agile way of working to encounter QR's challenges.

7   Threats of Validity

This section discusses the possible validity threats [13] to our empirical research design and our findings. First, we employed documentation research method [12] which is a reflexive approach to the analysis of documents that contain information about the phenomenon we wish to study. There is a possible validity threat related to the types of documents and the ability to use them as reliable sources of evidence on the social world. We think this threat is minimal because we used the most important repository of documents of the SAFe community of practitioners. The documents we reviewed form the basis for this community's education and certification programs. We were also conscious of researchers' bias. However, we mitigated this by including two academic researchers (the second and the fourth co-authors) next to the two industry researchers (the first and the third authors). This diversity of backgrounds was used to remove any bias and checking tacit assumptions about the reviewed documents. Furthermore, our interview study included 9 practitioners in two organizations. Their perceptions and experiences can not be generalized to all possible large-scale enterprises using SAFe. However, because these practitioners were with various roles and operated in very different cultural contexts (India and the Netherlands), we think that they cover a broad range of professional perspectives to QRs in SAFe. Acknowledging this diversity, we think it might well be possible to have similar findings if we included more participants from organizations similar to O1 and O2. As stated in [31], contextual similarity in terms of process-oriented thinking, experience with both agile and heavyweight development practices in large and very large projects, might lead to similar organizational mechanisms that might produce similar effects in other similar but different organizations (e.g. government agencies with 30000+ employees and large companies).

8   Conclusion

This paper investigated the possible remedies suggested by SAFe [5] to mitigate the effects of QRs challenges identified in a previous study [9]. We have examined SAFe with respect to those QRs challenges by (i) performing documentary analysis where the official SAFe literature has been investigated and (ii) conducting an interview-based study to understand the SAFe elements used by practitioners to cope with the QRs challenges. Our results show that SAFe contains 25 elements (e.g. roles, artifacts, events, practices; see Tables 3, 4, 5, 6) that are assumed to be used to mitigate the impact of the identified QRs. Nine of those elements were also mentioned by the practitioners involved in the interview-based study (see Table 8). We think that SAFe practitioners, due to the complexity of the SAFe framework, implement SAFe differently from the SAFe textbook [5]. In our opinion this difference in implementation could be the reason for the discrepancy between the SAFe elements identified through our documentary analysis and those identified in our exploratory interview-based study. Our follow-up research step will be to extend this work by investigating the actual reasons behind the discrepancy between the practical implementation of SAFe in real-world projects and the suggested implementation described by the SAFe authors [5]. The follow-up study will help us define a practical set of remedies to the QRs challenges identified in [9].

References

1. Smart, J.: To transform to have agility, don't do a capital A, capital T agile transformation. IEEE Softw. **35**, 56–60 (2018)
2. Conboy, K., Carroll, N.: Implementing large-scale agile frameworks: challenges and recommendations. IEEE Softw. **36**, 1–9 (2019)
3. Kalenda, M., et al.: Scaling agile in large organizations: practices, challenges, and success factors. J. Softw. Evol. Process **30**, e1954 (2018)
4. Bick, S., et al.: Coordination challenges in large-scale software development: a case study of planning misalignment in hybrid settings. IEEE Trans. Softw. Eng. **44**, 932–950 (2018)
5. Richard, K., Leffingwell, D.: SAFe 5.0 Distilled Achieving Business Agility with the Scaled Agile Framework, 1st edn. Pearson Education, London (2020)
6. Larman, C., Vodde, B.: Large-Scale Scrum more with Less. Pearson Education, London (2016)
7. Sutherland, J.: The Scrum@Scale guide - the definitive guide to Scrum@Scale: scaling that works. In: Scrum@Scale, pp. 1–19 (2019). https://www.scrumatscale.com/scrum-at-scale-guide/
8. Paasivaara, M., et al.: Adopting SAFe to scale agile in a globally distributed organization. In: ICGSE 2017, pp. 36–40 (2017)
9. Alsaqaf, W., et al.: Quality requirements challenges in the context of large-scale distributed agile: an empirical study. Inf. Softw. Technol. **110**, 39–55 (2019)

10. COLLAB.NET and VERSIONONE.COM: 14th Annual State of Agile Report. VersionOne (2020). https://stateofagile.com/?_ga=2.145189495.276092471.1591726593-100 8038165.1591726593#ufh-i-615706098-14th-annual-state-of-agile-report/7027494

11. Schwaber, K., Sutherland, J.: The scrum guide. Scrum.Org and ScrumInc, p. 19 (2017)

12. Appleton, J.V., Cowley, S.: Analysing clinical practice guidelines. A method of documentary analysis. J. Adv. Nurs. **25**, 1008–1017 (1997)

13. Yin, R.K.: Case Study Research Design and Methods. 5th Revise. Sage Publications Inc. (2013)

14. Alsaqaf, W., Daneva, M., Wieringa, R.: Quality requirements in large-scale distributed agile projects – a systematic literature review. In: Grünbacher, P., Perini, A. (eds.) REFSQ 2017. LNCS, vol. 10153, pp. 219–234. Springer, Cham (2017). https://doi.org/10.1007/978-3-319-54045-0_17

15. Kasauli, R., et al.: Requirements engineering challenges and practices in large-scale agile system development. J. Syst. Softw. **172**, 110851 (2021)

16. Moyon, F., et al.: How to integrate security compliance requirements with agile software engineering at scale? In: Morisio, M., Torchiano, M., Jedlitschka, A. (eds.) PROFES 2020. LNCS, vol. 12562, pp. 69–87. Springer, Cham (2020). https://doi.org/10.1007/978-3-030-64148-1_5

17. Beecham, S., et al.: Do scaling agile frameworks address global software development risks? An empirical study. J. Syst. Softw. **173**, 110823 (2021)

18. Ambler, S.W., Lines, M.: Disciplined Agile Delivery: A Practitioner's Guide to Agile Software Delivery in the Enterprise. IBM Press (2012)

19. Wagner, T.J., Ford, T.C.: Metrics to meet security & privacy requirements with agile software development methods in a regulated environment (2021)

20. Portman, H.: Scaling Agile in Organisaties. Van Haren Publ. (2017)

21. Kniberg, H., Ivarsson, A.: Scaling agile @ spotify - with tribes, squads, chapters & guilds (2012)

22. Hitchcock, D.: The practice of argumentative discussion. Argumentation **16**, 287–298 (2002)

23. Conklin, J.: Dialog mapping: reflections on an industrial strength case study. In: Kirschner, P.A. et al. (eds.) Visualizing Argumentation. CSCW, pp. 117–136. Springer, London (2003). https://doi.org/10.1007/978-1-4471-0037-9_6

24. Boyce, C., Neale, P.: Conducting in-depth interviews: a guide for designing and conducting in-depth interviews. Evaluation **2**, 1–16 (2006)

25. Benbasat, I., et al.: The case research strategy in studies of information systems. MIS Q. 369–386 (1987). https://www.jstor.org/stable/248684?seq=1#page_scan_tab_contents

26. Charmaz, K.: Constructing Grounded Theory: A Practical Guide Through Qualitative Analysis. Sage (2006)

27. Kassab, M., et al.: An ontology based approach to non-functional requirements conceptualization. In: 4th International Conference on Software Engineering Advances, ICSEA 2009, pp. 299–308 (2009)

28. Mart, S., et al.: Dealing with non-functional requirements in model-driven development : a survey. IEEE Trans. Softw. Eng. **45**(4), 818–835 (2021)

29. Putta, A., Paasivaara, M., Lassenius, C.: Benefits and challenges of adopting the scaled agile framework (SAFe): preliminary results from a multivocal literature review. In: Kuhrmann, M., et al. (eds.) PROFES 2018. LNCS, vol. 11271, pp. 334–351. Springer, Cham (2018). https://doi.org/10.1007/978-3-030-03673-7_24

30. Ebert, C., Paasivaara, M.: Scaling agile. IEEE Softw. **34**, 98–103 (2017)

31. Seddon, P., Scheepers, R.: Towards the improved treatment of generalization of knowledge claims in IS research: drawing general conclusions from samples. Eur. J. Inf. Syst. **21**, 6–21 (2011)

Capitalizing on Developer-Tester Communication – A Case Study

Prabhat Ram[1]([⊠]), Pilar Rodríguez[2], Antonin Abherve[3], Alessandra Bagnato[3], and Markku Oivo[1]

[1] M3S, Faculty of ITEE, University of Oulu, 90014 Oulu, Finland
{prabhat.ram,markku.oivo}@oulu.fi
[2] Faculty of Computer Sciences, Universidad Politécnica de Madrid, 28040 Madrid, Spain
pilar.rodriguez@upms.es
[3] Softeam, 75016 Paris, France
{antonin.abherve,alessandra.bagnato}@softeam.fr

Abstract. Communication between developers and testers can be a rich source of insights into software development processes and practices, which may not be easily discoverable from other means like retrospectives or project roadmaps. With the objective of deriving and capitalizing on potential development-related insights, we analyzed developer-tester communication in an industrial setting. We conducted a case study at a software-intensive Agile company, within the context of the development of one of their flagship products from 2016 to 2018. We applied Latent Dirichlet Allocation (LDA) to analyze communication between developers and testers, and then invited two case-company practitioners to study the results for insights into their developments processes. The findings reveal the case company's efforts to improve their product stability, the growing emphasis on addressing end-user concerns and other quality-related issues. The practitioners interpreted these findings as indicators of evolution in their development process. Based on these findings and the state of the art, we propose an *insight classification* to highlight insights discoverable from developer-tester communication. Recognizing LDA's potential for deriving insights, the practitioners are keen on incorporating it into their software development practices. The findings from this study serve as evidence for use and benefits of text-mining techniques like LDA in industrial setting, which other practitioners could adapt to elicit their own context-influenced insights. Furthermore, the *insight classification* can serve as a foundation for further investigation into the extent and type of insights discoverable from developer-tester communication.

Keywords: LDA · Topic modeling · Insights · Software evolution

1 Introduction

During software development, communication between developers and testers is documented in issue/bug trackers like Jira[1] and Mantis[2] in unstructured format. Unstructured

---

[1] https://www.atlassian.com/software/jira.
[2] https://www.mantisbt.org/.

© Springer Nature Switzerland AG 2021
L. Ardito et al. (Eds.): PROFES 2021, LNCS 13126, pp. 249–264, 2021.
https://doi.org/10.1007/978-3-030-91452-3_17

data are expressed in natural language [1], and so do not have a clear, semantically overt, and easy-for-a-computer structure [2]. Software engineering is a data-rich activity [3], and developer-tester communication are among the software artifacts that are produced in large volume, particularly as a result of modern software development methods like Agile software development (ASD) [1]. These artifacts may hold insights into software design, developers' knowledge and decisions, and overall software advancement [1]. Their analysis can produce actionable information [4] to complement, and even improve, the overall software development process [5, 6].

Developer communication can be used to classify developer emails based on their purpose [7], identify source code activities in mailing list discussions [8], summarize software artifacts [9], and identify software architecture knowledge [10] from discussions on forums like Stack Overflow[3]. Such insights have been used for recommending developers for bug triage [11], mentoring [12], and for code comprehension [13]. In these investigations, information retrieval (IR) techniques like Latent Semantic Indexing (LSI) and Latent Dirichlet Allocation (LDA) techniques have been preferred [7, 14–16]. LDA is more suitable for handling unstructured text, while retaining semantic richness, than other techniques like clustering and bag of words [17]. This may be why LDA is the most popular topic modeling technique for indexing, searching, and clustering large amount of unstructured data [5, 18]. Based on the surveys by Chen et al. [16] and Sun et al. [4], LDA has been used on source codes, requirement documents, bug reports, commit messages, and developer communication. However, its potential to derive insights from developer-tester communication remains unexplored.

In view of the potential insights discoverable from developer communication, exploration and analysis of developer-tester communication is also very likely to produce comparable results. If conducted in an industrial setting and during software product development, the results could help practitioners capitalize on their development data better by generating insights from them. Owing to such demonstrable positive findings, practitioners could expand and benefit from the use of this text-mining technique on other unstructured data, like change logs. To our knowledge, developer-tester communication in an industrial setting has not been studied, especially for discovering development-related insights. A study [19] similar to ours has used data-mining techniques to recover lost project knowledge from the informal communication conducted over instant messaging, and involved stakeholders from two startups to validate the results. However, in contrast to our study, the authors used a text-summarization algorithm and applied it only to developer communication.

With the objective of exploring developer-tester communication for development-related insights, we conducted a case study at a large software-intensive company using ASD. We targeted the unstructured data captured by Mantis, a bug-tracking tool used by the case company (CC). The data relates to discussion between developers and the testing team while addressing *issues*[4] revealed during testing, highlighted by the internal quality team, or reported by end users. We collected the data during the development of one of

---

[3] https://stackoverflow.com/.

[4] At the case company, the term *issue* is used to refer to bugs, anomalies, defects etc.

their flagship products *Modelio*, and we used LDA to analyze those data. We addressed our research objectives with the research question (RQ): *What software development related insights could be discovered from the developer-tester communication at the case company?*

We collaborated with two practitioners (henceforth stakeholders) from the CC. This was necessary to validate the LDA results, and understand their implications, particularly for the ongoing development of *Modelio*. Stakeholder involvement adds weight to our findings, as they are likely to elicit insights that are influenced by their development context. Based on these rationales, following are our study's contributions:

- In collaboration with stakeholders, we present empirical evidence of using LDA to elicit insights from developer-tester communication. Stakeholder-driven validation of the results helps retain the embedded development context. Since the results relate to one of the flagship products *Modelio*, the inferred insights carry a higher likelihood of influencing their ongoing software development processes and practices.
- We demonstrate the use of LDA in an industrial setting to elicit development-related insights, which the stakeholders claim would have remained undetected otherwise, even with the use of their classical monitoring tools and project roadmaps.
- Driven by the findings and state of the art, we propose a non-exhaustive *insight classification* to highlight examples of insights discoverable from developer-tester communication, recorded in issue trackers like Mantis.

In the remainder of the paper, we discuss LDA and related work in Sect. 2, research method in Sect. 3, followed by the study's results in Sect. 4. Discussion of the results is presented in Sect. 5, with limitations and threats to our research's validity in Sect. 6, and conclusion and future research directions in Sect. 7.

2 Background and Related Work

We first describe the LDA algorithm, which is central to our study, followed by a discussion on how our study relates to, and differs from, the state of the art.

2.1 LDA

LDA is one of the best topic modeling techniques to automatically extract topics from a corpus of text *documents* [20]. It creates statistical models to infer latent *topics* to describe a corpus. As a result, an unstructured corpus can be organized by their discovered semantic structure, represented by the topics embedded within the *documents* [21]. LDA identifies topics by using words that co-occur frequently in the *documents* of the corpus. This is due to the nature of natural language use, where frequently co-occurring words that constitute a *topic* are often semantically related [22]. Each *document* is a multi-membership of *topics*, which in turn is a multi-membership of words. This implies that each *document* can contain multiple *topics*, and conversely, each *topic* can appear in more than one *document*. By extension, each word can then appear in more than one *topic.* In this way, LDA can discover a set of ideas or themes that succinctly describe an entire corpus [20].

Formally, LDA infers for each of T topics an N-dimensional word membership vector $z(\phi 1{:}N)$ that describes the extent to which words appear in topic z. This membership vector describes the probability that each unique word appears in topic z. In addition, LDA infers for each *document d* in the corpus a T-dimensional topic membership vector $d(\theta 1{:}T)$, describing the extent to which each *topic* appears in d. This describes the probability that each topic appears in *document d* [21]. LDA makes these inferences using Bayesian techniques like Gibbs sampling [20].

2.2 Related Work

Anvik et al. [11] used Support Vector Machines on open bug repositories to identify relationships between developers and the bugs they fix, with the aim to propose a developer recommender system for bug triage. Similarly, Zhang et al. [23] used LDA to extract topics from bug reports, capture developers' interests and experiences vis-à-vis these bug reports, to propose a developer recommender system. To identify potential software development knowledge embedded in developers' discussions in mailing lists, Shihab et al. [8] used various heuristics to explore 22 GNOME projects. They identified that only a small group of developers dominate mailing list activity, and drew a correlation between mailing list activity and code activity, concluding that developers rely heavily on mailing lists to discuss source code changes. Also focusing on developers mailing list activity, Di Sorbo et al. [7] used natural language parsing to classify the mail content according to purpose of communication. The authors demonstrate the use of this approach to mine method descriptions from developers' communication. In a similar study, Panichella et al. [13] used Vector Space Model to automatically extract method descriptions from developer communications recorded in bug tracking systems and mailing lists. The authors used the approach to produce method descriptions from developer communication, and argued that such analysis could be used for code comprehension, which can be further used for source re-documentation.

Our study is similar to the above studies in the objective of extracting insights from unstructured data, such as developer communication. However, we target developer-tester communication, which may generate insights into both development and testing. Moreover, the study is conducted in an industrial setting, in collaboration with two stakeholders. According to a survey by Sun et al. [4] and the study by Zhang et al. [23], LDA has been used mainly for developer recommendations, which is marginally in contrast to our application of LDA on developer-tester communication. Excluding the study by Lima et al. [19], we have not found investigation similar to ours that involved stakeholders for interpreting and validating results.

Bertram et al. [24] classified issue trackers based on their potential utility for its users. The authors posit that issue trackers can act as a *knowledge repository, boundary object, communication and coordination hub,* and *communication channel.* We adapt this classification to propose a non-exhaustive *issue classification,* and highlight the development-related insights discoverable from developer-tester communication, recorded in issue trackers like Mantis. Although the foundation for this *classification* is our single case study, but by adapting the knowledgebase from [24], we aim to extend its relevance, encouraging further research to review, refine, or refute it.

3   Research Method

We followed the guidelines recommended by Runeson and Höst [25] to conduct the case study and answer the RQ.

3.1   Research Context

The CC is a large-size company, offering commercial services and solutions across multiple domains. The CC claims to follow *customized agile,* as it uses various software development methods that adhere to Agile principles, such as iterative development, but does not have any predefined sprint cycles. For the case study, we focused on one of their flagship products, *Modelio,* a modeling tool for model-driven development. A collocated team of nine practitioners works on *Modelio's* development. During our period of interest, the CC worked on and released three different versions of this tool.

3.2   Data Collection

For our study, we used data from the bug-tracking tool *Mantis.* The *issueDescription* and *testFeedback* fields in this tool record communication between the developers and testing team in natural language. The *issueDescription* field records *issues* raised by the testing team and even end users, and the developers respond with a fix. The testing team attempts to resolve the *issue* based on this response, and records the outcome in the *testFeedback* field. The data were collected for the years 2016 (189 entries), 2017 (571 entries) and 2018 (493 entries). *Mantis* 2019 dataset was too inadequate (66 entries) to be included in our study. By 'entries', we mean the total unique textual entries extracted from each year's dataset, both *issueDescription* and *testFeedback* fields taken together.

3.3   LDA Application and Data Analysis

We divided the *Mantis* dataset into three subsets, year wise. The year-based division approximates well to the three *Modelio* versions developed in 2016, 2017, and 2018. Moreover, a division of less than 12 months would have resulted in too few entries to produce any meaningful results, as we learned from the unintelligible topics produced from the analysis of *Mantis* 2019 dataset. Another reason for the year-based division is our previous study [26], where the same division logic was adopted to provide empirical evidence for the use and benefits of a metrics program in an industrial setting.

For applying LDA, we used the *tidytext*[5] format, where the text to be analyzed is stored as a table with one-*token*-per-row. Generally, a *token* is a single word, but can even be an *n-gram* (*n* words taken together), sentence, or paragraph [27]. A representative

---

[5] https://www.tidytextmining.com/tidytext.html.

example of how we applied LDA to our dataset can be found here[6]. We created a *tidytext* data-frame for *issueDescription* and *testFeedback* corpora for each of the three subsets. In the context of LDA, *issueDescription* is the corpus, and the individual entries therein are the *documents*. This means that the 2016, 2017 and 2018 *Mantis* subsets have 189, 571 and 493 *documents*, respectively. Next, we preprocessed the *issueDescription* corpus by performing *tokenization*, splitting the *documents* into individual *tokens* (words). We used the *tidytext* R package[7] to perform this step, converting the text into *tidytext* format. Next, we removed stopwords, which are common English-language words like *"the"*, *"of"*, *"it"*, etc. Typically, numbers are also removed, but the corpus contained mentions of *Modelio's* different versions (e.g. *3.8.00*, *3.8.01*), instruction set architecture (e.g. *x86*, *64*), and operating system platforms (e.g. *10.0*). We retained them to avoid losing *tokens* of potential significance. Next, *tokens* like *'xmldiagramreader.java'* would typically be split into *'xmldiagramreader'* and *'java'* before applying LDA. However, we decided against it, because the original text holds more meaning, and is easily identifiable and interpretable for the stakeholders.

The preprocessing steps helped standardize the *issueDescription* corpus, which was done for every *testFeedback* corpus as well. Next, we calculated terms frequency–inverse document frequency (TF-IDF) for *issueDescription* corpora. TF measures how frequently a word occurs in a *document*. IDF also measures word frequencies, but by decreasing the weight for commonly used words and increasing it for words rarely used in the corpus. Combined, TF-IDF measures frequency of a word, adjusted for how rarely it is used, which helps identify how important a word is to a *document* in a corpus [27]. Although not necessary for topic modeling in general, TF-IDF is useful in exploring data and deriving information that can help inform topic modeling.

Next, we applied LDA to every *issueDescription* subset separately, to elicit *topics* that best describe each subset. The most essential input for LDA is the number of topics, which are typically user defined. After several attempts, we settled on different number of topics for different subsets. This decision was dictated by 'γ' distribution, which measures the probability of each *document* belonging to a topic. Higher number of topics result in too sparse distribution, indicating that the *documents* are not being sorted well into different topics. Decreasing the number of topics results in less clear division among topics, with multiple concepts clubbed under one topic. In addition, the stakeholders reviewed and validated the *topics*, aiding our decision on the number of *topics*.

LDA application divided every *issueDescription* corpus into x semantically similar but distinct *issues*-related topics. We wanted to explore if patterns observed in these topics had corresponding patterns in how the testing team addressed them. Based on the γ distribution, we joined each *issues*-related topic, and their corresponding *documents*, with the tokens generated from the *testFeedback* corpus. Independent analysis of the *issueDescription* corpus would have produced *topics* about only the *issues* the development team worked on in a given year, without any insight into their possible causes and how they were addressed. Similarly, analyzing the *testFeedback* corpus in isolation

---

would have produced *topics* that provide some visibility into the testing efforts, but without the key insight into the *issues* those efforts were directed at. By combining the two corpora, we could explore one-to-many relationship between the distinct *issue*-related *topics* and how they were addressed by the testing team.

The LDA results were shared with the *Product Development Team Lead* and the *R&D Head* at the CC, the two stakeholders that we collaborated with. We asked them to study the findings to determine their significance from their development perspective, identify *issue*-related *topics* and the one-to-many relationship between these *topics* and the *testFeedback tokens*. Since LDA generates *topics* without labeling them, we asked the stakeholders to label them manually. Automatic labeling is an objective exercise [28]. Due to highly contextual knowledge embedded in unstructured data, we argue that manual labeling is preferable to automatic labeling, and that the stakeholders are in an ideal position to identify and interpret the *topics'* significance. The stakeholders provided their interpretations in under a week. We posit that this effort spent would be less if the LDA results are reviewed full-time, as part of daily work, instead of as a non-urgent task for an industry-academia collaboration. After receiving the stakeholders' interpretations of the results, we held an hour-long joint meeting with both the stakeholders for further clarification on their interpretations and claims made therein, which helped us answer the *RQ*.

4   Results

We first present the *topics* and their significance for each Mantis subset, interpreted by the stakeholders. Next, based on this empirical evidence, and the software development knowledge that issue trackers tend to capture [24], we present an *insight classification*, to characterize the potential of developer-tester communication for development-related insights. The LDA results the stakeholders studied and validated are available in the Appendix[8]. The R code for LDA application can be found here[9], but the Mantis raw data cannot be shared due to confidentiality reasons.

4.1   Development-Related Insights from Developer-Tester Communication

The *topics* for all the Mantis subsets and their interpreted significance, based on their relation with the *testFeedback* tokens, is presented in Table 1. A more detailed table with a sample of both *issueDescription* and *testFeedback* tokens the stakeholders used to infer the *topics'* significance is available in the Appendix. The '*NA*' entries mean the stakeholders could not find any meaningful one-to-many relationship between *testFeedback* *tokens* and the corresponding *issues*-related *topics*.

Mantis **Topics.**   The stakeholders claim that the six topics for the 2016 subset reflected their project structure and implementation of their product's lower layers. There was major work for redesigning the model kernels, and the related *issues* were identified in the topic '*Core feature/Integration*'. Stakeholders also claim that *issues* identified by

---

[8] https://doi.org/10.5281/zenodo.4761727.

[9] https://github.com/prabhatram/devtester_topicmodeling.

Table 1. *Topics* extracted from *Mantis* dataset and practitioners' interpretation

No.	Topic	Practitioners' interpretation
Mantis 2016 subset		
1	Diagram	Implementation of the tool's *diagram* component
2	*Modelio* extensions	*Modelio* API to integrate new functionality
3	Core feature/Integration	Integration aspects of the tool and model storage layers
4	Project configuration	Project configuration and its external elements
5	Interoperability, Import/export	OS incompatibilities and issue reproducibility in different environment/version of *Modelio*
6	Model creation	*NA*
Mantis 2017 subset		
1	Project lifecycle	*NA*
2	Diagram	*Diagrams* worked on during the development in 2017
3	Workbench support	Feature containing *workbench* implementation
4	BPMN metamodel evolution	*NA*
5	BPMN metamodel evolution	BPMN diagram implementation and import/export feature
6	ArchiMate metamodel support	*NA*
7	BPMN diagrams	
Mantis 2018 subset		
1	General customer support	Customer relations
2	BPMN metamodel	*NA*
3	Methodological links	
4	*Modelio* module (extensions for *Modelio*)	Solution dedicated for the tool's module development
5	Document view	*NA*
6	Collaborative work/constellation	Collaborative work with Constellation
7	Diagrams	*Diagrams* definition, implementation, commands and controllers in Eclipse RCP

the above topic and *'Project configuration'* highlight several non-development related anomalies that were relevant to the key components of *Modelio*. Overall, these topics reveal development process themes that could not have been discovered from sources like a project roadmap. The stakeholders regard these topics as evidence of development activities to improve stability of the core components of *Modelio*.

Of the seven topics for the 2017 subset, stakeholders could not find any relation between four of the topics and the corresponding *testFeedback* tokens. The tokens were too generic to provide visibility into how the *issues* were addressed. Still, the stakeholders identified an overarching theme, characterizing their development activities for that year. The focus was on implementation of new *Modelio* meta-model, as evidenced in the *'BPMN metamodel evolutions'* and *'ArchiMate metamodel support'* topics. Stakeholders identified two topics for the same *issue* of *'BPMN metamodel evolutions'*. Reducing the number of topics led to failure in identifying any relationship between the *issues* and the *testFeedback tokens,* and so we decided to retain this redundancy. Doing so helped the stakeholders identify a relation between one of the *'BPMN metamodel evolutions'* topics (#5) and the corresponding *testFeedback tokens,* thereby validating the decision to have seven topics for the 2016 subset. Next, the *'Workbench support'* topic also suggested the focus on development of new features. The topics *'BPMN metamodel evolution'* and *'BPMN diagrams'* highlighted the significant work that had begun on integrating BPMN standard. Stakeholders also claim that *issues* highlighted by the *'Diagram'* topic would have remained undetected without the use of LDA. Stakeholders also found *issues* related to user interface components, while *issues* related to *Modelio* core components, present in the 2016 subset, did not recur. This suggested that the development activities in 2017 grew closer to addressing end-user concerns.

Of the seven topics for the 2018 subset, no relation were found among three of the topics and the corresponding *testFeedback* tokens. Overall, these topics suggested a mixture of development activities for the year. The *'General customer support'* topic suggested an emphasis on addressing end-user reported *issues*, which were absent from both 2016 and 2017 findings. The stakeholders claim that this insight would have gone unnoticed if they had relied on their classical monitoring tools. The topics of *'Methodological links'* and *'Document view'* indicate new features development. However, the four topics of *'BPMN metamodel'*, *'Modelio module (extensions)*, *'Collaborative work/Constellation'* and *'Diagrams'* carry more significance. Stakeholders interpreted that the team emphasized on general quality improvement of several features, a development activity missing from both 2016 and 2017. Overall, 2018 development activity focused on general quality improvements of the products delivered.

Mantis is used to manage *issues* discovered by the quality team and reported by end users. *Issues* discovered by the quality team on newly developed features are more critical than those reported by end users, as density of the former is directly proportional to the quality of the development team's work. In 2016 and 2017, most topics point towards development of new features, which stakeholders interpret as quality problems with the products delivered, and under-representation of *issues* related to the quality of existing features (*GUI, end-user reported issues*). This may suggest either poor management or smooth resolutions of these *issues.* Conversely, there is an under-representation of *issues* related to development of new features in 2018. Stakeholders view this as their development process evolving from addressing issues affecting *Modelio's* core components, to addressing issues reported by end users and implementing general improvements. This is indicative of improvement in *Modelio's* quality, with its core components stabilizing, giving stakeholders more time to address end user reported concerns and the overall product quality.

Based on the stakeholders' interpretation, and the overarching development themes identified therein, we posit three development-related insights. First, bulk of the development activities in 2016 centered on developing new features and improving *Modelio's* stability by working on its core components. Second, in 2017 and particularly 2018, development activities focused on addressing overall product quality and *issues* reported by the end users. Viewing these development activities together, the third insight relates to how the development process evolved from emphasizing development of new features and *Modelio's* internal quality (core components stability) to emphasizing *Modelio's* external quality (end-user *issues*). Stakeholders point out that this evolution was natural, but would have remained undetected without this study.

Insights Classification. Based on the insights interpreted from the topics and the state of the art, we propose the following non-exhaustive *insight classification*, to characterize insights discovered from developer-tester communication recorded in *Mantis* (Fig. 1).

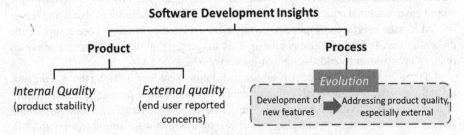

Fig. 1. Insight classification

Stakeholders were specific in their interpretation of how different topics for different years afforded them visibility into their development processes and practices. Piecemeal, the insights highlighted the efforts to address and improve the *Modelio's* quality, both internal (core component stability) and external (end-user *issues*). Cumulatively, the insights are indicative of an evolution in the CC's development process from 2016 to 2018, as development efforts evolved from focusing on new features development to addressing product's quality, especially external quality.

5   Discussion

We first elaborate on the development-related insights the stakeholders inferred, and how they improve upon the benefits reported in the state of the art. We also discuss the '*insight classification*' from the standpoint of existing literature, and the relevance and utility that companies similar to the CC may derive from it.

5.1 Development-Related Insights from Developer-Tester Communication

Despite the abundance of data generated as a result of modern software development methods like ASD, software development is still a risky endeavor, as existing tools are still inadequate at facilitating decision-making [3]. Software analytics can help address this shortcoming by automating processes to extract actionable information from data [29]. Still, companies struggle to capitalize on their development data, as a clear purpose for data collection [30, 31] and interpreting that data's significance [3] still remain a challenge. Our study's findings can help with both these challenges, especially for unstructured data that represent most of the development data produced [1]. The development-related insights that can be generated from unstructured data, with the help of text-mining techniques like LDA, could help companies capitalize on their data.

In contrast to the LDA benefits reported in the current literature, our exploration-centric approach helped identify insights of developers' and testers' engagement in addressing product stability, *issues* reported by end users, and general product quality, in addition to an overarching theme of process evolution. Stakeholders argue that these insights would have gone unnoticed without the study. These findings may be case specific, but they are evidence of LDA's use for extracting development-related insights in an industrial setting. LDA also helped the stakeholders discover transversal activities that was not documented in their project plan, something that their classical monitoring tools could not have detected. Insights related to addressing end-user reported *issues* and general quality improvements are part of background work and difficult to assess over time, as they are unplanned and, therefore, not monitored. Consequently, the stakeholders are now open to using LDA to analyze their development data at regular intervals. Incorporating a text-mining technique into the development process can help the CC create awareness among other stakeholders about the topics that may provide an early indicator of changes or problems warranting further attention.

In general, stakeholders are interested a system's history and how it evolves to understand their software development process [4]. Within the context of software evolution, how and why a software system changes can provide insights into both the specific software system and the software development as a whole [16]. LDA applied to the three-year Mantis data provided the CC stakeholders the historical knowledge, and the LDA *topics* helped them understand how and why their product development evolved, highlighting an evolution in their development process. Stakeholders' tacit contextual knowledge contributed to their interpretation of the LDA results, which lends plausibility to the above claim. Although LDA was applied to old data, the findings offer the stakeholders visibility into the development process of one of their flagship products, which can be leveraged to manage the development of future *Modelio* versions.

LDA results could be seen as summarization [15] of the developer-tester communication at the CC, which could be a useful way of presenting reusable software engineering knowledge to stakeholders [32]. Even though stakeholders-driven validation of LDA topics is seen as a critical requirement [33], this practice is not widely adopted [34], which reinforces our decision to include the stakeholders from the CC to study and validate the LDA results. In agreement with Hindle et al. [35], the stakeholders identified most of the relevant topics due to their familiarity of the concepts (conveyed by *tokens*), but had difficulty interpreting and labelling some, due to the *topics'* lack of significance.

Furthermore, our study supports another finding from Hindle et al. [35], where most topics labelled by the stakeholders matched their perception of the development processes and activities for *Modelio* between 2016 and 2018. Overall, our study's findings are indicative of the importance and the necessity of including stakeholders to validate LDA results, when conducted in an industrial setting.

Based on the classification of issue trackers' utility by Bertram et al. [24], Mantis' use as a *coordination and communication hub* and *communication channel* is typical of any issue tracker. Mantis is used by developers, testers, and the quality team for addressing *issues*, and so its utility as a *boundary object* is also evident at the CC, where stakeholders utilize the stored data based on their custom needs and purposes. Most importantly, the overall process evolution the stakeholders interpreted points to Mantis serving as a *knowledge repository*, storing organizational knowledge that is difficult to detect otherwise. With this insight, and the potential future use of LDA at the CC to derive more such insights, stakeholders can plan their future development of *Modelio* better. For example, the stakeholders claim that once *Modelio's* core components were stabilized, the team could focus on the *issues* reported by the end users. *Modelio's* core components stability points to the product's *internal quality*, as the related *issues* were identified before the use of the tool by end users [36]. Conversely, *issues* reported by the end users relate to *Modelio's* external quality, as these *issues* were identified by them while using it [36]. The stakeholders can leverage this knowledge to estimate and allocate their efforts optimally. The *classification* is more relevant for other researchers and practitioners, interested in investigating insights that developer-tester communication may hold, and which could be extracted using text-mining techniques like LDA.

6   Limitations and Threats to Validity

LDA is typically applied to large datasets, with thousands and millions of documents [37, 38]. Our dataset may be very small, but there exists no standard for sample size. The dataset should be large enough to generate distinct but not redundant topics, and small enough for topics that are not too broad and heterogeneous [39]. Although the small dataset is a limitation, stakeholders were able to extract distinct *topics* and non-trivial insights characterizing their development process from 2016 to 2018.

The number of topics is another limitation of our study. Similar to ideal sample size, there is no standard for ideal number of topics in LDA. Sbalchiero and Eder [39] provide a guide to aid in this decision, but those recommendations appear to be for sample sizes that are larger than ours. Informed by the γ distribution and stakeholders' validation, we have tried to address this limitation to some extent.

We address threats to our study's validity based on the guidelines recommended by Runeson and Höst [25]. We acknowledge that the developer-tester communication documented in Mantis does not capture the process of identifying and addressing *issues* in their entirety. Since the CC employs multiple tools in their software development, investigation of Mantis' data can provide only partial visibility into their development processes and practices. Even though the stakeholders claimed that the LDA topics helped highlight an evolution in their development process, the findings are still limited by the extent of information shared among the developers and the testers through Mantis.

By including the *Product Development Team Lead* and the *R&D Head* in our study, we mitigate the threat to our study's *construct validity* to some extent. These stakeholders were better judges of the significance and validity of the *topics*, and how these *topics* represent the process of identifying and addressing *issues*.

Absence of contextual knowledge and other confounding factors interfere with the validity of interpretations of LDA *topics*. In our study, we relied on the CC stakeholders to interpret our findings and comment on its validity, as they possessed the necessary contextual knowledge to justify proper interpretation of their data. This helps us strengthen the *internal validity* of our study, but the potential of *confirmation bias* threatens it at the same time [40], and we acknowledge this tradeoff.

Being a single case study, *external validity* of our findings is affected. However, the objective of our study is to explore development-related insights that could be extracted from unstructured data using LDA, in an industrial setting. We hope that the positive findings help trigger more exploratory investigation to discover the extent of knowledge that can be extracted from such unstructured data. To this effect, we proposed an *insight classification*, which may be of utility to organizations with context similar to the CC. Similarly, interested researchers could build upon the *classification*, and conduct similar investigations to refine and supplement it.

Only one author was involved in collecting the data and applying LDA, and in creating the *classification*, which can affect the *reliability* of the study. However, our findings have been studied and validated by the collaborating stakeholders and the co-authors of this study, which helps mitigate the threat to our study's *reliability*.

7 Conclusion

Modern software development methods like ASD produce voluminous unstructured data on a daily basis, which may hold insights not easily discoverable from other means. Data related to developer communication have been leveraged to classify developer communication, propose developers for bug triage, aid in code comprehension, etc. However, the potential of developer-tester communication in generating development-related insights remains unexplored, especially in industrial setting.

We conducted a case study at a large software-intensive Agile company to explore development-tester communication for their potential to generate development-related insights. We applied LDA on this communication data from year 2016 to 2018, and invited two stakeholders to study and validate the results. Unexpectedly, they were able to find insights related to the development efforts to address their flagship product's internal quality, external quality and general improvements. The stakeholders identified another insight of an overarching theme of process evolution, as their development efforts evolved from addressing new features and internal quality to emphasizing on its external quality. The stakeholders claim that without the study, these insights may not have been discovered. Now, stakeholders are keen on incorporating LDA in their development process to keep track of these insights, despite the additional efforts the technique demands. We also proposed an *insight classification* to characterize the insights that we discovered. Companies will similar development context could use these insights to guide their analysis of developer-tester communication unstructured data. Interested researchers are encouraged to critique and improve upon this *classification*.

As part of future work, we plan to develop software metrics that help the stakeholders monitor and track the LDA *topics* they are interested in. This real-time tracking of the significant *topics* can remove the requirement of conducting LDA every x months to derive insights. Instead, stakeholders can apply LDA only when there are legitimate and major changes to the project, resulting in different sets of *topics*, which in turn could be used to update the metrics.

References

1. Haiduc, S., Arnaoudova, V., Marcus, A., Antoniol, G.: The use of text retrieval and natural language processing in software engineering. In: Proceedings - International Conference on Software Engineering, pp. 898–899 (2016)
2. Schütze, H., Manning, C.D., Raghavan, P.: Introduction to Information Retrieval. Cambridge University Press, Cambridge (2008)
3. Buse, R.P.L., Zimmermann, T.: Information needs for software development analytics. In: In 2012, the 34th International Conference on Software Engineering (ICSE), pp. 987–996 (2012)
4. Sun, X., Liu, X., Li, B., Duan, Y., Yang, H., Hu, J.: Exploring topic models in software engineering data analysis: a survey. In: 2016 IEEE/ACIS 17th International Conference on Software Engineering, Artificial Intelligence, Networking and Parallel/Distributed Computing, SNPD 2016, pp. 357–362. Institute of Electrical and Electronics Engineers Inc. (2016)
5. Thomas, S.W., Hassan, A.E., Blostein, D.: Mining unstructured software repositories. In: Mens, T., Serebrenik, A., Cleve, A. (eds.) Evolving Software Systems, pp. 139–162. Springer, Heidelberg (2014). https://doi.org/10.1007/978-3-642-45398-4_5
6. Bettenburg, N., Adams, B.: Workshop on mining unstructured data (MUD): because "mining unstructured data is like fishing in muddy waters"! In: Proceedings - Working Conference on Reverse Engineering, WCRE, pp. 277–278. IEEE (2010)
7. Di Sorbo, A., Panichella, S., Visaggio, C.A., Di Penta, M., Canfora, G., Gall, H.C.: Development emails content analyzer: intention mining in developer discussions. In: Proceedings - 2015 30th IEEE/ACM International Conference on Automated Software Engineering ASE 2015, pp. 12–23 (2016)
8. Shihab, E., Bettenburg, N., Adams, B., Hassan, A.E.: On the central role of mailing lists in open source projects: an exploratory study. In: Nakakoji, K., Murakami, Y., McCready, E. (eds.) JSAI-isAI 2009. LNCS (LNAI and LNB), vol. 6284, pp. 91–103. Springer, Heidelberg (2010). https://doi.org/10.1007/978-3-642-14888-0_9
9. Vassallo, C., Panichella, S., Di Penta, M., Canfora, G.: CODES: mining source code descriptions from developers discussions. In: Proceedings of the 22nd International Conference on Program Comprehension, pp. 106–109 (2014)
10. Soliman, M., Galster, M., Salama, A.R., Riebisch, M.: Architectural knowledge for technology decisions in developer communities: an exploratory study with StackOverflow. In: Proceedings - 2016 13th Working IEEE/IFIP Conference on Software Architecture, WICSA 2016, pp. 128–133. IEEE (2016)
11. Anvik, J., Hiew, L., Murphy, G.C.: Who should fix this bug? In: Proceedings - International Conference on Software Engineering 2006, pp. 361–370 (2006)
12. Canfora, G., Di Penta, M., Oliveto, R., Panichella, S.: Who is going to mentor newcomers in open source projects? Proceedings of ACM SIGSOFT 20th International Symposium on the Foundations of Software Engineering, FSE 2012, pp. 1–11 (2012)
13. Panichella, S., Aponte, J., Di Penta, M., Marcus, A., Canfora, G.: Mining source code descriptions from developer communications. In: IEEE International Conference on Program Comprehension, pp. 63–72 (2012)

14. Panichella, A., Dit, B., Oliveto, R., Di Penta, M., Poshynanyk, D., De Lucia, A.: How to effectively use topic models for software engineering tasks? An approach based on genetic algorithms. In: Proceedings - International Conference on Software Engineering, pp. 522–531 (2013)

15. Nazar, N., Hu, Y., Jiang, H.: Summarizing software artifacts: a literature review. J. Comput. Sci. Technol. **31**(5), 883–909 (2016). https://doi.org/10.1007/s11390-016-1671-1

16. Chen, T.-H., Thomas, S.W., Hassan, A.E.: A survey on the use of topic models when mining software repositories. Empir. Softw. Eng. **21**(5), 1843–1919 (2015). https://doi.org/10.1007/s10664-015-9402-8

17. Sinoara, R.A., Scheicher, R.B., Rezende, S.O.: Evaluation of latent dirichlet allocation for document organization in different levels of semantic complexity. In: 2017 IEEE Symposium Series on Computational Intelligence, SSCI 2017 – Proceedings, pp. 1–8 (2018)

18. Blei, D.M.: Introduction to probabilistic topic models. Commun. ACM. **55**, 77–84 (2012)

19. Lima, M., Ahmed, I., Conte, T., Nascimento, E., Oliveira, E., Gadelha, B.: Land of lost knowledge: an initial investigation into projects lost knowledge. In: International Symposium on Empirical Software Engineering and Measurement, September 2019 (2019)

20. Blei, D.M., Lafferty, J.D.: Topic models. In: Text Mining, pp. 101–124. Chapman and Hall/CRC (2009)

21. Thomas, S.W., Adams, B., Hassan, A.E., Blostein, D.: Studying software evolution using topic models. Sci. Comput. Program. **80**, 457–479 (2014)

22. Thomas, S.W., Adams, B., Hassan, A.E., Blostein, D.: Modeling the evolution of topics in source code histories. In: Proceedings of the 8th Working Conference on Mining Software Repositories, pp. 173–182 (2011)

23. Zhang, T., Yang, G., Lee, B., Lua, E.K.: A novel developer ranking algorithm for automatic bug triage using topic model and developer relations. In: Proceedings - Asia-Pacific Software Engineering Conference, APSEC, pp. 223–230. IEEE (2014)

24. Bertram, D., Voida, A., Greenberg, S., Walker, R.: Communication, collaboration, and bugs: the social nature of issue tracking in small, collocated teams. In: Proceedings of the 2010 ACM Conference on Computer Supported Cooperative Work, pp. 291–300 (2010)

25. Runeson, P., Höst, M.: Guidelines for conducting and reporting case study research in software engineering. Empir. Softw. Eng. **14**, 131–164 (2009)

26. Ram, P., et al.: An empirical investigation into industrial use of software metrics programs. In: Morisio, M., Torchiano, M., Jedlitschka, A. (eds.) PROFES 2020. LNCS, vol. 12562, pp. 419–433. Springer, Cham (2020). https://doi.org/10.1007/978-3-030-64148-1_26

27. Silge, J., Robinson, D.: Text Mining with R: A Tidy Approach. O'Reilly Media, Inc. (2017)

28. Allahyari, M., Kochut, K.: Automatic topic labeling using ontology-based topic models. In: Proceedings - 2015 IEEE 14th International Conference on Machine Learning and Applications, ICMLA 2015, pp. 259–264 (2016)

29. Krishna, R., Agrawal, A., Rahman, A., Sobran, A., Menzies, T.: What is the connection between issues, bugs, and enhancements? In: 2018 IEEE/ACM 40th International Conference on Software Engineering: Software Engineering in Practice Track (ICSE-SEIP), pp. 306–315 (2018)

30. Bizer, C., Boncz, P., Brodie, M.L., Erling, O.: The meaningful use of big data: four perspectives - four challenges. SIGMOD Rec. **40**, 56–60 (2011)

31. Holmström Olsson, H., Bosch, J.: Towards data-driven product development: a multiple case study on post-deployment data usage in software-intensive embedded systems. In: Fitzgerald, B., Conboy, K., Power, K., Valerdi, R., Morgan, L., Stol, K.-J. (eds.) LESS 2013. LNBIP, vol. 167, pp. 152–164. Springer, Heidelberg (2013). https://doi.org/10.1007/978-3-642-44930-7_10

32. Silva, C., Mariane, C.: Reusing software engineering knowledge from developer communication. In: ESEC/FSE 2020 - Proceedings of the 28th ACM Joint Meeting European Software Engineering Conference and Symposium on the Foundations of Software Engineering, pp. 1682–1685 (2020)

33. Asuncion, H.U., Asuncion, A.U., Taylor, R.N.: Software traceability with topic modeling. In: Proceedings - International Conference on Software Engineering, pp. 95–104 (2010)

34. Hindle, A., Bird, C., Zimmermann, T., Nagappan, N.: Relating requirements to implementation via topic analysis: do topics extracted from requirements make sense to managers and developers? In: 2012 28th IEEE International Conference on Software Maintenance (ICSM), pp. 243–252 (2012)

35. Hindle, A., Bird, C., Zimmermann, T., Nagappan, N.: Do topics make sense to managers and developers? Empir. Softw. Eng. **20**(2), 479–515 (2014). https://doi.org/10.1007/s10664-014-9312-1

36. Gezici, B., Tarhan, A., Chouseinoglou, O.: Internal and external quality in the evolution of mobile software: an exploratory study in open-source market. Inf. Softw. Technol. **112**, 178–200 (2019)

37. Pettinato, M., Gil, J.P., Galeas, P., Russo, B.: Log mining to re-construct system behavior: an exploratory study on a large telescope system. Inf. Softw. Technol. **114**, 121–136 (2019)

38. Noei, E., Zhang, F., Zou, Y.: Too many user-reviews, what should app developers look at first? IEEE Trans. Softw. Eng. 1–12 (2019)

39. Sbalchiero, S., Eder, M.: Topic modeling, long texts and the best number of topics. Some problems and solutions. Qual. Quant. **54**, 1095–1108 (2020)

40. Salman, I., Turhan, B., Vegas, S.: A controlled experiment on time pressure and confirmation bias in functional software testing. Empir. Softw. Eng. **24**, 1727–1761 (2019)

Toward a Technical Debt Relationship with the Pivoting of Growth Phase Startups

Orges Cico[1(✉)], Terese Besker[2], Antonio Martini[3], Anh Nguyen Duc[4],
Renata Souza[5], and Jan Bosch[2]

[1] Norwegian University of Science and Technology, Trondheim, Norway
orges.cico@ntnu.no
[2] Chalmers University of Technology, Göteborg, Sweden
{besker,jan.bosch}@chalmers.se
[3] University of Oslo, Oslo, Norway
antonima@ifi.uio.no
[4] University of South-Eastern Norway, Notodden, Norway
anh.nguyen.duc@usn.no
[5] Universidade Federal da Bahia, Salvador, Brazil
renatamss@ufba.br

Abstract. Context: Pivot has been a common strategical tactic of startups by shifting course of actions to adapt to environmental changes to the companies. Among many factors influencing the decisions of pivot or preserve, technical characteristics of the product and its evolution are possible triggering factors. We have learned that technical debt is an inherent phenomenon in startups that hinders later growth. However, we do not yet know how technical debt might lead to pivoting in startups and what TD processes we observe in different pivoting scenarios. Aim: Our goal is to evaluate how technical debt influences pivoting in growth-phase startups. Methodology: We conducted an empirical study on 11 software startups in Norway and Brazil and analyzed qualitative data using thematic analysis. Results: We identified three ways that technical debt influences pivoting: (1) direct, (2) indirect, and (3) no-influence. Managing and avoiding technical debt significantly reduces the likelihood of technology pivoting and restrains indirect effects on other pivoting types. Contribution: Our study will enable practitioners to address the influence of technical debt on pivoting in growth-phase software startups. Future researchers can benefit from our findings by conducting exploratory studies and providing educated recommendations.

Keywords: Software startups · Technical debt · Pivoting

1 Introduction

Technical debt (TD) has become a practical problem in software practices in the past decade. Software startups encounter TD challenges in different life-cycle

L. Ardito et al. (Eds.): PROFES 2021, LNCS 13126, pp. 265–280, 2021.
https://doi.org/10.1007/978-3-030-91452-3_18

phases because product compromises are always needed to meet urgent demands. Most software engineering compromises influence the accumulated "debt", which needs to be paid at some point in time to assure long-term project sustainability [7]. Facing TD is becoming even more of an urgent need for many software startups [5,21]. Such startups are known to accumulate TD during their transition from the early phase to the growth phase.

Pivot is a common phenomenon in different stages of software startups, where the companies change the course of actions to survive or grow further. We mainly attribute pivoting at an early phase to startups' desire to explore potential products, measure market effects, and learn from the results. Startups face significant challenges in overcoming TD [1,5,13] and pivoting [16], especially in the growth phase. Previous authors emphasize that having less technical debt could give a startup more room for pivoting and product evolution in the long term [13]. TD affects startups' quality and productivity when they shift to the growth phase with stable resources [12]. TD hinders the maintainability and evolvability of software. In turn, TD can commence pivoting, leading growth-phase startups to significant challenges. There is little empirical evidence relating pivoting to TD during a startup's transition to the growth phase.

The aim of this paper is to investigate how TD affects pivoting in growth-phase startups, thus identifying TD processes in different pivoting scenarios. We formulated the following research questions (RQs):

RQ1: *How does technical debt influence pivoting in growth-phase startups?*
RQ2: *How are technical debt processes associated to pivoting types in growth-phase startups?*

Based on the available literature on TD and pivoting, we first provide an analysis of the pivoting dilemma in growth-phase startups. Then, we interview growth phase startup practitioners about their approach to coping with TD and their perceptions of how TD affected pivoting while transitioning to the growth phase. Combining these findings, we categorize the influence of TD on pivoting and the growth phase TD processes in pivoting scenarios. The different categories we identify in this paper are based on the pivoting concepts in software startups [4] and our experience in growth-phase startups' TD [5,8]. Specifically, we identify three manners that TD influences pivoting in growth-phase startups: (1) direct, (2) indirect, and (3) no-influence. Managing and avoiding technology debt significantly reduces the likelihood of technology pivoting and restrains indirect effects on other pivoting types. Moreover, we propose several hypotheses that suggest exciting new research areas on TD and pivoting relationship theories.

The rest of the paper is structured as follows. Section 2 presents research background. We present our study's design and methodology in Sect. 3. Section 4 presents the results and key findings. Section 5 discusses the findings. Finally, Sect. 6 concludes the study and identifies opportunities for future work.

2   Background and Related Work

2.1   Growth Phase Startups' Pivoting: A Dilemma

Recently, startup research has proliferated as a subfield of software engineering. In this subfield, although Bajwa et al. [3,4] have conducted several studies exploring the practices of pivoting in early phase startups, research that includes pivoting—especially in growth-phase startups—is still in its infancy. We observe a lack of proposals on good versus bad practices when startups need to pivot in relation to startup phases and pivoting types. Many authors seem to agree with the idea provided by Terho et al. [20] that pivoting mainly occurs in the early phase; according to these authors, once the business model is established, fine-tuning is more likely to take place.

Based on Muzellec et al. [15], the transitions of startups from one stage to another can be characterized under different categories. Finance is one of the most important factors for startup survival. In the early stages, funding is commonly based on selfcontributions, in the form of self-investment (by bootstrapping between jobs) or loans (from relatives or friends). Other funding options in the early stage of startup formation can come from pre-seed or crowdfunding. In later stages, when a Minimum Viable Product (MVP) has been developed and iteration with the market is a must (do-or-die approach), the need for larger funding amounts from venture capitalists (VCs) and angel investors (AIs) becomes obvious. Finally, if the startup has developed a fully operational product or service, then the market, either local or global, decides the startup's growth potential. After successfully growing in the market startups transition to a more mature phase, resembling more an ordinary company.

The transition of startups is also marked by shifting the startup strategy and the methodological evolution from ad-hoc or customized development practices [17] to more principled approaches. Strategical and methodological changes signify pivoting of the startup, which might drastically change the whole company. According to Ries [17], a pivot is a *"structured course correction designed to test a new fundamental hypothesis about the product, strategy, and engine of growth."*. Pivoting allows startups to continuously improve an idea through product creation and a validation loop. A startup pivots due to a need to shift its strategy to accommodate changes in industry or technology, customer needs, or factors that impact its triple bottom line. Direct and indirect feedback gathered in the product validation phase facilitates the startup pivoting process. Ries [17] presents ten different types of pivoting (Zoom-in, Zoom-out, Customer segment, Customer need, Platform pivot, Business Architecture, Value Capture, Engine of Growth, Channel Pivot, Technology Pivot).

There is only one study that addresses pivoting at various stages of the startup lifecycle (including the growth phase) by Nguyen-Duc et al. [16]. The authors provide evidence that pivots can happen in different phases of a startup's lifecycle. However, the discussion of pivoting in growth phase is relatively brief. Several other studies have addressed software startups' pivoting with a primary focus on early-phase startups [3,6,10,20]. Giardino et al. [9] explores pivoting in early phase startups while attributing startup failure to the neglect of pivoting. Similarly, studies from Bosch et al. [6] address pivoting at early-stage software startups. The study attempts to relate pivoting decisions to architectural decisions. Terho et al. [20] state that pivoting influences the hypotheses in the lean canvas model. The authors claim that pivoting typically happens early in the startup's life. Bajwa et al. [3, 4] provides an overview of startups' pivoting factors at the early stage, which are mainly attributed to technology and customer segments. The number of experimentation loops is higher in startups' early phase, significantly decreasing in the growth phase. Pivoting in growth-phase startups becomes more of a practitioners' dilemma, and very few studies have addressed the topic. As a startup matures, pivoting is a challenge that involves higher risks.

2.2 TD and Pivoting in Growth Phase Startups: A Preliminary Analysis

Recently, Avgeriou et al. [2] stated: "The term technical debt refers to delayed tasks and immature artifacts that constitute a 'debt' because they incur extra costs in the future in the form of increased cost of change during evolution and maintenance.". Software startups typically encounter TD challenges in different lifecycle phases because product compromises are always needed to meet urgent demands. Most software engineering compromises influence the accumulated "debt" that needs to be paid at some point to assure long-term project sustainability [4].

Another recent study has argued for the need for models, frameworks, methods, and tools to track and manage TD [14]. However, few studies have presented empirical evidence related to TD perceptions in startups. Two in particular focus on TD perception in early-phase startups [1, 11]. A more recent study uncovers four perceptual dimensions of TD (ignore, accept, avoid, and manage) in growth-phase startups [8]. Studies on startups' pivoting and its relationship to TD are scarce. One in particular argues that having less TD could give a startup more room for pivoting and product evolution in the long term [13]. However, the study provides no evidence of how TD is related to different pivoting scenarios in various startup lifecycles. Of these two studies, the first focuses on an innovative perspective of various TD perceptions [8] and the other [13] concerns the relationship between TD and pivoting. We thus argue for the need to deepen understanding of the influences of TD and pivoting.

3   Exploring the Practitioners' Point of View

To conceptualize the role of TD in software startups' pivoting, we interviewed chief executive officers (CEOs) with extensive experience in software practices. We focused our questions on identifying how they perceived TD in relation to ten pivoting scenarios.

3.1   Case Selection

We primarily collected data from startups located in Norway and Brazil. We selected the sample population using the purposive sampling technique. Purposive sampling is a form of non-probability sampling in which researchers rely on their judgment when choosing members of the population to participate in their study [19]. To conduct our study, we purposively chose startups that are in the growth phase. The primary motivation of our choice is because reaching growth signifies that the startup has faced and overcome significant challenges, some of which leading to pivoting scenarios. Some criteria we used to select our startups are: (1) startup was in series A financing; (2) up to 5 years old product commercialization; (3) entered the growth phase in the last 2 years; (4) self-owned or independent headquarters; (5) positive return income in the past 2 years;

3.2   Case Demographics

Specifically, we interviewed six CEOs and five CTOs with more than four years of hands-on experience with software engineering practices in their respective startups, Table 1. Notably, all startups are in the growth phase, and all the interviewees are co-founders of their startups, with active roles in product lifecycle development.

3.3   Interview Design and Data Collection

We performed an empirical study on multiple startup cases based on an interview template for data collection. Writing the interview questions beforehand allowed us to focus our interview questions in connection to the RQs.

The interview process took place in three parts. In the first part, the interview questions primarily addressed demographic information about the startup (duration: 5–10 min). The second part focused more on a broad context of the software and technological aspects of the startup (10–15 min). The third part concentrated on the perception of TD and its relationship to pivoting (30–40 min). We focused the last part of the interview on two key questions that help answer our RQs:

- How have you coped (involving four processes such as ignored, accepted, avoided, managed) with TD while transitioning from the early phase to the growth phase?
- How has TD affected the pivoting (selecting one or more of the ten pivoting types) of your startup while transitioning to the growth phase?

One author obtained the answers from seven startups located in Norway and another from four startups in Brazil. Transcription and data analysis were conducted separately by two authors, followed by discussions and disagreement resolutions with the rest of the co-authors.

Table 1. Software startups' sample demographics.

Startup case #	Role	Country/ City	Product/Service	Founded/ Commercial	Clients
Startup 1	CEO	Norway/ Trondheim	SaaS - Real Time planning for the Ocean Space	2012/2015	30+
Startup 2	CEO	Norway/ Trondheim	Privacy and cybersecurity tools	2015/2016	50+
Startup 3	CEO	Norway/ Trondheim	web based digital retrospectives	2016/2017	20+
Startup 4	CEO	Norway/ Trondheim	Platform for organizing and sharing information on the internet	2018/2019	10+
Startup 5	CEO	Norway/ Trondheim	3D vision cameras and software for next generation robotics	2017/2018	100+
Startup 6	CEO	Norway/ Oslo	Optimal wind farm layout services based Google PaaS	2015/2017	80+
Startup 7	CTO	Norway/ Oslo	Real estate business intelligence	2017/2019	70+
Startup 8	CTO	Brazil/ Sao Paolo	Fintech company offering accounting services	2012/2015	60+
Startup 9	CTO	Brazil/ Bahia	Legal assistant offering data based on API web services	2014/2016	100+
Startup 10	CTO	Brazil/ Sao Paolo	Fintech working on prepayment of credit card receivables	2016/2016	40+
Startup 11	CTO	Brazil/ Bahia	Energy SaaS to support SMEs' contracting of energy	2019/2019	1000+

3.4   Data Analysis

First, we carefully transcribed data to obtain significant evidence that would help us answer our research question. We then used the thematic analysis approach [18]. The coding process consisted of identifying recurring patterns and themes within the interview data. The steps to conducting the systematic analysis consisted of the following: (1) **Reading the transcripts.** This step initially involved quick browsing and correction of the automatically transcribed data from the audio recordings. (2) **Coding.** During this step, we focused on choosing and labeling relevant words, phrases, or sentences and even larger text fragments or sections related to TD phenomena. (3) **Creating themes.** After gathering all the codes, we decided on the most relevant ones and created different categories or themes; (4) **Labeling and connecting themes.** We decided on which themes were more relevant and defined appropriate names and relationships for them; (5) **Drawing the results summary.** After deciding on the themes' importance and hierarchy, we generated a summary of the results (cf. Sect. 4) and discussed them in relation to previous studies (cf. Sect. 5).

4 The Relationship Between Technical Debt and Pivoting in Growth Phase Startups

We identified several factors that influenced how the CEOs and CTOs of the startups perceived TD's influence on pivoting while transitioning to the growth phase. In Fig. 1 we provide a detailed overview of the thematic analysis summarized into two major groupings, which are as follows: (1) TD's influence on the pivoting type and determining factors (Sect. 4.1), and (2) TD processes in pivoting scenarios and corresponding considerations (Sect. 4.2).

Based on the practitioners' answers, we grouped the implications of TD for pivoting into three types—TD directly influencing pivoting, TD indirectly influencing pivoting, and TD not influencing pivoting—each helping to answer our RQ1. Direct effects, as the name suggests, deal with the direct impact of TD on pivoting when not determined by other factors. Indirect effects can be defined as the impact of TD on pivoting determined by other factors. We define a lack of influence when pivoting is not impacted by TD, whether directly or indirectly. Moreover, we map TD processes (managing and avoiding) occurring in growth-phase startups to pivot types—helping to answer our RQ2. In Sects. 4.1 and 4.2, we provide a detailed explanation of the relationship found between TD and pivoting.

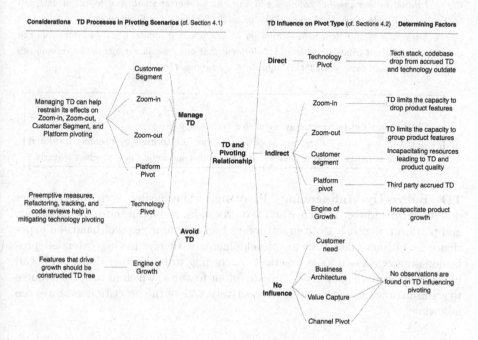

Fig. 1. Thematic analysis of TD relationship to pivoting in growth-phase startups.

4.1   TD Influence on Pivoting Types

TD Directly Influencing Pivoting. TD can have a direct influence on pivoting. Specifically, two of the practitioners described a direct influence of TD on technological pivoting. The practitioners reported over ten years of tech experience, and one had co-founded over fifteen startups. They argued that accruing TD leads to an inevitable technology pivoting scenario. Both practitioners claim that accruing TD within their products has led to entire tech stack and code base replacement. Specifically, the CEO from startup 1 reports:

"...Yes, so we've done a couple of technology pivots when we started out ... we could say that we're on the third iteration of different technology at the moment ... Yes, you could say it is because of technical debt ..." [Quote 1 - Startup 1]

Whereas, one CEO states the following:

"...But that platform couldn't really do what we do today...so we basically had to redo the whole platform because of all the technical debt..." [Quote 2 - Startup 3]

A TD induced technology pivot might cause challenges (as will be discussed later) but generally leads startups toward sustainable technology solutions. This means that products can better accommodate more features with a more robust tech stack.

"...With our technology stack right now, we can push new features a lot faster, it is much easier to change things around..." [Quote 3 - Startup 2]

Practitioners supported the idea that TD is inevitable, and that technology becomes outdated with time. Thus, at least a partial technology pivot is likely to happen in the development of every startup.

"...I think for our product changes will happen, no matter what, and technical debt will happen, so our code needs to be changeable as well..." [Quote 4 - Startup 3]

"...But that's the problem with technology so technology is almost like a fashion ... and in the end it's all about choosing tools and a platform that has enough support in the community and thus help avoid technical debt ..." [Quote 5 - Startup 1]

Key findings:

- Technology outdate certainly leads to a technology pivot.
- TD can lead to a technology pivot long before the technology becomes outdated because startups will continuously struggle to accommodate new product features.

TD Indirectly Influencing Pivoting. Specifically, two practitioners described the indirect influence of TD on zoom-in, zoom-out, customer-segment, and platform pivoting. Both practitioners had over four years of hands-on experience in business and software development, with one having extended professional knowledge of agile practices. According to both practitioners, TD can hinder a startup's capability to drop or adopt features, which in turn contributes to zoom-in or zoom-out pivoting, respectively. One of the practitioners states the following:

"...I'd say indirectly, yes, it [zoom-in pivoting] is related to technical debt, but not that much that technical debt that we have already fired but more about avoiding future technical debt we prefer to stick to one particular functionality ..." [Quote 6 - Startup 4]

Another example provided by one of the practitioners is the fact that in complex systems, the usage of third-party solutions might increase the risk of TD from other developers external to the startup. The utilization of third-party solutions contributes to product limitations encouraging platform pivoting. One of the CEOs reports the following:

"...it's connected to other people's technical debt. Well kind of looking at it in relation to those other systems ... you could also say technical debt is there and can be related to switching our system..." [Quote 7 - Startup 6]

Furthermore, unexpected customer-segment pivoting might push resources away from development teams, which in turn leads to accruing further TD that influences the outcome in reaching new customers with successful software products.

"...because we changed from B2B to B2C sales take so much resources from our team and it means that I have to do sales, rather than programming and coding and creating better products..." [Quote 8 - Startup 4]

Only one participant reports pivoting in engine growth, which is tightly related to developing and market testing only necessary features and adopting growth hacking. In this case, TD was not directly connected to the pivoting; however, the practitioner claimed that TD being left unchecked could drastically incapacitate the startup from achieving product growth.

"...We are doing growth hacking ... not developing new features that are not necessarily well thought out... but then we are avoiding technical debt..." [Quote 9 - Startup 1]

Key finding:

- TD can hinder startups' software development or product growth capabilities, and consequently, become an indirect contributor to technological and non technological pivoting.

TD Not Influencing Pivoting. None of the practitioners presented any connection between TD and customer need, business architecture, value capture, or channel pivoting.

Three of the practitioners (Startup 5, 8 and 9) did not observe any direct or indirect connection between technical debt and any of the pivoting types. Only one of the startups argues that the connection of TD with pivoting is beneficial at the early phase to obtain a proof-of-concept. However, this finding is anecdotal for our research and helps little in understanding the role of TD now that the startup is in growth phase:

"...We are doing growth hacking ... not developing new features that are not necessarily well thought out... but then we are avoiding technical debt..." [Quote 10 - Startup 10]

Key findings:

- No practitioners have been able to find an obvious relationship between TD and business-oriented pivot types.
- About 30% of growth-phase startups do not report any direct or indirect influence of TD on pivoting.

4.2 TD Processes in Pivoting Scenarios

Based on the reported analysis of the relationship between TD and pivoting and the practitioners' answers, we can map pivoting types according to TD processes. As discussed with the practitioners, this can help in mitigating the role of TD in startup pivoting. According to Cico et al. [8], we observe two main TD processes in growth-phase startups: managing TD and avoiding TD. In contrast, early phase startups lean more towards ignoring or accepting TD.

Managing TD and Pivoting: Managing TD, as defined by Cico et al. [8], includes recognizing, analyzing, monitoring, and measuring TD. Managing TD is perceived by practitioners as beneficial in delaying technology pivoting. Practitioners considered practices such as refactoring, TD tracking, and code reviews to aid in mitigating technology pivoting.

"...We track it, you cannot commit any technical debt to the repository without adding a comment in the code that this is technical debt and track it in a Jira issue...we want to keep our technology stack operational as long as possible..." [Quote 11 - Startup 3]

"...lot of sort of prototyping turned into production software that tends to generate technical debt and that cost us to spend some efforts on refactoring ... we can then push pivoting in time..." [Quote 12 - Startup 2]

However, one of the practitioners claimed that in particular cases, technology becomes outdated and so managing TD might not be the right solution. The interviewee leaned more toward the option of choosing a long-standing technology (Node.js or Python) to delay technology pivot. Two practitioners report the following:

"...choose something [Node.js] that we can live with for a while and to manage that technical debt and the risk involved..." [Quote 13 - Startup 3]

"...The restrictions that we had with previous technology in distributing and managing of the spreadsheets ... was deciding role for changing direction and moving to Power Bi ... and we will stick to the technology for features it has been offering ..." [Quote 14 - Startup 7]

"...Now we use Python, as I told you. And our definition is based on the concepts of Clean Architecture ... We need to reduce the technical debt to evolve the system [avoid technology pivoting] ..." [Quote 15 - Startup 11]

Yet another practitioner supports the argument and considers technology as fashion *(cf. Quote 5 – Startup 1)*; in the end, is all about choosing the latest technology with the most community support. In doing so, it is easier to maintain or avoid technical debt and, in turn, technology pivoting.

Practitioners also reported a positive association between managing TD and cases where TD has an indirect influence on pivoting *(cf. earlier analysis)*. Specifically, properly managing TD can lead to smoother transitions in choosing a specific feature to be the basis of the entire product *(zoom-in)* or many features to become a single product *(zoom-out)*. Practitioners made a similar consideration for platform and customer segment pivoting, where TD management can help restrain its effects.

Avoiding TD and Pivoting: Avoiding TD is defined by Cico et al. [8] as a proactive strategy to identify all potential software cycles (production–test–release) where TD can occur and to take measures for preventing it. Avoiding TD is typically a burden put on developers when technology pivoting is not an option at a mature startup stage. One practitioner claims the necessity of immediately adopting state of the art toolchains which help in avoiding TD and in turn abrupt technology pivot:

"...We also have a big focus on moving forward when it comes to tool chains...whenever there's a new version of a tool chain, we jump on it immediately, so we can get small increments... instead of switching our code base to a new one..." [Quote 16 - Startup 6]

For several other practitioners avoiding TD-similarly to managing TD-is bound to the technology choice, but with more scrupulous measures-such as code generalization-performed ahead and the adoption of best practices only. The proper technology choice delays technology pivot which in turn can trigger less TD (an observation brought as an opposite argument to the original question asked but demonstrates the strong bond between TD and pivoting).

"...I might with this [pivoting] be stretching it to our product UX...We are generalizing, yeah we're keeping it general, which is a way to avoid technical debt as well..." [Quote 17 - Startup 3]

One practitioner reports the actual connection between avoiding TD and engine of growth pivoting where implementation of necessary features that drive growth should be constructed TD free *(cf. **Quote 9 – Startup 1**)*.

Key finding:

– Managing and avoiding TD significantly reduces the likelihood of technology pivoting and restrains effects on other indirect effects of TD in pivoting.

---

5 Discussions

5.1 TD Influence on Pivoting in Growth-Phase Startups

In our study, we focus on highlighting the influence of TD on pivoting in software startups transitioning to the growth phase. Although we have a limited number of participants, our study's qualitative nature permitted us to obtain legitimate results that focus on deeply understanding the influence of TD on pivoting. Although this study focuses on a particular niche context, namely, startups transitioning to the growth phase, our results reveal unnoted differences from previous studies. Thus, we can offer practitioners and researchers unique insights. Nevertheless, this study has limitations as discussed in Sect. 5.3.

Previous studies have focused on uncovering and addressing TD influence on pivoting in early-phase startups only [4]. We focus more on investigating how TD influences growth-phase startups. We argue that our investigation is of interest because of the following: (1) the TD influence on pivoting is understudied in previous research [3,4,6,8,9,12,20], and (2) we observe the need for startups to consider at least one pivoting type to keep up with the market's evolution. However, if pivoting occurs because startups cannot overcome TD thresholds, then there is a high impact on startups' overall success [5]. In growth-phase startups, failure leads to greater socio-economic impacts.

Our findings enable us to emphasize three ways by which TD influences pivoting. Specifically, we found that TD can have a (1) direct, (2) indirect, or (3) no-influence on pivoting. The line is very thin between the influence and no-influence of TD on various pivoting types related to technology and business activities. We also push our efforts further in mapping TD processes (management and avoidance) in growth-phase startups with pivoting types.

We learn from our results that the discussion on whether TD has any influence on growth-phase startups' pivoting is not sterile. Early studies have provided marginal arguments on TD influence on pivoting [1,13], specifically focusing on early-phase startups. The reasons for this may vary, but we argue that the research community has yet to reach maturity in TD in general and on its influence on pivoting in particular.

5.2   Benefit to Researchers and Practitioners

Researchers can benefit from our study in the following ways: (1) by having better insights on how TD influences various pivoting types in growth-phase startups, (2) by mapping different TD processes to pivoting types, (3) by collecting similar data that could help in surveying the startups' TD and pivoting relationship in various startup lifecycle phases, and (4) by providing guidelines/recommendations on how to cope with pivoting influenced by poor TD approaches for startups in various development phases. Practitioners can benefit from our study in the following ways: (1) Consolidating their perception of TD influence on pivoting. Three influence manners can be identified (direct, indirect, and no-influence). We also uncover TD processes that allow understanding of TD's influence on various pivoting types. Consolidation can help startups choose among the best practices in coping with TD influence on pivoting in different startup development phases; (2) Learning to adopt TD processes efficiently, which can help restrain unexpected pivoting scenarios; (3) Understanding when TD can become a risk that leads to technology-related pivoting and when it actually can help startups achieve their market goals without the necessity to pivot.

5.3   Threats to Validity

This study is prone to limitations owing to its qualitative nature. However, our intention is not to generalize but rather deepen our understanding on the relationship between TD and pivoting, which is often overlooked by most researchers.

According to Suri [19], the threats to validity in qualitative research are primarily related to the following: (1) **External Validity.** External threats to validity in qualitative studies are related to the sample size and limited context under consideration. We admit that due to the limited number of cases larger sample size is required to generalize the results. To mitigate this threat to validity, we plan to recruit more samples and interview other roles in the startups *(follow-up interviews and questionnaires)*; (2) **Internal Validity.** Internal threats to validity in qualitative studies are related to data extraction and analysis. To mitigate this threat to validity we have carefully coded and categorized the transcriptions while gradually summarizing our findings from the most significant data; (3) **Construct validity.** In our cases, is related to previous knowledge about TD. The maturity level of the startups proved that they were all familiar with the concept. We used an instrument similar to previous research instruments in investigating TD, although applied with a different investigation scope and lenses. Consequently, we argue that this threat to validity is almost non-existent; (4) **Descriptive validity.** Although we have tried to gather as much information as possible, we admit that some aspects might not have been covered. To mitigate this threat to validity, we have used audio recordings of the interviews to verify the descriptive data back in time and stored the rest of the data electronically.

5.4   Hypotheses

Conducting interviews on a small sample in two distinct countries helped us reduce the bias of the obtained results, although fully eliminating them is not possible (cf. Sect. 5.3). Based on these results, we draw five hypotheses, thereby completing the first half of our investigation. We intend to corroborate our hypotheses by: (1) Conducting questionnaire surveys with a large sample of growth-phase software startups, including the ones that participated in the interview process, and (2) Performing triangulation with artifact analysis of our findings. While identifying the relationship between TD and pivoting, we can make assumptions (hypotheses) worth investigating in the research community.

Hypotheses:

H1: The influence of TD on technology pivot is direct and unequivocal. (cf. Section 4.1)

H2: TD accruing leads to technology pivot at some point. (cf. Section 4.1)

H3: TD has an indirect influence on both technological and business pivoting. (cf. Section 4.1)

H4: TD is not related to business-oriented pivot types (cf. Section 4.1)

H5: Managing or avoiding TD reduces its direct or indirect influence on various pivoting types (cf. Section 4.2)

Startups' lifetime usually does not outpace the core technology used or the tech stack. In H1 and H2, we argue that TD in growth-phase startups has a direct influence and higher impact on technology pivot than the technology outdate. As reported in our findings, accommodating new features that are highly in demand in the market may become practically impossible because of the accrued TD, leading to a technology pivot. Researchers can corroborate both hypotheses based on more quantitative data, enabling practitioners to make educated decisions about resilient technological choices (e.g., tech stack and code base).

In H3, we do not rule out the potential indirect influence that TD might have on various pivoting types, which is also reflected in the summary of our analysis in Fig. 1. For instance, zoom-in, zoom-out, customer-segment, platform pivot, and engine of growth are some of the pivoting types that are indirectly influenced by TD. Reasons for this vary from limitations in startups' own or third-party product code to incapacitated resources or business growth, as indirectly affected by TD. By gathering further empirical evidence, researchers would be able to corroborate and eventually discover more factors that lead to the indirect influence of TD on various pivoting types.

In H4, we argue that in some cases, pivoting choices are only related to business activities, such as customer need, business architecture, value capture, and channel pivot. This is why none of the startups could connect TD to business-oriented pivoting, and in particular, around 30% of the startups could not connect TD to any pivoting type at all. Researchers can gather further evidence from a quantitative perspective, which would help uncover the extent to which pivoting is related to TD from a technological perspective or business activities.

In H5, we suggest that such activities as TD management and avoidance, which are often encountered in growth-phase startups, can mitigate the overall effects of TD on pivoting. Especially, as illustrated in Fig. 1, technology pivoting is closely related to both TD management and avoidance. Likewise, customer-segment, zoom-in, zoom-out, and platform pivot types are related to TD management, and only the engine of growth pivot type is related to TD avoidance. We observe that managing TD helps restrain various technology-related issues, and thus, undesired technological pivoting. However, if the startup is expected to have healthy product growth, it should take adequate measures to avoid TD. Researchers can deepen the understanding of TD management and avoidance with pivoting by relying on this and previous research [8].

6   Conclusions and Future Work

We explored how startups perceive TD influence on pivoting in the growth phase. After interviewing six CEOs and five CTOs from eleven software startups from two countries, we identified three ways by which TD influences pivoting: 1) direct, 2) indirect, and 3) no-influence. TD influence on technology pivoting is direct and unequivocal. Nevertheless, growth-phase startups commonly adopt new technologies if they foresee the benefit of such technologies in easily accommodating product features. We also find that TD can hinder the development capabilities of startups, thus leading to technological and non-technological pivoting. Moreover, we argued that outlier startup cases exist, where pivoting is not related to TD. However, the startups might have pivoted because of other factors before TD actually played any particular role in their pivoting decision. We also do not know if growth-phase startups can avoid TD-induced pivoting by simply managing or avoiding TD.

It will be worthwhile for both researchers and practitioners to investigate and validate our claims. Nonetheless, our findings spark an intriguing debate on the influence of TD on pivoting when startups have reached their growth phase. Our study can help improve startup awareness about the TD processes (e.g., management or avoidance) that startups need to adopt as preemptive pivoting measures. Our results reflect patterns encountered in growth-phase startups. In conclusion, startup research has matured sufficiently in categorizing pivoting and TD processes but has not yet related one to the other. The orthogonal nature of the relationship between TD and pivoting seems to suggest exciting new areas of TD and pivoting theories.

We urge for this topic to receive the attention it deserves in the research community. Our proposed hypotheses merits further investigation in qualitative and quantitative studies. In the future, we plan to collect more data by surveying and interviewing a larger sample. The triangulation will allow us to generalize our findings and provide a clear roadmap and guidelines to be exploited by the research and practitioner community actively participating in software startups.

References

1. Apa, C., Jeronimo, H., Nascimento, L.M., Vallespir, D., Travassos, G.H.: The perception and management of technical debt in software startups. In: Nguyen-Duc, A., Münch, J., Prikladnicki, R., Wang, X., Abrahamsson, P. (eds.) Fundamentals of Software Startups, pp. 61–78. Springer, Cham (2020). https://doi.org/10.1007/978-3-030-35983-6_4
2. Avgeriou, P., et al.: Managing technical debt in software engineering (dagstuhl seminar 16162). In: Dagstuhl Reports, vol. 6. 4. Schloss Dagstuhl-Leibniz-Zentrum fuer Informatik (2016)
3. Bajwa, S.S.: Pivoting in software startups. In: Nguyen-Duc, A., Münch, J., Prikladnicki, R., Wang, X., Abrahamsson, P. (eds.) Fundamentals of Software Startups, pp. 27–43. Springer, Cham (2020). https://doi.org/10.1007/978-3-030-35983-6_2
4. Shahid, S., et al.: Start-ups must be ready to pivot. IEEE Softw. 34(3), 18–22 (2017)
5. Besker, T., et al.: Embracing technical debt, from a startup company perspective. In: 2018 IEEE International Conference on Software Maintenance and Evolution (ICSME), pp. 415–425. IEEE (2018)
6. Bosch, J., Veen, V.D., Salvador, J.: Pivots and architectural decisions: two sides of the same medal? In: Chalmers Publication Library (CPL), pp. 310–317 (2013)
7. Brown, N., et al.: Managing technical debt in software-reliant systems. In: Proceedings of the FSE/SDP Workshop on Future of Software Engineering Research, pp. 47–52. ACM (2010)

8. Cico, O., Souza, R., Jaccheri, L., Nguyen Duc, A., Machado, I.: Startups transitioning from early to growth phase - a pilot study of technical debt perception. In: Klotins, E., Wnuk, K. (eds.) ICSOB 2020. LNBIP, vol. 407, pp. 102–117. Springer, Cham (2021). https://doi.org/10.1007/978-3-030-67292-8_8

9. Giardino, C., Wang, X., Abrahamsson, P.: Why early-stage software startups fail: a behavioral framework. In: Lassenius, C., Smolander, K. (eds.) ICSOB 2014. LNBIP, vol. 182, pp. 27–41. Springer, Cham (2014). https://doi.org/10.1007/978-3-319-08738-2_3

10. Giardino, C., Paternoster, N., Unterkalmsteiner, M., Gorschek, T., Abrahamsson, P.: Software development in startup companies: the greenfield startup model. IEEE Trans. Softw. Eng. **42**(6), 585–604 (2016)

11. Holvitie, J., et al.: Technical debt and agile software development practices and processes: an industry practitioner survey. Inf. Softw. Technol. **96**, 141–160 (2018)

12. Jabangwe, R., et al.: An exploratory study of software evolution and quality: before, during and after a transfer. In: 2012 IEEE Seventh International Conference on Global Software Engineering, pp. 41–50. IEEE (2012)

13. Klotins, E., et al.: Exploration of technical debt in start-ups. In: 2018 IEEE/ACM 40th International Conference on Software Engineering: Software Engineering in Practice Track (ICSE-SEIP), pp. 75–84. IEEE (2018)

14. Martini, A., Besker, T., Bosch, J.: Technical debt tracking: current state of practice: a survey and multiple case study in 15 large organizations. Sci. Comput. Program. **163**, 42–61 (2018)

15. Muzellec, L., Ronteau, S., Lambkin, M.: Two-sided internet platforms: a business model lifecycle perspective. Ind. Mark. Manag. **45**, 139–150 (2015)

16. Nguyen-Duc, A., Seppänen, P., Abrahamsson, P.: Hunter-gatherer cycle: a conceptual model of the evolution of software startups. In: Proceedings of the 2015 International Conference on Software and System Process, pp. 199–203 (2015)

17. Ries, E.: The lean startup: How today's entrepreneurs use continuous innovation to create radically successful businesses. Currency (2011)

18. Runeson, P., Höst, M.: Guidelines for conducting and reporting case study research in software engineering. Empir. Softw. Eng. **14**(2), 131 (2009)

19. Suri, H., et al.: Purposeful sampling in qualitative research synthesis. Qual. Res. J. **11**(2), 63 (2011)

20. Terho, H., Suonsyrjä, S., Karisalo, A., Mikkonen, T.: Ways to cross the Rubicon: pivoting in software startups. In: Abrahamsson, P., Corral, L., Oivo, M., Russo, B. (eds.) PROFES 2015. LNCS, vol. 9459, pp. 555–568. Springer, Cham (2015). https://doi.org/10.1007/978-3-319-26844-6_41

21. Tom, E., Aurum, A.K., Vidgen, R.: An exploration of technical debt. J. Syst. Softw. **86**(6), 1498–1516 (2013)

Towards a Common Testing Terminology
for Software Engineering and Data Science
Experts

Lisa Jöckel[1(✉)], Thomas Bauer[1], Michael Kläs[1], Marc P. Hauer[2], and Janek Groß[1]

[1] Fraunhofer Institute for Experimental Software Engineering IESE, Fraunhofer-Platz 1,
67663 Kaiserslautern, Germany
{lisa.joeckel,thomas.bauer,michael.klaes,
janek.gross}@iese.fraunhofer.de
[2] Algorithm Accountability Lab, TU Kaiserslautern, Gottlieb-Daimler-Strasse 48,
67663 Kaiserslautern, Germany
hauer@cs.uni-kl.de

Abstract. Analytical quality assurance, especially testing, is an integral part of software-intensive system development. With the increased usage of Artificial Intelligence (AI) and Machine Learning (ML) as part of such systems, this becomes more difficult as well-understood software testing approaches cannot be applied directly to the AI-enabled parts of the system. The required adaptation of classical testing approaches and the development of new concepts for AI would benefit from a deeper understanding and exchange between AI and software engineering experts. We see the different terminologies used in the two communities as a major obstacle on this way. As we consider a mutual understanding of the testing terminology a key, this paper contributes a mapping between the most important concepts from classical software testing and AI testing. In the mapping, we highlight differences in the relevance and naming of the mapped concepts.

Keywords: Analytical quality assurance · Machine learning evaluation ·
Data-driven model · Quality characteristics · Artificial intelligence testing ·
Definitions · Concept mapping · Target application scope

1 Motivation

In complex software-intensive systems, analytical quality assurance (QA) activities, especially software testing, have proven to be crucial for achieving high product quality. Due to the increasing relevance of Artificial Intelligence (AI) and Machine Learning (ML) as part of software systems, the question arises how AI/ML-enabled systems, and especially their AI/ML-based components, should be tested. The functionality of such components, which we refer to as *data-driven components* (DDCs), is not explicitly defined by a specification and implemented by a programmer within the code. Instead, it is given by a – usually complex and not human-understandable – model that is automatically derived from a data sample via a learning algorithm. Due to properties such

© Springer Nature Switzerland AG 2021
L. Ardito et al. (Eds.): PROFES 2021, LNCS 13126, pp. 281–289, 2021.
https://doi.org/10.1007/978-3-030-91452-3_19

as limited specification and understandability, the transfer of classical test approaches is not trivial.

In the field of AI, the QA of DDCs has so far played a minor role and has mainly been done by applying specific evaluation criteria such as accuracy to a previously unseen subset of the available data. As the application of AI is being extended to ever more domains, including safety-critical areas such as autonomous driving, industrial automation, or medical applications, the demand for QA has also increased in recent years. New techniques are being proposed and quality aspects like fairness, robustness, and explainability are becoming more important. Although some approaches for testing DDCs are described in the literature [1] including some very sophisticated ones, their relation to classical software testing and system QA is not covered sufficiently yet.

We see the potential to exploit experiences and concepts from the field of classical software testing for the QA of AI-based systems and components. To this end, collaboration and direct exchange between experts from both fields are important. This is, however, impeded by different terminologies and meaning of terms, which leads to misunderstandings and makes it more difficult to relate to work from the respective other field.

Contribution: In this paper, we make a first step towards a common terminology. We use established terms from classical software testing as a basis to map corresponding concepts from the field of AI to it, pointing out differences and key challenges in transferring known concepts. The proposed mapping was developed in an interdisciplinary collaboration among the authors, who have many years of experience in at least one of the two fields, partly in both. We intend this to be a stimulus and a basis for discussions aimed at building a common understanding between experts of both fields.

In Sect. 2, we will describe some background regarding DDCs. Section 3 provides an overview of related work on testing terminology. Section 4 presents a mapping between testing terminology for classical software and AI. Section 5 concludes the paper.

2   Background on Data-Driven Components

In this section, we provide some background on DDCs that is relevant for understanding the discussions on the test concepts in Sect. 4. To this end, we will briefly describe a typical DDC lifecycle as well as supervised learning, and introduce an example use case.

As QA is done throughout the lifecycle of a DDC, we use an adapted lifecycle for DDCs [2] that allows differentiating the purposes of QA measures and datasets (see Fig. 1). Multiple datasets are needed for different purposes (e.g., training, validation, testing) during the DDC lifecycle. As the functionality of DDCs is derived from and evaluated on data, this is a key aspect that needs to be treated with caution. In the DDC lifecycle, the *specification* defines, among other things, the task of the AI, its target application scope (TAS) [3], and its required quality characteristics. The TAS is related to the operational design domain in the automotive domain. It defines in which context and under which conditions the DDC is considered applicable; hence, it is an important building block for testing and needs to be reflected by the test dataset. During *construction*, the data-driven model (DDM) is built as core of the DDC. Its input-outcome relationship is derived from a data sample, i.e., a training dataset composed for the intended task. The expected behavior of DDCs is therefore only specified for a subset of all possible input data. For previously unseen inputs, the expected behavior cannot be fully assured. We distinguish two phases of analytical QA activities during design time according to their purposes: (1) *Analysis* activities aim at finding potential weak points to improve the DDM, like explainability approaches. The results from the analysis are fed back to the construction phase. (2) *Testing* activities aim at providing quantitative evidence for the specified requirements, which are generated on a test dataset that is representative for the TAS. This differentiation into analysis and testing is a distinct feature of the lifecycle of DDCs, as eliminating faults based on incorrect outcomes is difficult [4]. The analysis and testing phases take place before the AI component is deployed. During *operation*, monitoring activities are needed to ensure that the application is in line with the specification. In the remainder of this paper, our focus will be on *analytical QA activities in the testing phase.*

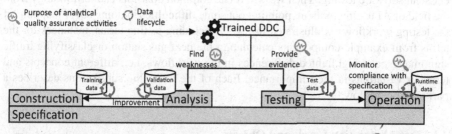

Fig. 1. Lifecycle model of a DDC with analytical quality assurance for different purposes.

Techniques for building DDCs can be grouped by the degree of supervision they need, which in turn influences the possibilities and raises different challenges for testing. Our focus is on *DDCs using supervised learning techniques*, where there is ground truth information for the outcomes, i.e., each data point is labeled with its expected outcome.

We will later refer to an example DDC whose task is traffic sign recognition (TSR), i.e., classification of the traffic sign type on a given input image, on German roads.

3   Related Work on Testing Terminology

Software testing has been a fundamental discipline in software engineering since the very beginning. Therefore, processes, terms, and definitions for software testing have been defined since the 1980s, leading to standards such as IEEE 829 for Software Test Documentation [5], and the IEEE 610 Standard Computer Dictionary [6], which still represent the basis for fundamental terms and definitions in software testing. They have been updated step by step and have been tailored for new domains and system classes [7], as well as being supplemented with new concepts, e.g., test coverage [8].

In contrast, the testing of AI-based software systems has only gained importance in recent years [4]. As there are many challenges related to the testing of AI [4, 9], a transfer of concepts and the corresponding terminology from classical software testing is not trivial. Lenarduzzi et al. provide a mapping between terms that are misleading or used differently in software engineering and AI [10]. Some works provide an overview of what has been done so far in transferring testing concepts, including the definition and relations of some testing terms [1, 4, 9]. These terms include, e.g., test input generation, adequacy criteria, oracle, testing level, online and offline learning. However, the number of considered terms is rather selective and not clearly oriented on the workflows for software and AI testing, which would improve relating the terminology of both fields to establish a common understanding. To the best of our knowledge, a comprehensive mapping between the terminologies – considering differences and common aspects as well as their relations to the testing workflows – has not been performed yet.

4 Mapping of Software and AI Testing Terminology

In this section, we will first provide an overview of the basic workflow and terminology in classical software testing. Then we will relate common concepts and terminology from the field of AI testing to them, pointing out some difficulties in doing so. A mapping of the testing workflows is illustrated in Fig. 2, including testing terms, instances for the terms from example components calculating the next gas station or classifying traffic sign images, and highlighted differences in the workflows, i.e., different concepts and terms or variations in their importance. Each of the following subsections describes a part of the workflow.

4.1 Test Abstraction Levels and Objects

Software Testing. In software engineering, *testing* is defined as "an analytical QA activity in which systems, subsystems, or components are executed under specified conditions, the results are observed or recorded, and an evaluation is made of some aspect of the system or component" [6]. This means that testing is performed on specific abstraction levels (component, integration, system) [12] when executable artifacts such as program code or executable models become available as test objects. A *test object* or test item is defined as "a software or system item that is an object of testing" [5] and implements a (sometimes implicit) specification. A *specification* is "a document that specifies, in a complete, precise, verifiable manner, the requirements, design, behavior, or other characteristics of a system or component, and, often, the procedures for determining whether these provisions have been satisfied" [6]. The test object is tested against the requirements, i.e., the required capabilities of the system or system component [6], and against quality characteristics. In this work, we focus on software *component testing*, which is defined as "testing of individual hardware or software components or groups of related components" where a *component* is "one of the parts that make up a system [...] and may be subdivided into other components" [6]. Each component contributes to a specific function or set of functions of its associated system.

AI Testing. We consider DDCs to be a counterpart to classical software components. A DDC may consist of sub-components that are organized in pipelines that include some data pre- and post-processing in addition to the trained DDM [13]. Since data pre- and

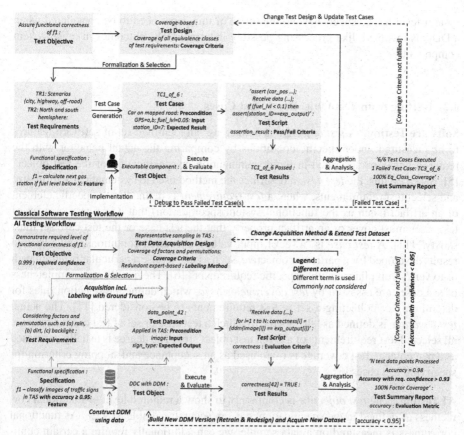

Fig. 2. Comparison of testing workflows for classical software (top) and AI (bottom).

post-processing can be addressed with software testing approaches, AI testing focuses on the DDM. As isolated testing of the implemented training algorithm does not reveal whether the trained model successfully derived the intended behavior from the training data, the trained DDM is considered to be the *test object*. Yet, as the behavior of the DDM is learned from data, ensuring that the data itself meets certain requirements becomes increasingly important. Although data is not an 'executable artifact' on its own, but only in combination with the model, certain characteristics of the dataset can be checked (e.g., inclusion of edge cases) with regard to the intended task of the DDC and its TAS. Contrary to classical software components, the behavior of the DDC cannot be described in a complete and verifiable manner as part of the *specification* as its functionality is not defined by the developer but is derived from data. For testing, functional correctness is mostly regarded as a *quality characteristic* (others might be fairness, robustness, and explainability). However, unlike in software testing, requirements on functional correctness need to be given a probabilistic sense (e.g., stop signs are correctly detected with a probability of 91%) as the input-outcome relationship cannot be fully specified and uncertainty in the DDC outcomes cannot be fully eliminated. For integration- and system-level tests, aspects beyond the scope of this paper need to be considered when a DDC is involved, like processing possibly incorrect DDC outcomes in other system components.

4.2 Getting from Test Objective to Test Cases

Software Testing. A *test objective* is defined as "an identified set of software features to be measured under specific conditions by comparing the actual behavior with the required behavior described in the documentation or specification of the test object" [5]. Based on this, the *test design* describes the method used to systematically formalize and select test requirements, where a *test requirement* is defined as "a specific element of an artifact (such as the functional system specification) that a test case or a set of test cases must cover or an artifact property that the test case or the test case set must satisfy" [11]. A *test case* is "a set of input values, execution conditions, and expected results developed for a particular objective, such as to exercise a particular program path or to verify compliance with a specific requirement" [6]. The quality and completeness of test cases are assessed by *test coverage criteria*, which define the selection rules for determining or collecting a set of test requirements to be considered [11]. The actual *test coverage* is defined as "the degree to which a test case or set of test cases addresses all selected test requirements of a given test object" [6]. The degree is usually expressed as a percentage. Test coverage is often used as an acceptance and stopping criterion for specifying test cases [8].

AI Testing. The *test objective* is commonly to show a required level of functional correctness as defined in the specification, e.g., an accuracy of at least 95%. As functional correctness is measured on a data sample, we can additionally require a certain confidence in the evaluation, e.g., requiring a confidence of 99.9% that the actual accuracy is not lower than 95%. This way, we reduce the risk of wrongly assuming an accuracy level that is too high.

In general, DDCs have to be tested on data that was not used during the development of the DDC, i.e., the *test dataset*, which also contains ground truth information for supervised models. Each data point can be seen as a *test case* providing the model input and the expected outcome, e.g., an image showing a stop sign as model input with the corresponding sign type as expected outcome. Execution preconditions are usually not defined explicitly, but implicitly, as the inputs should be collected from the TAS. Determining the expected outcome, i.e., the ground truth, is more difficult in most cases than for classical software components as the labeling is mainly done manually, not always unambiguous, and sometimes involves the observation of complex empirical processes, e.g., when we need to determine whether a certain cancer therapy was successful. This limits the amount of data available and the freedom in designing test cases. Sometimes, this issue is addressed by simulations to generate labeled synthetic data or data augmentations to add changes to a data point in a way that the ground truth is still known [14]. However, due to limitations regarding the realism of such data, it is not clear to which degree the testing performance can be transferred to real inputs during operation. Commonly, the *test dataset is acquired* by a representative sample for the

TAS (without defining test requirements). The method for labeling the data with ground truth information is also part of the data acquisition.

In analogy to classical software testing, *test requirements* could be defined. For the example DDC, this could be done by considering relevant factors influencing the input data quality, e.g., rain or a dirty camera lens. Here, *test coverage criteria* would be based on the influence factors and their permutations. However, defining test requirements in this way involves expert knowledge and is often not done explicitly in practice, which potentially leads to important influence factors not being (sufficiently) considered in the data, such as snow-covered traffic signs. Other possible coverage criteria are related to code coverage in classical software, like neuron coverage for neural networks demanding neurons to exceed a defined activation level [15]. Coverage criteria are often difficult to transfer to DDCs as they usually operate in an open context with many unforeseeable situations. Additionally, small changes in the input might lead to large variations in the outcome [16]. Therefore, the stopping criterion for testing is mostly handled trivially by stopping when all data points in a given test dataset have been processed. However, this does not necessarily reveal to which extent the test objective is addressed.

4.3 Test Execution and Evaluation

Software Testing. For the test execution, specific *test scripts* have to be derived from the test cases to enable a connection to the execution environment and the test tools, to stimulate the test object with concrete signals, messages, as well as function calls, and to record the system responses for the subsequent evaluation [12]. The actual response is compared with the expected response defined in the test case and implemented in the test script to determine the *test result*, i.e., whether or not a specific test case has passed or failed [7]. The *test summary report* includes a summary of the test activities and results, considering failed test cases and achieved coverage level [5]. For the failed test cases, the underlying faults are localized and fixed to improve the test object. Insufficient coverage leads to changes of the test design and, hence, an updated set of test cases.

AI Testing. *Test scripts* in the sense of software testing do not play a prominent role in AI testing. The reason is that DDCs are commonly stateless software components with well-defined, simple interfaces (e.g., taking as input an image of a defined size and providing as outcome a sign type). Thus, there is no need for individual scripts implementing different test cases but just for a single script that loads the test dataset, executes the DDC with each input, and then computes the *test results* applying the evaluation criteria, e.g., correctness of the DDC outcome, on each pair of obtained/expected outcomes. AI *test reports* commonly focus on aggregated results for the relevant evaluation metric, e.g., accuracy, without indicating which test cases failed. The reason is that unlike in software testing, where faults causing a specific failure can be localized and fixed in the test object individually, no concept equivalent to a fault exists for DDMs. The DDC will thus only be revised if the test report indicates that the test objective is not met. In such cases, a new DDM has to be constructed and a new test dataset needs to be acquired to avoid the situation that the construction of the new DDM can make use of knowledge about the test data to be applied later. The test objective might require that the evaluation metric result is met with a given confidence. If the test report indicates that the uncertainty in the evaluation metric result is too high, i.e., the evaluation metric result with confidence is lower than the required evaluation metric result, the test dataset may be extended by acquiring additional test cases, thereby reducing the uncertainty in the evaluation metric result.

5   Conclusion

In classical software testing, well-elaborated test concepts and processes exist. Due to the different nature of DDCs, transferring known test concepts to AI is not trivial and their applicability is not easy to assess. Therefore, we propose intensifying the exchange of experience between experts from both communities. In this paper, we contribute to this by encouraging discussions on mapping terminology from software testing to AI.

We focused on supervised DDCs, well aware that unsupervised or reinforcement learning might raise further challenges, e.g., no ground truth information being available. Furthermore, the benefits of AI testing vary from classical software testing. While insufficient or incorrect behavior of the DDC might be revealed, this rarely provides information on how the behavior came to happen (e.g., due to the model hyperparameters, insufficient training data, or the training process) and thus how to improve the DDC. Additionally, we only have only a partial specification for DDCs based on a data sample, and therefore some uncertainty always remains in the outcomes. This raises the question of how test evidences need to be interpreted and what this implies in relation to classical test evidences and the expected runtime performance; i.e., the validity of the test results cannot be guaranteed for situations outside the TAS, which are often difficult to detect.

Acknowledgments. Parts of this work have been funded by the Observatory for Artificial Intelligence in Work and Society (KIO) of the Denkfabrik Digitale Arbeitsgesellschaft in the project "KI Testing & Auditing" and by the project "AIControl" as part of the internal funding program "KMU akut" of the Fraunhofer-Gesellschaft.

References

1. Zhang, J.M., Harman, M., Ma, L., Liu, Y.: Machine learning testing: survey, landscapes and horizons. IEEE Trans. Softw. Eng. (2020). https://doi.org/10.1109/TSE.2019.2962027
2. Kläs, M., Adler, R., Jöckel, L., et al.: Using complementary risk acceptance criteria to structure assurance cases for safety-critical AI components. In: AISafety 2021 (2021)
3. Kläs, M., Sembach, L.: Uncertainty wrappers for data-driven models – increase the transparency of AI/ML-based models through enrichment with dependable situation-aware uncertainty estimates. In: Romanovsky, A., Troubitsyna, E., Gashi, I., Schoitsch, E., Bitsch, F. (eds.) SAFECOMP 2019. LNCS, vol. 11699, pp. 358–364. Springer, Cham (2019). https://doi.org/10.1007/978-3-030-26250-1_29
4. Riccio, V., Jahangirova, G., Stocco, A., et al.: Testing machine learning based systems: a systematic mapping. Empir. Softw. Eng. **25**, 5193–5254 (2020)
5. IEEE Standard for Software and System Test Documentation. IEEE Std. 829 (2008)

6. IEEE Standard Glossary of Software Engineering Terminology. IEEE Std. 610:1990 (1990)
7. ISO/IEC/IEEE Standard for Software Testing – Part 1: Concepts and definitions. ISO/IEC/IEEE 29119-1:2013 (2013)
8. Utting, M., Pretschner, A., Legeard, B.: A taxonomy of model-based testing approaches. Softw. Test. Verif. Reliabil. **22**(5), 297–312 (2012)
9. Felderer, M., Ramler, R.: Quality assurance for AI-based systems: overview and challenges. In: SWQD 2021 (2021)
10. Lenarduzzi, V., Lomio, F., Moreschini, S., Taibi, D., Tamburri, D.A.: Software quality for AI: where we are now? In: Winkler, D., Biffl, S., Mendez, D., Wimmer, M., Bergsmann, J. (eds.) SWQD 2021. LNBIP, vol. 404, pp. 43–53. Springer, Cham (2021). https://doi.org/10.1007/978-3-030-65854-0_4
11. Ammann, P., Offutt, J.: Introduction to Software Testing. Cambridge University Press, Cambridge (2016)
12. Burnstein, I.: Practical Software Testing – A Process-Oriented Approach. Springer Professional Computing. Springer, Heidelberg (2003).https://doi.org/10.1007/b97392
13. Siebert, J., Jöckel, L., Heidrich, J., et al.: Construction of a quality model for machine learning systems. Softw. Qual. J. – Spec. Issue Inf. Syst. Qual. (2021). https://doi.org/10.1007/s11219-021-09557-y
14. Jöckel, L., Kläs, M.: Increasing trust in data-driven model validation – a framework for probabilistic augmentation of images and meta-data generation using application scope characteristics. In: Romanovsky, A., Troubitsyna, E., Bitsch, F. (eds.) SAFECOMP 2019. LNCS, vol. 11698, pp. 155–164. Springer, Cham (2019). https://doi.org/10.1007/978-3-030-26601-1_11
15. Pei, K., Cao, Y., Yang, J., Jana, S.: DeepXplore: automated whitebox testing of deep learning systems. In: SOSP 2017 (2017)
16. Hendrycks, D., Dietterich, T.: Benchmarking neural network robustness to common corruptions and perturbations. In: ICLR 2019 (2019)

Towards RegOps: A DevOps Pipeline for Medical Device Software

Henrik Toivakka[1,3]([⊠]) [iD], Tuomas Granlund[2,3] [iD], Timo Poranen[3] [iD], and Zheying Zhang[3] [iD]

[1] Mylab Oy, Tampere, Finland
henrik.toivakka@mylab.fi
[2] Solita Oy, Tampere, Finland
tuomas.granlund@solita.fi
[3] Tampere University, Tampere, Finland
{timo.poranen,zheying.zhang}@tuni.fi

Abstract. The manufacture of medical devices is a strictly regulated domain in the European Union. Traditionally, medical software compliance activities have been considered manual, document-centric, and burdensome. At the same time, over the last decade, software companies have maintained competitiveness and improved by relying on essential practices of DevOps, such as process automation and delivery pipelines. However, applying the same principles in medical software can be challenging due to regulatory requirements. In this paper, we utilize a systematic approach to align the essential medical device software regulatory requirements from the standards IEC 62304 and IEC 82304-1 and integrate them into the software delivery pipeline, which is the main contribution of our work. The outcome supports practitioners to establish more efficient software delivery models while maintaining compliance with the medical device standards.

Keywords: Medical device software · Medical device standards · Regulatory compliance · DevOps · RegOps

1 Introduction

The EU regulation strictly controls the manufacturing of medical devices. In order to place a medical device on the EU market, the manufacturer must prove the conformity of the product with the applicable EU regulatory requirements. With a CE mark, the manufacturer affirms conformity to regulatory requirements, and a medical device without a CE mark cannot be sold or distributed, even free of charge. In addition to specific product-related requirements, the processes by which the device is being manufactured and maintained must comply with the regulations. Both standalone and embedded medical software products are regulated under the same EU regulation as physical devices.

The DevOps paradigm has significantly changed the way how software is being developed today. The technology transformation is supported by modern toolchains that

L. Ardito et al. (Eds.): PROFES 2021, LNCS 13126, pp. 290–306, 2021.
https://doi.org/10.1007/978-3-030-91452-3_20

are designed with automation in mind. In addition, public cloud platforms offer flexible computational environments with high availability, automated infrastructure, and reliable software delivery. As the software development industry continues to improve, relying on the DevOps best practices [1], it seems inevitable that DevOps will become the norm regardless of the industry. However, certain DevOps key practices, such as short lead time for changes and high deployment frequency, can be problematic from a medical device compliance perspective [2].

In this work, we aim at improving the medical device software development process by utilizing the automation capabilities of the DevOps paradigm while achieving compliance with the regulations. We focus on standalone medical software and strive to combine the DevOps goals of short process lead time and efficiency with regulatory goals of product safety and clinical effectiveness. To achieve the goal, we systematically address the most relevant medical device regulatory requirements, align them with DevOps automated software delivery concept, and propose a software delivery pipeline compliant with the regulatory requirements. Our research is based on several years of hands-on engineering of standalone software medical devices in the industry, covering in-house development and consulting roles.

The rest of the paper is structured as follows. In Sect. 2, we provide the background for the paper. In Sect. 3, we present the basics of DevOps practices and a reference model for continuous software delivery in an unregulated environment. In Sect. 4, the requirements of the standards IEC 62304 and IEC 82304-1 are aligned. In Sect. 5, we present our proposed Regulated DevOps (RegOps) pipeline for regulated continuous software delivery. Finally, in Sect. 6, we discuss the proposed pipeline and draw some conclusions.

2 Background

In the EU region, the manufacturing of medical devices is regulated by Medical Device Regulation (MDR) and In Vitro Diagnostics Regulation (IVDR). According to the legislation, a medical device must be clinically effective for its intended medical purpose, and it must be safe to use. Therefore, medical devices are classified according to their potential risk for a person's health. Determining the correct device classification is essential, as the device class defines applicable conformity assessment procedure and the extent of a third-party conformity assessment body involvement within the process. Thus, the intended purpose and technical properties of a device define how heavily it is being regulated. In addition, also the technical documentation of the device is part of the product. It is not uncommon that regulatory requirements are seen as burdensome activities for the manufacturers [4].

The EU regulatory framework can be interpreted to consist of four layers: 1) Union harmonized legislation, 2) national legislation, 3) harmonized standards, and 4) guidance documents endorsed by the Medical Device Coordination Group (MDCG) [3]. Arguably, the most convenient way to conform with the EU legislation is to utilize harmonized, European versions of the international standards that apply to the device in question as they provide *presumption of conformity* to legislation. At present, there are no software-specific harmonized standards against MDR and IVDR, which creates a certain level of uncertainty as to which are the appropriate standards to apply. However, the EU Commission's recent standardization request [5] is an excellent source of information to get an insight into the expectations of regulatory authorities. For all medical software, the applicable set includes general requirements for health software product safety (IEC 82304-1), software life cycle process (IEC 62304), risk management process (ISO 14971), usability engineering (IEC 62366-1), quality management system requirements (ISO 13485), and security activities in the product life cycle (IEC 81001-5-1). Depending on the intended purpose and technical properties of the software product, also other standards may be relevant.

From our experience, the appliance of medical device standards to software manufacturing can significantly slow down the development process. The time delay between development and release can be measured with the *process lead time* of a software change, which essentially means the latency between initiation and completion of a process [6]. Modern software development paradigms, such as DevOps, could assist in reducing the process lead time. However, a clear, universally accepted definition for DevOps and the related practices/activities does not exist. Despite that, DevOps tries to close the gap between the development (Dev) and the operations (Ops) [7] with a set of practices that developers and operators have agreed upon. From the technological viewpoint, the goal of DevOps is to reduce and join repetitive tasks with process automation in development, integration, and deployment [8]. In practice, process automation is implemented in the Continuous Integration and Continuous Delivery (CI/CD) pipelines. A pipeline consists of an automated and repeatable set of software life cycle processes. The key to efficient software delivery is automation, repeatability, and reliability of the software deployment [9].

In this paper, the concept of DevOps leans towards process automation and pipelines, which can perform automated tasks repeatedly to shorten the process lead time and reduce the risks related to the software delivery with deterministic deployment practices. For this reason, the term DevOps pipeline is used as the primary term for referring to a set of sequential activities/tasks that can be performed repeatedly and reliably.

3   DevOps and Pipelines

In this section, we present an overview of the key characteristics of DevOps that are relevant from the viewpoint of software integrity and delivery process automation, followed by a reference *Continuous software delivery model* [10].

3.1   Building Blocks for a DevOps Pipeline

A DevOps pipeline helps teams to build, test and deploy software through a combination of tools/practices. Common tasks performed by a DevOps pipeline are software integration and deployment. Continuous Integration (CI) is the practice of integrating new code frequently, preferably as soon as possible [11]. The pipeline builds the software, runs an automated set of verification tasks against the software, and places the built software artifact into the dedicated software artifact repository [6]. A software artifact is a piece of software, such as a binary file, which can be copied into different computational environments [9]. The artifact repository stores the builds generated by the CI pipeline alongside the metadata of the build [9]. The purpose of the CI is to prevent the code from diverting too much between the developers and keep the code constantly intact, ready for release. CI is enabled by storing the code in a source code repository, which any modern distributed version control system, such as Git, can offer.

Continuous Deployment is a concept for an automated software delivery model. By applying this practice, the software is deployed into a specific computational environment after all automated verification activities are passed, without a human-made approval, but not necessarily available to end-users [9, 10]. To establish the practice, a high level of automation in the software development, testing, and delivery processes is required [6]. The pipeline handles the deployment to different computational environments. Staging environments are utilized for testing and verifying the functionality of the software. Finally, the production environment is the environment for the final end-users of the software product.

3.2 DevOps Pipeline Reference Model

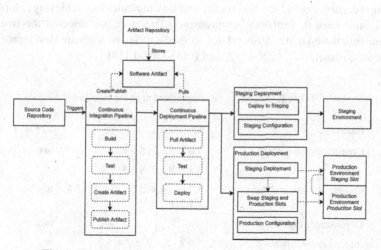

Fig. 1. Continuous software delivery model, adapted from [10].

For this work, we chose a Continuous software delivery model presented by Google [10] as the primary reference for the concept of the DevOps pipeline, as illustrated in Fig. 1. We also considered models from Humble and Microsoft [9, 12]. Google's model was selected because, based on our own experience from the industry, it is well-fitting for practical use. In addition, it illustrates the basic pipelines and relationships between different concepts well.

In the reference model, the software verification and delivery are highly automated. A check-in into the source code repository triggers the CI pipeline, which builds the software and runs automated checks and tests against the generated build. Software artifacts are created and published into the artifact repository. If the CI pipeline passes successfully, the build is deployed into the staging and the production environments. The software can be tested and verified in the staging environment manually before being released to the end-users. However, if the CI pipeline fails, the original developer is notified to fix the defects. A failing build will not be deployed.

The reference model was altered to present the sequential order of the CI/CD pipelines and the activities more accurately. Finally, the model was polished with the concept of Blue-Green Deployment [9], which enables more frictionless deployments. In practice, there are two identical copies of the customer environment present, which are swapped on software release. Thus, the rollback can be performed by swapping the slots back to the original position if any problems occur. However, databases can be quite challenging to manage while using this technique; thus, the issue should be recognized in the system's architectural design.

4   Integration of Regulatory Requirements into the DevOps Pipeline

We aim to improve the medical device software development process by utilizing the automation capabilities of DevOps pipelines while simultaneously achieving compliance with the most central regulatory requirements. Therefore, we selected the two most important international standards related to medical device software development for this research, namely IEC 62304 [13] and IEC 82304-1 [14].

Table 1. Requirements implemented in the pipeline.

Gate ID	Gate title	62304 reqs	82304–1 reqs
G1	Continuous Integration	5.6.3, 5.6.5, 5.6.7, 5.7.4	n/a
		7.3.3, 8.1.2, 8.1.3, 9.8	
G2	Change Review and Approval	5.3.6, 5.4.4, 5.5.5, 5.6.1 5.7.4, 8.1.2, 8.1.3	n/a
G3	Deployment Pipeline	n/a	n/a
G4	Integration Verification	5.6.2 - 5.6.7, 5.7.4, 5.7.5	n/a
		7.3.3, 8.1.3, 9.8	
G5	Manufacturer Release Approval	5.6.6, 5.7.4, 5.7.5, 5.8.1	6.2, 6.3, 7.1, 8.3
		5.8.3, 5.8.4, 5.8.6, 5.8.7	
		7.3.1, 7.3.3, 8.1.3, 9.8	

Although the selected standards do not cover all regulatory requirements that must be met to place the product on the EU market, in our experience, they represent exactly the part of the requirements that can benefit from technical DevOps practices.

4.1 Requirements of the Selected Standards Aligned

In our research, we aimed to identify the requirements from the standards that can be automated or which can otherwise be implemented in a similar pipeline process as illustrated in Fig. 1. In our systematic approach, first, we went through both standards and collected the requirements at the level of numbered clauses. Second, we divided the requirements into three categories:

1. requirements that could be implemented in a pipeline (presented in Table 1),
2. requirements that could be partially implemented in the pipeline (presented in Table 2), and
3. requirements excluded from the pipeline (presented in Table 3).

Finally, we mapped the requirements from categories 1 and 2 to different logical stages, presented as Gates, in our pipeline. Because of the nature of medical device regulatory requirements, certain Gates in our model are not fully automated but instead contain manual, human-made decision steps. It should be noted that the process to divide the requirements into categories and further map them to logical stages was done iteratively.

The IEC 62304 contains three software process rigor levels based on the risk level of the software. The levels are A, B, and C, from the lowest risk level to the highest. Even if rigor levels A and B allow the exclusion of certain clauses of the standard, our pipeline addresses the full spectrum of the requirements, making it suitable for also the software with the highest risk classification.

4.2 Burdensome Requirements Arising from the Standards

From a compliance perspective, the essential aspect of the development process is that all regulatory requirements are considered and implemented appropriately. These requirements create an additional layer of challenge to the usual complications related to software projects. The standards IEC 62304 and IEC 82304-1 contain some burdensome requirements, the automation of which could significantly improve the efficiency of the development process.

As discussed previously, the importance of documentation is crucial in medical device software development. As the software evolves during every development iteration and change, the corresponding technical documentation must be kept up to date, often challenging and laborious if done with manual processes. For instance, IEC 82304-1 requires the manufacturer to have comprehensive accompanying documentation containing information regarding the safety and security of the software product. These documents include, for example, instructions for use and the technical description. The standard contains fairly detailed requirements on the content of accompanying documentation. Furthermore, IEC 62304 further extends the requirements for technical documentation to include details of the documents that must be produced during different development lifecycle activities and tasks. For example, IEC 62304 requires the manufacturer to create software architecture and detailed design documentation for software units.

The requirements related to Software of Unknown Provenance (SOUP) can be a particularly troublesome area for manufacturers as IEC 62304 requires appropriate management of SOUP items according to its comprehensive rules. SOUP refers to a software or part of the software that is not intended for medical use but is incorporated into a medical device. SOUP also includes parts of software that have been developed before the medical device development processes have been available. The manufacturer must identify and list all SOUP components and specify functional, performance, system, and hardware requirements for the identified components. These documents are part of the product's required technical documentation.

5 RegOps Pipeline for Medical Software

This section presents our proposed pipeline for the medical device software, the RegOps pipeline, which builds on the reference pipeline illustrated in Fig. 1, and the results of Sect. 4. To ensure compliance against the regulatory requirements, the RegOps pipeline contains both automated and manual activities. The DevOps stages are modeled as Gates, with acceptance criteria that must be met before software release activities can proceed to the next stage. When the software release has passed all Gates, the regulatory requirements implemented within the RegOps pipeline have been fulfilled for that specific version of the software product. The RegOps pipeline is illustrated in Fig. 2 and presented in more detail later in this section.

It is worth noting that the RegOps pipeline relies on specific technical infrastructure details. For instance, we assume that the manufacturer manages product-related user requirements, software requirements, risks, anomalies, and change requests in electronic systems that can be integrated with the Version Control System (VCS). The RegOps pipeline itself can be implemented with a modern DevOps tool-set that is extended with customized improvements to support regulatory compliance.

5.1 Gate 1: Continuous Integration

The CI is the first stage of the RegOps pipeline. When new code is checked into the source code repository, the software build is triggered. In addition, automated verification activities and static code analysis are performed, and the product documentation is generated. Finally, the software artifact is published in the software artifact repository. The associated documentation is published into the dedicated documentation storage and made available for review.

In the *Integration testing* step, the covered regulatory requirements involve software unit verification, software integration testing, and the documentation of the results (IEC 62304 clauses 5.6.3, 5.6.5, 5.6.7, 5.7.1), which the CI stage can perform depending on the test automation coverage. However, the verification activities that are not covered by the test automation must be tested later manually, increasing the process lead time. In addition, IEC 62304 requires identifying and avoiding common software defects (clause 5.1.12), and the implementation of this requirement can be partly automated by performing a *Static code analysis* against the source code. The coding conventions,

Table 2. Requirements partially implemented in the pipeline.

62304 req.	Qualifying remarks
5.1.12	The planning activities are performed before the pipeline, but the pipeline can support the requirement by utilizing automated Linter-tools etc.
5.3.1 - 5.3.4	Even if the design activities are performed before the pipeline, the pipeline can support the implementation of the requirement by automating the creation of architecture documentation
5.4.1	Even if the design activities are performed before the pipeline, the pipeline can support the implementation of the requirement by an automated creation of architecture documentation. In practice, the automated generation of documentation is assisted by using annotations to document the software structure
5.5.2	Even if process establishing activities are performed before the pipeline, the pipeline is a tool to implement the requirement
5.5.3	Even if the design and specification activities are performed before the pipeline, the pipeline can support the verification of the software unit implementation
5.7.1	Even if test establishing activities are performed before the pipeline, the pipeline is a tool to implement the requirement, i.e. performing the tests
5.7.3	Retesting is performed in pipeline implicitly, whereas risk management activities must be performed before pipeline
5.8.2	Anomaly management can be automated to a certain degree, and the documentation generation and verification can be done within the pipeline
5.8.5	Planning tasks, incl. the software development plan and management of the development process are performed before the pipeline. However, infrastructure code can be part of the documentation, and pipeline participates in the creation of the documentation
5.8.8	Technical practices can be implemented. However, practices such as user access management for the pipeline infrastructure, are managed outside of the pipeline
6.3.2	See details from 5.8 requirements
7.1.3	Even if the evaluation activities are performed before the pipeline, the pipeline can support the implementation of the requirement by checking that evaluation exists and offering a convenient tool to update the evaluation if it is missing
7.4.3	See details from 7.1, 7.2, and 7.3 requirements
8.2.3	See details from 5.7.3, and 9.7
82304 req.	**Qualifying remarks**
4.4, 4.7	Even if requirements management is done mainly before pipeline, use requirement may need to be updated as a result of verification and validation activities
7.2	Contents of documentation is created before the pipeline, but the pipeline can support the requirement by automating the compilation of the documentation

errors not detected by compilers, possible control flow defects, and usage of variables that have not been assigned are audited during the analysis [15].

The major source of concern related to SOUP management, as discussed previously, is significantly reduced by automatically tracking SOUP components, which can also be done using static code analysis [17]. In practice, the pipeline performs *SOUP analysis* by identifying the SOUP items from the software (IEC 62304 clause 8.1.2). However, the IEC 62304 requirements for the manufacturer to specify functional, performance, and hardware specifications for SOUP components must still be implemented appropriately (clauses 5.3.3, 5.3.4). The required specifications are documented either before the commit or in Gate 2, at the latest. Finally, various vulnerability analyses could be performed to find any vulnerability risks arising from the SOUP items. As an example, OWASP dependency-check tool [16] is an efficient security utility to find vulnerabilities from third-party components.

In the *Generation of documentation* step, the software documentation is automatically compiled, to the extent possible. For example, the required architecture documentation (IEC 62304 clauses 5.3.1, 5.3.2) can be generated by using an augmented C4 software architecture model [17] by appropriately annotating the source code packages. The generated decomposition diagram represents the actual state of the software structure. In general, the source data for documentation content can be pulled from different data sources, and the generated documentation is stored in the VCS with the software source code. Automatic document creation also enables implementing other IEC 62304 requirements, such as refining the system into software units (clause 5.4.1) and documenting traceability (clause 7.3.3). In addition, the step contributes to implementing requirements related to software system testing verification (clause 5.7.4), system configuration documentation (clause 8.1.3), and test documentation (clause 9.8). Finally, IEC 82304-1 requirements for accompanying documents (clause 7.2), as discussed earlier, can be implemented.

To summarise, the CI stage does most of the heavy lifting in the RegOps pipeline. It performs the automated part of the software integration verification and prepares the software artifacts and the documentation for the following stages of the pipeline. Aside from all the activities, CI should be a repeatable and quick process to give feedback for the developers [18].

5.2   Gate 2: Change Review and Approval

Not all regulatory requirements can be implemented by automation, and certain specific required tasks need manual verification. Such verification activities are often characterized by the fact that they are related to the outcomes of the previous steps. The second stage of the RegOps pipeline, the Change Review and Approval stage, is the first manual phase of the pipeline. Its purpose is to ensure systematic analysis and endorsement of the change made, both in source code and documentation. The stage builds on the pull-based development model [19]. A pull request is the developer's way of announcing that their work has been finished and is ready for further actions [20]. In practice, after the code is committed and pushed into the source code repository, the pull request is created automatically by the pipeline.

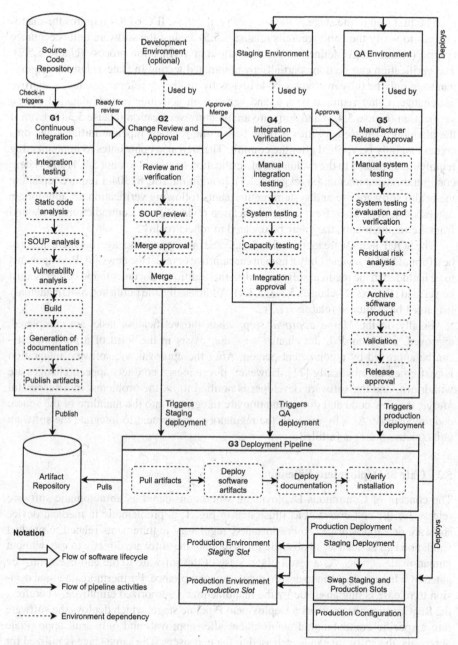

Fig. 2. Our proposed RegOps Pipeline with the regulatory activities emerging from the requirements of the standards IEC 62304 and IEC 82304-1 applied.

The first step in the stage is *Review and verification*. IEC 62304 requires the manufacturer to verify the software units (clause 5.5.5) against the software unit acceptance criteria (clause 5.5.3) defined in the software unit verification process (clause 5.5.2). The verification can be done partially by automated testing in Gate 1, but the requirement can only be fully met with a code review by another developer entitled to approve the change. Other required review and verification activities include detailed design verification (clause 5.4.4) and software architecture verification (clause 5.3.6). Even if the planning of these activities is done before the RegOps pipeline initiates, the outcomes can only be verified after the commit. The step also contributes to implementing requirements related to the evaluation of verification strategies (clause 5.7.4) and system configuration documentation (clause 8.1.3). In addition, IEC 82304-1 requires updating the health software use and system requirements following verification, as appropriate (clauses 4.4, 4.7). Therefore, in the verification review, if any contradictions are found from the requirements, they may be updated to reflect reality.

The SOUP items were identified and analyzed in the previous stage, but there needs to be a formal *SOUP review*. Only a human can approve or reject the new SOUP components to be included in the medical software. Also, the additional documentation contents must be verified (IEC 62304 clauses 5.3.3, 5.3.4). Additionally, the published SOUP anomaly lists must be evaluated (clause 7.1.3).

Finally, in the *Merge approval* step, when the verification tasks are completed, approved, and recorded, the change-set - that exists in the form of a pull request - can be approved by a competent person. After the approval, the software integration is performed automatically [21]. However, if any merge conflicts appear, changes are withdrawn, and the software developer is notified to fix the problems. In a successful *Merge*, the new code and documentation are integrated into the mainline of the source code repository. As a by-product, the regulatory requirement to integrate the software units (clause 5.6.1) is fulfilled.

5.3   Gate 3: Deployment Pipeline

The concept of Continuous Deployment, when considered as an automatic software release for the end-user and as illustrated in Fig. 1, is problematic in medical device software development [2, 2]. For instance, regulatory requirements related to product validation can be seen as an obstacle for deploying the software directly to use, without human-made actions. As a result, the release of the software to the end-users must be gated by a human decision to ensure regulatory compliance. Furthermore, the final decision to release is human-made by the manufacturer's authorized employee. Therefore, the RegOps pipeline contains a Deployment Pipeline stage, which deploys the software into a specific computational environment after approval, and only with appropriate approvals, the software can be released to the end-users. The same stage is utilized for all deployments; only the destination computational environment differs. As the software change advances through the pipeline gates, it is deployed into inspection of other developers, QA experts, and finally, to be used in real life.

Technically, the Deployment Pipeline pulls the software artifact generated by the CI stage. The software artifact is then deployed into the destination computational environment. The documentation accompanied by the software is also published in a dedicated location for further review. Finally, the software deployment is verified automatically by performing a set of smoke tests, which verify that the software is up and running. If the software does not start or the smoke tests fail, the developer is notified immediately to fix the problem.

Our research did not identify any specific requirements from the addressed standards to be implemented in the Deployment Pipeline stage. However, as the deployment is a crucial part of the system, the software change cannot be approved unless the deployment is performed successfully. Also, the deployment must be gated by a human decision. For instance, Gate 4 and Gate 5 contain specific approval activities, which essentially trigger the software deployment.

5.4 Gate 4: Integration Verification

As a result of the actions performed in previous stages, the software is deployed into the Staging Environment, which is as accurate a copy as possible of the final use environment [22]. Hence, the software product can be reviewed as a whole. In addition, the software artifacts deployed to the Staging Environment are already reviewed by another person and automatically tested for possible defects. However, there may be a need to perform *Manual integration testing*: not all test cases can be automated, and test automation cannot be used for exploratory testing. Any additional tests can be performed in the Staging Environment to test and verify that the software integration has been performed successfully (IEC 62304 clause 5.6.2). The software integration and regression testing (clauses 5.6.3 - 5.6.7) are finished at this stage.

The software system's functionality is verified through *System testing*, which ensures that the software system meets its intended requirements and performs as designed. The system testing must be carried out in a computational environment that closely corresponds to the actual use environment to ensure reliable test results. In Gate 4, the part of the system testing that is automated is carried out (clauses 5.7.1, 5.7.3, 5.7.5, 7.3.3, 8.2.3, 9.8), and, again, the stage contributes to implementing requirements related to software system testing verification (clause 5.7.4) and system configuration documentation (clause 8.1.3). A high degree of automation coverage enables efficiency by reducing the burden of manual work during the later stages. Furthermore, as automated system testing can take a considerable amount of time, it is only carried out in Gate 4, allowing fast feedback for the developers from earlier stages in the pipeline [23]. In a scenario where any anomalies are found during the system testing, the pipeline will not proceed. The identified anomaly is escalated to the problem resolution process (clause 5.7.2). Finally, the development team is notified with an automatic problem report (clause 9.1).

The performance of the system is tested by running a set of relevant tests in the *Capacity testing* step. The capacity testing provides a way for the manufacturer to analyze the behavior of the system under stress. For example, any change in the software could introduce performance issues, which can be detected early by running performance tests against the system.

The last step in Gate 4 is *Integration approval* after all other integration verification activities are completed. Technically, the approval triggers the Deployment Pipeline, which then deploys the software into the QA Environment. The QA Environment is the final environment for testing and verification before the software can be released.

5.5 Gate 5: Manufacturer Release Approval

In Gate 5, the software is system tested, the system testing is evaluated and verified, and the software product is validated before the final release. The activities performed in this stage are primarily manual or require human inspection.

The test cases that could not be automated are performed in the QA environment (clauses 5.6.6, 5.7.5, 7.3.3, 9.8) within the activity of *Manual system testing*. Depending on the test automation coverage, this stage may require significant amounts of resources. However, even with comprehensive test automation coverage, exploratory testing is recommended [24].

After the system testing has been completed, the system testing activities must be evaluated and verified within the formal *System testing evaluation and verification* step. In practice, the system test results are evaluated and verified as stated in IEC 62304 (clauses 5.7.4, 5.8.1). Essentially, all relevant test cases are verified to have been performed properly. Furthermore, according to IEC 62304, any anomalies found from the product must be documented and evaluated (clause 5.8.2, 5.8.3). In addition, the risk control measures are to be verified (clause 7.3.1). Finally, the residual risk level of the medical device product must be reduced to or remain at an acceptable level before the release to the end users can happen. These requirements are implemented in the *Residual risk analysis* step.

Before the final release, the manufacturer must ensure that all activities mentioned in the software development plan are completed (clause 5.8.6). The software and documentation artifacts created by the CI are labeled with a release version tag (clause 5.8.4). However, IEC 82304-1 extends this requirement to require a Unique Device Identifier (UDI) (clause 7.2). The software artifacts are transferred into a permanent archive (IEC 62304 clause 5.8.7). The archived software artifacts and documentation are used to install the product into the computational environment where it will be used. From a technical perspective, the medical device software product is ready to be released at this point. First, however, the manufacturer must perform the *Validation* according to the validation plan (IEC 82304-1 clauses 6.2, 6.3, 8.3). Essentially, the manufacturer must obtain reliable evidence of the software to fulfill its intended purpose.

Finally, when the software product is technically intact and verified to conform to the regulatory requirements, the software can be released and deployed into the customer environment by formal *Release approval*. In the pipeline, we utilized the Blue-green deployment, which practically means deployment into the staging slot of the environment, as discussed earlier. This practice allows customer organizations to familiarise themselves with the product as it is common that they have their validation processes. Then, when it is time to release the software to the end-users, the staging slot can be swapped with the production slot, making the software available for real-world use.

It should be highlighted that the pipeline implements some of the regulatory requirements implicitly, such as documenting how the release was made, the repeatability of the release, and re-releasing the modified system (clauses 5.8.5, 5.8.8, 6.3.2). These are the core principles of the pipeline.

6 Discussion and Conclusions

In this paper, we have collected the most central regulatory requirements related to medical software, that is, requirements from the standards IEC 62304 and IEC 82304-1, and integrated the aligned requirements into our proposed software delivery pipeline. The resulting RegOps pipeline aims to reduce the lead time of the software delivery while at the same time maintaining compliance with regulatory requirements. We identified 110 requirements from the standards, of which 26 are fully implemented, and 20 are partially implemented within the pipeline. The remaining 64 requirements, shown in Table 3, were scoped out.

Ideally, the use of the RegOps pipeline could enable early customer feedback from healthcare practitioners by allowing them to test the software in the staging slot of their computational environment before the software is released into medical use. In addition to collecting feedback, this allocated environment could be used to perform customer-specific acceptance testing and validation activities. First, however, it must be ensured that the unreleased software is not used for patient treatment in any circumstances.

The paper's primary contribution for medical device software industry professionals is to provide a conventional and pragmatic approach to deliver software for real-world use. As the medical regulations introduce rather unique requirements in the software industry, such as a demand for extensive and traceable documentation, the automation capabilities of the pipeline are precious in the automatic generation of documentation. Furthermore, when the whole delivery process is implemented within the pipeline, it is implicitly deterministic and in control by nature in the form of version-controlled infrastructure code - a feature that regulatory professionals appreciate. For researchers, our consolidated regulatory requirements can act as a baseline for future extensions in the use of DevOps practices in the medical domain. Finally, for those interested in only DevOps, our pipeline could offer a new perspective and ideas for their work.

As a limitation in our proposed approach, we acknowledge that the RegOps pipeline does not alone fulfill every applicable regulatory requirement associated with a medical software product. Therefore, it is only a part of the overall solution for regulatory compliance. As discussed previously, in addition to these standards, other regulatory requirements must also be taken into account when designing and implementing the medical device manufacturing process.

In the future, we intend to perform a case study to validate our proposed approach's applicability in real-world use and to develop the concept further. Then, the pipeline could be expanded to apply to the entire manufacturing process while retaining the mindset for process automation. Finally, the applicability of the proposed pipeline could be explored in the field of embedded medical devices, in which case additional regulatory requirements related to electrical equipment need to be taken into account.

Table 3. Requirements scoped out of the pipeline.

62304 req.	Explanation
4.1	Applies to the whole organization and all its functions
4.2	Applies to the entire product development process
4.3	The software process rigor level is decided outside of the pipeline
	However, it affects how many requirements are applicable for the product
4.4	The model is intended to support software development done in compliance with the standard
5.1.1 - 5.1.9 5.1.11, 6.1, 8.1.1	Planning activities are performed before the verification activities
5.1.10	Applies to the entire product development process. However, the pipeline needs to be addressed in the supporting items management
5.2.1 - 5.2.6, 5.4, 5.3.5, 5.4.2 5.4.3, 5.5.4, 7.1.1 7.1.2, 7.1.4, 7.2.1 7.4.1, 7.4.2, 8.2.1	The software requirements management and technical design activities are performed before the verification activities
5.5.1, 6.3.1	The implementation activities are performed before verification activities
5.6.8, 5.7.2	However, anomalies detected in the pipeline can be automatically forwarded to the software problem resolution process
6.2.1 - 6.2.6	Problem and modification analysis activities are performed before pipeline
7.2.2, 8.2.2	The software requirements management, technical design, and implementations activities are performed before verification activities
8.2.4	Change requests, change request approvals, and problem reports are managed outside of the pipeline
8.3	Configuration item history is stored in VCS
9.1 - 9.7	Software problem resolution is managed outside of the pipeline

(continued)

Table 3. (*continued*)

82304 req.	Explanation
4.1	Applies to general product documentation
4.2, 4.3, 4.5, 4.6	The requirements management and technical design activities are performed before the pipeline
6.1	Planning activities are performed before the pipeline
8.4, 8.5	Post-market activities are performed after the pipeline

Acknowledgements. The authors would like to thank Business Finland and the members of AHMED (Agile and Holistic MEdical software Development) consortium for supporting this work.

References

1. Forsgren, N., Smith, D., Humble, J., Frazelle, J.: 2019 Accelerate State of DevOps Report. DevOps Research and Assessment & Google Cloud (2019)
2. Granlund, T., Mikkonen, T., Stirbu, V.: On medical device software CE compliance and conformity assessment. In: IEEE International Conference on Software Architecture Companion (ICSA-C), pp. 185–191. IEEE (2020)
3. Granlund, T., Stirbu, V., Mikkonen, T.: Towards regulatory-compliant MLOps: oravizio's journey from a machine learning experiment to a deployed certified medical product. SN COMPUT. SCI. **2**, 342 (2021)
4. Laukkarinen, T., Kuusinen, K., Mikkonen, T.: DevOps in regulated software development: case medical devices. In: 2017 IEEE/ACM 39th International Conference on Software Engineering (ICSE-NIER), pp. 15–18. IEEE (2017)
5. A standardisation request regarding medical devices to support Regulation (EU) 2017/745 and (EU) 2017/746. https://ec.europa.eu/growth/toolsdatabases/mandates/index.cfm?fuseaction=search.detail&id=599. Last accessed 2 Jul 2021.
6. Kim, G., Humble, J., Debois, P., Willis, J.: The DevOps Handbook: How to Create World-Class Agility, Reliability, and Security in Technology Organizations. IT Revolution Press, Portland (2016)
7. Wettinger, J., Breitenbücher, U., Leymann, F.: DevOpSlang – bridging the gap between development and operations. In: Villari, M., Zimmermann, W., Lau, K.K. (eds.) Service-Oriented and Cloud Computing. ESOCC 2014. LNCS, vol. 8745, pp. 108–122. Springer, Berlin, Heidelberg (2014). https://doi.org/10.1007/978-3-662-44879-3_8
8. Laukkarinen, T., Kuusinen, K., Mikkonen, T.: Regulated software meets DevOps. Inf. Softw. Technol. **97**, 176–178 (2018)
9. Humble, J., Farley, D.: Continuous Delivery: Reliable Software Releases Through Build, Test, and Deployment Automation. Addison-Wesley, Boston (2010)
10. Google Cloud Architecture Center. https://cloud.google.com/architecture/addressingcontinuous-delivery-challenges-in-a-kubernetes-world. Accessed 21 May 2021
11. Fowler, M.: Continuous Integration. https://www.martinfowler.com/articles/continuousIntegration.html. Accessed 1 June 2021

12. Microsoft Documentation: DevTest and DevOps for microservice solutions. https://docs.mic rosoft.com/en-us/azure/architecture/solution-ideas/articles/devtest-microservice. Accessed 8 July 2021
13. IEC/EN 62304:2006/A1:2015. Medical device software - Software life-cycle processes (2015)
14. IEC 82304-1:2016. Health software – Part 1: General requirements for product safety (2016)
15. Wichmann, B., Canning, A., Marsh, D., Clutterbock, D., Winsborrow, L., Ward, N.: Industrial perspective on static analysis. Softw. Eng. J. **10**(2), 69–75 (1995)
16. OWASP Dependency-Check Project. https://owasp.org/www-projectdependency-check/. Accessed 12 July 2021
17. Stirbu, V., Mikkonen, T.: CompliancePal: a tool for supporting practical agile and regulatory-compliant development of medical software. In: 2020 IEEE International Conference on Software Architecture Companion (ICSA-C), pp. 151–158. IEEE (2020)
18. Duvall, P., Glover, A., Matyas, S.: Continuous Integration: Improving Software Quality and Reducing Risk. Addison Wesley, Boston (2007)
19. Sadowski, C., Söderberg, E., Church, L., Sipko, M., Bacchelli, A.: Modern code review: a case study at Google. In: Proceedings of the 40th International Conference on Software Engineering: Software Engineering in Practice, pp. 181–190. Association for Computing Machinery, New York (2018)
20. Fowler, M.: Pull Request. https://martinfowler.com/bliki/PullRequest.html. Accessed 1 June 2021
21. Ståhl, D., Bosch, J.: Automated software integration flows in industry: a multiple-case study. In: Companion Proceedings of the 36th International Conference on Software Engineering, pp. 54–63. ACM (2014)
22. Morales, J., Yasar, H., Volkman, A.: Implementing DevOps practices in highly regulated environments. In: Proceedings of the 19th International Conference on Agile Software Development: Companion, Article 4, pp. 1–9. ACM (2018)
23. Laukkanen, E., Mäntylä, M.: Build waiting time in continuous integration – an initial interdisciplinary literature review. In: IEEE/ACM 2nd International Workshop on Rapid Continuous Software Engineering (2015)
24. Shah, S., Cigdem, G., Sattar, A., Petersen, K.: Towards a hybrid testing process unifying exploratory testing and scripted testing. J. Softw. Evolut. Process **26**(2), 220–250 (2014)

Author Index

Printed in the United States
by Baker & Taylor Publisher Services